Socio-Economic Effects and Recovery Efforts for the Rental Industry:

Post-COVID-19 Strategies

Maximiliano Korstanje
University of Palermo, Argentina

A volume in the Advances in Hospitality, Tourism, and the Services Industry (AHTSI) Book Series

IGI Global
PUBLISHER of TIMELY KNOWLEDGE

Published in the United States of America by
IGI Global
Business Science Reference (an imprint of IGI Global)
701 E. Chocolate Avenue
Hershey PA, USA 17033
Tel: 717-533-8845
Fax: 717-533-8661
E-mail: cust@igi-global.com
Web site: http://www.igi-global.com

Library of Congress Cataloging-in-Publication Data

Names: Korstanje, Maximiliano E., editor.
Title: Socio-economic effects and recovery efforts for the rental industry : post-COVID-19 strategies / Maximiliano Korstanje, editor.
Description: Hershey, PA : Business Science Reference, [2021] | Includes bibliographical references and index. | Summary: "This book presents chapters discussing theoretical and empirical approaches on the importance of the renting industry and sharing economy to help in the recovery of tourism, hospitality and service industries in a post-COVID-19 world"-- Provided by publisher.
Identifiers: LCCN 2020058397 (print) | LCCN 2020058398 (ebook) | ISBN 9781799872870 (hardcover) | ISBN 9781799872887 (paperback) | ISBN 9781799872894 (ebook)
Subjects: LCSH: Lease and rental services. | Tourism. | Hospitality industry. | COVID-19 (Disease)--Economic aspects.
Classification: LCC HD9999.L4362 S63 2021 (print) | LCC HD9999.L4362 (ebook) | DDC 333.33/8--dc23
LC record available at https://lccn.loc.gov/2020058397
LC ebook record available at https://lccn.loc.gov/2020058398

British Cataloguing in Publication Data
A Cataloguing in Publication record for this book is available from the British Library.

Advances in Hospitality, Tourism, and the Services Industry (AHTSI) Book Series

ISSN:2475-6547
EISSN:2475-6555

Editor-in-Chief: Maximiliano Korstanje, University of Palermo, Argentina

MISSION

Globally, the hospitality, travel, tourism, and services industries generate a significant percentage of revenue and represent a large portion of the business world. Even in tough economic times, these industries thrive as individuals continue to spend on leisure and recreation activities as well as services.

The Advances in Hospitality, Tourism, and the Services Industry (AHTSI) book series offers diverse publications relating to the management, promotion, and profitability of the leisure, recreation, and services industries. Highlighting current research pertaining to various topics within the realm of hospitality, travel, tourism, and services management, the titles found within the AHTSI book series are pertinent to the research and professional needs of managers, business practitioners, researchers, and upper-level students studying in the field.

COVERAGE

- Food and Beverage Management
- Leisure & Business Travel
- Destination Marketing and Management
- Health and Wellness Tourism
- Cruise Marketing and Sales
- Tourism and the Environment
- Customer Service Issues
- Service Training
- Service Design
- International Tourism

IGI Global is currently accepting manuscripts for publication within this series. To submit a proposal for a volume in this series, please contact our Acquisition Editors at Acquisitions@igi-global.com or visit: http://www.igi-global.com/publish/.

The Advances in Hospitality, Tourism, and the Services Industry (AHTSI) Book Series (ISSN 2475-6547) is published by IGI Global, 701 E. Chocolate Avenue, Hershey, PA 17033-1240, USA, www.igi-global.com. This series is composed of titles available for purchase individually; each title is edited to be contextually exclusive from any other title within the series. For pricing and ordering information please visit http://www.igi-global.com/book-series/advances-hospitality-tourism-services-industry/121014. Postmaster: Send all address changes to above address.

Titles in this Series

For a list of additional titles in this series, please visit: http://www.igi-global.com/book-series/

Strategic International Restaurant Development From Concept to Production
Angelo A. Camillo (Sonoma State University, USA)
Business Science Reference • © 2021 • 497pp • H/C (ISBN: 9781799843429) • US $195.00

ICT Tools and Applications for Accessible Tourism
Celeste Eusébio (University of Aveiro, Portugal) Leonor Teixeira (University of Aveiro, Portugal) and Maria João Carneiro (University of Aveiro, Portugal)
Business Science Reference • © 2021 • 356pp • H/C (ISBN: 9781799864288) • US $215.00

Impact of New Media in Tourism
Maria Gorete Dinis (GOVCOPP, Polytechnic Institute of Portalegre, Portugal) Luís Bonixe (ICNOVA, Polytechnic Institute of Portalegre, Portugal) Sónia Lamy (ICNOVA, Polytechnic Institute of Portalegre, Portugal) and Zélia Breda (GOVCOPP, University of Aveiro, Portugal)
Business Science Reference • © 2021 • 389pp • H/C (ISBN: 9781799870951) • US $195.00

Growth of the Medical Tourism Industry and Its Impact on Society Emerging Research and Opportunities
Manjeet Singh (Central University of Jammu, India) and Subbaraman Kumaran (Alliance University, Bangalore, India)
Business Science Reference • © 2021 • 189pp • H/C (ISBN: 9781799834274) • US $195.00

Global Development of Religious Tourism
Emilia Alaverdov (Georgian Technical University, Georgia) and Muhammad Waseem Bari (Government College University, Faisalabad, Pakistan)
Business Science Reference • © 2021 • 366pp • H/C (ISBN: 9781799857921) • US $195.00

Innovation and Entrepreneurial Opportunities in Community Tourism
Jakson Renner Rodrigues Soares (Universidade da Coruña, Spain & Universidade Estadual do Ceará, Brazil)
Business Science Reference • © 2021 • 358pp • H/C (ISBN: 9781799848554) • US $195.00

IGI Global
PUBLISHER of TIMELY KNOWLEDGE

701 East Chocolate Avenue, Hershey, PA 17033, USA
Tel: 717-533-8845 x100 • Fax: 717-533-8661
E-Mail: cust@igi-global.com • www.igi-global.com

Editorial Advisory Board

Table of Contents

Detailed Table of Contents

The sharing economy developed rapidly with the increase in consumption expenditures in a period when low interest rates and access to credit were easy before the 2008 Financial Crisis and entered into serious competition with companies operating in the traditional economy. The use of sharing economy tools has increased as a result of sustainability, environmentalism, desire for new experiences, local tourism, and authentic searches. The sharing economy, whose main motivation is to reintroduce idle products to the market, has changed its priorities over time and turned into a profit-oriented structure, and large companies increased their revenues by increasing the number of users. The criticisms emerging as a result of employment losses, reservation cancellations, reimbursement requests, lack of social security of employees, and therefore not being able to benefit from COVID-19 aids have revealed the missing parts of the sharing economy.

Leasing emerges as an important practice that meets the needs of companies that do not want to spend their equity on investment goods or whose equity is not sufficient to acquire investment goods. At this point, investors prefer financial leasing and operational leasing methods to provide economic benefits and profits from the use

result of the research, it has been revealed that 23 news reports have been made on different news sites related to the subject. Based on this news, it has been concluded that the COVID-19 pandemic has influenced the second home tourism in behavioral, environmental, and economic aspects. Some deductions have been made about the matter through these results.

Tourism is a fragmented and information-oriented sector covering tour operators, travel agencies, hotel sales representatives, associations, meeting offices, transportation, car rental, airlines, cruise, souvenirs, restaurants, hotels/motels, and entertainment. The car rental sector, which is an important part of the tourism sector, is growing day by day, and the number of customers is increasing rapidly. The success of the car rental sector, which produces support services within the growing tourism sector, is considered very important for the development of tourism. The COVID-19 pandemic has engulfed the globe and has already had an enormous impact on life as we once knew it. With airplanes grounded, millions of people in quarantine, and hundreds of travel bans in place, COVID-19 has brought the global tourism industry to a grinding halt along with the rental industry. The study determines the current situation of the car rental sector and presents some suggestions.

Without any doubt, coronavirus disease slumped global economies in an unparalleled crisis, one of the worst downturns since 2008. COVID-19 not only affected negatively the tourism industry but also other service sectors. To some extent, governments have adopted two different dispositions against the virus. While some nations imposed a strict lockdown, others privilege the consumption and domestic circuits of payment. In its history, the tourism industry has never faced a crisis of this caliber, and its impacts remain unsure even to date. Although the interests and studies evaluating the impact of COVID-19 have captivated the attention of countless scholars, less attention has been given to the rent-a-car industry, which occupies a central position in the tourist system. As substitute competitors of train, bus, and airplanes, the rent-a-car organizations seem to be a quintessential actor of the tourist system. Of course, because we live in a world without tourists, empirical-based studies do not abound these days.

The boom of short-term rental (STR) intensifies the debate on overtourism because of some negative effects on destinations. Conversely, the STR was a way out in moments of crisis. Until now, only a few studies extend the analysis outside the limits of individual cities; that's why this case-study research was conducted by the analyses of Airbnb listings and the tourists' spatial distribution in Lisbon Metropolitan Area (LMA). For this purpose, this chapter uses two cartographic tools: 1) Airbnb listing from Inside Airbnb Project of Lisbon and 2) Geotaggers' World Atlas (map of sites that tourists took photos). Also, institutional Lisbon urban planning plans fed this study. Methodologically, combining the selected maps is a way to understand tourism spatial analysis by bringing together data on supply-side (rooms) and demand-side (distribution of tourists). The analysis demonstrates that a time-spatial distribution of visitors and the STR throughout the LMA could contribute to avoiding tourism congestion and proper distribution of economic benefits.

The turn of the century has brought many mega threats for the West, such as terrorism, natural disasters, and virus outbreaks including SARS, H1N1, Ebola, and now COVID-19. An invisible micro-organism suddenly paused our progress towards a globally interconnected flat world. We now realize that super-structures driving economic development cannot grow in specific directions without destroying themselves in certain other directions. The precautionary logic suggests the rational planning aided by our technological progress ought to alleviate most of these problems. The manner in which we deal with disasters like COVID-19, however, does not inspire confidence. Application of the precautionary logic did not avert a calamity, and recovery efforts are now guided by some crude forms of post-facto, post-cautionary logical thinking. Tourism as well as hospitality is now in crisis.

In a global context of social metamorphosis, it is important to understand how and why the reconfiguration of work experiences comes about in relation to the modifications produced by the digitalisation of society. All areas of people's lives are colonised by the logic of the digital, and the different work experiences are affected. This chapter aims to explore the connections between these two critical dimensions of the social structuration process in Latin America, which have reached a superlative role in the context of the COVID-19 pandemic. In order to do that, it considers "digital labor" and particularly the work of deliveries by platforms as a paradigmatic experience that condenses the tendencies mentioned. The selected argumentative strategy proposes to contextualize the expansion of "digital labor" in the region by drawing from the analysis of secondary data, and from primary data generated through virtual ethnography oriented to capture the experiences of workers (deliveries by platforms).

Preface

The Impacts of COVID-19 in Renting Subservice Industries: Born of a New Digitalized Capitalism?

When I was invited by IGI global to edit a book regarding the renting industry I cast some doubts about the future—if not the success—of the Project. Some little scholars focus on the problem of the rent-a-car sector in the tourism industry, however, the efforts deserved my time and attention. I started from the premise that COVId19 not only changed the industry forever but it opens the industry to new opportunities and challenges. The renting industry, above all, does not limit to rent-a-car companies, it includes better Airbnb, the renting of houses, cruises, and other transport means. I worked in the selection and edition of highly-reputed authors who can very well make a significant contribution to the book. They come from different countries and of course speak different languages, in which case, it was the first barrier: how may I homogenize (standardize) all received chapters into the same spirit?

If the Western hemisphere prospered and evolved according to the industry of travels no less true was that COVID19 paralyzed the global and commercial world as never before. The pandemic not only confronts the idea of mobilities but also in the belief we need to move for travelling. Physical displacement, which was the precondition for modern tourism and mobilities, set the pace to new concepts as virtual tourism where travellers remain immobilized in the comfort of their homes. This point led me to think that probably the renting subsector would occupy a central position in the future tourism trends, a point which I had not taken seriously in consideration. This begs another interesting question, when does a journey start?

Some voices claim that travels begin at the time the tourist imagines future destinations whilst others argue convincingly that the travel commences when the ticket is finally purchased. Are tourism and dreams inextricably intertwined?

To respond to this above-noted question, we need to discuss the nature of tourism. Far being a growing industry, tourism seems to be a rite of passage that dislocates the tourist´ identity at least temporarily to be finally introduced in a new status, a renovated status. As MacCannell (1976) puts it, tourism should be defined as a catalyst mechanism that revitalizes all our daily frustrations. Without tourism, in this way the concept narrows to the tribal totem, the social cohesion would be undermined. In the same ways, dreams fictionalize our realities condensing a piecemeal part of social reality whilst recreating a landscape that is real only when we sleep. In consonance with this, Erik Cohen contends that the figure of play seems to be vital to understand –and discuss- the nature of tourism. By playing to be what in reality we want to be is the quintessential feature of tourism. To some extent, Cohen accepts the liminoid space as well as the rite of passage is important elements of tourism, but they are not enough to explain the phenomenon. He revolves around the notion of play as a concrete manifestation of liminality. To put the same in other terms, Cohen says overtly that beyond tourism consumption lies the needs of living a bored or exciting life; in a nutshell, the quest for excitement –in terms of Elias & Dunning- is what tourists are looking for to gaze at (Cohen 1985).

The COVID-19 affects negatively not only tourism but also other sub-service industries. However, some renting service sectors –as those associated with digital technologies, rent-a-car systems, and so forth- are being revitalised towards new forms of production and consumption. This point speaks to readers of a new digital society oriented to a new division of labour. These emerging new means of production (more decentralized than the industrial society) gives novel forms of leisure practices and consumption. The chapters gathered by this volume deals with a wide spectre of a post-COVID-19 society. The book includes themes as the precaritization of work or unemployment, the economic crisis derived from the strict lockdown worldwide, the importance of the rise of new forms of mobilities, as well as the regulation of shared economy without mentioning the importance of E-commerce to domesticate the human body. The social distancing, which was imposed by the governments, creates a gap between the self and the "Other", a gap which is filled by the digital technologies and the renting subsector. To what extent the effects are beneficial -or not- appears to be only a question of time.

The first section contains three relevant chapters which discuss the role of financial leasing, E-commerce and sharing economy to mitigate the devastating effects of COVID19 in capitalist economies. In the first chapter, Volkan Kaymaz highlights the importance of sharing economy –with a focus on Turkey- to overcome the barriers of the economic downturn of 2008. The sharing economy proved to be an efficient instrument to improve the profit-oriented structure energized by sub-service sectors and the tourism industry. The same lessons this crisis left leads to rethinking the next courses of action to alleviate poverty in a post COVID19 context. The second chapter, which is authored by Mikail Kar, discusses the financial leasing and operational leasing practices that are used to finance the tourism industry in times of crisis. His main thesis holds that leasing emerges as an important practice meeting the needs of companies that are not inclined to spend resources on investment goods.

In the third chapter, Aldana Boragnio & Constanza Faracce Macia bring the case of e-commerce and the food industry during the pandemic. Per their viewpoint, the pandemic led many persons to use digital platforms and e-commerce to consume goods and services. They describe how food practices have been radically shifted because of the lockdown and the dilemmas of stay at home. Authors innovate in a novel understanding of food and care.

The second section, complementarily, focuses on four chapters aimed at presenting study cases of renting sub-service sector. This issue ranges from rent-a-car companies, which characterize new forms of mobilities to second home tourism and short rental development toward de-growth tourism. In the fourth chapter, Ali Anair dissects the complexity of tourism accommodation in the new normal. The pandemic boosted new forms of consumption associated with second home tourism. The fifth chapter –on the ink of Bayram Akay- reviews the future of cars and truck renting systems. Although the tourism industry grinds to a halt the renting industry offers a fertile ground for tourism growth. The rent-a-car sector which was historically overlooked by policymakers and scholars in tourism fields offers a new form of transport in the new normal. The same conclusions are reached by me in the sixth chapter. I outline the statistics, profits and losses of a specific rent-a-car company in Argentina. The outcomes should not be extrapolated to other cases but they illustrate the future of the tourism sub-service sector in the years to come –above all replacing other classic transport modes like public transport which includes the cruises, the airplane or trains-. Flavio N. Santos –in the seventh chapter- interrogates furtherly on the short term rental development to overcome the barriers of Overtourism in Portugal, Europe. Over-tourism situates today as one of the main problems of the industry in terms of sustainability. The short-term Rental model (STR) revitalizes the negative effects of over-tourism in the context of social distancing and lockdown.

The third section, finally, organized with four fine works as well, covers the macro and micro-sociological aspects of the Pandemic. Chapters integrating this section discuss critically the effects of COVID-19 in our customs, emotions, social relations and labour. The social distancing generates a new climate of depersonalization where digital technology and labour precaritization prevail. To put things simply, we witness the transformation of the classic digital –at least as the concept was thought by postmodern sociologists- technology in pandemic days. This section evinces the dark side of technology and the pandemic. In the eighth chapter, I declare the "end of hospitality" at least as we know it. The different travel bans associated with the strict lockdown disposed of for the government to stop the mass-contagion has radically shifted the ways we understand and perceive the "Non-Western Other". In this new normal, the foreign tourists who historically were seen as ambassadors of democracy and economic prosperity have become *undesired guests.* Adrian Scribano & Florencia Chahbenderian introduce readers to the world of digital technologies, labour and emotions. The chapter looks to shed light on the aftermaths of the pandemic in the division of labour. Centred on public and private reports, they offer an interesting model to understand what they dubbed as the politics of sensibilities in post-pandemic landscapes. Echoing this Maria Victoria Mairano places the digital delivery platforms under the critical lens of scrutiny. The crisis generated by COVID-19 divides the world into two sides, service platform companies and the rest of the industry. Whereas the former has been significantly benefited by COVID-19 paving the ways for a new decentralised virtual economy the latter has gone through a terminal crisis. This chapter explores the rise of new politics of sensibilities based on depersonalization and the precaritization of labour. Lastly, Pedro Lisdero analyzes the future of labour in western digital societies. The COVID-19 affirms previous changes linked to the metamorphosis (precaritization) of the labour in developing economies. Digital technologies not only mediate between consumers and produces but domesticate the consumers´ bodies that are sold and exchanged as commodities.

Once again, I would thank authors and reviewers for the high-quality products I obtain as well as IGI Global staff who have brought support as long as the editorial project takes place. Although the future of the capitalist system, as well as the service sector, remains obscure by these days, the present chapters give some light on the socio-economic effects of COVID in society.

REFERENCES

Cohen, E. (1985). Tourism as play. *Religion*, *15*(3), 291–304. doi:10.1016/0048-721X(85)90016-8

MacCannell, D. (1976). *The tourist: A new theory of the leisure class*. University of California Press.

Acknowledgment

A project of this caliber is always a difficult task. I do thank to my family, my wife Maria Rosa Troncoso and my sons and daughter, Benjamin, Olivia and Ciro. I want to express my gratitude to all authors who generously donated part of the time as well as reviewers and IGI global staff. Basically, the present editorial project would be never possible without their academic support.

Section 1

Chapter 1
Regulated Sharing Economy in the New Normal

Volkan Kaymaz
Istanbul Yeni Yuzyil University, Turkey

ABSTRACT

The sharing economy developed rapidly with the increase in consumption expenditures in a period when low interest rates and access to credit were easy before the 2008 Financial Crisis and entered into serious competition with companies operating in the traditional economy. The use of sharing economy tools has increased as a result of sustainability, environmentalism, desire for new experiences, local tourism, and authentic searches. The sharing economy, whose main motivation is to reintroduce idle products to the market, has changed its priorities over time and turned into a profit-oriented structure, and large companies increased their revenues by increasing the number of users. The criticisms emerging as a result of employment losses, reservation cancellations, reimbursement requests, lack of social security of employees, and therefore not being able to benefit from COVID-19 aids have revealed the missing parts of the sharing economy.

INTRODUCTION

Although sharing is an innocent and non-monetary concept, it started to take a different turn with the emergence of sharing platforms. The sharing economy spread to societies with a positive image by causing idle products or products that are used on very few days of the year to be brought back to the economy, thus reducing purchases, and changing perceptions about sustainability. Sharing economy allows the owned products or services to be used by others in a short term. Sharing economy is a term

DOI: 10.4018/978-1-7998-7287-0.ch001

describing digital platforms that connect consumers to a service or product through a mobile app or website (Cockayne, 2016). The sharing economy covers different sectors and a wide range of organizational forms, from for-profit initiatives to non-profit initiatives (Acquiera et al. 2017). The system, in which money is included in the sharing process and mediated by platforms, started with the social media sites established in the late 1990s with the partial widespread of the internet (Botsman & Rogers, 2010). Economic recessions such as the 2008 Financial Crisis pushed the search for cheap goods and services, and the global widespread use of smartphones increased the popularity of the sharing economy.

Basically, there are two different types of sharing economy, asset hubs and peer-to-peer networks (Rauch & Schleicher, 2015). While asset hubs rent their goods and services for a short term, the peer-to-peer network provides a connection between the host and the users. Besides accommodation and car sharing, the sharing economy spans many sectors, including education, finance, goods, public services, and the workplace. The sharing economy ensures that the capital costs of products are reduced and used effectively. Any idle goods can be included in the sharing economy. Borrowing has become an important alternative instead of buying household goods, cars, and houses.

Sharing economy offers broader and cheaper access to services for customers in the short term (Bardhi &Eckhardt, 2012). As a result of the development of technology, sharing platforms reduce transaction costs thanks to companies that provide services with websites and smart phone applications, and search costs are also reduced by making it easier to compare alternative prices published on the platforms. Thanks to the intermediaries that bring together consumers and people who have the opportunity to profit from their idle products, a new economy style has emerged, and it has reached a level that can compete with many institutions operating in the traditional economy in a short time. Moreover, due to the flexibility of supply, relatively inexpensive services reach the entire target customer without information asymmetry with the use of internet networks. Supply flexibility is one of the important advantages of sharing economy. By analyzing the situation of the market, hosts can quickly share their products actively or withdraw from the sharing upon the change in total demand in the short term. For example, with the app, Uber drivers can quickly add or remove themselves from the existing driver supply, and similarly, other suppliers can easily list and remove their selection of goods or services they offer (Zervas et al. 2017). In addition, sharing economy employees or intermediaries can provide a cost-free transition to platforms that make fewer interruptions, and provide more profit opportunities by using alternative applications, thus ensuring that the market remains constantly dynamic. In the demand part, users can act flexibly and sort according to the prices, user points and characteristics of the products that are subject to sharing, thereby minimizing search costs. The results of the survey conducted in Amsterdam showed that the most important reason for choosing the sharing economy is economic reasons, on the other hand, environmental reasons and sustainability factors are also effective (Böcker & Meelen, 2017).

The increase in small earnings over time, the diversification of the shared products, and the increase in total demand in proportion to the number of users of the platforms increased the interest in the sharing economy. Growing interest in the sharing economy is changing the behavior of people whose main motivation is sharing. With the profit of products, vehicles, homes and even experiences that are subject to sharing, individuals have started working full-time on sharing platforms., Even by making new purchases, has created new products to share or improved existing products. As a result, the sharing economy has become an alternative to traditional economics.

Although it has become profit-oriented, considering its benefits, and properly regulated, it is understood that the sharing economy benefits society by increasing efficiency (Koopman et al., 2015; Hong & Lee 2018). Car and home sharing platforms are the leading contributors to the sharing economy. Although car sharing dates back to the 1950s in Europe (Shaheen et al., 1999), the emergence of Uber and similar customer satisfaction oriented platforms dates back to 2009. Uber's ability to inform users in advance about the cost of the ride and the estimated time of the ride, and transparency increase platform selection. Studies show that platforms are preferred by service quality and cheaper price, and Greenwood & Wattal (2015) reveals that alcohol-related accidents and loss of life have decreased with the widespread use of Uber. Home rental services provide price advantage by increasing alternatives and offer individuals a freer and more sterile environment. The use of goods that are difficult for most people to buy becomes easier thanks to the sharing economy. For example, a luxury car, a seaside mansion by the ocean can be experienced even for a few days without buying.

Rapid Growth of Sharing Economy

Interestingly, the scale of the sharing economy has grown along with the causes that led to the 2008 financial crisis, namely variables such as excessive borrowing, lack of regulation, increased spending and mortgage lending. The global recession and supply-demand shocks caused by the outbreak, which began in 2020, have caused economic losses in the sharing economy for both platforms and landlords, and many participants are turning to traditional rental methods where they expect less fluctuation in income rather than short-term rental income.

Initiatives that have succeeded in the sharing economy have set an example, and many new ventures have entered the industry, and many have failed. In addition, many companies valued beyond estimates and even became unicorns shortly after were established like an Airbnb. Including the fast growth of the sharing economy among its economic targets, China targets sharing economic's potential contribution to the GDP as 10%. Successful enterprises have increased investments in the sector, investments in the sector increased by 8.49% in 2014 compared to the previous year (Cognizant, 2016). There are many reasons for the rapid growth of the sharing economy. A new class of consumers is born with the millennium generation. The new understanding of consumption is open to different experiences, does not have an attachment to owning, therefore does not buy a product that is not used continuously; but it is shaped by the behavior of people who want to experience it. Platforms, which have expanded their user base over the years, generally provided services to young people when they were first established, while the number of participants increased over time, and they also served to high income and older people.

The aim of this study is to examine the economic and sociological effects of platforms operating in the sharing economy. In addition, another purpose is to investigate the need for regulation by considering the existing situations of the service providers, customers, competitors, and the public sector. In cases where regulation is needed, it is to examine what kinds of sanctions are possible by taking into account various examples and to touch upon the hypothetical consequences of these sanctions.

How to Read This Chapter

However, the sharing economy, which was understood to be fragile, affected the structure of the tourism sector, and the hosts, which were brought into the tourism sector with little known virgin areas, caused changes in the employment structure of the tourism sector. In the first section of the study, the reflections of the sharing economy on the tourism sector are examined, and the changes the sector has undergone, and the new opportunities created are mentioned. Covid-19 has caused global economies to lose value far beyond predictions. The coexistence of supply and demand shocks led to a decrease in the share of expenditures in the budget, which is of secondary importance to reducing expenditures. In addition, the closure of the country borders, the measures are taken, and restrictions have negatively affected the tourism sector. Sharing tourism has also experienced huge losses and fragilities have surfaced within the sector. In the second section, the effects of Covid-19 on sharing tourism are examined and inferences about the future are made. In the last section, regulations that can be applied and applied at global and local levels are discussed in order to overcome the vulnerabilities that arise and to prevent the problems caused by the sharing economy.

SHARING TOURISM

With the increase in globalization and the ease of transportation, the shares of tourism revenues in the country's gross domestic product increase. In OECD countries, while tourism contributes 4.4% to GDP, 6.9% of the employees are employed in the tourism sector (OECD, 2020). The tourism industry provides direct or indirect income to many sectors such as food and beverage, transportation, accommodation, travel agencies, culture, and sports events. The increasing demand in the tourism sector has led to the development of the sharing economy and to the increase in the quality of the service it provides. Economic developments and sociological changes, the different demands of millennials, have increased interest in the sharing economy, and niche markets have emerged. Younger consumers seek and spend on services and experiences more than ever. European Commission (2016) reports that one third of 25 to 39 year olds have used sharing economy services and that they are three times more likely to do so than those over 55 years of age. One of the sectors where platforms are most widely used is tourism. With increasing access to information and changing demands, free and independent travel will become more prominent. The growth of social media, increased interactivity, and technology making platforms functional have increased the market for the sharing economy. Social media and review sites will be more powerful in creating destinations image and directing tourist flows.

While the tourism industry is changing shape, companies providing tourism services face economic problems from time to time. British origin Thomas Cook, who had financial problems for a long time and could not find new loans, announced his bankruptcy in 2019, while Airbnb was breaking an income record. Although Thomas Cook's bankruptcy does not mean much by itself, indirect or direct effects have affected the entire tourism industry. Tourists receiving services, hotels booked, Airlines, side sectors waiting for additional expenses of potential tourists, and insurance companies have faced the negative consequences of this situation. The bankruptcy of Thomas Cook and the growth of Airbnb's corporate value also revealed a significant projection about the new era. Airbnb, one of the biggest actors of the sharing economy, despite its establishment in 2008, company competed with the largest hotel chains and passed most of them in valuation. Although the service they provide is basically the same, they offer different or even partially incomplete service compared to traditional hotels in terms of service experience, the changing perception of tourism and price advantage in recent years has increased the use of Airbnb and this has made them one of the world's giants in the accommodation sector.

Theoretically, a tourist can meet all their needs without leaving the sharing economyA tourist; With car sharing applications such as Uber, Blablacar Lyft Zipcar, they can rent the vehicle required for transportation; can meet their food demands with newly developed applications such as Uber Eats, VizEat, EatWith; by renting bicycles and scooters, they can travel around; with Airbnb, HomeAway etc's. applications can be accommodated. Sharing economy has become one of the main players of the sector, instead of providing complementary services within the tourism sector. In addition to providing many advantages to consumers, it has also created an opportunity for hosts to earn money.

One of the reasons for the development of sharing services in the tourism sector is sustainability. Thanks to the sharing economy, individual demand for the purchase of transportation vehicles may decrease, and new investments or large hotel chains are not required for accommodation. Car rental practices reduce traffic congestion (Li, Hong, & Zhang, 2016). Thanks to the services, there is no need for the rides required to find customers, thus reducing fuel consumption (Kisi, 2018).

Increasing competition in the tourism sector leads to the emergence of new enterprises and service differentiation. One of the other important reasons for the development of sharing tourism is that it offers accommodation in authentic and relatively less explored places, as well as a price advantage. Within the framework of sharing economy practices, more sustainable and environmentally friendly tourists have led to the emergence of a new tourist concept. The increase in tourism demand for rural areas prevented the decrease in the population of villages and towns, and migration to cities due to employment was partially reduced (Belotti, 2019). Moreover, when this new tourism concept is small-scale and environmentally friendly, it reduces the need for large hotel chains and new construction. The new tourist understanding defines the tourists who are more connected to local destination, and local economies and take it as their duty to experience the life styles and consumption styles of the local people (Molz, 2013) For example, Japan offers new alternatives for tourists to experience daily routines (OECD, 2016) Airbnb partners have also begun to provide such services, and local organization companies allow tourists to increase their interaction with local people and culture.

In addition to working as a hotel operator, the hosts of Airbnb and similar companies have started to earn additional profits from the customers provided by the system, working as a tourist guide. The most important reason for the choice of sharing tourism is the price advantage. A study conducted by Airbnb (2014) in Montreal, Canada shows that people who spend 2.7 nights and 760 CAD in traditional stays but when they choose Airbnb for accommodation average of 5 nights they spend 909 CAD.

Although the sharing economy was considered a complete alternative to the traditional economy when it first appeared, some traditional companies adapting to the New Order are also trying to take advantage of the current situation.The solutions of the sharing economy are beginning to be used by the traditional tourism sector. Even hotel chains can benefit from sharing platforms by integrating them into their services (Akbar & Tracogna, 2018). Hilton Hotels partners with Uber to provide guests with easy access to local restaurants and popular spots (OECD, 2016).

THE EFFECTS OF THE 2020 PANDEMIC ON THE SHARING ECONOMY AND THE TOURISM SECTOR

Economic activity of the new era, which began to take shape under the influence of sharing platforms, decreased under the influence of Covid-19, and the epidemic that spread all over the world prevented people from manufacturing and social activities. Due to the inability to prevent the pandemic and the inability to find the Covid-19 vaccine, the thought that economies would grow in a V-shape towards the end of 2020 and the effects of the pandemic could end has not been realized. Covid-19, which caused the third largest decline in the stock market in history, caused a great loss of income in countries with a high share of tourism revenues in GDP. Increasing economic uncertainty due to the pandemic caused the delay of expenditures. While total expenditures contracted, the structure of expenditures changed, the demand for food and cleaning goods increased, but especially tourism expenditures decreased. Negative expectations of households for the future have led to reduced non-mandatory spending. Declining confidence in economies pushed individuals to save for precautionary reasons. This situation was not only due to social constraints but also due to economic uncertainty. Countries such as Spain, Portugal, Italy, and Greece, whose economies rely heavily on tourism revenue, have announced negative economic growth rates for 2020.

The decrease in travels during the pandemic has negatively affected the demand for car rental. In May 2020, Hertz, one of the world's largest car rental companies, filed for bankruptcy postponement. Postponement or cancellation of organizations such as balls and weddings has reduced the rental of clothes and accessories. University students have returned to their hometown, thus reducing their demand for rental housing. The cancellation of holidays and local festivals has also reduced the demand for house rentals.

Like all sectors, sharing economies and the tourism sector are negatively affected by the pandemic period. During the period of a supply shock, platforms and hosts in the sharing economy encountered demand shock. In March 2020 borders in the European Union were shut and nearly all travel stopped because of Covid-19. Pandemic the huge blow to the tourism industry one of the blocks main economic sectors. Tourist guides have been out of work, many hotels have suffered financial losses, and occupancy rates have fallen. The industry is forecast to lose 100 million jobs in 2020, according to the World Travel and Tourism Council. The International

Figure 1. International tourist arrivals

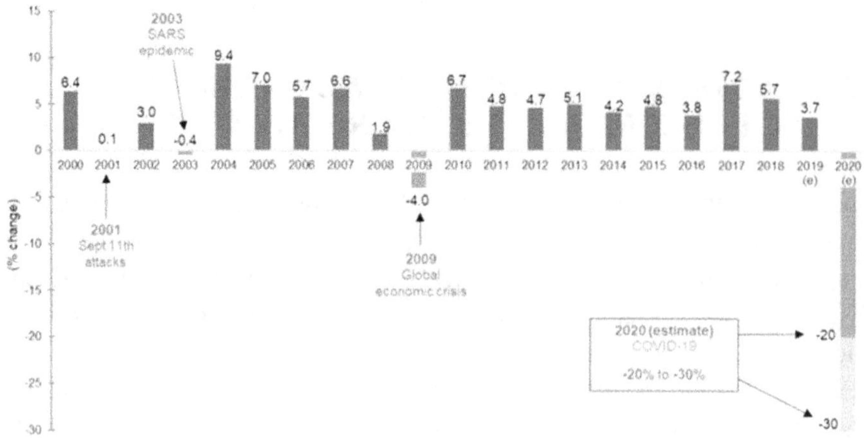

Air Transport Association estimates that total revenue for airlines will fall by $ 314 billion in 2020.

During the period of economic crisis and pandemic, tourism fell back in the ranking of cities, which led to a decrease in demand. Other sectors are feeling less of a decline in demand, while the tourism sector is experiencing a greater loss of revenue. Economic crises or social events rapidly change the volume of tourism demand on an international and national scale or preferred destinations differ depending on the factors. The 9-11 September Terrorist Attack is one example of this. At a more local level, coups or terrorist attacks in many developing countries in the past rapidly reduce the demand for tourism. While the tourism sector has a flexible demand structure, traditional tourism supply is stricter and cannot rapidly shift its investments to different sectors. In 2003, the SARS virus signaled that pandemics could be the notorious enemy of the tourism industry. It took 8-10 months to completely eliminate the effects of the SARS virus, which is much less effective compared to Covid-19, and for the tourism industry to reach the previous year's demand. The 2009 Financial Recession affected the whole world, especially the United States of America, and stocks depreciated, which led to a decrease in new investments and an increase in unemployment rates. However, as the sharing economy offered services to consumers at lower prices in the period when it emerged as a new alternative, it has not suffered as much as traditional firms, at least in domestic tourist activity. Covid-19, which is much more deadly and contagious compared to the SARS virus, again caused great damage to the tourism industry. According to estimates, the number of tourists is expected to decrease by at least 20%. Although the vaccinations that started in 2021 are perceived positively by the markets, social life is still far from returning to the old normal. Therefore, potential losses await the tourism industry in 2021.

Traditional companies, which were regulated during the pandemic process, had to take strict measures against the spread of the virus. Hotels had to work with less capacity, and it was stipulated that new guests should not be admitted to the rooms within 2 days after the residents' departure. European Commissioner has presented a rescue plan for the tourism industry to recommend vouchers and said of refunds for canceled travel sanitary measures for hospitality and transport services and the reopening of some borders. Hotels have introduced new protocols based on the health measures of the country in which they are located. New gadget purchases and implemented protocols increased the costs.

The closure of people, postponement, or cancellation of social activities have negatively impacted the rental industry. Before Covid-19, individuals rented things like cars and clothes for social events; however, the widespread use of remote work and social restrictions reduced this spending. Rental reservation data shows Beijing saw a 96% drop in Airbnb's bookings from January to March 2020 (Batool et al. 2020). A comparison of the previous year's January 2020 and August 2020 data shows that the pandemic causes Airbnb hosts (about 14 million) in about 6.5 times the economic loss compared to the Airbnb platform itself (Chen et al. 2021). Uber Eats has ceased operations in 8 countries due to the pandemic.

The situation of the enterprises in the sharing economy remained partially uncertain. Contrary to its name, the sharing economy has caused consumers to be more individual, and the tourism industry has partially taken on a new normal. Especially in the pandemic process, alternatives have started to be preferred instead of traditional methods. Holiday plans are made using platforms instead of travel agencies; trips are made using Uber and similar platforms instead of buses or planes. Individuals have started to prefer camping holidays in touch with nature rather than collective holiday areas, hotels, and holiday villages. In addition, a new form of tourism by renting houses and yachts has become widespread in local areas.

However, the change in consumer preferences is not enough to limit the financial losses of the tourism industry or sharing economy. While Airbnb was considering participating in the stock exchange in 2021, it experienced a huge loss of value, and the company, which grew over 40% from 2017 to 2020, had to dismiss some people employed at the headquarters for economic reasons. Before the pandemic, low interest rates worldwide increased demand for rental industries, investment in the sector increased, home sales accelerated, and service providers bought goods, tools, and equipment for use in homes; however, due to the negative demand shock, revenues fell, and debts became unpaid. Regardless of who or what their excuses were, Airbnb canceled the reservations requested during the pandemic period and ensured the refund of the fees. Some travel agencies didn't cut off and hide their money to use in the future.

Airdna data shows that demand for rental homes is declining and Airbnb's revenues are falling. According to Airbnb data, there was a 53% decrease in US reservations between February 3 and April 13 (Hossain, 2021). Refunds of canceled reservations in the sharing economy, especially Airbnb, emerged as one of the problems. In fact, while platforms act as organizers between hosts and guests, the global crisis has limited the effectiveness of the decisions to be taken and increased the discussions. Airbnb declared that guests would receive a refund if they cancel their reservations, while hosts criticized not being consulted during the decision-making process while contributing to the company. On the other hand, prices crashed in the pandemic process created opportunities that could be used badly. The user who received a cancellation from Airbnb and took back the paid deposit, had the opportunity to stay in another house at a much more affordable price.

The sharing economy provided timely solutions to urgent needs after major disasters. After Hurricane Sandy in 2012, Airbnb launched its Disaster Response Program to assist in the event of a disaster. Airbnb has made updates to the app to automatically contact displaced people to meet their accommodation needs and to automatically communicate with hurricane affected and surrounding hosts to see if there is extra space. Willing hosts were then able to share their homes with disaster victims for free. Airbnb (2020) announced that it has allocated $ 250 million to support Airbnb hosts worldwide who have experienced reservation cancellations related to COVID-19 and have to pay back the fees.

REGULATION REQUIREMENT IN SHARING ECONOMY

The advancement of technology and the removal of barriers bring people closer together. Although sharing platforms have many positive features, the sector has faced new problems and has been criticized from various angles. The idea that platforms that are not fully regulated create unfair competition and other social problems necessitated a further examination of the issue. Although sharing is a concept that is positive and compatible with human nature, platforms operating under the title of sharing economy, or "sharing companies" as many companies describe themselves, can in some cases lead to harmful or controversial consequences. Already, instead of sharing platforms, it generates revenue by making short-term rental activities (Sundararajan, 2016) by deducting from hosts and guests. When the regulation debates arise, the central governments have a positive view of the sharing economy actors that directly contribute to economic growth; (Hong & Lee, 2018), however, it can be understood from the practices and regulations that local governments take a more defensive and protectionist attitude towards the sharing economy because they directly confront lame competition, social problems, or complaints.

Although it has increased the use of inert products, the sharing economy has improved since it emerged. A new era has begun in which homes, cars and other products are bought only for profit within the sharing economy. While hosts started to demand houses for rent on platforms and use mortgage loans to increase their income, different sectors of the economy were affected differently in this process. On the other hand, although the rented or shared things are cheaper than their alternatives, the sharing economy did not present a more egalitarian situation in terms of economic equality, on the contrary, a new tool has emerged that allows the owners to liquidate their physical capital. Sharing economy marketplaces have flourished particularly within the field of travel and tourism. In addition to their benefits, platforms have also changed the existing dynamics in various aspects. Airbnb created an experience anyone who is a host who can also become a tour guide. Airbnb does this for hospitality, but on the other hand professional tour guides may be unemployed. Middle class people become real entrepreneurs in the tourism sectors but in the busiest cities average rent has increased.

The fact that it is a relatively new concept, and the social security and rights of employees are blurred has proven that economic damages and destructions can be deep in the covid-19 period. The fact that many employees serving on platforms are unemployed due to sudden shrinking demand and cannot benefit from the cash benefits provided by governments reveals the need to increase regulations in the sharing economy. Platforms see employees as service partners and individual employees. The cutoffs of the platform from hosts and customers have become questionable. As the companies got bigger, the cutoffs they made also increased. As platforms become stronger in the market, network effects are also increasing. Therefore, platforms are also criticized for using power asymmetries to achieve the value created by employees and customers (Bauwens & Kostakis, 2014). Growing platforms are beginning to encounter various problems. It has been criticized that some users go out of the platform and make a rental agreement with the host, which may lead to informal accommodation.

During the Covid-19 process, each country has introduced very strict measures and new regulations, especially hotels, for traditional tourism organizations and conducts direct inspections. Although Airbnb takes new measures that change the quality of service, the absence of an audit mechanism other than the point system reveals the inadequacy of the sharing economy. There are also some difficulties in collecting taxes from the platforms. It is controversial to what extent such organizations serving in more than one country will provide tax on their income (Minifie & Wiltshire, 2016). For example, Airbnb leaves its local tax liability to users in Turkey, while the company itself makes a profit, but does not pay the tax on the earnings it receives.

The social security status of people serving on the platforms is also questionable. Social security taxes are not paid even when people leave their current jobs and take full-time work on the platforms.

One of the social problems is that on platforms, it is possible for hosts to discriminate based on race and sexual orientation by accessing customer information (Ahuja & Lyons, 2017). The problem of subjectivity also arises with the review comments written by customers and hosts and the scores they give. In order to avoid mutual trust problems, the platforms must take additional measures. Edelman, Luca, and Svirsky (2016) found evidence of racism, where guests with African - American names are 16% less likely to be accepted than guests with white names. Since it is still a developing area, solutions are sought after the problems encountered. For example, people found to be racist by the company could be removed from the platforms. On the other hand, both hosts and guests can be punished in various ways by creating a penalty point system, such as driver's license points.

Airbnb hosts usually rent houses to guests who come for tourism, while in the tourism sector, hotels have to meet certain standards such as fire safety, emergency health support. The security of private life also causes problems in short-term rented houses. While many hosts do not have any experience with hospitality, they also lack the official licenses required for this type of business. Although the service quality of the guests is the focus for the hosts, the externalities that occur cause many negativities. Complaints of local people are generally security concerns, noise and security issue related to the deterioration of neighborly relations, which is one of the problems that hosts also fear and frequently encounter. Damage to the house by the guest is one of the problems. On the other hand, short-term rental causes the rents paid by the residents to increase and the housing supply to be insufficient.

Airbnb has stopped renting homes to users under the age of 25 in Canada due to noise and violence. It is stated that Canada has been determined as a pilot country to start the implementation. While the complaints against the short-term guests by the local people are increasing, the increase in rental prices and the damage to daily life and social life are the subjects of complaints. Major cities (for example, Chicago) require hosts to register and obtain a license to list and rent their place on sites like Airbnb. (Ganapati and Reddick, 2018). London and Amsterdam restricted short-term rented houses and decided that they could be rented for a maximum of 90 and 60 days, respectively, within a year (Wachsmuth & Weisler, 2018). Barcelona city council imposed a fine on Airbnb for advertising hostels without any licenses (Buhalis et al. 2020) and increased inspections of the owners of the houses that provide accommodation services.

The issue of what laws the companies involved in the sharing economy are subject to is also controversial. Such companies, operating in more than 190 countries, must comply with local laws. Otherwise, free market conditions are damaged and unfair competition is born. Achieving localisation and establishing local partnerships will be important in the future to ensure the continuity of such companies. Airbnb's terms of use do not comply with European Union (EU) law. For example, the company tells its users that guests cannot sue the host for personal or other damages in the EU. It also says that the terms of use can be changed without giving customers the option to cancel. Such conditions can be applied in the USA, but are prohibited in Europe.

Domestic or foreign tourists usually make their decisions by listing their alternatives according to price and user ratings, therefore feedback is important for both hosts and guests; however, subjective or misuse of comments can lead to misdirection of decision makers in the market and harming the conditions of perfect competition. Considerable attention to the comments made the sharing economy known as a reputation economy (Gandini, 2016). During the Covid-19 era, direct inspections were carried out while each country introduced very strict measures and new regulations, especially hotels, to traditional tourism organizations. Although Airbnb takes new measures that change the quality of service, the absence of an audit mechanism other than the point system reveals the inadequacy of the sharing economy. Interestingly, 95% of the ratings in Airbnb reviews are above 4.5 points, and only 1% of the ratings are below 3 points in Uber (Stemler, 2017). The lack of a scoring system increases the likelihood of encountering surprise shocks. The application of the mutual scoring system causes the two sides to give each other high points. The fact that the points given are anonymous and that users can meet with each other by going outside the system perhaps requires a third agent employed by Airbnb.

Finally, taxi troops in many cities around the world rallied against car sharing platforms. Taxi unions argue that car-sharing platforms have an unfair advantage as they are exempt from public safety regulations. Taxi operators are typically subject to municipal licensing for public safety and other purposes. In most cities in the USA, licenses are issued in a limited coin system that is limited and may interfere with new taxi service operators (Rauch & Schleicher, 2015; Rogers, 2015). Taxi associations advocate either to abolish municipal regulations on taxi operations or to subject car-sharing services to similar regulations. Uber has faced sanctions from Bulgaria, Turkey, Denmark, Hungary, China and many other countries, and has also been criticized for the fact that the drivers it employs are considered subcontractors before the law. While the developing sharing economy faces various problems, the damage to the entire tourism sector during the pandemic period reveals all the problems of the system directly.

CONCLUSION

Although there are many reasons for economic crises, external factors such as natural disasters and pandemics, which are difficult to predict, also cause significant economic losses, increase the unemployment rate, change the share of the spending groups in the budget and shrink demand for various sectors. Covid-19, which spread all over the world in 2020 and deeply affects the economies, caused the GDP of countries to shrink, economic shrinkage and the coexistence of supply-demand shocks caused economic recessions. Increasing economic uncertainty, travel restrictions, and loss of income from potential customers led to tourism being one of the sectors most affected by the adverse effects. While tourism has been transforming in recent years, the sharing economy is intertwined with the tourism sector, so tourism losses have also negatively affected the sharing sector. Both platform owners and hosts suffered significant economic losses in this process; however, hosts working full time in the sharing economy faced much greater revenue losses compared to platforms. While the depreciation of the sharing economy and the increasing criticism and complaints of the hosts revealed the fragility of the sharing economy, the regulatory activities of the states and local administrators were questioned. This study discusses how regulation activities can be carried out without harming the free market economy. As a result, the activities of regulatory institutions are important for the rapidly growing sharing economy and the related tourism economy to take more robust future steps. In this process, it has emerged that hosts need to find alternative sources of income regardless of sharing economy platforms.

REFERENCES

Ahuja, R., & Lyons, R. C. (2017). *The Silent Treatment: LGBT Discrimination in the Sharing Economy*. Trinity College.

Airbnb. (2014). *New Study: Airbnb Community Contributes C$54.6 million to Montreal Economy*. https://www.airbnb.com.tr/press/news/new-study-airbnb-community-contributes-c-54-6-million-to-montreal-economy

Airbnb. (2020). *$250M to support hosts impacted by cancellations*. https://www.airbnb.com.au/resources/hostinghomes/a/250m-to-support-hosts-impacted-by-cancellations-165

Akbar, Y. H., & Tracogna, A. (2018). The sharing economy and the future of the hotel industry: Transaction cost theory and platform economics. *Intenatioal. Journal of Hospitality Managament*, *71*, 91–101. doi:10.1016/j.ijhm.2017.12.004

Aurélien, A., Daudigeosb, T., & Pinksec, J. (2017). Promises and paradoxes of the sharing economy: An organizing framework. *Technological Forecasting and Social Change*, *125*, 1–10. doi:10.1016/j.techfore.2017.07.006

Bardhi, F., & Eckhardt, G. M. (2012). Access-Based Consumption: The Case of Car Sharing. *The Journal of Consumer Research*, *39*(4), 881–898. doi:10.1086/666376

Batool, M., Ghulam, H., Hayat, H. M., Naeem, M. Z., Ejaz, A., Imran, Z. A., Spulbar, C., Birau, R., & Tiberiu, T. H. (2020). *How COVID-19 has shaken the sharing economy? An analysis using Google trends data.* Economic Research-Ekonomska Istraživanja. doi:10.1080/1331677X.2020.1863830

Bauwens, M., & Kostakis, V. (2014). From the Communism of Capital to Capital for the Commons: Towards an Open Co-operativism. *tripleC: Communication, Capitalism & Critique. Journal for a Global Sustainable Information Society*, *12*(1), 356–361.

Böcker, L., & Meelen, T. (2017). Sharing for people, planet or profit? Analysing motivations for intended sharing economy participation. *Environmental Innovation and Societal Transitions*, *23*, 28–39. doi:10.1016/j.eist.2016.09.004

Botsman, R., & Rogers, R. (2010). *What's mine is yours: The rise of collaborative consumption*. HarperBusiness.

Buhalis, D., Andreu, L., & Gnoth, J. (2020). The dark side of the sharing economy: Balancing value co-creation and value co-destruction. *Psychology and Marketing*, *37*(5), 689–704. doi:10.1002/mar.21344

Chen, G., Cheng, M., Deborah Edward, D., & Xu, L. (2021). COVID-19 pandemic exposes the vulnerability of the sharing economy: A novel accounting framework. *Journal of Sustainable Tourism*, 1–18. doi:10.1080/09669582.2020.1868484

Cockayne, D. G. (2016). Sharing and neoliberal discourse: The economic function of sharing in the digital on-demand economy. *Geoforum*, *77*, 73–82. doi:10.1016/j.geoforum.2016.10.005

Dalir, S., Mahamadaminov, A., & Olya, H. G. T. (2020). *Airbnb and taxation: Developing a seasonal tax system. Tourism Economics.* . doi:10.1177/1354816620904894

Edelman, B. G., Luca, M., & Svirsky, D. (2016). *Racial discrimination in the sharing economy: Evidence from a field experiment.* Harvard Business School Working Paper 16-069. Retrieved from https://papers.ssrn.com/abstract=2701902

European Commission. (2016). *The use of collaborative platforms*. Flash Eurobarometer 438.

Ganapatia, S., & Reddick, C. G. (2018). Prospects and challenges of sharing economy for the public sector. *Government Information Quarterly*, *35*(1), 77–87. doi:10.1016/j.giq.2018.01.001

Gandini, A. (2016). *The reputation economy: Understanding knowledge work in digital society*. Palgrave Macmillan. doi:10.1057/978-1-137-56107-7

Gossling, S., & Michael Hall, C. (2019). Sharing versus collaborative economy: How to align ICT developments and the SDGs in tourism? *Journal of Sustainable Tourism*, *27*(1), 74–96. doi:10.1080/09669582.2018.1560455

GreenwoodB.WattalS. (2015). *Show Me The Way To Go Home: An Empirical Investigation of Ride Sharing and Alcohol Related Motor Vehicle Homicide*. Fox School of Business Research Paper 15-054. http://ssrn.com/abstract=2557612 doi:10.2139srn.2557612

Guttentag, D. A., & Smith, S. L. J. (2017). Assessing Airbnb as a disruptive innovation relative to hotels: Substitution and comparative performance expectations. *International Journal of Hospitality Management*, *64*, 1–10. doi:10.1016/j.ijhm.2017.02.003

Hong, S., & Lee, S. S. (2018). Adaptive governance and decentralization: Evidence from regulation of the sharing economy in multi-level governance. *Government Information Quarterly*, *35*(2), 299–305. doi:10.1016/j.giq.2017.08.002

Hossain, M. (2021). The effect of the Covid-19 on sharing economy activities. *Journal of Cleaner Production*, *280*, 124782. doi:10.1016/j.jclepro.2020.124782 PMID:33106734

Kisi, N. (2015). The Reflections of Sharing Economy in the Transportation Sector: Uber Sample. *Journal of International Management and Social Researches*, *5*(10), 57–68.

Koopman, C., Mitchell, M. D., & Thierer, A. D. (2015). The sharing economy and consumer protection regulation: The case for policy change. *The Journal ofBusiness, Entrepreneurship & The Law, 8*(2).

Li, Z., Hong, Y., & Zhang, Z. (2016). Do ride-sharing services affect traffic congestion? An empirical study of Uber entry. SSRN *Electronic Journal*. Retrieved from https://ssrn.com/abstract=2838043

Minifie, J., & Wiltshire, T. (2016). *Peer-to-peer pressure: policy for the sharing economy. Report*. Grattan Institute.

Molz, J. G. (2013). Social Networking Technologies and the Moral Economy of Alternative Tourism: The Case of Couchsurfing.org. *Annals of Tourism Research, 43*, 210–230. doi:10.1016/j.annals.2013.08.001

OECD. (2016). *OECD Tourism Trends and Policies 2016*. OECD Publishing. doi:10.1787/tour-2016-

OECD. (2020). *OECD Tourism Trends and Policies 2020*. OECD Publishing. doi:10.1787/6b47b985-

Rauch, D., & Schleicher, D. (2015). *Like Uber, But for Local Governmental Policy: The Future of Local Regulation of the 'Sharing Economy'*. George Mason Law & Economics Research Paper 15-01. doi:10.2139srn.2549919

Shaheen, S., Sperling, D., & Wagner, C. (1999). A Short History of Carsharing in the 90's. *The Journal of World Transport Policy and Practice*, *5*(3), 18–40.

Srineck, N. (2016). *Platform Capitalism*. Polity Press.

Stemler, A. (2017). Feedback loop failure: Implications for the self-regulation of the sharing economy. *Minnesota Journal of Law, Science & Technology*, *18*(2), 673–712.

Sundararajan, A. (2016). *The sharing economy: The end of employment and the rise of crowdbased capitalism*. MIT Press.

Wachsmuth, D., & Weisler, A. (2018). Airbnb and the rent gap: Gentrification through the sharing economy. *Environment and Planning A. Economy and Space*, *0*(0), 1–24.

World Tourism Organisation. (2020). *COVID-19: Putting People First*. Author.

Zervas, G. & Byers J. W. (2017) The Rise of the Sharing Economy: Estimating the Impact of Airbnb on the Hotel Industry. *Journal of Marketing Research, 54*(5).

ADDITIONAL READING

Belk, R. (2014). You are what you can access: Sharing and collaborative consumption online. *Journal of Business Research*, *67*(8), 1595–1600. doi:10.1016/j.jbusres.2013.10.001

Benkler, Y. (2004). Sharing nicely: On shareable goods and the emergence of sharing as a modality of economic production. *The Yale Law Journal*, *114*(2), 273–358. doi:10.2307/4135731

Cognizant. (2016). *The Rapid Rise of the Sharing Economy*. https://www.cognizant.com/perspectives/the-rapid-rise-of-the-sharing-economy-part1

Connolly, J. M. (2020). No Uber, no tourists? Public attitudes toward municipal regulation of the sharing economy. *Local Government Studies*, 1–16. Advance online publication. doi:10.1080/03003930.2020.1794844

Gong, Y., & Janssen, M. (2012). From policy implementation to business process management: Principles for creating flexibility and agility. *Government Information Quarterly*, *29*(Supplement 1), S61–S71. doi:10.1016/j.giq.2011.08.004

Ključnikov, A., Krajčík, V., & Vincúrová, Z. (2018). International Sharing Economy: The Case of AirBnB in the Czech Republic. *Economia e Sociologia*, *11*(2), 126–137. doi:10.14254/2071-789X.2018/11-2/9

Lacy, P., & Rutqvist, J. (2015). *Waste to wealth: The circular economy advantage*. Palgrave Macmillan UK.

Lee, D. (2016). How Airbnb short-term rentals exacerbate Los Angeles's affordable housing crisis: Analysis and policy recommendations. *Harvard Law & Policy Review*, *10*(1), 229–254.

Miller, S. R. (2016). First Principles for Regulating the Sharing Economy. *Harvard Journal on Legislation*, *53*, 147–202.

Salvioni, D. M. (2016). Hotel Chains and the Sharing Economy in Global Tourism, Symphonya. *Emerging Issues in Management*, *1*, 31–44.

Thees, H., Pechlaner, H., Olbrich, N., & Schuhbert, A. (2020). The Living Lab as a Tool to Promote Residents' Participation in Destination Governance. *Sustainability*, *12*(3), 1120. doi:10.3390u12031120

Todisco, M. (2015). Share and share alike? Considering racial discrimination in the nascent room-sharing economy. *Stanford Law Review Online*, *67*, 121–129.

Tussyadiah, L. P., & Marianna Sigala, M. (2018). Shareable tourism: Tourism marketing in the sharing economy. *Journal of Travel & Tourism Marketing*, *35*(1), 1–4. doi:10.1080/10548408.2018.1410938

Wachsmuth, D., Kerrigan, D., Chaney, D., & Shillolo, A. (2017). Short-term cities: Airbnb's impact on Canadian housing markets. Policy report, Urban Politics and Governance research group, School of Urban Planning, McGill University, Canada.

Wallsten, S. (2015). The competitive effects of the sharing economy: How is Uber changing taxis? Technology Policy Institute, 22.

Wirtz, J., So, K. K. F., Mody, M. A., Liu, S. Q., & Chun, H. H. (2019). Platforms in the peer-to-peer sharing economy. *Journal of Service Management*, *30*(4), 452–483. doi:10.1108/JOSM-11-2018-0369

Wosskow, D. (2014). *Unlocking the Sharing Economy: An Independent Review*. Department for Business, Innovation and Skills.

KEY TERMS AND DEFINITIONS

COVID-19: It is the final name given by the world health organization to a newly discovered virus from the coronaviridae family, known as 2019-ncov.

Pandemic: Is any deadly infectious disease reaching a "global" dimension that will affect the whole world.

Regulation: Is all kinds of regulatory measures taken by the state or local administrators in the economy in order to ensure efficiency in the economy and to eliminate inefficiencies caused by market failures.

Sharing Economy: Is the set of services that are competitive and complementary to the traditional economy in some areas, based on not having, but using or receiving services for the duration of the need.

Tourism: Tourism is all of the economic, cultural, technical measures and studies carried out to attract tourists to a country or a region. It is the most important sub-sector of the service sector.

Chapter 2
Financial Leasing and Operational Leasing:
An Early Assessment of the Impact of COVID-19 Pandemic

Mikail Kar
Bursa Uludag University, Turkey

ABSTRACT

Leasing emerges as an important practice that meets the needs of companies that do not want to spend their equity on investment goods or whose equity is not sufficient to acquire investment goods. At this point, investors prefer financial leasing and operational leasing methods to provide economic benefits and profits from the use of goods, not ownership. This study discusses the financial leasing and operational leasing practices that are frequently used for financing and assesses the use of these methods in the tourism and hospitality markets and the effects of the COVID-19 pandemic. In addition, the study also makes recommendations by making predictions about changes and innovations that may occur after the pandemic crisis.

INTRODUCTION

It is both difficult and ineffective for firms to meet the resources they need to reach their goals by continuing their development, entirely from their equity capital. Therefore, companies finance some of their needs in various ways and methods instead of purchasing them with cash. At this point, leasing emerges as an important practice that meets the needs of investors that do not want to spend their equity on

DOI: 10.4018/978-1-7998-7287-0.ch002

investment goods or whose equity is not sufficient to acquire investment goods. Leasing is based on the idea that the main benefit and profit arising from the use of the goods, not from the ownership. The main reason for the need of firms for investment goods is the economic benefit they will obtain as a result of the operation of this investment good. In other words, companies that are aiming for maximum profit want to increase the profit obtained as a result of the use of this product rather than having ownership of the product. For this reason, leasing becomes an important alternative for companies to acquire investment goods. With leasing, companies can both get rid of some of the burdens caused by the right of ownership and provide and renew products faster according to the needs of the day.

Leasing methods are one of the most common needs meeting methods in the tourism and hospitality markets. Although there are many reasons for this, the main reasons include the asset structure these sectors have and use, the excess of capital-intensive investments in the market, seasonal changing needs, close relations with various sectors that require different specialties and changing demands with changing lifestyles. The choice of leasing methods provides companies in the sector with significant competitive advantages. In this sector, which is constantly being renewed and where international competition is high, the leasing method is an important advantage. Tourism and hospitality companies that meet their needs with this form of financing can mobilize their existing resources for different opportunities and do not have problems with cash flow. In this sector, the leasing method is preferred both as an alternative to the purchasing method in terms of substitution relationship and is used in a complementarity relationship.

Tourism and hospitality expenditures are considered as discretionary expenditures rather than mandatory, and demand elasticity is argued to be extremely high. Therefore, the tourism and hospitality sector is known as one of the fastest and most affected sectors by crisis, uncertainty, and fluctuations. This sector, which has experienced quite painful experiences from past crisis periods, is also strongly affected by the Covid-19 pandemic, which affects the world today, directly and indirectly. As of the period when the study was prepared (2020-December), the effects of the Covid-19 pandemic, which caused more than 70 million cases and more than 1.5 million deaths, are increasing rapidly and predictions about when it will end are not clear. At the end of the epidemic, it is not possible to predict how much the overall effects of this process will be and what will be the total destruction it will create in the tourism and hospitality sector in particular. Curfew, travel restrictions, and business activity stops imposed by many countries directly affect the sector, while the economic difficulties and psychological effects caused by the pandemic indirectly reduce the demand for the sector in quality and quantity.

This chapter of the book discusses the financial leasing and operational leasing practices that are frequently used for financing and discuss the use of these methods in the tourism and hospitality markets and the effects of the Covid-19 pandemic. In addition, the study also provides suggestions by making predictions for the post-crisis changes and innovations in the tourism and hospitality markets and leasing contracts after the pandemic. For this purpose, the study is structured with seven sections. After this introduction, the definition, history, and types of leasing are examined in general in the second section. In this section, the definitions, processes, and advantages and disadvantages of financial leasing and operational leasing are explained in detail and a comparative evaluation of these methods is made. In the third section, the tourism and hospitality markets is covered and financial leasing and operational leasing usage in these markets are discussed. In the fourth section, crises in tourism and hospitality markets and the effects of the Covid-19 pandemic are discussed. In the fifth section, the impact of the Covid-19 pandemic on financial leasing and operational leasing agreements and the expectations after the crisis are discussed. In the sixth section, with the help of observational information and emerging new literature, suggestions are made for the strategies to be developed during and after the pandemic process. The study concludes with the conclusion section in which a general evaluation is made.

LEASING

Aristotle's approach that wealth is caused by the use of property rather than ownership than property rights, and Adam Smith's discourse that capital accumulation is caused by the operation of the means of production, not the ownership of the means of production, are accepted as the basis of today's leasing practices in an economic approach. According to the International Finance Corporation(IFC), leasing is a way to access financial resources and it can be defined as a contract made between two parties, as one of the parties allows the other to use an asset for a certain period and for certain payments. IFC states that leasing is based on obtaining income by using an asset rather than holding it as ownership. Although there are different definitions of different types of leasing, according to the European Federation of Equipment Leasing Company Associations (LEASEUROPE), leasing can generally be defined as a contract signed between the lessor and the lessee for a certain period of time and the lessor, the legal owner of an asset, provides an asset for use to the lessee, the user of the asset, for a specified period of time, in return for set payments. So, leasing is generally the use of a property owned by the lessor to the lessee for a certain period of time and for a certain price, with a contract signed between the lessor and the lessee (Tongxia et al., 2016; Bennett & Bradbury, 2003; IFC, 2005; IFC, 2006; Mayes & Nicholas, 1988; Carter et al., 1996).

Although the history of leasing is taken as far as the Sumerians' renting agricultural tools in various sources in 2000 BC, leasing in the contemporary sense emerged in the United States in the 1930s, in Europe in the 1960s, and in developing countries in the 1970s. In the efforts to get out of the Great Depression, the leasing business became widespread and its current structure after the Second World War began to take shape. In today's sense, making lease agreements starts with the leasing company "United States Leasing Corporation" established in San Francisco in 1952. Leasing first spread from the USA to the UK. In the UK, the first leasing contracts in a contemporary sense, besides its historical background, start with the leasing company "The Merchantile Leasing Company" established in 1960. Leasing, which entered Europe through the UK, spread rapidly and the European Federation of Equipment Leasing Company Associations (LEASEUROPE) was established in 1972 by the national leasing associations of 15 European countries. Leasing, which spread all over the world in the 1970s with the influence of multinational companies, gained an international character in the 1980s. Leasing, which had a relative slowdown during the great oil crisis, started to rise again in the 1980s. Leasing has become a part of the economic order as an important financing method with the various incentive applications of the countries over time (Mayes & Nicholas, 1988; Vasiliou, 2008; Teodorescu, 2014; Carter et al., 1996; Ezzell et al., 2001).

Apart from the differences arising from the types and applications, there are four basic elements in today's leasing transactions: the lessor, the lessee, the goods subject to the lease, and the lease agreement. The lessor is the owner of the asset to be leased and transfers the right to use the asset to the lessee for a certain period and amount in order to gain profit. These organizations, which are called leasing companies, are generally established with the aim of leasing assets and purchase the asset notified by the lessee and lease it to the lessee. These organizations may be the producers of the relevant goods from time to time. The lessee is the company or person who wants to get the right to use the property in return for the rent to be paid for a certain period of time. The lessee obtains the right to use the asset subject to the lease and provides an economic benefit from that asset for a certain period of time and pays rent for a certain period in return. The leased goods are the goods that the lessee needs and wants the right of use to achieve his goals. The properties of the goods in question are usually determined by the lessee and the lessor is notified and asked to buy and lease it. Depending on the type of leasing, these goods can be a very simple and small item, or it can be a very large and costly property. Finally, a lease agreement is a formal agreement between the lessor and the lessee that shows the conditions under which the property to be leased, sets out the obligations, and legally binds the parties. (Bennett & Bradbury, 2003; IFC, 2005; IFC, 2006; Mayes & Nicholas, 1988; Vasiliou, 2008)

Leasing practices have become a rapidly accepted and widely used financing method for investors due to the attractive advantages they offer compared to a cash purchase or loan use. Since the main purpose of leasing is to finance investments, it can be seen in many different goods today. It is quite long to count them one by one, but to give a few examples in general headings; air transportation vehicles, land transportation vehicles, sea transportation vehicles, metal processing machinery, production machinery, packaging machinery, construction and business machinery, audio and video equipment, medical devices, electronic and optical devices, press and broadcast equipment, office equipment, tourism equipment, real estate, patent rights, all kinds of intellectual and industrial rights, raw material and semi-finished goods, computer software, film, videotape, games, patents and license agreements on reproduction rights.

Leasing can be divided into various types in terms of the duration of the contract, the parties, the subjects, the liabilities of the property, the scope, the payment type, and the quality of the leased property. Some of these types are Direct-Indirect Leasing, Term-Revolving Leasing, Full Pay Out-Non Full Pay Out Leasing, Domestic-International Leasing, Individual-Blanket Leasing, First Hand-Second Hand Leasing, Short Term-Long Term Leasing, Investment Goods-Consumption Goods Leasing, Open End-Net Leasing, Sublease, Leveraged Leasing, Private Leasing. However, there are two main categories of lease agreements; these are financial leasing and operational leasing. Since the main purpose of this study is to explain these types of leasing, these applications are examined in detail in subtitles.

Financial Leasing

The most widely used type of leasing, and even the type that comes to mind when it comes to leasing, is financial leasing. The clearest and most used definition of financial leasing is made by the European Federation of Equipment Leasing Company Associations as financial leasing is a contract signed between the lessor and the lessee for a certain period of time, which leaves the use of the property selected by the lessee and purchased by the lessor to the lessee in exchange for certain payments. In the United States, according to the Financial Accounting Standards Board (FASB), if a lease covers at least 75% of the useful life of the asset subject to the lease, if the lessee is given the option to purchase ownership of the asset at the end of the lease for a very low price, and if the reduced value of the minimum lease payments to date at the inception of the lease is at least 90% of the present value of the leased asset the transaction is defined as a financial leasing. Financial leasing is a type of long-term lease that transfers control over the leased property economically to the lessee and turns the lessee into the de-facto owner of the property, although the property right of the leased property remains legally in the financial leasing company. In other words, financial leasing is a type where all risks and benefits arising from owning an asset are transferred. In this method, the lessee has the right to use the whole or almost all of the economic life of the leased property and undertakes all risks and benefits other than ownership. In addition, if the lessee terminates the lease at any time, all losses arising from termination are covered by the lessee and the losses arising from the changes in the fair value of the residual value belong to the lessee (Duke et al., 2009; Contino, 2002; Bennett & Bradbury, 2003; IFC, 2005; IFC, 2006)

Financial leasing processes may vary between countries depending on structural regulations and legal systems. There may be process differences especially, between national and international financial leases. However, the general processes are very similar. A typical finance leasing takes place between three parties: the lessee, the lessor company, and the seller of the item. First of all, the lessee who wants to acquire the relevant good finds the seller of the product suitable for his wishes and agrees on the properties of the property. Then, the party that wants to become a lessee applies to the leasing firm and requests that it be allocated a limit and that a financial lease be made for the relevant property. The financial leasing institution evaluates the application and decides whether it will be able to make a financial leasing and, if so, its conditions, and informs the party willing to lease. Contract terms are determined and signed by negotiating between the lessor and the lessee. After the contract is signed, the leasing company, which makes the financial leasing, pays the seller of the goods and ensures the delivery of the property to the lessee. After that, the lessee makes the necessary payments to the lessor on time in line with the conditions specified in the contract (Duke et al., 2009; Contino, 2002; Bennett & Bradbury, 2003; IFC, 2005; IFC, 2006).

As stated before, financial leasing stands out as the most preferred type of leasing. The reason why financial leasing is preferred so much is that it includes significant advantages over cash purchase, using credit, and other leasing types. Highlights of these advantages are as follows;

- 100% of the relevant investment can be financed
- Payment plans are flexible and can be tailored to the lessee's cash flow
- The leasing process is very fast compared to the bank loan process
- The leasing agency does not impose restrictions on the lessee's administrative practices
- Does not limit credit opportunities as it does not affect credit rating and limits
- Provides lessee protection against adverse economic conditions caused by market uncertainties
- At the end of the contract, it provides the opportunity to own the relevant property for a low price or free of charge

- Usually does not require a separate collateral
- Protects property from seizure in case of possible bankruptcy
- Provides tax advantages depending on country regulations
- Eliminates some proprietary procedural actions

In addition to these important advantages, it is possible to mention the disadvantages of financial leasing. These can be briefly listed as;

- Deprives of discount incentives applied to direct purchases in investments
- Termination of the financial lease agreement is very difficult and very costly for the lessee.
- High-interest rates are applied in financial leasing transactions
- Since the lessee does not own the property, the tenant cannot mortgage the property and show it as security.
- There is a significant exchange rate risk in foreign currency contracts.

Operational Leasing

Operational leasing is a type of leasing in which all risks and benefits arising from the ownership of the asset to be leased are not transferred. In this method, which is one of the most common types of leasing in practice, the ownership of the asset remains with the lessor and the lessee leases the related asset only for a very short period of its economic life. The fact that the contract period is shorter than the economic life of the product subject to the transaction means that the discounted form of the lease payments paid by the lessee to the lessor company during the contract period is below the current purchase price of the product. Accordingly, the residual value risk lies with the lessor. In this form of leasing, it is used in cases where the payment amounts in the contract made for the leased goods are not enough to meet the cost values. Therefore, companies that leasing out can subject the same asset to more than one lease within its useful life. In an operational leasing, the lessor is usually either the manufacturer or the seller of the leased asset. In these transactions, the leasing company usually produces or buys the asset subject to lease before the lessee requests it. Thus, all risks related to this asset are borne by the lessor before the lease is realized (Contino, 2002; Bennett & Bradbury, 2003; IFC, 2005; IFC, 2006)

In operational leasing, which is a very flexible leasing type, the lessee can easily meet their short-term needs, while the lessor can rent the relevant goods more than once, taking into account the economic life. At this point, the basic point in operational leasing is that the need is short-term, it is preferred for rapidly aging goods or equipment with very high purchasing costs. In operational leasing, all kinds of maintenance, repair, insurance expenses, damages, and losses within the lease term of the leased property belong to the lessor. The lessee does not have any responsibility for the maintenance of the property, and his sole responsibility is limited to paying the lease payments that he has committed during the contract period. In addition, although a certain period is specified in the contract, the contract can be terminated with prior notification before the end of this period. Sometimes, fines may be charged if the tenant goes to such a contract termination, although these penalties are usually not very high (Contino, 2002; Bennett & Bradbury, 2003; IFC, 2005; IFC, 2006).

Although the processes in operational leasing transactions may differ in details between countries, they are generally similar. There are two main actors in operational leasing, mainly the lessor and the lessee. The lessee finds the leasing company with the product he wants to make an operational leasing for a short time and makes sure that the relevant property has the desired features. After deciding on the properties of the property, the lessee and the lessor negotiates the terms of the lease and reach an agreement on a contract. After signing the contract, the property is delivered to the lessee. After the delivery, while the lessee pays his monthly rents, the lessor follows and performs the necessary maintenance, repair, and other official transactions arising from his ownership (IFC, 2005; IFC, 2006; Contino, 2002; Bennett & Bradbury, 2003).

Operational leasing also has significant advantages over purchasing, using credit, and other leasing types. Highlights of these advantages are as follows;

- It frees the tenant from the obligation to stick to the economic life of the property
- Flexible plans
- It is the most suitable method for short-term assets in seasonal projects.
- It facilitates the follow-up of technology and saves you from the obligation to work with goods that are outdated and lose their technological efficiency.
- Provides professional support as important issues such as maintenance and repair are taken care of by the lessor
- Does not affect credit rating and limits
- Provides the advantage of avoiding financial risks such as currency and interest rate risks
- Provides various tax advantages depending on the regulations in the countries
- It provides a significant time saving since transactions such as tax and insurance are carried out by the lessor

In addition to these positive aspects of operational leasing for the investor, some negative aspects can also be counted. The highlights of these are as follows;

- The leased product may not be a brand new product
- If the lessor is not expert and fast enough in maintenance and repair, there may be too much breakdown and time loss
- There are high fees
- Usage method can be intervened
- Different mortgages or guarantees may be requested
- The property cannot be shown as a mortgage in other applications

A Comparison Between Financial Leasing and Operational Leasing

Financial leasing and operational leasing, which are important financing methods for investors, differ from each other in terms of various features as the two most used leasing methods. Although operational leasing is sometimes referred to as an advanced form of financial leasing, significant differences arise due to attention to the essence of the methods. An important way to better understand these leasing methods is to evaluate them comparatively. Below, these leasing types are compared in terms of six prominent features and content (Contino, 2002; Bennett & Bradbury, 2003; IFC, 2005; IFC, 2006)

Firstly, the prominent difference between these two types of leasing is who will retain the ownership of the asset at the end of the contract period. If there is an agreement that the ownership of the asset will pass to the lessee at the end of the contract period or during the period, the contract in question is a financial leasing. If the lessee has to return the leased asset to the lessor at the end of the contract period, the contract is an operational leasing.

Secondly, the important feature in the comparison of the two leasing methods is the leasing price. The discounted value of the lease fees paid to the lessor on the day the contract is signed provides important information about the type of leasing. The discounted amount of the rent paid by the lessee to the lessor in operational leasing is well below the current market price of the leased asset. However, in financial leasing, the discounted amount of the rent paid by the lessee to the lessor is very close to or above the current market price of the leased asset.

Thirdly, another important point that differentiates financial leasing and operational leasing from each other is the lease term. It can be said that financial leasing is medium and long term and operational leasing is short term. If the lease term covers a large part of the economic life (more than 75%) of the leased asset, the contract is deemed to be a financial leasing. If the contract period covers a short part of the economic life (less than 75%) of the product in question, it is considered as an operational leasing.

Fourthly, the difference between the requirement of collateral can be counted while making the lease. Lessors that provide financing to investors by leasing can request collateral from the lessee in order to reduce their own risks. Since the amount to be collected from the lessee through the lease in financial leasing transactions is close to the whole value of the product in question, the relevant product is considered as collateral and no additional collateral is required. However, since the rents in operational leasing are considerably lower than the economic value of the goods, the relevant product is not accepted as collateral and additional collateral can be requested.

Fifthly, the termination possibilities are among the factors that differentiate these two leasing methods. At this point, operational leasing is a very flexible type of leasing compared to financial leasing. The possibility of contract termination in financial leasing is very low and the sanctions are very heavy. However, in operational leasing, the option of termination is generally included in the contracts as an option, provided that it is notified in advance and incurred low costs.

Sixthly, these two types of leases differ in terms of the services offered by the lessor. In the operational leasing method, expenses such as all kinds of maintenance, repair, and insurance costs related to the asset are covered by the lessor. In financial leasing, maintenance and repair expenses are covered by the lessee, while insurance and tax expenses are the responsibility of the lessor.

LEASING AND TOURISM AND HOSPITALITY MARKETS

The Tourism and hospitality markets, which are considered as invisible exports, have become one of the most vital markets in the world economy with its rapid growth after the second half of the 20th century. It can be said that factors such as population growth, economic and social development, changes in working conditions, transportation facilities, and international convergence are effective in the rapid rise of these markets, which are important sources of income for both developed and developing countries. Rapid growth in terms of quantity and quality rapidly increases the need for vehicles, facilities, land, and equipment in the sub-components of this market such as accommodation, food and beverage, recreation, entertainment, and transportation. The sector can respond to the increasing demand by financing investments quickly and effectively. In the tourism and hospitality market, which is a capital-intensive sector, it is difficult for equity to suffice investments. At this point, financial leasing and operational leasing come to the fore as one of the most frequently used financing methods in making new investments and in the development and modernization of existing investments in the sector (Koh & Jang, 2009; Whittaker, 2008; Jang et al., 2008; Vujovic et al., 2018).

Considering that the demand elasticity of the expenditures made by consumers in the tourism and hospitality market is high, it is clear how important new investments, modernization, and updating are in this sector. Compared to many other markets, this sector should appeal to the consumer's tastes and dreams as well as mandatory needs. It can be seen as one of the basic requirements for the sector to provide the goods and services used by the consumers in their daily lives and to offer more in better quality. In addition, it is not enough to make these investments for one period. In parallel with the developments and innovations in the world, these assets should be renewed and changed in line with the tastes and preferences of the consumers. In this respect, both the need for high funding at the beginning and the need for renewal and modernization over time make the leasing methods one of the important fund resources of the sector (Jang et al., 2008; Vujovic et al., 2018).

The tourism and hospitality industries, together with its sub-services, mainly arise with the need for facility, land, vehicle, and equipment. At this point, it can be said that financial leasing is used more for facilities and lands, and operational leasing is more common for vehicles and equipment. It is seen that financial leasing is mostly used in financing the land and facilities, since the land and facilities determined and built for tourism and hospitality have very high costs and are not used for different purposes, and it is very difficult to rent or sell them. Leasing companies do not prefer operational leasing much, considering the high risk in this type of financing. In addition, the investor is also willing to prefer financial leasing as he does not want to be deprived of its residual value. However, in the procurement of vehicles and equipment, although finance leasing is also seen, operational leasing is preferred. For example, in air transport, companies expand their aircraft fleets through operational leasing. In addition, buses, minibuses, and automobiles used to provide transportation of personnel and/or consumers are provided by operational leasing and can be easily renewed over time. Companies operating in the maritime transport prefer mainly operational leasing in the supply of transportation and accommodation vehicles such as ships and yachts. In addition, equipment such as information processing machines and equipment, door systems, televisions, elevators, heating and cooling devices, hot water systems, steel cases, floor-sweeping and cleaning devices, ice cream and ice machines, cabinets, furniture, sound systems, gambling machines, kitchen appliances are also goods obtained by operational leasing. Moreover, some companies rent all products based on fabrics such as bed sheets, duvet covers, mattresses, quilts, and towels used in their facilities through operational leasing, provided that the washing and cleaning are undertaken (Koh & Jang, 2009; Whittaker, 2008).

As discussed in the previous titles, financial leasing and operational leasing have significant advantages and disadvantages compared to other financing methods. When this situation is evaluated specifically in terms of the tourism and hospitality market, these methods have features that can provide benefits and create disadvantages specific to the sector. At this point, many advantages and disadvantages can be counted, but the prominent ones are stated below;

Investors prefer to managership more in the tourism and hospitality market rather than investing by purchasing directly. Especially foreign capital avoids the risk of purchasing fixed assets and does not prefer it. At this point, leasing options are effective in attracting entrepreneurs who will make the investments needed by the market.

There are seasonal peaks and troughs in terms of demand in the tourism and hospitality sector in general. In this respect, cash flows are not distributed homogeneously to all periods of the year. In bank loan financing, the determination of the terms of the installments is more fixed and strict. This situation cannot generally be adapted to the cash flow patterns of tourism and hospitality businesses. In order for companies to pay their loan debts regularly, they need to make separate resource planning and transfer resources from periods when their returns are high to periods when their returns are low. Although this situation creates a separate cost, sometimes incomplete calculations can cause a waste of resources and sometimes high penalties. However, since the rental payment periods can be determined flexibly as a result of the negotiations of the parties in leasing transactions, periods suitable for the cash flow of the companies can be determined as the payment period. This allows companies to meet their financing needs with lower risks and costs.

The tourism and hospitality market is a market that may require cash from time to time due to its unique characteristics. In this respect, it is very important for companies to have liquidity. Since financing through leasing can meet 100% of the required investment and does not restrict other credit limits and opportunities, it allows the investor to keep a significant part of their equity in liquid form and to use these resources more efficiently and effectively in other areas.

The entrepreneur takes the investment risk and gets a profit in return. There is a high possibility of making mistakes in the tourism and hospitality market, which is established with great costs, as in all other investments. Investors can make mistakes in their investments, sometimes completely and sometimes only in a specific choice. Sometimes, the investment made before may be unnecessary under the changing conditions. At this point, leasing contracts, especially operational leasing, can offer the entrepreneur a way out by offering the possibility of cancellation. In other words, the cancellation and renewal possibilities in the lease contracts are very relaxing for the investor.

As stated before, many investments in the tourism and hospitality sector need to be modernized and updated in parallel with the developments and innovations in the world and changes in the tastes and preferences of the consumers. At this point, especially in operational leasing, the tenant can change the old, outdated, and technologically behind goods. Since such risks remain with the lessor, the operational leasing provides the investor with a dynamic renewal process.

In addition to the stated advantages of financial leasing and operational leasing, the sector-specific disadvantages can be expressed as follows;

Investments can be made with very high costs in the tourism and hospitality market, which is a capital-intensive market. Leasing costs are generally higher than loan costs. Companies that have already invested by bearing high costs increase their costs and therefore the risk they undertake by choosing leasing methods.

In operational leasing, the lessee is deprived of the residual value of the property at the end of the lease term. The residual value may reach substantial amounts if the relevant property is leased for a shorter period than the end of its useful life. The lessee who returns the goods at the end of the contract is deprived of this value. In projects that are successful in the tourism and hospitality market, the value increase in land and buildings can be quite high over time. In this case, purchasing is more advantageous than leasing.

Since tourism and hospitality companies do not have the ownership of the assets acquired through leasing, they cannot mortgage those assets against their debts, so they may encounter problems when borrowing. Since the leased assets do not appear in the assets of the companies, the enterprises are seen as smaller and weak than they are.

It is very difficult to set an upper limit on tourism and hospitality investments that are basically considered luxury goods and appeal to tastes and preferences. More beautiful and better quality will always be a target in this market. If leasing is used frequently and uncontrolled, the business may fall into payment difficulties in the future, as leasing allows to overcome budget limitations and to make high investments with a small amount of equity.

CRISIS IN TOURISM AND HOSPITALITY MARKETS AND COVID-19 PANDEMIC

Crisis is used to express the situations that arise as a result of an unforeseen social, economic, or psychological development that seriously shakes the normal process and the existing solutions are inadequate in solving the encountered problem. Crisis creates social and economic losses by occurring unexpectedly, preventing activities that are accepted as usual, and leaving extremely negative traces with its effects and results. The crisis in the tourism and hospitality market can be defined as events that threaten the usual activities of tourism and hospitality-related companies, create a negative opinion by creating the impression that the tourism region is not safe, and cause tourism businesses to disrupt their activities or shut down due to the decrease in tourism and hospitality demand and expenditure. The crises affecting the tourism and hospitality market can be grouped under five different headings: crises caused by economic problems, crises caused by terrorism and war situations, crises caused by political problems, crises caused by social and cultural conflicts, and crises caused by natural and environmental factors. Since tourism demand is elastic, the tourism and hospitality market is affected more rapidly and deeply by the emerging crises compared to other sectors. The effects of the crisis on the tourism and hospitality market are examined under five different headings: the effect on the number of tourists and tourism revenues per tourist, the effect on the enterprises, the effect on the sector employees, the effect on the country's economy, and the effect on the related sectors (Glaesser, 2003; Ritchie, 2004; Hao et al., 2020; Bremser et al., 2018;).

Despite its relatively young age, the tourism and hospitality market in the world has faced many different types of crises. One of these types is the crisis originating from health threats that can be presented as a type of crisis caused by natural and environmental factors. Contagious and epidemic diseases that threaten human health can affect the travel decisions of tourists and cause crises in the tourism and hospitality sector. Cases such as sars, mers, ebola, cholera, swine flu that have emerged in the past years have negatively reflected in the tourism and hospitality markets of the countries. Therefore, epidemics or viruses that threaten human health seriously affect tourism and hospitality activities and are the source of the crises that will occur in these sectors (Ritchie, 2008; Mao et al., 2010; Bremser et al., 2018; Kalyankar, 2020).

A new epidemic that is emerging today is the Covid-19 pandemic. The Covid-19 pandemic that emerged towards the end of December 2019 has affected the whole world. As of the beginning of December 2020, when these lines are written, the total number of cases in the world has exceeded 70 million and the total number of deaths has exceeded 1.5 million. With the ongoing Covid-19 pandemic, international trade and travel were suspended, schools were closed, organizations, congresses, festivals were canceled, and some workplaces were closed. It seems inevitable that the Covid-19 pandemic will deeply envelop the economies of the country, leading to losses in production, employment, and income. The epidemic, which is said to be in an upward trend, is expressed as an unprecedented disease in the world and therefore a crisis situation. Other than the Covid-19 virus, no other event in the world has affected the whole world so much and has not caused such a large-scale travel restriction. Therefore, along with travel restrictions, there have been major cancellations in all commercial activities related to tourism and hospitality such as transportation, entertainment, sports and cultural events, hotel reservations, and festivals and this situation has seriously affected the global tourism and hospitality market. Therefore, not knowing how long this pandemic will increase and how long it will continue causes concern in the tourism and hospitality sector (Hao et al., 2020; Gössling et al. 2020; Chang et al., 2020; Kalyankar, 2020).

The effects of the pandemic on the tourism and hospitality sector can be examined under two main headings as direct effects and indirect effects. Direct effects are the effects of restrictions. It has been prevented that individuals not only travel to other countries, regions, or places but leave their homes from time to time. Consequently, in the early stages of the pandemic, there was a great decrease in the number of tourists and tourism revenues worldwide. This effect is clear and obvious. However, the effects of the restrictions are expected to return to normal after the virus is controlled and the easing of restrictions. In fact, it can be expected that consumers who cannot travel as they wish due to restrictions will have a greater desire to travel after the restrictions are lifted (Gössling et al., 2020; Lapointe, 2020).

When the indirect effects are considered, it is possible to consider it by dividing it into two main headings. These are economic effects and psychological effects. Considering its economic impacts, tourism expenditures will decrease as a result of the decrease in the incomes of consumers and this situation will cause mass tourism to be affected at first. In all economies the spending collapse (demand shock) that has erupted in important service sectors, especially transportation, tourism, and trade, will gradually deepen and rapidly spread to all economies. On top of all these, with the financial shocks, real economies are likely to shrink together with demand and supply shocks. It is the basic expectation of the economic theory that this expected economic collapse, along with other crises, will greatly affect the demand for tourism and hospitality, which has already elastic demand.

Finally, the psychological effect of the pandemic will come into question. Even if this pandemic is brought under control, it is an approach accepted by all segments that nothing can be the same as before. As a result, there is a terrible epidemic period experienced by people and the significant effects that this has left on psychologies. At this point, people are expected to be affected at different levels in proportion to the degree of the situations they have experienced and witnessed during this pandemic process. Time will tell the extent of these effects and how long they will last. However, it is clear that this psychological effect will reduce the demand for tourism and hospitality even if the epidemic is brought under control. In addition, the success of countries in the epidemic process will also affect the possibility of traveling to that country. At this point, it is expected that countries that can respond well to the epidemic, quickly control it, the health system does not collapse and offer a healthy tourism opportunity will attract more tourists than before, while travel to countries that are the source of the virus, the health system fails in troubled periods and are considered insufficient to offer healthy tourism will be avoided (Lapointe, 2020; Chang et al., 2020; Kalyankar, 2020).

LEASING AND COVID-19 PANDEMIC

An important point to be discussed in the analysis of the effects of the Covid-19 pandemic is leasing contracts. The sanctions that tourism and hospitality firms with many financial leasing and operational leasing contracts will face in the current situation and the developments that will occur after the pandemic are very important for the future of the market.

Firstly, it can be looked at the status of existing contracts signed by lessor (leasing companies) and lessee (tourism and hospitality companies). As part of the fight against the pandemic, many restrictions and sanctions were taken by the authorities, and these decisions directly or indirectly affected the activities of the tourism and hospitality firms. In this pandemic, there is an unpredictable and unforeseen situation for the lessor and the lessee. This extraordinary situation is neither caused by the lessee nor the lessor. As of the developing process, the conditions have changed against the lessee, which will make it impossible for the lessee to fulfill the promises made through the contract. However, it is not clear how this situation will affect the existing contracts. In this case, it is necessary to discuss the situation and put forward what needs to be done in line with these changing conditions. At this point, dividing leasing contracts into two parts provides convenience in terms of the analysis of the topic. The first of these is the situation where a similar situation is predicted and written into the contract while the contracts are being made. The second is the situation where similar conditions are not covered in the contract. These two situations should be evaluated separately.

1. *Inclusion of Extraordinary Situations in the Contract:* One of the most important advantages of choosing leasing is their flexibility. In this respect, the parties can conclude a leasing contract with their mutual free will, without being subject to any form of the condition, provided that it is not contrary to the mandatory provisions of the law, public order, and general moral rules. It is possible that in these leasing agreements concluded between the parties, they have established special provisions regarding such extraordinary situations experienced globally. If such a situation is in question, these special provisions of the contract should be examined first and the outcome of the leasing should be decided within the framework of these provisions. At this point, a solution should be sought in whatever is stipulated in the contract such as deferring payments, cancellation of contracts, renegotiation of contract terms.
2. *Extraordinary Situations Not Included in the Contract:* If there are no special clauses in the contract for such extraordinary situations; This time, it will be necessary to examine the outcome of the lease agreements within the framework of the general provisions of the law. It is also necessary to examine this situation

by dividing it into two parts. The first is the situation in which the activities of the relevant lessee are completely banned and stopped within the scope of the measures and restrictions taken by the central administration, and the second is the partial suspension of the activities of the relevant enterprise or the situation of the business coming to a halt due to the measures and restriction decisions taken.

a. *2a- Situation in terms of the lessee whose activities are completely discontinued:* Considering that the lessee pays the rent in return for the use of the leased property for the purpose of use in the lease agreements, it can be concluded that the lessee, who is not responsible for the impossibility of the use of the leased property, will not be temporarily liable for paying the lease fee to the lessor. In such temporary impossibilities, the date of performance of the debt is postponed until the date when the impossibility of execution disappears.
b. *2b- Situation in terms of the lessee whose operations are partially discontinued and/or indirectly affected:* The central authorities have partially stopped the activities of some enterprises, not completely, that is, restricted their activities. Some businesses, on the other hand, did not face direct activity restrictions, but were indirectly affected by the restrictions and their activities came to a halt. It clearly states that if the conditions existing during the establishment of the contract change in an unpredictable manner and the balance in the contract becomes unbearable for a party as a result of this change, the principle of strict commitment to the contract cannot be expected from the said party. In this context, the lessee shall have the right to request the adaptation of the contract to the new conditions and to return from the contract if this is not possible. The lessee will request an adaptation from the court, but if it is not possible to adapt the contract, termination may occur.

The second situation to be evaluated is how to shape the innovations in leasing opportunities in the tourism and hospitality market after Covid-19 pandemic. At this point, it is obvious that tourism and hospitality businesses that have gone through a long crisis period will need financial resources. It is obvious that the demand of market actors, who could not provide cash inflows in the past, for leasing opportunities will increase. In particular, the demand for operational leasing is expected to increase. On the other hand, it is inevitable that innovations will occur in the content of the leasing agreements with the experiences gained. How to act in such extraordinary situations will be included in the contracts considering the expectations of both parties. Such innovations to reduce risk will obviously increase costs. Considering how interest rates will increase depending on the economic crisis that the pandemic will cause, it is expected that the costs of leasing contracts will increase even more. In other words, an increase in costs and a decrease in demand and prices are an expectation for market. As a result, time will show in which direction the total effect will be, but there are various expectations that will create the opposite effects.

POST-COVID-19 PANDEMIC STRATEGIES

Crisis processes are basically analyzed in three phases: pre-crisis phase, crisis phase, and post-crisis phase. The pre-crisis phase is when action can be taken to prevent or reduce the effects of potential crises. Unfortunately, the tourism and hospitality market was not prepared for the Covid-19 pandemic process. The crisis stage refers to the point at which the effects of the crisis are felt and cannot be reversed by being relatively out of control. This phase, unfortunately, started with direct cessation, travel bans, and leaving home restrictions for the tourism and hospitality market. The sector, which could not take precautions before the crisis, was shocked by the rapid and widespread restrictions and did not know what to do. The post-crisis phase is the reconstruction period in which the measures taken are implemented. The fact that no international organization has yet been able to reveal how this crisis will progress, where its peak will be and when the end trend will start increases the uncertainties even more. However, as the pandemic process cannot be fully predicted, the evaluations made for the post-crisis period remain theoretical and the opinions put forward cannot go beyond different scenarios. Therefore, it is very difficult to make post-crisis assessments and to support them with data. But ultimately, there is no other way than to come up with new ways and ideas based on old experiences (Bremser et al., 2018; Gössling et al., 2020; Chang et al., 2020).

Considering the high consumer demand elasticity, the inability to store the product produced and supplied in the market, and the fact that the crisis was caused by an easily transmitted and fatal disease, it is a fact that the tourism and hospitality sector will be affected more by this process and some of its effects may be permanent for many years. However, with the tourism and hospitality market being a very sensitive sector against crises, old experiences have shown that the sector is recovering rapidly after crises and can perform surprisingly well. In addition, considering the contributions it makes to the country's economy, the elimination of the effects of this crisis will be evaluated as a problem not only for the relevant companies or the sector but also of the countries and a solution will be sought. At this point, central authorities should set up an information center without leaving all the burden to the company and the sector, and determine a management consisting of sector representatives and experts, and produce alternative solutions for what to do on behalf of the sector during and after the crisis (Gössling et al., 2020; Hao et al., 2020; Chang et al., 2020).

The central authority should focus primarily on what it can do during the crisis. First of all, pioneering steps should be taken and measures should be implemented to ensure the survival of companies during the crisis period. It is necessary to inform businesses about the measures and restrictions to be implemented, to save them from unnecessary expenses, and to help them with government support in their compulsory expenses. Their debts to the state should be urgently postponed in the long term and supported with tax cuts. In times of crisis, enterprises should be prevented from falling into liquidity shortages due to uncertainty and from entering into a high-interest loan impasse with the measures taken.

Secondly, it is necessary to work on what needs to be done to revive the sector after the crisis. It should be understood that such crises in the tourism and hospitality market are always the harbinger of the change in the understanding of sectoral service, and it is necessary to produce proactive solutions for controlled and healthy tourism. It should be ensured and explained not only that the vehicle, facility, and region are safe, but also the success of the country's fight against Covid-19 pandemic and a country where foreigners can spend their holidays without any problems. Central authorities should reconsider the standards they have previously determined within the framework of the pandemic, and high standards should be determined from the points of cleanliness, hygiene, and health. State-controlled modernizations should be provided for common use areas of consumers such as pools, elevators, door handles, remote controls, toilets and bathrooms, open buffet restaurants in the tourism and hospitality market. New standards for health, cleanliness, and hygiene for tourism and hospitality businesses should be audited with certificates to be issued. It is clear that there will be big and radical changes in consumer demands. These should be revealed with the expert staff formed and arrangements should be made at this point. It should be studied in what ways and methods can be implemented in the tourism and hospitality market innovations such as the robot age will begin, contactless services will be intensified, social distance will be preferred, individuality will come to the fore. With the innovations, it will make in the state health system and the guarantees it will provide to foreign visitors, tourism will be able to keep it active, even if the pandemic continues (Bremser et al., 2018; Gössling et al., 2020; Chang et al., 2020; Lapointe, 2020).

Since financial leasing and operational leasing is one of the most popular means of financing the tourism and hospitality market, the central authority should also work on this point. During the crisis period, tourism and hospitality firms should prevent them from terminating their activities due to their existing contracts and they should also enable them to obtain the fund needs that will arise after the crisis in a fast, low-interest, and long-term. Market representatives who have difficulties in lease payments during the crisis should be supported with a solution formula that their lessor is not victimized, and the debts should be spread over long terms. The legal basis for reviewing existing contracts in accordance with the new norm should be established. In addition, it is very important not to expose lessee to exchange and inflation risks in leasing transactions to be carried out by ensuring price stability rapidly. With political stability and an environment of social and cultural peace, attractive messages should be created for foreign visitors and investors. State support for new investments should also be extended to renewal projects that highlight pandemic measures.

FUTURE RESEARCH DIRECTIONS

This study discusses financial leasing and operational leasing and the use of these leasing methods in the tourism and hospitality markets. In the study crises in tourism and hospitality markets and the effects of the Covid-19 pandemic are examined. The effects of the Covid-19 pandemic and the strategies put forward for the post-Covid-19 period have been based on observational information and emerging new literature. These studies can be developed with the support of data that can be obtained in the future. In addition, the effects of the measures to be taken can be observed and evaluated, and new measures and solutions can be proposed. In addition, each country and region can be evaluated individually and comparative analyzes can be made.

CONCLUSION

All humanity gains a new experience with what they have recently experienced. It can be said that the world will not be the same as before and new order definitions will emerge with the concept of "new normal". The Covid-19 virus, which emerged in December 2019 and has been spreading globally since then, deeply affects the tourism and hospitality sector as well as all other effects. At this point, the impact of this pandemic on this sector, and especially on financial leasing and operational leasing agreements, which are highly preferred in the sector, emerges as an important issue. In this study, financial leasing and operational leasing, which are the most used leasing methods in the world, and the use of these leasing methods in the tourism and hospitality market are discussed and effects of the Covid-19 pandemic at this point are evaluated. In addition, in the study, suggestions were made for the changes and innovations that may occur after the crisis in the tourism and hospitality market and leasing contracts.

The ability to overcome this crisis with the least damage and the emergence of the economies will only be possible if all actors find a solution together. If a solution cannot be found together, it is clear that all parties will suffer in the long run. Longer-term and permanent solutions should be produced instead of short-term profit targets or loss minimization approaches. This can be possible with the solution that the central authority, lessor, and lessee will put forward together. In this period, each actor accepting to bear certain costs will ensure that all parties will get more profitable results in the long term.

In order to discuss the effects of the Covid-19 pandemic and post-pandemic strategies in a more reliable and healthy way, it is necessary to see the peak of the crisis and examine the ending trend.

REFERENCES

Bennett, B. K., & Bradbury, M. E. (2003). Capitalizing non-cancelable operating leases. *Journal of International Financial Management & Accounting*, *14*(2), 101–114. doi:10.1111/1467-646X.00091

Bremser, K., Alonso-Almeida, M. M., & Llach, J. (2018). Strategic alternatives for tourism companies to overcome times of crisis. *Service Business*, *12*(2), 229–251. doi:10.100711628-017-0344-7

Carter, L. Barger, T. & Kuczynski, I. (1996). *Leasing in emerging markets*. World Bank IFC Lessons of Experience Series 3.

Chang, C. L., McAleer, M., & Ramos, V. (2020). A charter for sustainable tourism after COVID-19. *Sustainability*, *12*(9), 3671. doi:10.3390u12093671

Contino, R. M. (2002). *The complete equipment-leasing handbook*. AMACOM American Management Association.

Duke, J. C., Hsieh, S. J., & Su, Y. (2009). Operating and synthetic leases: Exploiting financial benefits in the post-enron era. *Advances in Accounting, Incorporating. Advances in International Accounting*, *25*(1), 28–39. doi:10.1016/j.adiac.2009.03.001

Ezzell, J. R., & Vora, P. P. (2001). Leasing versus purchasing: Direct evidence on a corporation's motivations for leasing and consequences of leasing. *The Quarterly Review of Economics and Finance*, *41*(1), 33–47. doi:10.1016/S1062-9769(00)00060-0

Glaesser, D. (2003). *Crisis management in the tourism industry*. Butterworth-Heinemann Publications.

Gössling, S., Scott, D., & Hall, C. M. (2020). Pandemics, tourism and global change: A rapid assessment of COVID-19. *Journal of Sustainable Tourism, 29*(1), 1–20. doi:10.1080/09669582.2020.1758708

Hao, F., Xiao, Q., & Chon, K. (2020). COVID-19 and China's hotel industry: Impacts, a disaster management framework, and post-pandemic agenda. *International Journal of Hospitality Management, 90*, 102636. doi:10.1016/j.ijhm.2020.102636 PMID:32834356

IFC. (2005). *Leasing in development: lessons from emerging economies*. International Finance Corporation.

IFC. (2006). *Leasing handbook, international finance corporation*. World Bank Group.

Jang, S., Tang, C., & Chen, M. (2008). Financing behaviors of hotel companies. *International Journal of Hospitality Management, 27*, 478–487. doi:10.1016/j.ijhm.2007.08.010

Kalyankar, M. D., & Patil, P. (2020). Impact of Covid-19 pandemic on the tourism sector. *UGC Care Journal, 31*, 611–617.

Koh, J. H., & Jang, S. (2009). Determinants of using operating lease in the hotel industry. *International Journal of Hospitality Management, 28*(4), 638–640. doi:10.1016/j.ijhm.2009.03.002

Lapointe, D. (2020). Reconnecting tourism after COVID-19: The paradox of alterity in tourism areas. *Tourism Geographies, 22*(3), 633–638. doi:10.1080/14616688.2020.1762115

Mao, C., Ding, C., & Lee, H. (2010). Post-SARS tourist arrival recovery patterns: An analysis based on a catastrophe theory. *Tourism Management, 31*(6), 855–861. doi:10.1016/j.tourman.2009.09.003 PMID:32287733

Mayes, D. G., & Nicholas, C. S. (1988). *The Economic Impact of Leasing*. Macmillan Press. doi:10.1007/978-1-349-09523-0

Ritchie, B. (2008). Tourism disaster planning and management: From response and recovery to reduction and readiness. *Current Issues in Tourism, 11*(4), 315–348. doi:10.1080/13683500802140372

Ritchie, B. W. (2004). Chaos, crises and disasters: A strategic approach to crisis management in the tourism industry. *Tourism Management, 25*(6), 669–683. doi:10.1016/j.tourman.2003.09.004

Teodorescu, C. D. (2014). The leasing-evolutions and trends. *Economic Insights - Trends and Challenges*, *3*(2), 85–92.

Tongxia, L., Rahimie, K., & Qaiser, M. (2016). The determinants of leasing decisions: An empirical analysis from Chinese listed SMEs. *Managerial Finance*, *42*(8), 763–790. doi:10.1108/MF-06-2015-0166

Vasiliou, D., & Ipirotis, N. (2008). *Financial management (theory and practice)*. Rosili Publishing, Chapman and Hall/CRC.

Vujovic, S., Arsic, L., & Premovic, J. (2018). Financing in tourism: basic models of financing the accommodation offer. *J Hotel Bus Manage*, *7*(2), 185.

Whittaker, C. (2008). Hotel operator motives in UK sale and leaseback/ managementback transactions. *International Journal of Hospitality Management*, *27*(4), 641–648. doi:10.1016/j.ijhm.2007.07.031

ADDITIONAL READING

AlBattat, A. R., & MatSom, A. P. (2014). Emergency planning and disaster recovery in Malaysian hospitality industry. *Social and Behavioral Sciences*, *144*, 45–53. doi:10.1016/j.sbspro.2014.07.272

Ang, J., & Peterson, P. P. (1984). The leasing puzzle. *The Journal of Finance*, *39*(4), 1055–1065. doi:10.1111/j.1540-6261.1984.tb03892.x

Beattie, V., Goodacre, A., & Thomson, S. (2000). Operating leases and the assessment of lease-debt substitutability. *Journal of Banking & Finance*, *24*(3), 427–470. doi:10.1016/S0378-4266(99)00045-X

Cooper, C. (2012). *Essentials of tourism*. Pearson.

Deloof, M., Lagaert, I., & Verschueren, I. (2007). Leases and debt: Complements or substitutes? Evidence from Belgian SMEs. *Journal of Small Business Management*, *45*(4), 491–500. doi:10.1111/j.1540-627X.2007.00224.x

Endo. (2006). Foreign direct investment in tourism – flows and volumes. *Tourism Management*, *27*, 600-614.

Korstanje, M., & Seraphin, H. (2017). Revisiting the sociology of consumption in tourism. The Routledge Handbook of Consumer Behaviour in Hospitality and Tourism, 2-16.

Korstanje, M. E. (2011). The fear of traveling: A new perspective for tourism and hospitality. *Anatolia, 22*(2), 222–233. doi:10.1080/13032917.2011.597935

Morais, A. I. (2013). Why companies choose to lease instead of buy? Insights from academic literature. *Academia (Caracas), 26*(3), 432–446. doi:10.1108/ARLA-07-2013-0091

Oliner, S. D., & Rudebusch, G. D. (1992). Sources of the financing hierarchy for business investment. *The Review of Economics and Statistics, 74*(4), 643–654. doi:10.2307/2109378

Senbeto, D. L., & Hon, A. H. (2020). The impacts of social and economic crises on tourist behaviour and expenditure: An evolutionary approach. *Current Issues in Tourism, 23*(6), 740–755. doi:10.1080/13683500.2018.1546674

Sharpe, S. A., & Nguyen, H. H. (1995). Capital market imperfections and the incentive to lease. *Journal of Financial Economics, 39*(2-3), 2–3, 271–294. doi:10.1016/0304-405X(95)00830-8

KEY TERMS AND DEFINITIONS

Crisis: Crisis is the situations that arise as a result of an unforeseen social, economic, or psychological development that seriously shakes the normal process and the existing solutions are inadequate in solving the encountered problem.

Financial Leasing: Financial leasing is a contract signed between the lessor and the lessee for a certain period of time, which leaves the use of the property selected by the lessee and purchased by the lessor to the lessee in exchange for certain payments. In this method, the lessee has the right to use the whole or almost all of the economic life of the leased property and undertakes all risks and benefits other than ownership.

Financing: Financing is the provision of the resources a firm or individuals need to cover their expenses.

Lease Agreement: Lease agreement is a formal agreement between the lessor and the lessee that shows the conditions under which the property to be leased, sets out the obligations, and legally binds the parties.

Leasing: It is a financing method realized with a contract signed between the lessor and lessee for a certain period of time. The lessor provides an asset for use to the lessee for a specified period of time, in return for set payments.

Lessee: Lessee is the company or person who wants to get the right to use the property in return for the rent to be paid for a certain period of time.

Lessor: Lessor is the owner of the asset to be leased and transfers the right to use the asset to the lessee for a certain period and amount in order to gain profit.

Operational Leasing: Operational leasing is a type of leasing in which all risks and benefits arising from the ownership of the asset to be leased are not transferred. In this method the ownership of the asset remains with the lessor and the lessee leases the related asset only for a very short period of its economic life.

Tourism and Hospitality Market: Tourism and hospitality market is where the supply and demand of tourism and hospitality goods and services meet.

Tourism and Hospitality Market Crisis: Events that threaten the usual activities of tourism and hospitality-related companies, create a negative opinion by creating the impression that the tourism region is not safe, and cause tourism businesses to disrupt their activities or shut down due to the decrease in tourism and hospitality demand and expenditure.

Chapter 3
"Taking Care of Yourself at Home": Use of E-Commerce About Food and Care During the COVID-19 Pandemic in the City of Buenos Aires

Aldana Boragnio
National Council for Scientific and Technical Research (CONICET), Argentina & CIES, Argentina

Constanza Faracce Macia
Center for Research on Consumption, Sensibilities, and Creativity (CICSEC), University of Palermo, Argentina

ABSTRACT

This chapter presents some reflections on the changes regarding the use of electronic commerce and digital platforms during the period of preventive and mandatory social isolation decreed in the country during the COVID-19 pandemic, based on the new services food services, food delivery service, and new practices around "home care." To this end, a survey was conducted on eating practices during the first part of the isolation period in April-May 2020, and a digital ethnography was performed on new services around food and "home care" during the subsequent period. The expository strategy is as follows: 1) the theoretical approach on the sociology of bodies/emotions and its relationship with consumption and enjoyment is described, 2) virtual ethnography is defined based on its advantages as a methodology of social inquiry, 3) research results focused on the acceleration of electronic commerce and consumption "at home" are presented during the ASPO, and 4) some final reflections are made.

DOI: 10.4018/978-1-7998-7287-0.ch003

INTRODUCTION

Because of the COVID-19 pandemic, in Argentina, on March 20, 2020, through decree No. 297/20, the Social, Preventive and Mandatory Isolation (ASPO, for its acronym in Spanish) entered into force. The executive order disposed not only the social distancing but also the confinement (lockdown) of the citizens living in urban and rural areas. In consequence, a whole sector of economy has downfallen or tittered on the brink of collapse. It is safe to say there was an increase in the unemployment rate oscillating from 8.9% in December 2019 to 13.1% in June 2020 (Mercado de Trabajo, 2020). This economic downturn not only affected the entire country – so to speak in the fields of health and employment- but also accelerated an identity crisis at all levels: commodities, manufactured goods, industrializations and small consumption. Domestic consumption, as well as the industry of travels and subservice sectors was negatively affected by the global pandemic. In fact, the market often adjusts to the environmental conditions. In this case, the higher levels of fear and uncertainty paralyzed the domestic demand creating a cut-off in wages, tariffs, and business. The capitalist world, at least as we know it, was radically changed as never before. The fall of employment associated to the bankruptcy of thousands firms and companies give a grim shot for the next decades (Operti and Mesquita Moreira, 2020). Against this background, there were clear transformations in the ways of conducting business, especially in the food and care sectors. Many businesses and services had to be reconfigured to the new daily realities and delivery and self-employment practices were reinforced, giving rise to the appearance of new individual mechanisms linked to obtaining income or not losing it. In this vein, the renting industry still offers a fertile ground to understand the dilemmas and opportunities this pandemic gives.

In the present chapter, we present some reflections on the new food services and its relationship for using of digital and platforms new practices around the "home care" during the ASPO declared in the country on 20 March 2020. A survey was conducted on feeding practices during the isolation period in April-May of that year and a digital ethnography was carried out on the new services around food and "home care" during the subsequent period. The expository strategy will be as follows: a) the theoretical approach on the sociology of bodies/emotions and its relationship with consumption and immediate enjoyment will be described, b) virtual ethnography is based on its advantages as a methodology of social inquiry, c) research results are presented, focused on the acceleration of electronic commerce and consumption "at home" during the ASPO, d) some final reflections will be made.

CONSUMPTION FROM SOCIOLOGY OF BODIES/EMOTIONS APPROACH

From the lens of the sociology of bodies/emotions, emotions are not just another sociological object, but rather they become a lens from which to interpret social reality. Emotions are understood in their social character, that is, as incorporated and constructed from the interaction of subjects with the social world and with others, a process that they necessarily carry out through their bodies. In this way, the opposition between bodies and emotions loses meaning (Scribano, 2012).

The bodies/emotions of social agents are understood as products (and reproducers) of the politics of sensibilities. By the latter it is understood:

"1. A set of cognitive-affective social practices. 2.Aimed at the production, management and reproduction of horizons of action, disposition and cognition. 3.These horizons refer: (a) to the organization of daily life (day-to-day, wakefulness/sleep, food/withdrawal, etc.); (b) to the information used to order preferences and values (adequate/inappropriate; acceptable/unacceptable; bearable/unbearable) and (c) to the parameters for time/space management" (De Sena and Scribano, 2020: 45).

Thus, the politics of the sensibilities contextually organize the ways of feeling and, therefore, guide the actions of the agents, configuring sociabilities, experiences and sensibilities that contribute to the production and reproduction of societies. Currently, we are urged to think about the connections between emotions, sensibilities and the reproduction of societies while, from this conceptual scheme, inhabiting normalized societies for immediate enjoyment through consumption is thrown as a diagnosis (Scribano, 2015, 2017).

Although consumption was related to capitalism since its inception, from the historical transformations in the mode of production, the theoretical reflections around the notion have been modified (Scribano, 2013). In the 1960s, perspectives emerged from various disciplines (history, anthropology, sociology and cultural studies) that differed from both classical political economy and the conception of the consumer from the Critical Theory of the Frankfurt School. While the former comprises an autonomous individual who rationally consumes to satisfy his vital human needs, the later defines a passive and manipulated mass society, a victim of advertising traps (Aristizábal García, 2020).

In opposition, the social sciences theorized the purchase of goods as an activity that serves to establish and maintain social relationships, surrounded by multiple moral and evaluative meanings for people who carry them out, evaluations that will only be such within a given society. Thus, understanding consumption as an aspect that crosses the multiple edges of social life enables its understanding as a social practice that organizes the actions of subjects. These views move away from the moral interpretations of consumer practices, which place them as negative or positive action in themselves, as well as their association with material needs or access to certain levels of income. Consuming goods of a certain type, with money obtained in one way or another, for oneself or to share with others, was understood as a practice that acquires different social meanings, depending on the historical, cultural and economic moments in which it is carried out (Aristizábal García, 2020).

As this backdrop, consumption is detached from the chain that unites increased production - greater consumption - unlimited progress, which allows us to visualize that the proliferation of consumption can be sustained in societies with high levels of inequality (Dettano, 2019). This is related to Marcuse's conception that forms of consumption as the acquisition of things produced were displaced by consumption for enjoyment (Scribano, 2013).

Starting from this idea, it is possible to establish that, in the 21st century, "the connections between consumption, enjoyment and objects acquire the procedural structure of addictions: there is an object that releases moments of containment/ adaptation to a specific state of sensibilities with such power/capacity that its absence demands its immediate replacement/reproduction" (Scribano 2015: 47). Thus, consumption functions as an ephemeral mechanism for reducing anxieties: it is consumed, it is enjoyed and the anxieties are appeased at the moment in which the object of enjoyment is being consumed. Therefore, it can only be enjoyed in the here and now, which produces a parenthesis that suspends the daily flow of life of the subjects and disengagement in time/space that only makes sense in its indefinite reiteration. This is how enjoyment acquires its character immediately, giving rise to the compulsive and pre-reflective repetition of the act of consuming. With these characteristics in the mind, memory facilitates the efforts made erasing part of the knowledge how objects are manipulated; and it is at this point that a stabilized and a-conflictive life is formed through immediate enjoyment and consumption (Scribano, 2013; Dettano, 2020).

In this scheme, the act of immediate enjoyment gives meaning to the action of consuming, constituting a moral of immediate enjoyment through consumption that becomes an imperative that organizes people's daily lives, while at the same time guiding the accepted sensibility and acceptable of the time:

Immediate enjoyment "in-consumption", being a substitute strategy for social synthesis, occupies at least three simultaneous positions in the action coordination processes: a) it is a bridge with the others, b) it is a way to elaborate the presentation social of the person and fundamentally shelters the contradiction of being an individual act carried out in front of the Others. (Scribano, 2015: 49)

Having said this, it is possible to understand the *immediate enjoyment* from consumption as an element that constitutes the identity of the subjects in the process of interaction with others, this being a central aspect to understand the current social structuring processes, since it was strongly deepened and reconfigured with the acceleration of the technological transformations of the last ten years from the so-called "digital acceleration" (Scribano, 2020: 230). Consuming to be seen consuming and "having a good time" enhances the imperative of enjoyment, which must not only be experienced but must also take on a public state and be related, shown and experienced in front of others. Thus, "everything that is experienced must be represented in public, transmitted massively while recognized/approved by many" (Scribano, 2015: 41) and today, in the era of the Internet, broadcasts for billions of subjects and the living of Instagram, this takes on other dimensions.

In sum, the mandate of enjoyment associated with consumption is a great organizer of the politics of sensibilities in contemporary societies. There, consumption and immediate enjoyment are combined as two central elements that make the conditions of existence of the societies of the Global South bearable (Borock, 2008; Warde 2016; Korstanje 2017).

METHODOLOGY: INTERNET FROM AN INTERNET

To study complex sociological dimensions in an ever-changing society, we adopt a qualitative research strategy based on digital ethnography. Since this type of approach seeks to deepen the meanings and meanings that social practices acquire within the framework of the daily life of the subjects (Taylor and Bogdan, 1987). As debated, this new century demands new methodologies. Hence, it is essential to develop new methodologies that frame to the new cosmologies of a global capitalism. New technologies and their impact on sensibilities, on the senses and their stimulation, on the transformations in daily life, in sociability and in the ways of speaking / listening/writing/reading, invites us to think about the ways in which we can get closer to knowing this new reality and the social practices.

The Internet emerges in the late 1960s when a small university community of scientists and students launch to new discoveries while creating the ARPANET. From the modifications of this network came the Internet and, with the beginning of its commercialization in 1980, it expanded far beyond its first roots in research, coming to include both a wide community of users and a growing commercial activity. With the rapid expansion of personal computers, browsers, and World Wide Web (WWW) technology in its first decades of existence, the Internet-enabled user's easy access to global information and generated new phases of commercialization (ISOC, 2009). This is how the advent of 4.0 companies took place, which was strongly radicalized at the beginning of the 21st century, promoting the rapid development of Social Networks and the consequent increase in their commercial value. Among these factors, in the line of lower levels of production costs of mobile devices, as well as the expansion of internet access and the rise of new modes of communication change daily the routine of people. In consequence, the digital technology has drawn the borders of human relations (Scribano and Lisdero, 2019). It must be said that the use of digital tech associates mainly to social networks, such as WhatsApp, Facebook and Instagram and to multiple apps that are part of the daily practices. Therefore, by incorporating them from different modes of inquiry enables access to various aspects of social reality (Boragnio, 2020b). Still further, the current digital/ virtual/mobile world requires us to enter a set of new practices where sociabilities, experiences and sensibilities are inscribed, configuring new possibilities, assumptions and limitations for social research. So it becomes necessary to investigate from methodologies that allow us to approach new phenomena by using technologies no longer as "new" but as phenomena installed in the everyday life. Approaching the XXI century from the XXI century is an essential need for sociology, from which it becomes essential to "… review the binary divisions between "the virtual/the real", "the online/the offline in the understanding of the experiences that are hatched in our societies" (De Sena and Lisdero, 2015: 98). In consonance with this, digital ethnography mediates between the human relations and the virtual world. Anchored in the assumptions of traditional ethnography, it is an inquiry strategy in which "… the researcher must immerse himself or herself in the world of the Internet" (De Sena and Lisdero, 2015: 72), seeking to understand the meanings that They are built from the interaction in the virtual space between users, which can be personal profiles, services, companies, brands or "influencers".

Cyberspace is understood as a new social space, in which certain senses, feelings and meanings are configured that, in Hine's words, "cross the border between online and offline over and over again" (2004: 21). It is at this point that digital ethnography presents new advantages for the observer since it allows us a progressive approach as well as a systematic record of the online world as a space for continuity of the offline, in which specific interaction dynamics are found, with their own logic, but which are historically situated cultural practices. Therefore, while increasing the capacity to collect information and allow recording at the same time as observation in a more efficient way in relation to time, which requires us "… a constant and persistent epistemological vigilance (see Bourdieu)" (De Sena and Lisdero, 2015: 94).

Without being a simple sum of qualitative techniques, in this strategy, a variety of support techniques are assumed, such as the registration of publications, the conduct of surveys through online forms, interviews by video calls or through chats, among many others. (Domínguez Figaredo, 2007). The chapter synthesizes a survey oriented to inquiry on food practices with emphasis on the purchase, cooking and consumption of food in Argentine homes during the first month of isolation. The survey, which was self-administered, ranged from March 25 to April 25 with 472 responses.

As stated, the ethnography was conducted on Instagram, on the new services that emerged during the ASPO period in relation to eating practices and "home care". The choice of Instagram responds to the fact that it is currently the social network that shows the highest growth, with more than 1 billion active users per month, of which 65% are between 18 and 34 years old. In addition, Argentina is on the list of the 20 countries with the largest number of users in the world, along with three other countries in Latin America (Brazil, Mexico and Colombia) (DIGITAL 2020, 128). The commercial value of social networks is proportional to the number of active users and Instagram has the particularity of allowing interaction between the consumer and brands, companies, services or products through images or photographs with descriptions and comments. In addition to the name of the brand or organization, the registration of multiple hashtags (#) with different reasons, special circumstances, contests, etc. is allowed. (Caerols Mateo et al., 2013). Next, we will present an analysis of some of the results of the research work in relation to consumption and immediate enjoyment, exposing how these are related and modified during the ASPO period in the Metropolitan Area of Buenos Aires.

ONLINE CONSUMPTION, ENJOY "AT HOME"

From Online Shopping to Electronic Commerce

In the days earlier than the pandemic, online shopping was not very widespread in Argentina. From the survey conducted during the first month of ASPO in the country, we learned that 3.56% indicated that they had made purchases prior to the isolation decree online. After the ASPO started, this number had an almost imperceptible increase, since 4% of those surveyed made their purchases online. Now almost 9 months later, it can be seen that online commerce is still a small field.

The Survey of supermarkets and wholesale self-services carried out by the National Institute of Statistics and Censuses (INDEC) indicated that, by February 2020, the sales of supermarkets through the online channel were 1.4% of total sales (INDEC, 2020a) and by March 2020 they were 1.8% (INDEC, 2020b). On the other hand, for July of the same year, these rose to 6.1% of total sales, which represents "a positive variation of 437.40% compared to the same month of the previous year" (INDEC, 2020c: 5). This is a large increase relative to the year-on-year period, but, at the same time, it is a smaller percentage of the total sales of everyday food and cleaning products nationwide. Otherwise, online sales of non-essential products took a strong boost after the dispatch of non-essential purchases was enabled, on April 20, 2020. The data indicates that e-commerce in Argentina grew by 84% in turnover during this month compared to an average month in the first quarter of the year. In this way, two clearly differentiated stages appear in online shopping, the pre and post opening of the store, where consumption growth accelerates by 111% in turnover, 54% in purchase orders and 87% in units of products sold (El Comercio…, 2020). At a closer look, the data for the first semester indicates how this increase is stable in the time. Purchases of non-essential products through online channels during the first semester had an increase of 106% in relation to the same period of 2019, mainly the sales units increased -63% more- and then, 30% more than purchase orders (KANTAR, CACE, 2020). It is eloquent to see how more quantity was sold and more times, which exposes the intense development of e-Commerce and its expansion.

Based on these data, we understand that the COVID-19 pandemic and the lockdown changed the way the Argentine consumer purchases, by obligation and by habit. At the beginning of the ASPO, the need to buy without leaving home encouraged the increase in online consumption; later, the incorporation of the habit allowed new modes of purchasing. According to data from the Argentine Chamber of Electronic Commerce, in the second quarter of 2020, 1 in 10 Argentines bought online for the first time during ASPO and 2 out of 10 purchase orders came from new customers (KANTAR, CACE, 2020: 22).

These changes in the consumption of food and basic necessities were to be expected since they were the most required during the early days of the ASPO. In this sense, the online commerce of supermarkets had to develop rapidly in response to consumer demand. But this increase was compounded by the use and expansion of digital platforms for small orders –mainly those for food delivery and shipments– thus allowing us to expand the possibilities of purchase without leaving home. The reviewed information suggests that in the midst of the pandemic, the items that most expanded their sales nationwide were food delivery, food and mobile telephony. But, within these areas, what grew the most was the share of "last miller"[1] in food.

Figure 1. Mass consumer purchase orders at 2019 and 2020
Source: Self-Elaboration from data from CACE, 2020

Observing these data on the growth of "last miller" allows us to think not only about the increase in e-commerce but also about the new markets and consumption habits that this modality brings with it.

GO OUT TO EAT INSIDE

As we explained, in the first half of 2020 there was a substantial increase in sales in food and beverages. Many companies in the Food sector sold 30% more in units compared to the same period last year, but this implied a great effort for the gastronomic area. The closure of stores, restaurants and premises mainly implied a loss of sales, but, on the other hand, there was an event that generates a great impact on this market, the loss of contact with customers and the pause of consumption of "eating out" as a sensibility of the enjoyment of the XXI century in cities (Scribano, 2017).

With the entry of the new century, in Buenos Aires, Argentina, there was a proliferation process of night bars concentrated in the Palermo neighborhood, which acted as a counterpart to the socio-political-economic period of 2001-2003 in which a crisis occurred. manifested by the fall in the ability to access food - the increase in prices, unemployment and the decrease in income-generating transformations in the food consumption of urban populations. From these processes, the 'gourmet' world arises as a fundamental space in the structuring of urban consumption. And, although it might seem paradoxical, there is no contradiction in this regard, since "gourmet" or "Haute cuisine" was installed "as an occlusive on the question of hunger. The gourmet world has become a program, an aesthetic and an ethic in the face of lack of protection, hunger and the distribution of food" (Bruera, 2006: 32).

In this way, the material and social distances of the different social sectors are deepened from the distinction of the new gastronomic sensibility that focuses its focus on domestic life and consumption (Bourdieu, 1979). Thus, food is structured in two extremes: the daily one, which remains anchored at work, at home, in the dining room, in the simplification of the structure of the food, in the speed and in eating "anything" (Boragnio, 2020c), while the extra-daily is conformed as the "enjoyment meal" (Boragnio and Sordini, 2019) where consumption will act as a social organizer. Therefore, while a part of the population was excluded from the choice of daily food, another social sector feeds on the consumption of spectacularity and the commodification of both food and eating understood as a sensitive symbolic experience.

With the suspension of consumption and daily work that the COVID-19 crisis produced, the restaurant businesses had to adapt to the new reality, redefine their stores and, on other occasions, redefine their role in the market, since the experience of eating, framed in a specific time and space, is organized as commensality linked to the workload (Boragnio, 2018) and the gastronomic sensibility that functions as a social differentiator. The act of "going out to eat", understood as a class experience, is "a ritual (hoisted) and mercantile (hoisted) relational practice that makes sense by being-with-others" (Lava, 2012: 215). Given this, gastronomic restaurants linked to "eating out" had to strategically modify services. In this sense, we find two great proposals: the first focused on eating what was eaten in restaurants, but at home and, the second, linked to the reproduction of the experience "at home".

Within the first axis, we can see that from the neighborhood restaurants to the most exclusive restaurants they made special menus to buy at the premises and eat at home under the 'take away' format. For this, special menus were created in order to provide daily food and/or at lower prices.

Figure 2.

Besides, those most exclusive and fashionable restaurants were specializing not only in food and dishes to eat at home, but also strengthened contact with customers, establishing the restaurant as an identity for consumers. Thus, we can see how the service was transformed, building a relationship with the customer where the restaurant's offer began to be organized based on demand.

As the days went by, restaurants began to offer delivery service - which is not a service that was offered in all restaurants, especially in haute cuisine restaurants.

Figure 3.

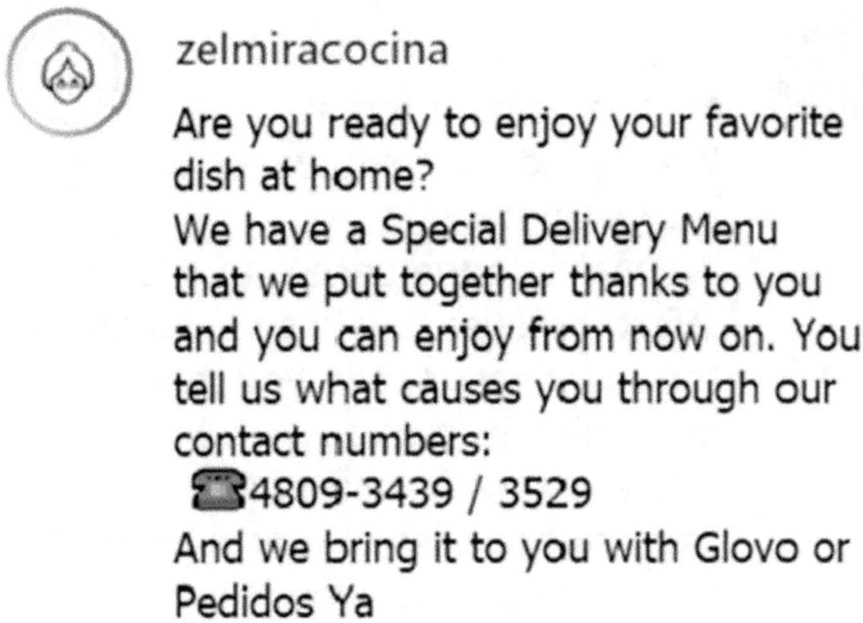

As delivery platforms multiplied and the possibility of "leaving home" became increasingly distant, businesses re-adapted not only including this service but also seeking to expand the offer with the sale of warehouse products or new services.

As we can see, the restaurants went from putting together special menus to modifying what was offered by rethinking the menu based on whether it is to eat at home and they also became pantries since they added to the service the possibility of buying products and/or raw materials. In this way, food service was added to be home pantries.

Along with these changes in the restaurant service that occurred during the first weeks, the second axis appears where the reproduction of the restaurant experience becomes central and this is sought from the transformation of the consumer into a chef.

In this case, we can see that the "onion with potato cream" –the restaurant's iconic dish– is offered to be only taken home and consumed indoors, while being transformed so that it arrives in the necessary conditions so that the client becomes the cook, the chef and the presenter of the same.

Figure 4.

cafesanjuanoficial

No two without three!

We started the third week, working with everything!

We maintain the price with a lot of effort, because you know, you go to the supermarket, and you realize that everything increases ...

But let's stay, because the neighborhood menu was born to be able to be close to you.

Remember that you can also buy the complete menu, vacuum packed, and we will deliver it to you -free of charge- next weekend!

The chef of an haute cuisine restaurant in the City of Buenos Aires called "Tegui", says in the propaganda of a delivery App transmitted on the networks:

"For Tegui at home, we choose the most emblematic dishes of the restaurant in the last 10 years. The idea is **to repeat the experience you had in the restaurant, to include yourself** *in a playful process where you finish cooking with our instructions, you are going to listen to music, you are going to play with us, you are going to try something that is a common delivery is impossible."* **[2]** *(emphasis ours)*

The restaurant, knowing its client, knows that cooking is part of the valued activities of "good living" (see Bourdieu). But at the same time, although the cooking techniques are known, they are not the practical heritage of all the subjects, so it sends instructions, steps, details of how to make not only the dish, but also music and details to replicate the experience of the restaurant from its identity, but including the consumer, as a cook and as an experimenter. In haute cuisine, being-with-others implies being seen, looking at and sharing the mutual gaze that is constitutive in the search for a lifestyle associated with "good living". Today, the uses of social networks transform being-with-others to a fundamental being seen online. In this sense, the Instagram platform is ideal since "it does not only socialize images, it shares experiences, practices of feeling and politics of sensibilities and through them a way of knowing and doing the world" (Scribano, 2017: 47). And, in this sense, having previously configured an identity reflected in a hashtag allows restaurants to maintain their presence, reproducing the "good life" no longer in a being-with-others but in a being-seen in the "good living" at home.

Figure 5.

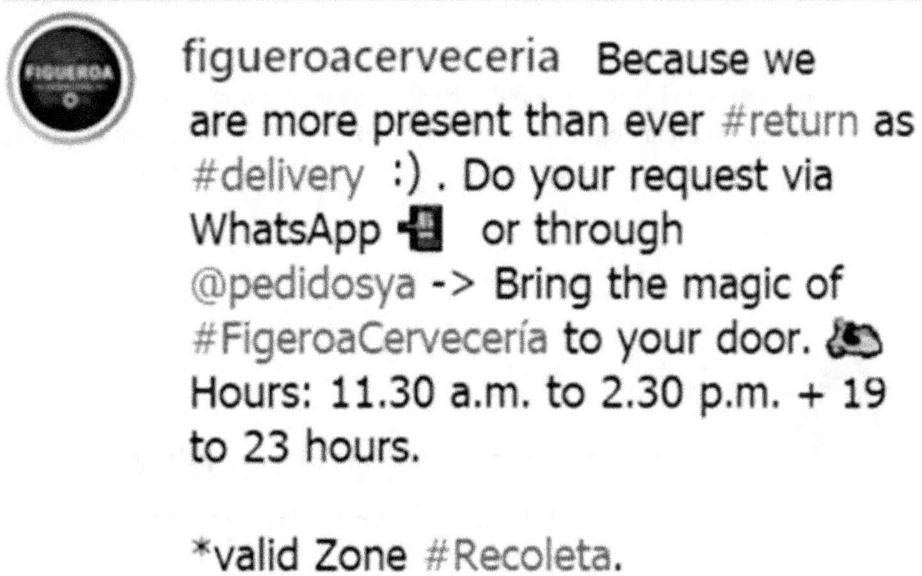

The expansion of these proposals was seen in all the haute cuisine restaurants in the city. But they also reached the delívery applications under the name "Foodi Box":

"What are the Foodi Box? They are magic boxes that store different gastronomic experiences that you ask for Rappi and end up at home"

Figure 6.

The Foodi box service was not only installed as a new home delivery service for food and haute cuisine but also as a service for well-known but not exclusive restaurants, neighborhood restaurants and even chain snack boxes of bars.

Figure 7.

Figure 8.

In the process of expanding the sensibility of the experience of "going out to eat" that expanded outside of haute cuisine –to other social sectors– a social space was formed in which a "we" is evoked that, although perhaps he does not understand the "good living", he knows about the legitimately valued experiences. In this case, the concept of "distinction" proposed by Bourdieu allows us to think of "going out to eat out" as a practice that seeks a relationship of proximity with the legitimate culture, in this case with the sensibility of enjoyment over time of leisure. As noted in the publications, this sensibility was reconfigured during the ASPO, since the growth in the use of delivery platforms and new services provided the possibility that consumption could be carried out at any day and at any time. Thus, this is imposed as the central axis that organizes the time of being at home. So much so that we find the same services not only in high-level gastronomy but also in cocktails, pastries, etc.

In this sense, if the food event was anchored in a daily way that is organized in the "eating any little thing" and, in an extra-daily way, in the "eating of enjoyment", thus organizing social times of eating, the "being at home" from the pandemic –where the hours and days took on another dimension linked to monotony– not only led to

Figure 9.

putting into practice strategies to sustain consumption, but it was also organized by immediate enjoyment. Enjoyment as an act and consuming as an action, in "the dialectic of their mutual interactions arranges life as a set of practices oriented towards them with the promise of operating as 'erasers' of memory of the effort" (Scribano, 2015: 48). In this way, we can see that during the ASPO a new sensibility related to enjoyment was set up around "going out to eat inside" that seeks to continue enjoying in a self-centered way, but now indoors.

CONSUMPTION AT HOME, ENJOY AT HOME, TAKE CARE OF MYSELF AT HOME

Deepening the changes that occurred during the ASPO by the hand of social networks and applications, we focus on the hashtags #mequedoencasa, #mecuidotecuido and #cuidarseencuarentena, from which we can observe various services and businesses that not only had to adapt but built a new service based on the times of the home. The first thing to take into account is the preponderance of the notion of care and, within this, of services related to aesthetics, proper nutrition and physical exercise. Online consultations with nutritionists are an example of this. From a strong modification that occurred in the first weeks due to the availability of time to cook on the one hand and the diversity of emotions, on the other, variations were generated in the daily routine of eating (Boragnio, 2021). Accompanying these changes, the services of nutritionist doctors appeared exponentially through online consultations that were promoted through Instagram. These types of consultations, although they had been carried out before, appeared as if they were essential for the social moment that was being lived, "today more than ever."

Figure 10.

In this modality, a series of tasks are delegated to the patient (analysis, taking measurements, photos) and "as if they were doing it in the office" they are given a diet plan, recipes, etc. As we can see, the service is not only about the consultation, but the follow-up is the main part. Social networks make it possible to monitor the patient and her behavior with the least time invested as possible. On the other hand, but in the same sense of care, we found a multiplicity of posts about the transformations carried out by gyms and personal trainers. First, there was the conversion of face-to-face classes to an online form, through digital platforms for coaches –mainly through Zoom– and through live Instagram transmissions in the case of gyms. These new ways of training could be observed both in large gym chains, with several branches, and in neighborhood gyms. The gyms also put their efforts into maintaining contact with the members to support the monthly fees. But, unlike gastronomy, they had experience in creating an identity with the brand as a place of sport, although they had to concentrate on configuring an identity of sport at home.

Figure 11.

licbaparicio

ONLINE INQUIRIES

... today more than ever we give you the possibility of accompanying you in this unique and difficult stage!

How is this?

✔ First-time patients: We ask you for a series of clinical and anthropometric data (we send you instructions for taking photos and measurements), we guide your needs and after the consultation we prepare the Food Plan, ideas of menus, recipes, sweet tips, etc.

And then we are communicated via WhatsApp for questions, queries, demonstration of dishes and delivery of material, and what is generated based on your needs.

✔ Patients who have already been seen and want to resume the nutritional approach: we schedule appointments and connect through a video call or meeting via zoom, we evaluate adherence, doubts, reorganize the eating plan if necessary, send new resources related to anxiety and emotions if they need and we monitor anthropometric parameters through measurements and photos, when we see each other again we perform body composition !! We have been doing this online for a long time and it works very, very well !!! Do not stay adrift waiting for this to end ... those who have not yet dared ... I wait for you !!

#nutritionenquarantine #nutritiononline #nutritionisadistance #nutritionzonasur #beingquarantined #adviceonlinenutrition

Figure 12.

Then, as the weeks went by, the classes opened my Instagram began to be combined with classes in private profiles for the partners, which were divided into activities. First, in the smaller gyms and then in some of the chains with the largest number of members, the necessary elements to perform exercises at home began to be rented. Sports activity at home poses a great limitation which is the availability of elements. Thus, the sale of products that allow home equipment is intended to recreate the appropriate conditions for physical exercise "at home", such as the rental of "combos" of CrossFit elements, mats, weights, supports that immobilize the bicycle, etc.

"From Megatlon we have been renting or selling spinning bikes, but they flew. I understand that there are many gyms doing it to make some cash, but ours happened more to provide a service and that the members continue doing the virtual spinning. We had started with a differential price for members and another for non-members, but when the demand was so great we decided to do it only to members. 90% was for sale and 10% for rent. We sold the bikes for a third of the value of a new one (approximately $ 120,000) and rented them to 10% of that value, but we had to provide the service". Raúl Wainraich, commercial director of the chain, told LA NACION. (La Nación, April 30, 2020)[3]

The sensibilities staged on Instagram link self-care based on an association between food, health and physical exercise, hand in hand with the individuation processes of some subjects that make themselves. That is why to analyze the type of consumption that emerges from the observed services, the concept of self-care is retaken, understood as a behavior that involves the adoption of (self) referential practices and the responsibility of permanent care-care -control of oneself. From this definition, it is possible to identify that the consumption patterns around taking care of oneself respond to the idea of what is healthy related to what is beautiful, and its scope from individual behavior, which has as a correlate the responsibility and blame of the subject around to the performance or nonperformance of these activities and the consequences derived from it (Boragnio, 2020a). In addition, taking up the new services during the ASPO, self-care associated with proper nutrition, health, and exercise is reinforced and identified as double care when it is carried out through practices retracted to the home. In this way, it is possible to assert that, by self-centering in the home of each person, new levels of individuation and self-responsibility are fostered. It is in these senses that some modes of individuation are deepened that, under the motto of taking care of oneself, configure a politics of sensibilities linked to the control of emotions, bodies and the self-regulation of daily life. Finally, we make one last mention, just to add it as an axis to take into account for other works. It is noteworthy that, in parallel to the reconversion of restaurants, the offer of services or products during the ASPO, new services also emerged that offer guidance for optimizing the use of social networks to improve sales. Either online writing courses in networks, workshops on the use of applications, community manager courses and the use of Instagram and its possibilities (feed, stories, hashtags, etc.) as dissemination of the business itself.

The 4.0 revolution has brought with it "new jobs", one of them is that of those that recommend that people buy the product/object and whose valuation is measured in relation to how many people follow these influencers on social networks (Scribano, 2020: 242). In this way, in a context of advertising migration towards social networks, Instagram is one of the main networks that enable mediation between the consumer and the services or products, giving rise to a new category of services related to good network management (Caerols Mateo et al., 2013). If, as Adrián Scribano indicates, "it is possible to notice that digital consumption at a global level and in Argentina is producing changes in companies, consumers and consumer channels that in turn are altering the politics of sensibilities" (Scribano, 2020: 234), it becomes central to wonder about the period of Social, Preventive and Mandatory Isolation as an accelerating process of these practices.

CONCLUSION

COVID-19 accelerated trends that had been observed in world trade, such as changes in the supply and demand of services, virtual practices and the exacerbation of the development of the commercial world of the intangible. These trends will increase in the coming years and will invite us to get used to living and competing in a world of e-commerce, virtual fairs, and changes in marketing where work increasingly includes new technologies in its production such as in its diffusion. In Argentina, the precarious situation of the economy has been reflected in an increase in prices, an increase in inflation and a continuous devaluation; it was quickly affected by the economic crisis caused by the COVID-19 pandemic. However, based on what has been developed, it is possible to establish that, in a context of uncertainty in which physical isolation was established as the main form of prevention, the suspension of consumption was not a durable or viable option.

Electronic commerce emerged as the main alternative to acquire basic necessities since it greatly reduces the physical contact involved in previous commercial transactions. Following this sense, both the survey and the inquiry on Instagram made it possible to approach the approach to the sensibilities associated with food practices, consumption and "taking care of oneself at home" during the ASPO, enabling the understanding of a daily life constituted by digitization, in which face-to-face relationships and those made in the digital world constantly intersect (Faracce Macia, 2020). When observing the emerging services during the ASPO, both in the gastronomic and nutritional fields and in the gyms, it was noticed the transfer of the experiences that in the pre-pandemic period were carried out outside the home towards the interior of this, entering the home both new objects and new activities through digital platforms. Thus, services and consumption modalities began to emerge in which it is sought to reproduce the experiences that in the pre-pandemic were carried out in other spaces, but within the home. In this case, social networks are not only the means of consumption, but they are installed as the way to make consumption visible to another, reinforcing mimetic consumption while maintaining the belief in a world lived to be seen, where "it is consumed to be seen consuming" (Scribano, 2015: 49).

In this way, the preponderance of services related to eating, enjoying and caring "at home" allowed us to visualize consumption patterns associated with the reordering of daily life turned towards the home, in which sensibilities linked to consumption, enjoyment and self-care as self-centered practices that show that "staying at home" did not mean a setback of the sensibilities linked to the imperative that connects enjoyment with consumption. On the contrary, there was a reconfiguration in the way of buying, but also of consuming, from an exacerbation of trends linked to the digital world, which already showed exponential growth in the previous period. That is why these processes cannot be explained without understanding that they occur on horizons of action, disposition and cognition already crossed by the digitization of life, tending to make these emerging forms of consumption acceptable.

Lastly, the diagnosis prior to COVID-19 maintains that our societies are normalized societies in the immediate enjoyment through consumption and, as we can observe after the above, this characteristic is deepened from the so-called "digital acceleration". In this sense, the pandemic not only slowed down consumption and sales as part of a global economic crisis but also deepened a daily reality that brought new forms. But, at the same time, reinforcing the processes of social structuring that are organized from the triangle of the capacity of consumption-enjoyment-purchase, which extends as part of the framework of the politics for sensibilities. Thus, in a stabilized and a-conflict society based on the compulsive and pre-reflexive repetition of the act of consuming associated with immediate enjoyment, the market quickly adapted to the confinement of the millions of inhabitants of large cities and, in this process, that the digital was constituted as the unavoidable path for the reordering of the daily life that we are witnessing in 2020 where the sensibilities of "eating inside" and "taking care of yourself at home", structured under the "stay at home", constituted continuous efforts to continue "consuming at home".

REFERENCES

Aristábal García, D. M. (2020). Estudios sociales sobre el consumo. Trayectorias disciplinares de un campo de estudio en construcción [Social Studies on Consumption: disciplinary routes in a field on underway construction]. *Revista de Estudios Sociales*, *71*(71), 87–99. doi:10.7440/res71.2020.07

Bocock, R. (2008). *Consumption*. Routledge. doi:10.4324/9780203131091

Boragnio, A. (2018). Disposable commensality: strategies for the selection of meals in the office. *Eureka: Social and Humanities*, *5*(2018), 16-28.

Boragnio, A. (2020a). Producción de subjetividades en el autocuidado alimentario cotidiano [Production of subjectivities in daily food self-care]. In R. Del Monaco & M. E. Epele (Eds.), *Tecnologías y Técnicas en Investigaciones Socioantropológicas de la Salud*. Estudios Sociológicos Editora.

Boragnio, A. (Ed.). (2020b). Etnografía virtual: un acercamiento a las sensibilidades desde el siglo XXI [Virtual ethnography: an approach to sensitivities from the 21st century]. In *Documentos del trabajo del CIES*. Buenos Aires: Estudios Sociológicos Editora. http://estudiosociologicos.org/portal/etnografia-virtual-un-acercamiento-a-las-sensibilidades-desde-el-siglo-xxi/

Boragnio, A. (2020c). Las emociones del comer cotidiano: mujeres entre el asco, la culpa y la vergüenza [The emotions of everyday eating: women between disgust, guilt and shame]. *Polis, Revista Latinoamericana, 55*, 56-70. https://www.polis.ulagos.cl/index.php/polis/article/view/1444/2613

Boragnio, A. (2021). Sensibilities of eating inside: Emotions and Food Practices in a time of pandemic. In *Emotionality of COVID19. Now and After: The War Against a Virus. Nova Scientia.*

Boragnio, A., & Sordini, V. (2019). Gustos y prácticas alimentarias de mujeres empleadas de oficinas públicas y mujeres destinatarias de programas alimentarios en Argentina [Food tastes and practices of women employees of public offices and women recipients of food programs in Argentina]. *Aposta. Revista de Ciencias Sociales, 81*, 69-86.

Bourdieu, P. (1979). *La Distinction. Critique sociale du jugement*. Les Éditions de Minuit.

Bruera, M. (2006). *La Argentina Fermentada. Vino, alimentación y cultura* [The Argentina Fermented. Wine, food and culture]. Paidós.

Caerols Mateo, R., Tapia Frade, A., & Carretero Soto, A. (2013). Instagram, la imagen como soporte de discurso comunicativo participado [Instagram, the image as a support for participated communicative discourse]. *Revista de Comunicación Vivat Academia, 15*(124), 68-78.

De Sena, A., & Lisdero, P. (2015). Etnografía virtual: Aportes para su discusión y diseño [Virtual Ethnography: Contributions for its discussion and design]. In *Caminos cualitativos. Aportes para la investigación en ciencias sociales*. CICCUS.

De Sena, A., & Scribano, A. (2020). *Social Policies and Emotions. A look from the global South*. Palgrave Macmillan. doi:10.1007/978-3-030-34739-0

Dettano, A. (2019). Leyendo al consumo desde las emociones sociales. Algunos recorridos y perspectivas posibles [Reading consumption from social emotions. Some possible routes and perspectives]. *Antropología Experimental*, (19), 2019.

Dettano, A. (2020). Introducción. Contorneando los relieves del consumo: una topografía posible del Siglo XXI [Introduction. Contouring the reliefs of consumption: a possible topography of the 21st century]. In Topografías del consumo. Ciudad Autónoma de Buenos Aires: Estudios Sociológicos Editora.

DIGITAL 2020. (2020). *Global Digital Overview: essential insights into how people around the world use the internet, mobile devices, social medirá, and ecommerce*. Author.

Domínguez Figaredo, D. (2007). Sobre la intención de la etnografía virtual [About the intention of virtual ethnography]. *Revista Electrónica Teoría de la Educación. Educación y Cultura en la Sociedad de la Información*, *8*(1).

El Comercio. (2020). https://www.cace.org.ar/noticias-el-comercio-electronico-crecio-84-en-abril

Faracce Macia, C. (2020). Políticas sociales y consumo en la Sociedad 4.0 [Social policies and consumption in Society 4.0]. In A. Dettano (Ed.), *Topografías del consumo*. Estudios Sociológicos Editora.

Hine, C. (2004). Etnografía virtual [Virtual Ethnography]. In Colección Nuevas Tecnologías y Sociedad. Barcelona: Editorial UOC.

INDEC. (2020b). https://www.indec.gob.ar/uploads/informesdeprensa/super_05_202A09BABB1B.pdf

INDEC. (2020c). https://www.indec.gob.ar/uploads/informesdeprensa/super_09_20DDB84A2C4B.pdf

INDEC. (2020a). https://www.indec.gob.ar/uploads/informesdeprensa/super_04_20FDF3CFC833.pdf

ISOC. (2009). www.isoc.org

KANTAR. CACE. (2020). https://cace.org.ar/uploads/estudios/estudiomidterm-2020.pdf

Korstanje, M. E. (2017). *Mobilities Paradox: a critical analysis*. Edward Elgar.

Lava, M. (2012) Des-mitificando el dicho popular: "sobre el gusto no hay nada escrito" [Demystifying the popular saying: "about taste there is nothing written"]. In Las tramas del sentir. Ensayos desde una sociología de los cuerpos y las emociones. Buenos Aires: Estudios Sociológicos Editora.

Mercado de Trabajo. (2020). https://www.indec.gob.ar/uploads/informesdeprensa/mercado_trabajo_eph_2trim20929E519161.pdf

Operti, F., & Mesquita Moreira, M. (2020). Impacto del coronavirus en el comercio y la integración: ¿qué hacer? [Impact of the coronavirus on trade and integration: What to do?]. *Banco Interamericano de Desarrollo*. Disponible en: https://blogs.iadb.org/integracioncomercio/es/coronavirus-comercio-integracion/

Scribano, A. (2012). Sociología de los cuerpos/emociones [Sociology of bodies/emotions]. *Revista Latinoamericana de Estudios sobre Cuerpos, Emociones y Sociedad*, *4*(10), 93–113.

Scribano, A. (2013). Una aproximación conceptual a la moral del disfrute: normalización, consumo y espectáculo [A conceptual approach to the morality of enjoyment: normalization, consumption and spectacle]. *RBSE – Revista Brasileira de Sociologia da Emoção, 12*(36), 738-750. http://www.cchla.ufpb.br/rbse/Index.html

Scribano, A. (2015). *¡Disfrútalo! Una aproximación a la economía política de la moral desde el consumo* [Enjoy it! An approach to the political economy of morality from consumption]. Ciudad Autónoma de Buenos Aires: Elaleph.com.

Scribano, A. (2017). *Normalization, enjoyment and bodies/emotions: Argentine sensibilities*. Nova Science Publishers.

Scribano, A. (2017, August). "Instaimagen: mirar tocando para sentir" [Instaimagen: look by touching to feel]. *RBSE Revista Brasileira de Sociología da Emoção*, *16*(47), 45–55.

Scribano, A. (2020). Consumo digital y sensibilidades de plataforma: algunas pistas para su análisis [Digital consumption and platform sensitivities: some clues for analysis]. In A. Dettano (Ed.), *Topografías del consumo*. Estudios Sociológicos Editora.

Scribano, A., & Lisdero, P. (2019). *Digital labor, Society and Politics of Sensibilities*. Palgrave Macmillan. doi:10.1007/978-3-030-12306-2

Taylor, S. J., & Bogdan, R. (1987). *Introducción a los métodos cualitativos de investigación* [Introduction to qualitative research methods]. Editorial Paidós.

Warde, A. (2016). *Consumption: A sociological analysis*. Springer.

ADDITIONAL READING

Alonso, L. E. (2005). *La Era del Consumo* [The Age of Consumption.]. Siglo XXI Editores.

Baudrillard, J. (1998). *Consumer Society*. Sage. (Original work published 1970)

Belk, R., Ger, G., & Åskegaard, S. (2003). The Fire of Desire: A Multisited Inquiry into Consumer Passion. *The Journal of Consumer Research, 30*, 326–351.

Campbell, C. (1998). Consumption and the Rhetorics of Need and Want. *Journal of Design History, 11*(3), 235–246.

Dettano, A., Sordini, M. V., & Chahbenderian, F. (2019). Social Policies, Conditional Cash Transfer Programs and Types of Indebtedness: Possible Articulations in Twenty First Century Argentina. *Advances in Social Sciences Research Journal, 6*(5), 276–292.

Falk, P., & Campbell, C. (Eds.). (1997). *The Shopping Experience*. Sage.

Scribano, A. (2018). Politics and Emotions. Houston USA. *Studium Press, llc*, 240.

Trentmann, F. (2016). *The empire of things*. Penguin Random House.

KEY TERMS AND DEFINITIONS

Consumption: Practices of use, acquisition of goods, services, subjects and experiences that, within the framework of a particular accumulation regime, implies ways of experiencing, being in the world and with the others.

Digital Ethnography: A qualitative method based on ethnography that is carried out through a massive communication platform such as the Internet.

Eating Practices: Are the result of multiple social relationships and cultural guidelines that constitute foodstuffs and organize them into dishes, meanings, and diners, becoming a space of class bodies with the main consequence of shaping those bodies.

Immediate Enjoyment: An act with pretensions of totality that suspends the flux of everyday life. It refers to a form of "intense" and "superficial" appropriation, restorative of objects for anxiety decrease through salvation technologies.

Isolation: The condition of being separated from other people, towns, countries, etc.

ENDNOTES

1 It refers to the last step in the supply chain in which the product is delivered to the customer.

2 https://www.instagram.com/p/CGtC5U5gUT6/

3 https://www.lanacion.com.ar/economia/liquidacion-bicicletas-gimnasios-alquilan-venden-equipos-hacer-nid2359735

Section 2

Chapter 4
Second Home Tourism During COVID-19:
The Case of Turkey

Ali Inanir
Burdur Mehmet Akif Ersoy Üniversity, Turkey

ABSTRACT

The COVID-19 pandemic, which emerged in Wuhan, China in 2019 and then spread rapidly around the world, has also become a factor affecting the tourism industry in many aspects. Second homes, which meet a significant part of the accommodation within the tourism sector, have also been affected in different levels by this pandemic. This research, which attempts to reveal the extent of the impact, has examined the news that appeared in the media during the COVID-19 process in Turkey. As a result of the research, it has been revealed that 23 news reports have been made on different news sites related to the subject. Based on this news, it has been concluded that the COVID-19 pandemic has influenced the second home tourism in behavioral, environmental, and economic aspects. Some deductions have been made about the matter through these results.

INTRODUCTION

The tourism industry is rapidly affected by the developments occurring in the world due to its highly fragile structure. As one of the most important of these developments, the Covid-19 pandemic that emerged in Wuhan, China in 2019, which the World Health Organization later declared a "global pandemic" on March 11, 2020, has affected many sectors positively or negatively in different aspects. The tourism

DOI: 10.4018/978-1-7998-7287-0.ch004

sector has also been one of the sectors most affected by this epidemic, positively or negatively in different aspects. As a matter of fact, especially according to the changes in the face of the process, differences in the behavior of tourists participating in tourism activities began to emerge.

Due to the risk of spreading the virus of the Covid-19 pandemic, there have been migrations from crowded places to less populated rural areas with the travel bans being relaxed during the summer period. In this process, the second homes, which have types such as holiday homes, cottages, recreational houses, bungalow houses, time properties, villas, cottages, cabins, summer houses, summer residences, chalets, entertainment houses, highland houses, village houses and winter houses, have started to become even more attractive in terms preventing close contact (Zoğal & Emekli, 2020). Depending on this situation, just like all over the world, second homes have become more preferred places by many guests than large-scale hotels in Turkey, which offers safe holidays in the Covid-19 process. Due to this development, the second home tourism phenomenon has gained momentum in Turkey during the Covid-19 process.

Turkey, where the research took place, has been visited by approximately 51.7 million tourists in 2019. In 2020, despite all the negativities, 14,486,632 tourists visited Turkey between January and November thanks to his safe holiday and rapid adaptation to the crisis. Approximately $8.1 billion in revenue has been made from tourists from different destinations such as Russia, Germany, Ukraine, Bulgaria and the UK (Ministry of Culture and Tourism, 2019; 2020). In 2020, the majority of tourists visiting Turkey preferred to stay in second homes in different regions of Turkey, especially in Aegean, Mediterranean and Marmara regions. The second homes have been undeniable in the accumulation of this revenue. Even if there is no statistical data on accommodation and income related to second home tourism, the media reports on this matter reveal its importance.

Depending on the developments in the second home tourism experienced during the Covid-19 process, this study aimed to examine the media reports about the issue in Turkey. According to this purpose, theoretical information on the concept and characteristics of second home, positive and negative effects of second homes, second home tourism in the world and second home tourism in Turkey have been presented in the study. In the second phase, in line with the purpose of the research, the news that are made regarding the issue between March 11, 2020 when the first pandemic case was observed in our country and December 13, 2020 when the efforts for research data collection commenced have been scanned in order to put forth the developments on second home tourism within the Covid-19 process in Turkey. According to the results obtained after the news has been examined in detail, deductions have been made regarding the developments related to second home tourism in the Covid-19 process in Turkey. It is thought that these inferences can show the ground for scientists who will do research on the subject and tourism stakeholders in the planning process of second homes.

SECOND HOME CONCEPT AND CHARACTERISTICS

The topic of second homes has been a topic of discussion amongst various researches in tourism and housing studies since 1930 (Ljungdahl, 1938; Sund, 1948). As a matter of fact, the concept of second home tourism is frequently used in the literature in the researches carried out in this field (Anabestani, 2004; Asgary et al., 2011; Vagner et al., 2011; Hiltunen et al., 2013; Velvin, 2013; Hall, 2014; Cengizoğlu & Özyılmaz, 2016; Larsson & Müller, 2019). Although there are definitions made in the international literature regarding the concept of second home, it is observed that there is no clear definition (Coppock, 1977; Jaakson, 1986; Hall & Muller, 2004; Czarnecki & Frenkel, 2014). Therefore, many researchers have identified second homes of different sizes and purposes.

The concept of second home has been expressed by the French Statistical Institute as areas that provide services to owners at certain periods of the year (Kısa, 1998). In a similar definition, it is defined as non-commercial places to stay for short-term holidays (Bieger, et al., 2007). In these definitions, it is revealed that the second homes are areas that can be used temporarily for accommodation purposes. The expression of non-commercial places is also a phenomenon that arises from the use of some second homes for accommodation purposes in winter or summer outside the existing homes of individuals.

Addressing the second home phenomenon extensively, Emekli (2014) has stated that they are located in a destination other than the place of residence, opened for recreational use at certain times of the year, located in places with high natural and cultural attractiveness (streams, lakes, hot springs, seashores, etc.), integrated with tourism and with real estate investment characteristics (Emekli, 2014). In this definition, it is noted that the second homes are accommodation enterprises used in tourism. Based on these definitions and inspired by the general literature review, it can be stated that the second homes have a number of characteristics. These characteristics have been obtained by researchers (Struyk & Angelici, 1996; İçöz, 2003; Eaten, 2008; Matteuicci, et al., 2008; Dias, et al., 2015) is put forward as follows.

Second homes are temporary residences with different types such as holiday homes, cottages, recreational houses, timeshare apartments, huts, cabins, summer houses, summer residences, winter houses, vineyards, entertainment houses, highland houses and village houses. Each type of these second homes can be used for different purposes.

Second homes are areas that allow visitors to relax and have fun alone with nature away from crowded areas. Therefore, they are indispensable facilities for those who want to relax and isolate themselves away from crowded groups and the noise of the city.

In addition to being able to use or rent second homes for recreational purposes, it has the effect of touristic structures in terms of creating season differences in terms of density in their destinations, providing economic benefits and revealing differences in physical and cultural structure. Therefore, they are important accommodation facilities that can rival large-scale hotels in tourism.

Second homes are facilities that can allow tourism activities to be carried out sustained due to the increasing demand in the regions where the number of touristic facilities is small and the loyalty of the requesters is high to the region and the public. Especially because of the low investment costs, they are regarded as areas where local people living in the region can invest with factors such as insurance and tax convenience.

Second homes are areas that seem suitable for individuals who want to take holidays according to their traditions and customs, with attractive prices in their own country. Therefore, second homes have an undeniable role in the development of domestic tourism, which is an important factor in tourism.

Finally, the second homes are places where visitors who work and have a good economic status or are in the middle-income group, on the other hand, who have earned the right to retirement but whose affording capacities are not very good, but who have a lot of leisure time. Therefore, second homes are areas that serve those who can participate in tourism activities at all times of the year. In this context, the second homes are facilities that have an important place in the dissemination of tourism over twelve months.

These characteristics of the second homes reveal a number of positive and negative effects on local communities and businesses in economic, social, cultural and environmental dimensions. Since these effects are important for the sustainability of second homes, it will be in order to be discussed in detail.

POSITIVE AND NEGATIVE EFFECTS OF SECOND HOMES

In general, factors such as industrialization, urbanization, population growth, the development of technology and the prolongation of human lifespan play an important role in the development of second homes. In addition, highlands, natural areas, countryside have been the factors that attracted people, and in the process of this situation, the second homes became important, nature-compatible accommodation facilities that met the demand (Retired, 2014). All these developments have caused

Figure 1. Positive and negative effects of second homes (Stettler & Danielli, 2008)

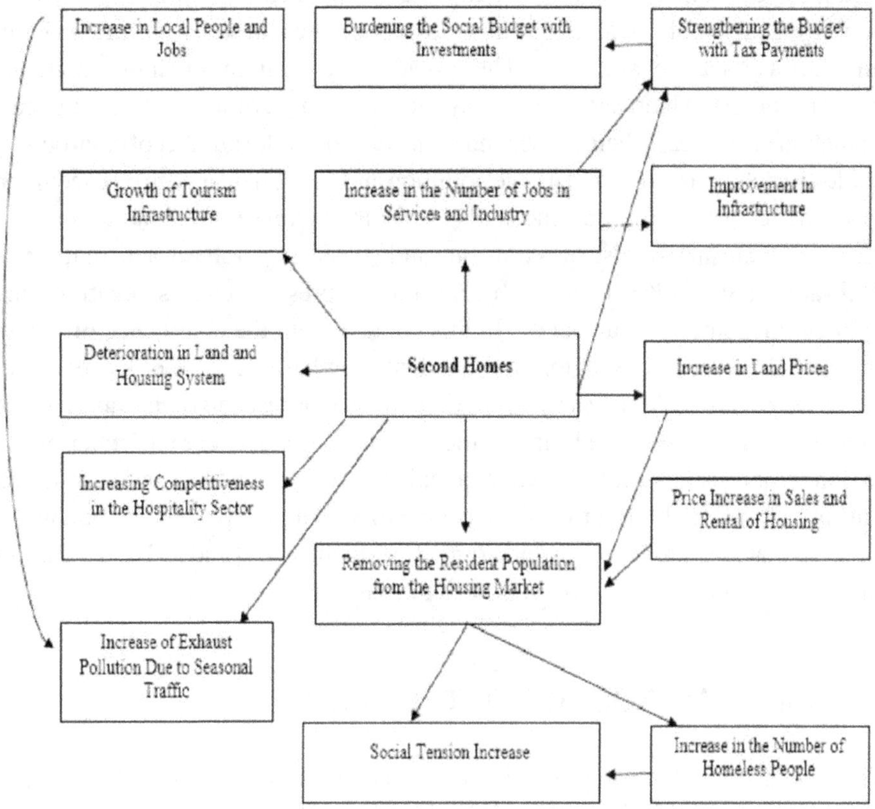

further positive and negative developments with the areas where the second homes are built. These developments are discussed in Figure 1.

Direct and indirect job opportunities are increasing in the service sector and industry sector in the areas where second homes are developing. It also occurs in areas where local people can work and be employed in places where the number of second homes is increasing. Due to these developments, the increased tax revenues reveal the improvement of the general and touristic infrastructure in the destination, as well as the increase in the welfare level of the society (Müller et al., 2004; Fleischer & Tchetchik, 2005). Meanwhile, a number of positive developments are also emerged in the hospitality sector in these areas. Especially hotels that want to survive in increasing competitive conditions need to adapt themselves to the conditions and improve the quality of service. With this obligation, businesses that adapt to developments and improve service quality can ensure increased customer satisfaction.

In addition to positive developments in the areas where the second homes are built, it can occur in a number of negative developments. Especially in case of over-carrying capacity, physical, environmental, economic and socio-cultural negativity can be seen (Asgary et al., 2011). The spread of second homes in large areas causes deterioration in the land and housing layout. At the same time, due to the increasing population in the areas where the second homes are located, a number of environmental problems such as air, noise and image pollution and traffic density can be encountered. However, according to Riebsame et al (1996); the increase of second homes in one area causes an inflationist pressure on land, housing purchase and rental prices (Riebsame et al., 1996). This state of inflationist pressure causes negativity in the socio-cultural structure of society. In this context, with the emergence of investors with global power in the region, the resident population can be observed to leave the housing market. At the same time, rising house prices and rents can give rise to homelessness of the people living in the region. This can cause a number of social tensions among second-home owners, local residents and visitors in the community (Philips, 1998). In the light of all these positive and negative developments, it is observed that the number of second homes both in the world and in Turkey continues with increasing momentum from past to present.

SECOND HOME TOURISM IN THE WORLD

When the historical development of second homes around the world is examined, it begins to appear during the period of Ancient Egypt and the Roman Empire (Rezvani, 2003). These houses have been built at that time by a small and wealthy group of society. By the 17th century, aristocrats and bourgeois living in Britain, France, Sweden and other European countries began to build second homes to evaluate their future. This has led to an acceleration of the development of second homes in Europe. After the second world war, the development of second homes gained significant momentum. The middle-income groups in particular have used second homes for tourism purposes, which significantly increased their numbers (Fesharaki, 1996).

Various factors have played a role in the development of second homes in the world and their use for tourism purposes. In particular, the renting of some or all of the housing of people with low-income levels has made the second home increase rapidly. In addition, due to the developments occurring in the public and private sectors, the number of participants in the second housing tourism has increased significantly due to the increase in the free time of individuals, increased income level because of increased employment opportunities, and development of transportation infrastructure. Communities migrating from village to city with industrialization began to acquire second homes in rural areas due to the boring living conditions given by city life, in this case increasing the pace of development of second homes and their use in tourism (Keshavarznia et al., 2013; Mirani & Farahani, 2015).

To this day, the presence of second homes with large houses around Moscow in Russia increases significantly due to the positive developments in the world for second homes. Although there is not very clear statistical data on this issue, it has been revealed that there are 17.000.000 second homes in Russia as of 2013 (Lipkina, 2013). It has been determined that, as of 2010, there were 4.600.000 second homes in the United States, which ranked second in the world in terms of the number of second homes (Armstrong & Stedman, 2013). In addition, Canada, another North American country, stands out in terms of the second home availability. As a matter of fact, the number of second homes increased from 444.900 in 1973 to 605.000 in 1992. However, in the cities of Ontairo and Ouebec, it has been determined that one third of the houses have been second (Salehinasap, 2005; Emekli, 2014). These developments have led to the acceleration momentum of the second home tourism for the evaluation of free time in the USA and Canada (Müller & Hoogendoom, 2013).

In addition to North American countries, the second home tourism began to develop in Europe since the 1940s (Kadıoğlu, 1990; Ceylan & Somuncu, 2020). Countries such as Spain, France, Portugal, Switzerland, England and Germany are pioneers in this regard. As a matter of fact, as of 2001, 3.300.000 second homes had emerged in Spain, the country that attracted the most attention regarding the number of second homes in Europe (Barke, 2007). It is known that there have been 1.500.000 second homes in France in 1970. In Portugal, an increase of approximately 23% in the number of second homes increased between 2001 and 2011. As of 2011, it is known that there have been 1.113.000 second homes. The number of second homes in Switzerland increased from 185.000 to around 419.000 with the increase of second homes in rural areas. As of 2005, there were 230.000 second homes in different concepts in Germany, where rural tourism is widely developed. In the UK, the number of second homes increased by 2.6% in 4 years from 229.186 in 2005 to 245.384 in 2009. (Dijst et al., 2005; Keshavarznia et al., 2013; Oliveria et al., 2015).

In Scandinavian countries such as Sweden, Denmark and Norway, second home ownership is known to be a habit, and the second number of dwellings was 400.000 in Sweden in the 1960s to 500.000 in 1996; the number in Norway from 190.000 to 339.000 in 1998; and in Denmark it increased from 145.000 to 195.000 in 1995. As another Scandinavian country, Finland had 423.000 second homes as of 1996. (Müller 1999; Komppula et al., 2008; Cengizoğlu & Özyılmaz, 2016). These developments revealed that the tourism of second homes in Scandinavian countries showed development momentum. In addition to these developments occurring in the world, second home tourism in different regions in Turkey has entered a serious growth trend.

SECOND HOME TOURISM IN TURKEY

When the way of life of the society in Turkey is taken into account, it is observed that the use of summer and winter houses for accommodation purposes takes place in accordance with the cultural structure. In Turkish history, principality and summer palaces used during Ottoman Era and highland and vineyard culture spread throughout Anatolia are the most conspicuous examples of habit (Kısa, 1998). As a matter of fact, while traditional livestock activities have been carried out in the highlands before 1950, recreation and tourism activities have been carried out in the following years and with this goal, investments such as highland house, hotel, second home and hostel are being made in the highlands. With the ministry of culture and tourism's highland tourism project, the ministry declared 26 plateaus, many of which in the Eastern Black Sea Region as tourist centers, and the ministry changed the traditional function of the highlands. In other words, the highlands have revealed the situation that the city community is a tourism destination for performing activities such as mentally refreshing, having fun, getting fresh air, being intertwined with natural life (Somuncu & Ceylan, 2015). These developments have rapidly spread the second home tourism activities in the Turkish highlands.

Besides the highlands, the number of second homes on Turkey's coastline has started to increase rapidly. As a matter of fact, due to the plans and policies implemented during the period from 1980 to 1990, the number of second homes has increased rapidly, causing environmental and economic problems in coastal areas where tourism is intense due to the impact of sea and sand. This situation has accelerated the development process of the second home tourism phenomenon on the coasts. In this direction, it is observed that the second homes are concentrated in the Mediterranean, Aegean and Marmara regions. As of 2008, 79,480 houses in the Mediterranean Region, 87,106 in the Aegean Region and 110,495 in the Marmara Region have been revealed by unclear statistical data. When examined on a provincial basis in these regions, it has been determined that there are 12,531 second homes in Mersin, 20,155 in Muğla, 17,354 in Aydın, 11,783 in Izmir and 7,902 in Balıkesir (Reader, 2016).

In addition, many tourist destinations in the south west of Turkey come to the forefront with the migration of foreigners (Yirik et al., 2015) and the second homes it owns through housing. As a matter of fact, it is observed that pensioners living in EU countries own many second homes in Marmaris, Bodrum and Alanya districts located in Muğla and Antalya provinces through housing acquisition (Kaiser, 2003; Yirik & Baltacı, 2016). Although there are no clear statistics on this subject, the number of second homes in Turkey increased significantly between 1990 and 2000, increasing from 102,400 in 1989 to 480.000 in 1999 (Manisa, 2007; Özsoy, 2015). According to the unclear data exhibited by the General Directorate of Population and Citizenship, it has been revealed that there were a total of 559,934 second homes in Turkey as of 2013.

The Ministry of Culture and Tourism in Turkey has carried out long-term studies in order to bring the second homes to the tourism sector. Accordingly, the ministry covered holiday sites, villas or other facilities within the scope of the "Regulation on the Certification and Qualifications of Tourism Facilities" and listed them in the qualifications necessary for tourism. With this regulation, which has been enforced in 2005, the field has been determined by setting the condition that the second homes should be located in cultural and tourism development destinations. In fact, in addition to common areas of use in the regulation, the services that must be provided and the materials that should be presented are discussed in detail (Kozak & Duman, 2011).

Similarly, the Ministry of Development has announced in 2018 that projects related to second homes should be created in the 2019-2023 Eleventh Development Plan. In this context, it has been proposed "to bring recreational facilities operating for social tourism purposes by public and private sector enterprises and buildings built on personal demand and need as alternative accommodations in order to diversify tourism and spread it over 12 months (Ministry of Development, 2018). With all these, due to the increasing demand, changes have started to emerge in Turkey regarding the second home tourism in the Covid-19 process.

SECOND HOME TOURISM IN THE COVID-19 PROCESS IN TURKEY

With the Covid-19 pandemic affecting the whole world, a number of changes in world tourism mobility began to emerge. In particular, the partial lifting of restrictions imposed by states during intense tourism periods has severely affected tourism mobility. These changes in the world also affected Turkish tourism and the second homes, which have an important place in tourism, in different aspects. Due to these developments, it is observed that many news has been made in the media about the impact of Covid-19 on second home tourism in Turkey. In this study, in order to reveal the developments related to the subject, the newspapers where tourism news is made and other news channels are scanned in detail with the help of search buttons.

During the search buttons, search buttons have been searched by writing words such as second home, secondary housing, second home, secondary house, holiday homes, cottages, recreational houses, bungalow houses, timeshare apartments, villas, huts, cabins, summer houses, summer residences, chalets, entertainment houses, highland houses, village houses and winter houses. News about the second homes in the Covid-19 process between 11.03.2020-13.12.2020 has been transferred to the Word file and then reviews have been carried out on the news.

It is observed that 23 news reports have been made about the subject. These news have been included in news websites such as Turizm Günlüğü (2 news), Turizmin Sesi (1 news), Türkiye Turizm (1 news), Hotel Newspaper (2 news), Turizm GM (4 news), Turizm Tatil Seyahat (1 news), Turizm Dosyası (3 news), Sözcü Newspaper (6 news), TRT News (1 news), Hürriyet News (1 news) ve Anadolu Agency (1 news). When the news on the news websites are examined, it has been determined that there have been/may be changes in behavioral, environmental and economic dimensions in Turkey in the trend towards second home tourism during the Covid-19 process. In this context, it has been revealed that there are changes in isolated life, contactless holiday, social distancing and hygiene regarding the holiday tendency of visitors in behavioral dimensions. In economic dimension, projects such as Hobbit houses and eco tourism routes for second homes have started to emerge. In the economic dimension, developments such as increased prosperity, increased demand and price increases for the second increasing housing trend have started to occur.

During the Covid-19 process, it is observed that visitors who want to participate in recreation activities and other tourism activities especially in different regions of Turkey generally start to prefer areas that they can isolate themselves away from city life.

Dumanlı Plateau, which is covered with yellow trees in Erzincan, provides picnics and recreational opportunities for visitors who want to get away from the city due to both the novel coronavirus (Covid-19) pandemic and the hot weather. (Özdemir, 2020).

With the new measures implemented with the start of the Covid-19 process, people are obliged to continue their lives without contacting each other. Due to this development, the idea of contactless holidays began to appear in visitors as a form of behavior. In order to meet this need, it has been seen that the second homes to meet the contactless holiday needs of tourists during the Covid-19 process serve as an important accommodation business in Turkey.

In the new period when the measures will continue, rental villas are expected to respond to the needs of the citizens who want to take a holiday without contacting other guests of the enterprises they are staying in. Sevil Albayrak Demir emphasized that the concept of rental villa holiday, which has become quite popular in recent years, is the most favorable option for contactless holidays, "While the practice of buffet is removed with the new arrangements made in the accommodation sector within the scope of the epidemic, the introduction of common areas and items such as pools, towels, sunbeds is also a risky and meticulous process. On the other hand, the increasingly preferred rental villa holiday concept provides a safe holiday where hygiene control is at the guest's side, away from the risks of living areas and kitchen sections and common areas that are only available to guests. (Turizmin Sesi, 2020).

Another necessity that corona virus has revealed in human life is the mandatory compliance with social distancing and hygiene rules. In this context, during the tourism activity, visitors especially in areas with social distances have been desired to carry out tourism activity. The second homes are usually built to spread over large areas. Due to this development, it is observed that this request of visitors is provided with second homes in Turkey. With this, it has been revealed that the necessary works have been carried out by the second home owners and marketers in order to fulfill the hygiene rules depending on the understanding of safe holidays before the start of the tourist season.

Having stated that the biggest factor in the orientation to rental villas is social distancing and hygiene concerns, Mat said, "We quickly stepped up and activated the disinfected villa options. We have made the disinfection procedures applied by expert teams in the villas to be added as notes to online advertisements. We are working on many measures, including disposable towel options. All villas rented with May are selected only from among the disinfected advertisements. The priority of our citizens is health." (Turizm Dosyası, 2020).

With the Covid-19 pandemic in the environmental dimension, new formations have begun to emerge. Due to this development, it is planned to develop projects in which dwarves will provide services in accordance with the isolated holiday logic and inspired by the Hobbit philosophy that natural products are presented to visitors.

İbrahim Ünsal says that they are in high demand due to the pandemic, and that these houses, which are very suitable for the structure of Olympos with plenty of oxygen in nature, will increase the demand even more. While every Hobbit house is looking out in the forest, perfect isolation can be achieved because it is designed not to see other houses. Organic vegetables and fruits produced in their own gardens will be used in the kitchen of the business, while eggs and cheeses will come from specially produced dairy. Dwarves will work in this business, which will serve on 35 acres with great views, just like in the film (Bayburs, 2020).

During the Covid-19 process, it is observed that studies have been carried out to determine new eco tourism routes in order to protect the environmental hobbit houses as well as the protection of natural life and to increase the level of well-being of local people.

General Director of Forestry Bekir Kocabey said, "The isolation process we are experiencing due to the pandemic will further expand ecotourism in the coming period. As General Directorate, we are working to provide our citizens with 19 unique ecotourism routes and a total of 350 km of hiking and cycling trails throughout Turkey where they can stay, hike, cycle, and explore nature with their children." Stating that another important contribution of eco-tourism, which is also of great importance in terms of nature love and the awareness of protecting forests, is to the local people, Karacabey said, "We have come a long way with our Ecotourism Branch Directorate, which we established 9 years ago. An important goal in this area is to provide financial resources to the local people in the regions where these routes are located." (Turizm Günlüğü, 2020).

With the serious increase of Covid-19, there has been a significant increase in demand in different regions of Turkey for the second types of houses such as camps, caravans, tents, bungalows, villas, detached houses and summer houses. Due to this increase in demand, the situation of increasing the prices of second homes has also started to emerge.

Covid-19, which caused habits to change all over the world, also caused preferences to differentiation in the tourism sector. Secluded facilities, where social distancing can be kept under control, came to the forefront in this process. In addition to the growing interest in rental summer houses, tents and caravans, bungalows, also in detached structures, spend this year with higher occupancy than last season. (Şahbaz, 2020).

Bodrum has reached the highest winter population in recent years. Many families continue to live in Bodrum due to the increased home office working order and distance education due to coronavirus. The district had a population of 170.000, which has now grown to 400.000. Therefore, housing and land prices increased in the district. (Turizm GM, 2020).

When the citizens who wanted to take a holiday preferred to rent summer instead of hotels due to the COVID-19 pandemic, hotels remained empty in coastal cities and summers have been full. There are no empty summers left in Kuşadası, Didim and Çeşme, where transportation is easy and the number of summers is large. The daily rent of the villa on a site with a pool increased by 150 percent to 2,500 liras this year from around 1.000 liras last year. The Covid-19 pandemic has changed this year's holiday preference. Despite the "Safe Tourism Certificate" requirement imposed on the hospitality sector, citizens who tried to stay away from crowded environments turned to summer villas. In coastal cities with hundreds of thousands of summers, there are almost no empty summers left. Those who did not want to come on holiday this year or wanted to get additional income preferred to rent their summer house. Prices doubled in Kuşadası, Çesme and Didim. The daily rent of the villa in a site with a pool increased by 150 percent to 2,500 liras this year from around 1.000 liras last year. (Sansür, 2020).

CONCLUSION AND EVALUATION

Changes in economic, socio-cultural, environmental, health and safety issues in the world directly affect tourism activities. However, these developments can cause significant changes in the second home market, which is an important pillar of accommodation in tourism. As a matter of fact, the covid-19 pandemic has been the most increasing demand for second homes recently (Zoğal & Emekli, 2020). As of December 12, 2020, the total number of cases in the world has been 70.228.447 due to the Covid-19 pandemic, and the number of those who lost their lives has been 1.592.187 (World Health Organization, 2020). In Turkey, the total number of cases on these dates has been record as 1.809.809 and the total number of deaths as 16.199 (Republic of Turkey. Ministry of Health, 2020). As a matter of fact, the increasing number of cases during 2020 and the limitations and releases that emerged afterwards affected the second home tourism in different aspects during the pandemic process in Turkey as it did all over the world.

As a result of the research, some changes in behavioral, environmental and economic dimensions began to emerge in the habits of tourists to take holidays with the Covid-19 process in Turkey. Consequently, for behavioral dimensions, tourists have started to show sensitivity in isolated life, contactless holidays, social distancing and hygiene. In order to achieve this sensitivity, it has been revealed that there are many tourist destinations in Turkey and it integrates itself into the process. In addition, in the studies carried out by the second homes in the existing houses for tourists to have a healthy holiday, it has been revealed that tourism activities can be carried out effectively during the Covid-19 process. As a matter of fact, despite all the negatives, the fact that approximately 14.486.632 tourists visited Turkey between January and November (Ministry of Culture and Tourism, 2020) and many of these tourists preferred second homes (Emekli & Zoğal, 2020) supports this result.

For the environmental dimension, with the Covid-19 process, it has been revealed that it is carried out in its efforts to implement new projects in accordance with natural life, with the logic of hiking, cycling, exploring and protecting natural life. It is also an important measure that turkey's natural structure is suitable for development in the implementation of these projects. The existing of many alternative tourism sources, especially in the Mediterranean Region, in different regions of the country, make it possible to carry out these targeted projects. One of the biggest advantages these projects can reveal is the rise in the welfare level of local people. This situation reveals that the second homes of different concepts to be built can contribute to the economic development of the region. Thanks to these areas, new employment areas will emerge for the local people and destinations with second homes will be developed thanks to the new taxes obtained. As a matter of fact, Deller et al. (1997) and Müller (1999) supports this result by revealing similar results in their research.

In the Covid-19 process, it has been concluded that there has been a significant increase in demand for different types of secondary houses, especially in the touristic regions of Turkey. Due to the increase in demand, the second home owners living in the region who did not want to participate in tourism activities this year started to rent out their facilities. All these developments have resulted in a significant price increase in house prices in the region when it comes to renting and purchasing. The increase in prices has also started to reveal inflationist pressure in touristic regions. As a matter of fact, due to inflationist pressure, the rising prices of goods and services in the region can put local residents in economic straits. However, the population growth situation caused by the increasing demand causes many problems on the specific local community in the region where the second homes are. As a matter of fact, many studies on the subject (Hoggart & Buller, 1995; Gallent et al., 2005; Marjavaara & Müller, 2007; Velvin et al., 2013) has come to the fore that the development of the second homes in one region brings many problems together.

In general, it is observed that the Covid-19 pandemic affects tourists, tourist destinations, local people living here, accommodation businesses and second homes, which are an important complement to accommodation, positively and negatively in many issues. It is important that new plans and policies are implemented as soon as we can in turn negative developments into positives in this process of impact. In this regard, first of all, efforts should be carried out to ensure that large-scale hotels in the region, which are severely affected by the increase in demand for second homes, can continue their sustainable activities. In this context, some restrictions may be imposed on the excessive construction, rental and sale of second homes in order to prevent unfair competition. This may also limit the inflationist pressure caused by second homes in the region. Secondly, studies should be carried out to prevent the situation of exceeding the physical, economic and social transportation capacity that may occur due to the excessive demand of the second homes. Studies on measuring the carrying capacity can be put forward in this regard. Finally, when normalization is returned after the Covid-19 process, detailed studies should be carried out by relevant institutions and academicians on the number of houses on a national, regional and local basis and the income obtained in the case of the use of second homes effectively in tourism.

REFERENCES

Armstrong, A., & Stedman, R. C. (2013). Culture clash and second home ownership in the U.S. northern forest. *Rural Sociology*, *78*(3), 318–345. doi:10.1111/ruso.12010

Asgary, A., Rezvani, M. R., & Mehregan, N. (2011). Local residents' preferences for second home tourism development policies: A choice experiment analysis. *Tourismos*, *6*, 31–51.

Barke, M. (2007). Second homes in Spain: An analysis of change at the provincal level 1981-2001. *Geography (Sheffield, England)*, *9*(3), 195–207. doi:10.1080/00167487.2007.12094200

Bayburs, Ö. K. (2020, July 13). Turizmde doğa dostu proje: Hobbit evleri [An environmentally friendly project in tourism: Hobbit Homes]. *Turizm Günlüğü*. https://www.turizmgunlugu.com

Bieger, T., Beritelli, P., & Weinert, R. (2007). Understanding second home owners who do not rent: Insights on the proprietors of self-catered accommodation. *International Journal of Hospitality Management*, *26*(2), 263–276. doi:10.1016/j.ijhm.2006.10.011

Cengizoğlu, F. P., & Özyılmaz, H. (2016). Adapting the secondary houses to the primary houses: Mersin sample. *Planning (Chicago, Ill.)*, *26*, 219–233. doi:10.14744/planlama.2016.83702

Ceylan, S., & Somuncu, M. (2020). Using for recreational aims of second homes in tourism areas: Case of Pelitköy (Burhaniye/Balıkesir). *Turkish Journal of Geographical Sciences*, *18*, 28–56.

Coppock, J. T. (1977). *Second homes.: Curse or blessing?* Pergamon Press.

Culture and Tourism Ministry. (2019). *Torism statistics*. Ministry of Culture and Tourism General Directorate of Investment and Enterprises.

Culture and Tourism Ministry. (2020). *Torism statistics*. Ministry of Culture and Tourism General Directorate of Investment and Enterprises.

Czarnecki, A., & Frenkel, I. (2014). Counting the invisible second home in polish statistical data collections. *Journal of Policy Research in Tourism, Leisure & Events*. Advance online publication. doi:10.1080/19407963.2014.935784

Deller, S. C., Marcouiller, D. W., & Green, G. P. (1997). Recreational housing and local governmentfinance. *Annals of Tourism Research*, *24*(3), 687–705. doi:10.1016/S0160-7383(97)00025-X

Dias, J. A., Correia, A., & Lopez, F. J. M. (2015). The meaning of rental second homes and places: The owners' perspectives. *Tourism Geographies*, *17*(2), 244–261. doi:10.1080/14616688.2014.959992

Dijist, M., Lanzendorf, M., Barendregt, A., & Smit, L. (2005). Second homes in Germany and the Netherlands: Ownership and travel impact explained. *Tijdschrift voor Economische en Sociale Geografie*, *96*(2), 139–152. doi:10.1111/j.1467-9663.2005.00446.x

Emekli, G. (2014). Importance of tourism geography for researching second homes and the development of second homes in Turkey. *Aegean Geographical Journal*, *23*, 25–42.

Fesharaki, P. (1996). *Rural geography*. Islamic Azad University Press.

Fleischer, A., & Tchetchik, A. (2015). Does rural tourism benefit from agriculture? *Tourism Management*, *26*(4), 493–528. doi:10.1016/j.tourman.2003.10.003

Gallent, N., Mace, A., & Tewdwr-Jones, M. (2005). *Second homes: European perspectives and UK policies*. Publishing Limited.

Hall, C. M. (2014). Second home tourism: An International revıew. *Tourism Review International*, *18*(3), 115–135. Advance online publication. doi:10.3727/154427214X14101901317039

Hall, C. M. & Muller, D. (2004). *Tourism, Mobility and Second homes: Between elite landscape and common ground.* Channel View.

Hiltunen, M. J., Pitkanen, K., Vepsalainen, M., & Hall, C. M. (2013). Second home tourism in finland: current trends and eco-social impacts. In Z. Roca (Ed.), *Second homes in Europe: from lifestyle to policy ıssues* (pp. 165–198). Ashgate.

Hoggart, K., & Buller, H. (1995). British home owners and housing change in rural France. *Housing Studies*, *10*(2), 179–198. doi:10.1080/02673039508720816

İçöz, O. (2003). *Travel agencies and tour operators management*. Turhan Publisher.

Jaakson, R. (1986). Second-home domestic tourism. *Annals of Tourism Research*, *13*(3), 367–391. doi:10.1016/0160-7383(86)90026-5

Kadıoğlu, Y. (1990). *Use of second homes in domestic and international tourism* (Unpublished master's thesis). B. Ü, İstanbul.

Kaiser, B. (2003). Life worlds of EU immigrants in Turkey. In E. Zeybekoğlu & B. Johanson (Eds.), Migration and Labour in Europe: views from Turkey and Sweden. Academic Press.

Keshavarznia, N., Sarvar, R., & Mahdavi, M. (2013). Environmental Impact of Second Home Development on Damash Village in Gilan Province Iran. *International Journal of Engineering and Advanced Technology*, *3*, 181–184.

Kısa, P. (1998). *Facade, mass and outdoor formation in second residential architecture* (Unpublished master's thesis). Trakya University, Edirne.

Komppula, R., Reijonenen, H., & Timonen, T. (2008). Vacation home owners' willingness to lease through an intermediary: a case study in two finnish ski resorts. In P. Keller & T. Bieger (Eds.), *Real estate and destination development in tourism* (pp. 285–300). Erich Schmidt Verlag.

Kozak, M., & Duman, T. (2011). Reviving second homes in tourism sectör: The case of Muğla-Datça Province. *Journal of Doğuş University*, *12*, 226–242.

Larsson, L., & Müller, D. K. (2019). Coping with second home tourism: Responses and strategies of private and public service providers in western Sweden. *Current Issues in Tourism*, *22*(16), 1958–1974. doi:10.1080/13683500.2017.1411339

Lipkina, O. (2013). Motives for Russian second home ownership in Finland. *Scandinavian Journal of Hospitality and Tourism*, *13*(4), 299–316. doi:10.1080/15022250.2013.863039

Ljungdahl, S. (1938). Sommar-Stockholm. *Ymer*, *58*, 218–242.

Manisa, K. (2007). *İkinci konutların turizm sektöründe yeniden kullanılabilmesine ilişkin bir model önerisi* [A model proposal for reuse of second homes in the tourism sector] (Unpublished Doctoral Thesis). Yıldız Tecnical University, İstanbul.

Marjavaara, R., & Müller, D. K. (2007). The development of second homes assessed property values in Sweden 1991-20021. *Scandinavian Journal of Hospitality and Tourism*, *7*(3), 202–222. doi:10.1080/15022250601160305

Matteucci, X., Lund-Durlacher, D., & Beyer, M. (2008). The socio-economic and environmental impact of second home tourism: the sounth pacific coast of nicaragua example. In P. Keller & T. Bieger (Eds.), *Real estate and destination development in tourism* (pp. 149–164). Erich Schmidt Verlag.

Mirani, S. Z., & Farahani, B. M. (2015). Second homes tourism and sustainable rural developmen in all around the world. *International Journal of Leisure and Tourism Marketing*, *4*(3/4), 176–188. doi:10.1504/IJLTM.2015.072076

Müller, D. K. (1999). *German second home owners in the Swedish countryside: on the internationalization of the leisure space* (Unpublished Doctoral Thesis). Umea University, Sweden.

Müller, D. K., Hall, C. M., & Keen, D. (2004). Second home tourism impact, planning and management. In C. M. Hall & D. K. Müller (Eds.), *Tourism, mobility and second homes: between elite landscape and common ground* (pp. 15–35). Channel View Publications. doi:10.21832/9781873150825-004

Müller, D. K., & Hoogendoom, G. (2013). Second homes: Curse of blessing? A review 36 years later. *Scandinavian Journal of Hospitality and Tourism*, *13*(4), 353–369. doi:10.1080/15022250.2013.860306

Okuyucu, A. (2016). *İkinci konutların ekonomik ve sosyo-kültürel etkileri konusunda bir araştırma: Yalova-Çınarcık Örneği* [A research on economic and socio-cultural effect of second homes. The case of Yalova-Çınarcık] (Unpublished Doctoral Thesis). Ankara University, Ankara.

Oliveria, J. A., Roca, M. N. O., & Roca, Z. (2015). Economic effects of second homes: A case study in Portugal. *Economia e Sociologia*, *8*(3), 183–196. doi:10.14254/2071-789X.2015/8-3/14

Özdemir, K. (2020, July 13). Erzincan dumanlı yaylası izole piknik imkanı sunuyor [Erzincan Dumanlı Plateau offers isolated picnic opportunities]. *Anadolu Ajansı*. https://www.aa.com.tr/tr

Özsoy, T. (2015). Use of secondary housing approach in marketing of Turkish tourism. *The Journal of KAU IIBF*, *6*, 1–18.

Phillips, M. (1998). Investigations of the British rural middle class: Part 2, fragmentation, identity, morality and contestation. *Journal of Rural Studies*, *14*(4), 427–443. doi:10.1016/S0743-0167(98)00031-X

Republic of Turkey Ministry of Development. (2013). *Eleventh development plan*. Ministry of Development.

Rezvani, M. (2003). Analyzing the process of establishment and developmen of second homes in rural areas of North of tehran province. *Geographical research Quarterly*, *45*, 59-73.

Riebsame, W., Gosnell, H., & Theobold, D. (1996). Land use and landscape chane in the Colorado mountains 1: Theory, scale and pattern. *Mountain Research and Development*, *16*(4), 395–405. doi:10.2307/3673989

Şahbaz, Y. (2020, July 28). Bungalovlara 'pandemi' ilgisi ['Pandemic' interest in bungalows]. *Anadolu Ajansı*. https://www.aa.com.tr/tr

Salehinasab, Z. (2005). *Tourism of second homes and their impacts on rural areas* (Unpublished Master's Thesis). Tehran University.

Sansür, L. (2020, July 19). Ünlü tatil beldelerinde kiralık villa furyası [The rush of rental villas in famous holiday resorts]. *Sözcü Newspaper*. https://www.sozcu.com.tr

Stettler, S., & Danielli, G. (2008). Image, truth and illusion in tourism promotion: the problem of he rapid spread of second homes in Switzerland and planning strategies. In P. Keller & T. Bieger (Eds.), *Real estate and destination development in tourism* (pp. 249–268). Erich Schmidt Verlag.

Struyk, R. J., & Angelici, K. (1996). The Russian dacha phenomenon. *Housing Studies*, *11*(2), 233–250. doi:10.1080/02673039608720854

Sund, T. (1948). Sommer-Bergen. Avisenes adresseforandringer som vitnesbyrd om bergensernes landopphold sommeren 1947. *Norsk Geografisk Tidsskrift*, *12*(2), 92–103. doi:10.1080/00291954808551651

Turizm, G. M. (2020, November 9). Bodrum'da Tarihi Nüfus Artışı Koronavirüs Kaçışları Sürüyor [Historical population increase coronavirus escape continues in Bodrum]. *Turizm GM*. https://www.turizmgm.com

Turizm Dosyası. (2020, May 22). Kiralık villa aramaları 4 kat arttı [Rental vılla calls ıncreased four tımes]. *Turizm Dosyası*. http://www.turizmdosyasi.com

Turizm Günlüğü. (2020, May 27). İşte pandemide nefes aldıracak 19 ekoturizm rotası [Here are nineteen ecotourism routes that will breathe in the pandemic]. *Turizm Günlüğü*. https://www.turizmgunlugu.com

Turizmin Sesi. (2020, May 8). Koronavirüs salgını temassız tatil devrini başlattı [Coronavirus epidemic started the contactless holiday era]. *Turizmin Sesi*. https://www.turizminsesi.com

Turkey Republic Health Ministry. (2020, December 12). *Covid-19 General Situation*. https://covid19.saglik.gov.tr

Vagner, J., Müller, D. K., & Fialova, D. (2011). Second home tourism in light of the historical political and socia geographical development of Czechia and Sweden. *Geografie (Utrecht)*, *116*(2), 191–210. doi:10.37040/geografie2011116020191

Velvin, J., Kvikstad, T. M., Drag, E., & Krogh, E. (2013). The impact of second home tourism on local economic development in rural areas in Norway. *Tourism Economics*, *19*(3), 689–705. doi:10.5367/te.2013.0216

World Health Organizations. (2020, December 12). *Covid-19 Number at Glance*. www.who.int/covid-19/information

Yirik, Ş., & Baltacı, F. (2016). Investigating the demographic particulars of aliens who setted in Antalya within the scope of second residence and the reasons for their choice. *Journal of Academic Researches*, *68*, 137–156.

Yirik, Ş., Uslu, A., & Küçük, F. (2015). Yerleşik Yabancıların Türkiye'ye İlişkin Sosyo Kültürel Algılarının Demografik Özelliklerine Göre İncelenmesi [Analysis of foreign residents' socio-cultural perceptions of Turkey according to their demographic characteristics]. *Journal of Bartın İİBF,* 263-282.

Zoğal, V., & Emekli, G. (2020). The changing meanings of second homes during Covid-19 Pandemic in Turkey. *International Journal of Geography and Geography Education*, *42*, 168–181.

KEY TERMS AND DEFINITIONS

COVID-19: The "global pandemic" of SARS-CoV-2.

Second Homes: For accommodation purposes in winter or summer outside the existing homes of individuals.

Tourism: One of today's largest industries promoting travel, consumption, eating, and entertainment.

Tourism Sector: Among the tourism enterprises operating in the fields and subjects of tourism; tourism related production, demand, customer etc. composed section.

Turkey: It is a country that has lands both in Asia and Europe.

Chapter 5
Renting Cars and Trucks

Bayram Akay
Burdur Mehmet Akif Ersoy University, Turkey

ABSTRACT

Tourism is a fragmented and information-oriented sector covering tour operators, travel agencies, hotel sales representatives, associations, meeting offices, transportation, car rental, airlines, cruise, souvenirs, restaurants, hotels/motels, and entertainment. The car rental sector, which is an important part of the tourism sector, is growing day by day, and the number of customers is increasing rapidly. The success of the car rental sector, which produces support services within the growing tourism sector, is considered very important for the development of tourism. The COVID-19 pandemic has engulfed the globe and has already had an enormous impact on life as we once knew it. With airplanes grounded, millions of people in quarantine, and hundreds of travel bans in place, COVID-19 has brought the global tourism industry to a grinding halt along with the rental industry. The study determines the current situation of the car rental sector and presents some suggestions.

INTRODUCTION

The travel and tourism industry not only impacts millions of individuals but also has the power to transform communities. Accounting for more than one-third of the global services trade, its growth rate facilitates the creation of more and better jobs requiring a diverse portfolio of skills and capabilities. With its continued resilience against socio-economic disturbances and other events, the travel and tourism industry contributed USD 8.9 trillion in total to the global GDP, accounting for nearly 10.3% of the total figure in 2019 (UNWTO,2020). This massive growth in the tourism industry also boosted the growth of other related industries, such as

DOI: 10.4018/978-1-7998-7287-0.ch005

car rental. Nowadays, tourists prefer renting cars to explore a new place as it gives them the flexibility of planning their own itinerary without the fear of relying on public transport system. Car rental services allow customers to travel to their choice of places as per their convenience. Further, the rising disposable income has also established the trend of more people taking short trips. Rather than taking their own vehicle, customers prefer renting cars; airport rentals are the most common as tourists rent a car immediately after landing in a new country and keep the car with them for the whole duration of their stay or drop them off at convenient drop-off points (Shah, 2019).

Car rental industry can date back to the 20th century when two important people (Walter L. Jacobs and John D. Hertz) auspicated this business in American. After the development of nearly one century, the revenue of car rental business per year has been up to one hundred billion US dollars, and it has become a significant role for the world economic development. For Instance, in the United States, about one third new cars are sold by the channel of rental every year; similarly, two millions which account for fifteen percent of new cars are sold by the same way in Japan (Yang et al., 2008).

Transportation services have an important role in tourism, which requires some sort of movement to or from locations. Car rental agencies, along with many other factors, have played a vital role in increasing the ease of transportation by providing a service that allows tourists to easily travel within their destinations. It seems that the importance of travel facilities, especially car rental business, will gain more attention and unavoidably car rental owners will have to provide more extensive and better quality services to be able to compete with the growing needs and expectations of international tourists (Ekiz et al., 2009). As car rental companies provide substitutional products, price and service quality are critical success factors. This underlines the importance of optimizing car rental logistics in terms of the utilization of the fleet of cars while maintaining a high degree of customer satisfaction, and makes it possible to provide a kind of caring service (Fink & Reiners, 2006).

This study deals with the renting car and trucks from the perspectives of the conceptual. This chapter organized the car rental industry and history, car rental sector in the world (U.S., Europe, Asia - Pacific, Africa, and Middle East), truck rental, car rental industry after COVID-19 and conclusion.

The Car Rental Industry and History

Car rental is the hiring of a motor vehicle from one party to another party. Rentals are generally made on an hourly, daily, weekly or monthly basis (Akay, 2015). The car rental sector provides billions of dollars of income to the economy of many countries. In the US with 19.272 car hire locations, more than 2.2 million cars in service in 2019, the car renter sector's contribution to the economy was about $32.018 billion (www.autorentalnews.com, 2019a). In the world, the car rental industry is most prevalent in the US, Europe and other developed countries. The sector is also growing in developing countries such as India, China and Brazil (Tyya, 2007). The car rental sector takes place in two forms: long-term car rentals (more than 12 months) and short-term car rentals (hourly/daily /monthly). Long-term car rental activities are mainly divided into operational renting and financial renting. Short-term car rental activities take place in two forms: daily car rental and one-year minimum rental (Gençler, 2012).

The history of most famous rent a car companies is initially associated with the automobile's appearance inside United States from 1900 to 1920 (Korstanje, 2011). In 1908, Ford Motor Company produced the Ford Model T, which was so low in price that it opened travel to the common middle-class American. In 1918, Walter L. Jacobs founded the first car rental company, Rent-A-Ford-Car Company, in Chicago, which grew rapidly from 23 to 565 cars by 1923 and was merged into John D. Hertz later. America car rental industry started to bloom since then, and expanded in operation scale in the 1990s. Today, large-scale car rental companies are distributed all over the world. In Europe and America there are world famous Avis Car Rental, Hertz Car Rental, Budget Rent A Car System, Inc., and Europcar. Taking Hertz Car Rental as an example, it operates from approximately 8,500 locations in 146 countries worldwide (Zhang et al., 2014: 83).

In recent years, one of the most significant trends in tourism has to be the increasing emphasis on individual, non-package holidays. More specifically, when tourist habits worldwide are analyzed, many tourists seem to favor a higher number of shorter breaks to short-distance, short-haul destinations, which in turn leads to increased mobility. Clearly, the continued growth of low-cost airlines and the increasing use of the Internet give holiday makers direct access to tourism service providers and, by extension, to ''self-service'' tourism (Palmer-Tous et al., 2007).

How to Read This Chapter

The first section synthesizes a short introductory discussion about the tourism, car rental and transportation services. The section proffers description and history of the car rental. The second section deals with the car rental industry in the world and its economic size. It also examines the status of the car rental industry according to geographical regions, which are car rental sector in the U.S.A., Europe, Asia – Pacific, Africa and Middle East. The third section dissects renting trucks about market segmentation, logistics business models and truck rental options. The last section examine future of the car rental industry after COVID-19 in the world.

CAR RENTAL SECTOR IN THE WORLD

As the car rental industry has organized very well in developed countries, it has achieved more growth in these places. The U.S. has the majority stake in the global car rental industry, followed by Europe and other developed countries. In addition, the sector is growing in developing countries such as India, China and Brazil (Tyya, 2007: 112). Economic factors such as the constant growth of the travel and tourism sector, the increased demand for entertainment and leisure activities, the increase in urban population and consumer spending power cause the growth in the sector. On the other hand, some difficulties, such as stringent emissions standards set to prevent environmental pollution, prevent the sector from growing (Business Wire, 2013:5). The global car rental market size was valued at $92,92 billion in 2019, and is projected to reach $214.040 billion registering a CAGR of 10.7% from 2020 to 2027 (see table 1).

Table 1. Global car rental market value

Years	Revenue (million $)
2012	59,504.
2013	61,943
2014	66,574
2015	69,876
2016	74,149
2017	79,045
2018	86,100
2019	92,920
2027	214,040

Source: https://www.alliedmarketresearch.com/car-rental-market, 2021.

In general, the car rental sector is divided into three market segments: travel, financial leasing and replacement car market. In this case, it can be regarded as TOURISM + BUSINESS + LOCAL market (Geraghty & Johnson, 1997: 109). The car rental sector takes place in two forms: long-term car rentals (more than 12 months) and short-term car rentals (hourly/daily /monthly). Long-term car rental activities are mainly divided into operational renting and financial renting. Short-term car rental activities take place in two forms: daily car rental and one-year minimum rental (Gençler, 2012). In operational renting, the rental company undertakes all variable and fixed costs such as maintenance, repair, insurance, tax and service follow-up (Kesenci, 2010: 83). In the financial leasing method, while the ownership of the vehicles is in the leasing company, costs such as maintenance, repair and depreciation expenses of the vehicles are undertaken by the leasing customer (Gezer & Çiçek, 2011: 175). The renting customer is responsible for all costs incurred during the use of the vehicle (fuel, accident, breakdown, bridge and highway crossings, traffic fines, etc.).

Table 2. Summary of types of vehicle hiring

Hiring type	Duration	Ownership of the	Services/maintenance included
Short term rental	Few hours to several weeks	Rental company	Yes
Medium-/Long terms rental	Up to 12 months	Rental company	Yes
Operating leasing	Over 12 months (typically up to 3 years)	Leasing company	Maintenance is often included.
Finance leasing	2-5 years – Depending on the type of vehicle	Leasing company	No (typically)
Hire purchase	2-5 years – Depending on the type of vehicle	Typically the user after the end of contract period.	No (typically)

Source: Tsamis et al., 2016: 20.

The car rental market is divided into several niche markets, including airport operators and major city agencies for business and leisure travel, replacement vehicle companies and fleet sellers (Raskop, 1994: 44). For example, Hertz carries out 80% of its operations in airports and 20% in city agencies (Bonoma, 1984: 149).

CAR RENTAL SECTOR IN THE U.S.

The car rental sector started in the U.S. in 1918 as a business line (William & Richard, 1995: 84). In the United States, the car rental and leasing industry emphasizes on 50 large companies that generate more than 80% of the total revenue thereof. Major companies include Enterprise Holdings, Hertz Global Holdings, Avis Budget Group, Ryder and U-Haul International. These companies conduct daily or long-term rental of passenger cars, recreational vehicles, trucks and trailers. Many U.S. based car rental companies have expanded to include international operations primarily at international airports and often through local vendors (Seay & Narsing, 2013: 113). In the U.S., large car rental companies such as Hertz, Avis, National and Budget operated in the sector. With the increasing airline competition in the 1980s, a small number of customers created the business and entertainment niche markets. Alamo and Dollar car rental companies implemented low prices to increase their market share in tourist destinations. The increase in tourist demand has changed the market shares in the car rental sector (Pachon, 2000: 6). In the U.S., market shares of businesses have risen dramatically, as many mergers and acquisitions have diminished. Table 3 shows the number of car rental companies, number of vehicles, number of branches, income and market shares in the U.S.

Table 3. U.S. car rental market fleet, locations and revenue (2020)

Company	U.S. Cars in Service (AVG.) 2020	U.S. Locations	2020 U.S. Revenue (in millions $)	2019 U.S. Revenue (in millions $)
Enterprise Holdings (Includes Alamo, Enterprise, National Car Rental)	1,100,000	6,000	14,715	17,800
Hertz (includes Dollar and Thrifty)	430,000	3,800	3,600	6,938
Avis Budget Group (includes Payless, not Zipcar)	350,000	3,200	3,800	5,500
Advantage Rent-A-Car	18,500	100	300	450
Fox Rent A Car	18,200	21	205	255
ACE Rent A Car	9,000	60	73	100
U-Save Auto Rental System (owned by FSNA)	5,500	124	22	37,5
NP Auto Group (Priceless & Next car)	7,500	100	60	52
Rent-A-Wreck of America	1,750	71	18	20
Independents	42.000	4,200	25	550
Total	**1,982,450**	**17,676**	**23,218**	**32,018**

Source: www.autorentalnews.com (2020b).

In the U.S., the car rental industry averaged 1.98 million units in its overall fleet in 2020, a 12.4% decline over 2019. As a result, revenue per unit, per month (RPU) dropped to $975 for the year, from $1,174 in 2019. The U.S. car rental market achieved a projected $23.22 billion in revenue for 2020, the lowest overall revenue since 2011, according to data collected by Auto Rental News. The 27.4% drop in total revenue for 2020 compared to revenue of $32 billion in 2019 is historically unparalleled, in fact much steeper than during the Great Recession when revenues only dropped 6.7% from 2008 to 2009.

CAR RENTAL SECTOR IN EUROPE

Europe has a more flexible and free way of car rental. Transportation is easy as the European-based passenger railway lines are much more than highways. Apart from Switzerland, automobiles offer transportation even to the smallest villages (Bestor, 2013:3). The European market is approximately half the size of the US market and top five countries (France, Germany, the United Kingdom, Spain and Italy) represent roughly 70% of the total market (www.nedrelid-ca.com, 2016). In Europe, there are two giant companies in operation such as Europcar and Godfrey which are European companies besides American car rental companies such as Hertz, Avis, Budget, Alamo, Dollar, National, Thrifty and Advantage. Businesses operate a total of 40,000 vehicles in Europe (Pran, 2006: 12).

Avis, the largest car rental organization in Europe, makes about half of all bookings (up to 5,000) through travel agencies. Renting cars with holiday purposes constitutes the most important part of the job with a ratio of 60%. Hertz is the world's largest car rental organization and is an influential car rental business especially in the U.S. business world. In Germany, Hertz has 50 tour operators, as well as co-operation agreements with Lufthansa and Ryanair airlines (Walter, 2010: 17). The European car rental market remains reasonably fragmented. There are five operators with a truly European-wide presence. These are five operators with market share (www.nedrelid-ca.com, 2016);

- Europcar and market share 19%,
- Avis Budget and market share 13%,
- Hertz and market share 12%,
- Sixt and market share 11%,
- Enterprise and market share 10%,
- Other Independents and market share 35%.

According to a regulation on the registration of motor vehicles, car rental companies have been allowed to transfer their vehicles to another EU country without having to re-register their vehicles during the holidays (the ability to use the vehicle used in the coasts through the summer in the Alps as well in winter holiday). Car rental companies have also saved a considerable amount since they can transfer their vehicles to another EU country without resorting to re-registration during holiday periods. Thus, it became cheaper to rent a car for tourists (http://ec.europa.eu). EU,

Directive no 2006/1 / EC has been issued for the road transport of goods for renting cars without a driver for tucks. The Directive allows the use of hired vehicles for the purposes of cross-border transport operations between Member States. It also gives Member States the possibility to restrict the use of hired vehicles with a total permissible laden weight of more than 6 tonnes used for own account operations (Tsamis et al.,, 2016: 15).

In Turkey, car rental companies operating in airports and big city centers in the past years provides services in many tourism regions as a result of rapid developments in the tourism sector (MEB, 2006). In Turkey, a total of 300.000 vehicles are used in the car rental sector, 50.000 of which are used daily (short-term) and 250.000 of which are corporate long-term corporate rentals. The asset size of the sector is 31.5 billion ₺ (TOKKDER 2020). Many multinational companies (Avis, Budget, Enterprise, Europcar, Sixty, Thrifty, Hertz, Leaseplan, Fleetcorp ect.) and local companies (Intersity rent a car, Derindere Filo Kiralama, Zeplin rent a car, GarentaDAY, Beyaz Filo Kiralama, Işıl Tur, Central rent a car, Lider Filo, Almira car rental service, Hedef Filo, Mengerler kiralama, Garanti Filo etc.) compete in Turkey.

CAR RENTAL SECTOR IN ASIA - PACIFIC

The Asia Pacific is one of the fastest growing regional markets for car rental due to the increasing population coupled with transportation issues in the region. Car rental service is very useful in Asian countries like India, Australia, Cambodia, Japan, China etc. There are many islands in Indonesia region which are the most attractive tourist destination. This helps to grow the car rental market in the Asia Pacific. Avis, Ola, Hertz, Didi Chuxing, Sixt, Zoomcar, Europcar, GrabTaxi, Uber, Hailo, Line Taxi, Blue Bird Eco Rent A Car, Carzonrent, Al-Futtaim Group are some leading car rental service providers in the Asia Pacific (https://globenewswire.com).

The car rental industry in China is in a large-scale development. In 2002, with Hertz, Avis and Europcar entering into the Chinese market and the rental car market opened to the world market. There are more than 400 car rental agencies in China's car rental market. Most of them operate in airports and in the mainland, in small and single cities (Li & Tao, 2009: 265).

In India, a developing market, as airlines are building new flight routes, hotel chains building new ones, car rental companies have opened new offices. Operating in more than 8,000 locations in 143 countries around the world, Hertz entered the Indian market by establishing a joint venture. The language and status of roads are important problems in the region where services are provided with driver and driverless options (Southan, 2011:42). The top income group emerging in India and China provides growth in rental vehicle trade in the Asia Pacific region (Car Rental Business, 2008: 4).

In Taiwan have emerged business opportunities for transportation equipment and rental business. In particular, there has been an increase in demand for long-term car rental services that allow businesses to reduce spending. The number of businesses in the sector, which was 140 in 2008, has reached 805 in 2012. The development of the tourism industry in Taiwan has also improved car rental services. The intensive demand for motorcycle renting in the country created car rental companies in the country, as well as motorcycle renting businesses (Wang, 2012: 8).

CAR RENTAL SECTOR IN AFRICA

There are large international franchise car rental companies (Hertz, Budget, Alamo, National and Enterprise) and local organizations operating on a regional scale in Africa (South Africa Tourism Report, 2019: 73). The rental value sales in South Africa for 2018 was 11.5 billion $, which grew by 5.7% to reach R12.1 billion in 2019. The Travel & Tourism Competitiveness Index (TTCI) ranked South Africa 43rd out of 140 countries in 2019 for the presence of major car rental companies in the country (South Africa Tourism Report, 2020: 25). In South Africa, Kenya, Zimbabwe and Uganda, car rental is available from websites of international companies such as Hertz and Avis (Maswera, Davson & Edwards, 2008). Among domestic organizations, First Car Rental provides services in all major airports, cities and tourist centers with 6,000 vehicles and 47 different office networks in South Africa and owns 11% of the market. The company offers a diverse range of products and services from economical vehicles to luxury groups at 4,500 rent-a-cars in 100 countries around the world (www.firstcarrental.co.za).

Budget Rent-a-Car is located in Botswana, Mozambique, and Namibia with 60 branch offices in South Africa. The organization has a fleet of 4,500 vehicles and a market share of 14%. It has muscle car retail organization with McCarthy organization and automobile sales, distribution and concession agreements with brands such as Alfa-Romeo, BMW and Peugeot (South Africa Tourism Report, 2019: 28). Addis Ababa, founded by an Ethiopian investor in 2008, rents and tours 40 different vehicles with the Budget Car Rental franchise in the region. In addition, on one of the popular tourist sites Lake Tana, it provides chartering with a boat with a carrying capacity of 10 people as well as tourist transportation (Tutu, 2011: 12).

CAR RENTAL SECTOR IN THE MIDDLE EAST

Most of the problems that global tourism has experienced in the last 30-40 years stem from events in the Middle East. The wars, the terrorist attacks, the stagnation caused by the increase in gasoline prices, inflation caused financial losses to tourism entrepreneurs in different parts of the world (Enderson, 2007: 152).

Since 2010, the Middle East has experienced an increase in the rental fleet. Mainly, increasing competition among rental players, ranging from pricing to quality, has led to the expansion of the regions' market. International companies operate on the franchise system in the Middle East market. Few major players are Hertz Corporation, Sixt, Avis Corporation, and Europcar (Research & Markets, 2019). For example, Sixt car rental operates as franchise in Bahrain, Egypt, Jordan, Kuwait, Lebanon, Oman, Qatar, Saudi Arabia and United Arab Emirates (http://se.sixt.de). The Avis Budget group also has offices in the Middle East.

TRUCK RENTAL

Truck rental includes hiring and leasing of heavy commercial trucks or light commercial vehicles. Truck rental primarily serve individuals, companies, and agencies who do not own their own truck fleets but undertake freight transport as a service. The continuously increasing demand for trucks from the logistics, industrial, and construction industries and the rapid population growth are some of the factors driving the global truck rental market. Truck rental curbs the level of vehicular pollution by reducing the volumetric sales of owned vehicles as well as on road vehicles. Such factors are promoting the growth of the truck rental industry at an exponential rate. Moreover, fleet owners are continuously working on cost cutting measures to offer cost efficient fleet solutions. Thus, to efficiently manage cost, fleet owners are adopting the option of truck rental to significantly reduce transport costs (www.marketresearchfuture.com).

The prominent players in the global truck rental industry are AMERCO (US), PACCAR Leasing Company (US), Penske Truck Leasing Co., L.P. (US), Ryder System, Inc. (US), Sixt SE (Germany), United Rentals, Inc. (US), Alamo (US), Advantage Rent-a-car (US), Avis Budget Group Inc. (US), Budget Car Rental (US), MAX Rental.lu AG (Luxembourg), and Europcar (UK). Budget Truck rental business is one of the largest local and one-way truck rental businesses in the United States. Budget Truck fleet is comprised of approximately 22,000 vehicles that are rented through a network of approximately 1,000 dealers and 480 Company-operated locations throughout the continental United States (Avis Budget Group, 2017).

The global truck rental market is segmented based on truck type, lease type, and region. On the basis of truck type, the global market has been divided into heavy commercial truck and light commercial vehicle. On the basis of lease rate, the global market has been divided into long term and full-service lease (www.marketresearchfuture.com). Long-term lease units are often painted with the lessee company's " logo" and cannot always be easily identified as leased trucks. Full -service lease contracts may provide a wide range of services including suggestions on appropriate vehicle specifications for products hauled, acquisition and disposal of vehicles, maintenance and repair, painting, insurance, fuel, tax stamps, and State permits. However, all lessors do not provide all these services nor do customers always purchase the complete range of services offered . Some leasing firms also process the enormous volume of paperwork required in truck operations — licenses, fuel use reports, servicing schedules, and regulatory reports (Renee, 2009: 10). New business models have emerged in the truck industry. Technological advancements find application in the truck industries (See table 4).

The market for the trucking industry is very huge. Many industries require trucking services. These include agriculture industry, mining industry, manufacturing industry, construction industry, fuel industry, supermarkets, wholesalers, distributors and raw materials suppliers. Companies and individuals need trucks to transport bulky goods (https://startupbizglobal.com/starting-trucking-business-plan). Truck rental companies have a range of options such as with payload, curtain-side, axle, semi, furniture, hiab, watercart, EWP, hard side, refrigerated, tipper, tractor, bulky, pull trailer, trombone, low loader, minilift, swinglift, flat deck, flatbed, and even combin of these.

FUTURE OF RENT-A-CAR SUBSECTOR IN A POST COVID-19 WORLD

The rapid spread of COVID-19 across the globe is having an enormous impact on the travel and tourism industry. The indirect and induced impact of travel bans is felt by sectors such as hotels and hospitality; car rentals, travel agents and tourist guides, among others. Tourism losses are growing bigger in parallel to the rapid spread of the disease. The shelter-in-place orders will cost the global airline industry over US$350 billion for the year 2020. Car rental businesses are heavily dependent on air travel since business travelers and vacationers often combine their car rental and flight reservations to save money and make the travel process more efficient, convenient, streamlined and stress-free. With international and domestic vacations on a complete freeze, its tough times for car rentals. The U. S. car rental giant Hertz, for instance, is already dangerously on the brink of bankruptcy as it desperately seeks last-minute extension on debt payments (www.businesswire.com).

Table 4. New logistics business models

Business Models	Business Models
Same-day delivery – *shutl.com*: Realization of shortest delivery times with attractive pricing on basis of a broad network of carriers and partnerships.	**City freight consolidation platform** – *Cargo hopper:* Provision of efficiently bundled shipments through electric transportation vehicles.
Own car as delivery box – *Volvo Drop-off/ Pick-up System:* Testing of a system that allow consumers to have their shopping delivered straight to their car.	**Digital logistics agents** – *Sennder*: Digital logistics agent and full forwarding service for entire transportation route. Avoiding different subcontractors reduces transportation costs. *InstaFreight* follows the same business model.
Route optimization – *Routific:* Smart trucks are navigated by GPS and telematics data to ensure optimized route and capacity utilization.	**FTL1) freight brokerage for shippers and carriers –** *Transfix*: Manufacturers & distributors can connect with a truck driver network shipping long-haul freight across the U.S. Parties are connected by a mobile app.
Smart Trucks – *DHL:* DHL combines advanced technology with dynamic route planning in its vehicles to increase efficiency in both pickup and delivery	**Shared logistics concept** – *Gogovan*: Offering of logistics-on-demand, e.g. in Hong Kong – Currently >26,000 registered drivers.
City freight consolidation platform – *CARGONEXX:* Brokerage service for bundling of shipments from different wholesalers/ manufacturers to serve customers within one specific area.	**Potential city logistics concepts –** *FreightExchange:* Without a specific time schedule, hitchhiking is the most efficient mean of transportation as operators can sell unused capacity to businesses that need to ship goods
Senden24 offers spontaneous urban instant delivery. For B2B, B2C and C2C. Service available 24/7. Pickup within 5 min. Delivery within 1 hour. On demand. Any place. Any time.	**RYTLE** provides the first holistic and interconnected concept of city logistics. Consists of a unique cargo bike called MOVR, a standardized BOX and a mobile HUB.
Smartlane is an easy-to-use web-based delivery management software focusing on automated tour planning and optimizing as well as simplified process controlling.	**Quiqup** is a London-based on-demand delivery company formed in 2014. Founded originally to let consumers order anything for local same hour delivery, Quiqup has since expanded its proposition to provide last mile delivery to businesses of any size and sector.

Source: Roland Berger GmbH, 2018: 9.

With the constant efforts of various countries to find the vaccine for the coronavirus, the virus will soon pass away. This will gradually make people step out of their houses and resume their regular life as it was before the pandemic. Once the customers get back to their daily routine, the demand for the things would also surge gradually. This includes demand for car rentals for traveling. The future of the car rental industry in the world after COVID-19 will be as follows (https://mytaxipulse.com, www.autorentalnews.com):

- Consumers will get very used to goods and services coming to their doorstep. When travel resumes, the car rental industry will need to adopt that mentality.

- Rental companies with more agile regulations and policies would flourish faster in the market.
- Rental companies that have maintained good connections with their customers will gain from these connections, as they will still have their trust.
- Era of the new normalcy will be motto "Fast Service + Friendly Service + a Clean Car = Good Customer Experience."
- Rental companies would assure the customers of hygiene and personal safety.
- Vehicle cleanliness and sanitization will be of most importance more than ever. A dirty rental will be a perceived health risk and a lost customer.
- Individual mobility will be preferred instead of public transportation (bus, plane, ship, train) for a long time post Covid-19.
- The smartphones, companies like Uber and electric and autonomous vehicles will have an important future of car rental.

CONCLUSION

The car rental sector consists of franchise international car rental companies (Hertz, Avis & Budget group, Sixt, Europcar. National and Enterprise), leasing companies (LeasePlan, Fleetcorp, ect.), and national businesses. Truck rental is provided by international car rental (Sixt, Alamo, Advantage Rent-a-car, Avis Budget Group, Europcar), leasing companies (Leasing Company, Penske Truck Leasing Co., Ryder System, United Rentals, ect.) and truck manufacturer companies (Volvo, Scania, BMC, Daimler AG.).

Cars in service and rental revenue have come into being an approximately stable scale in US (see table 3) due to the increasing competition and never-ending rate wars according to the Auto Rental News, so does other countries. According to UNWTO World Tourism Barometer (2021), international travel loss of USD 1.3 trillion in tourism revenues and international arrivals dropping by 74% due to Covid 19 in 2020. Covid 19 also negatively affected the number of vehicles and revenues in the car rental industry. The global car rental business is reached $ 89.6 billion after declining by -31.7% in the year 2020 (www.researchandmarkets.com). The industry is going through a difficult period due to travel restrictions, working home office, curfews and increasing unemployment. On the other hand, the necessity of social distance, hygiene and the use of masks negatively reflected on public transportation, which provides individual movement to the car rental sector. Thus, apart hotels, holiday sites and villas that provide individual accommodation have attracted attention in 2020.

Mobility is a mega trend and is likely to see both growth and new solutions and service offerings going forward. The car rental industry is a key service provider at the heart of the mobility universe and can be able leverage its existing capabilities to deliver mobility solutions adapted to an evolving market environment. This represents a potential growth driver for the sector, both in current and adjacent segments. The question is how to position oneself to best take advantage of the mobility megatrend. The industry will further adopt app-based booking, online booking, competitive service pricing, car sharing, cloud-based car rental software services and car rental ecommerce platforms, car rental software and self-service technologies during the post corona virus period.

REFERENCES

Akay, B. (2014). *Impact of Competition Determinants in Car Rental Sector on Operation Performance: A Research in Tourism Destinations* (PhD thesis). Sakarya University Institute of Social Sciences, Turkey.

Avis Budget Group. (2017). *Avis Budget Group, 2016 Annual Report.* Retrieved from https://www.annualreports.com/HostedData/AnnualReportArchive/a/NYSE_CAR_2016.pdf

Bestor, A. (2013). *What you should know about renting a car in Europe in 2013.* Retrieved from www.gemut.com

Bonoma, V. T. (1984). *Managing marketing: text, cases and readings.* Macmillan Inc.

Business Wire. (2013). *Global Car Rental Market Report: 2013.* Retrieved from ww.researchandmarkets.com

Car Rental Business. (2008). *Global strategic business report global industry analysts.* Retrieved from www.researchandmarkets.com/reports

Ekiz, E. H., Bavik, A., & Arasli, H. (2009). RENTQUAL: A new measurement scale for car rental services. *Tourism An International Interdisciplinary Journal, 57*(2), 135–153.

Enderson, J. C. (2007). *Tourism crisis: causes, consequences and management.* Elsevier Publishing. doi:10.4324/9780080466033

Fink, A., & Reiners, T. (2006). Modeling and solving the short-term car rental logistics problem. *Logistics and Transportation Review, 42*(4), 272–292. doi:10.1016/j.tre.2004.10.003

Gençler, G. (2012). *Beyaz Filo Oto Kiralama A.Ş. 01.01.2012-30.09.2012 Faaliyet Raporu.* Retrieved from www.beyazfilo.com

Geraghty, M. K., & Johnson, E. (1997). Revenue Management Saves National Car Rental. *Interfaces*, *27*(1), 107–128. doi:10.1287/inte.27.1.107

Gezer, Ö., & Çiçek, B. (2011). Binek Oto Kiralamalarında Vergi Uygulamaları. *Mali Çözüm Dergisi*, *11*(4), 161–176.

Jamal, T., & Budke, C. (2020). Tourism in a world with pandemics. *Journal of Tourism Futures*, *6*(2), 181–188.

Kesenci, Ç. A. (2010). *Araç kiralama sektörünün gelişimi ve ülke ekonomilerine etkileri. In Tüm Oto Kiralama Kuruluşları Derneği*. TOKKDER.

Korstanje, M. E. (2011). Rent-a-car industry: A case study in Argentina. *Tourismos*, *6*(1), 1–15.

Li, Z., & Tao, F. (2010). On determining optimal fleet size and vehicle transfer policy for a car rental company. *Computers & Operations Research Journal*, *37*(2), 341–350.

Maswera, T., Dawson, R., & Edwards, J. (2008). E-commerce adoption of travel and tourism organizations South Africa, Kenya, Zimbabwe and Uganda. *Telematics and Informatics*, *25*(3), 187–200.

Milli Eğitim Bakanlığı (MEB). (2006). *Konaklama ve Seyahat Hizmetleri Rezervasyon Sistemleri*. Mesleki Eğitim ve Öğretim Sisteminin Güçlendirilmesi Projesi.

Pachon, E. J. (2000). *Strategic and tactical fleet planning for the car rental industry*. University of Miami.

Palmer-Tous, T., Riera-Font, A., & Rossello-Nadal, J. (2007). Taxing tourism: The case of rental cars in Mallorca. *Tourism Management*, *28*, 271–279.

Pran, N. S. (2008). *Successful tourism: tourism practices* (Vol. 2). Sterling Publisher.

Raskop, R. R. (1994). *Is the public being taken for a ride? The car rental industry: its policies, practices and the public interest*. Golden Gate University.

Renee, L. G. (2009). *The Motor Vehicle Leasing & Rental Industry: Trends and Prospects*. Industry and Trade Administration.

Research & Markets. (2019). *Middle East Car Rental Market - Growth, Trends, and Forecast (2020 - 2025)*. Retrieved from https://www.researchandmarkets.com /reports/4987210/middle-east-car-rental-market-growth-trends#pos

Roland Berger Gmb, H. (2018). *Trends in the truck & trailer market*. Retrieved from https://www.rolandberger.com/fr/Insights/Publications/Trends-in-the-truck-trailer-market.html

Seay, S., & Narsing, A. (2013). Transitioning to a lean paradigm: A model for sustainability in the leasing and rental ındustries. *Academy of Strategic Management Journal, 12*(1), 113–124.

Shah, P. (2019). *Car Rental Market Research Report: P&S Intelligence.* Retrieved from https://www.researchgate.net/publication/337324851_Car_Rental_Market_Global_Industry_Analysis_and_Forecast_to_2024

South, A. T. R. (2019). *State of tourism report 2017/18.* Retrieved from https://www.tourism.gov.za/AboutNDT/Publications/State%20of%20Tourism%20Report%20(STR)%202017-18.pdf

South, A. T. R. (2020). *State of tourism 2018/19 report,* Retrieved from https://www.tourism.gov.za/AboutNDT/Publications/State%20of%20Tourism%20Report%20 2018-19.pdf

Southan, J. (2011). Trend driven: what's in store for car rental? *Business Traveler.* Retrieved from http://go.galegroup.com/ps/i.do?

TOKKDER. (2020). *Operational Leasing Sector Report Presentation – 2020.* Retrieved from https://tokkder.org/tokkder-dergi/3139

Tsamis, A., Gibson, G., Felix Kirsch, F., & Lohr, E. (2016). *Ex-post evaluation of Directive 2006/1/EC.* Retrieved from https://ec.europa.eu/transport /sites/transport/files/facts-fundings/evaluations/doc/2016-ex-post-evaluation-of directive -2006-1-ec-final-report.pdf

Tutu, J. (2011). *International tourism marketing -promoting BRC budget car rental and tour, Ethiopia* (Master's thesis). School of Tourism and Hospitality Management.

Tyya, N. T. (2007). *Hospitality & tourism industry employers.* Vault Inc.

UNWTO. (2019). *International Tourism Highlights, 2019 Edition,* Retrieved from https://www.e-unwto.org/doi/pdf/10.18111/9789284421152

UNWTO. (2020). *2020: worst year in tourism history with 1 billion fewer international arrivals.* Retrieved from https://www.unwto.org/taxonomy/term/347

Walter, F. (2010). *Einführung in die fremden verkehrs ökonomie* (10th ed.). Oldenburg Verlag.

Wang, C. C. (2012). Transport equipment rental & leasing. Taiwan industry reports. *Ref. Code, 19786*, 1–19.

William, J. C., & Richard, C. G. (1995). Evolutionary change in product management: Experiences in the car rental ındustry. *Interfaces, 25*(5), 84–104.

Yang, Y., Jin, W., & Hao, X. (2008). Car rental logistics problem: A review of literature. *IEEE International Conference on Service Operations and Logistics, and Informatics,* 2815–2819.

Zhang, M., Xie, Y., Huang, L., & Zhen, H. (2014). Service quality evaluation of car rental industry in China. *International Journal of Quality & Reliability Management, 31*(1), 82–102.

ADDITIONAL READING

Akay, B., & Türkay, O. (2014). Analysis of the customer complaints against car rental companies. *Electronic Journal of Vocational Colleges-December, 4*(4), 138–146.

Beech, J., & Chadwick, S. (2006). *The business of tourism management*. Prentice Hall.

Carfoot, G. (2008). Competition Hertz: The culture and practice of car audio competitions. *Journal of Media. Cultural Studies, 22*(5), 667–674.

Carroll, W., & Grimes, R. (1995). Evolutionary change in product management: Experiences in the car rental industry. *Tourism Management, 25*(5), 84–104.

Cheung, R., & Lam, P. (2009). How travel agency survive in e-business world? *Communications of the IBIMA, 10*(2), 85–92.

Cho, S., & Rust, J. (2008). Is econometrics useful for private policy making? A case study of replacement policy at an auto rental company. *Journal of Econometrics, 32*(12), 243–257.

Cho, S., & Rust, J. (2010). The Flat Rental Puzzle. *The Review of Economic Studies, 77*(2), 560–594.

Dolnicar, S. & Laesser, C. (2007). Travel agency marketing strategy: insights from Switzerland. *Journal of Travel Research. Online Journal, 12*(3), 1-41.

Enderson, J. C. (2007). *Tourism crisis: causes, consequences and management*. Elsevier Publishing.

Gronroos, C., & Sand, A. (1993). A winning service offer in car rental. *Management Decision Journal, 31*(1), 45–51.

Hanrahan, J., & Melly, D. (2019). Biosecurity risk and tourist communication in Ireland. *European Journal of Tourism Research, 22*, 45–61.

Jamal, T., & Budke, C. (2020). Tourism in a world with pandemics: Local-global responsibility and action. *Journal of Tourism Futures*, *6*(2), 181–188.

Mancini, M. (2012). *Access: Introduction to Tourism and Travel*. Wiley Publishing.

Marijanovic, K. (2010). Differentiation of car rental services in the Croatian market. *Preliminary Communication*, *22*, 113–128.

Pachon, E. J. (2000). *Strategic and Tactical Fleet Planning for the Car Rental Industry*. University Of Miami.

Raskop, R. R. (1994). *Is the public being taken for a ride? The car rental industry: its policies, practices and the public interest*. Golden Gate University.

Romagosa, F. (2020). The COVID-19 crisis: Opportunities for sustainable and proximity tourism. *Tourism Geographies*, *22*(3), 690–694.

Tang, C., & Deo, S. (2006). Rental Price and rental duration under retail competition. *European Journal of Operational Research*, *23*(11), 806–828.

Walker, J. (1999). Hire capacity of rental services. *Managing Service Quality*, *9*(2), 116–120.

KEY TERMS AND DEFINITIONS

Car Rental: Is the hiring of a motor vehicle from one party to another party. Rentals are generally made on an hourly, daily, weekly, or monthly basis. The car rental business is usually associated with a car that is hired for a period of 12 months or less. "Rental" of cars for a longer period is commonly referred to as leasing.

COVID-19: Is defined as illness caused by a novel coronavirus now called severe acute respiratory syndrome coronavirus 2 (SARS-CoV-2; formerly called 2019-nCoV), which was first identified amid an outbreak of respiratory illness cases in Wuhan City, Hubei Province, China.

Tourism: The act and process of spending time away from home in pursuit of recreation, relaxation, and pleasure, while making use of the commercial provision of services.

Transport: Is the easiest way of movement of humans, animals, and goods from one location to another.

Truck Rental: Includes hiring and leasing of heavy commercial trucks or light commercial vehicles.

Chapter 6
The Impact of COVID-19 on the Rent-a-Car Industry:
An Study Case With Focus in Argentina

Maximiliano Emanuel Korstanje
https://orcid.org/0000-0002-5149-1669
University of Palermo, Argentina

ABSTRACT

Without any doubt, coronavirus disease slumped global economies in an unparalleled crisis, one of the worst downturns since 2008. COVID-19 not only affected negatively the tourism industry but also other service sectors. To some extent, governments have adopted two different dispositions against the virus. While some nations imposed a strict lockdown, others privilege the consumption and domestic circuits of payment. In its history, the tourism industry has never faced a crisis of this caliber, and its impacts remain unsure even to date. Although the interests and studies evaluating the impact of COVID-19 have captivated the attention of countless scholars, less attention has been given to the rent-a-car industry, which occupies a central position in the tourist system. As substitute competitors of train, bus, and airplanes, the rent-a-car organizations seem to be a quintessential actor of the tourist system. Of course, because we live in a world without tourists, empirical-based studies do not abound these days.

DOI: 10.4018/978-1-7998-7287-0.ch006

INTRODUCTION

On December of 2019, The Socialist Republic of China experienced a new virus outbreak, in the city of Wuhan –to be more exact. Originally the situation was trivialized by authorities leading the world to an unexpected and global crisis. The virus rapidly disseminated to the four continents forcing governments to close their borders and cancelling all flights. To the date, CO-SARS-v2 (known as COVID-19) infected almost 23.472.214 persons causing 815.262 fatal victims (last updated on 08-24-2020). The most affected countries include the US (180.788 victims) followed by Brazil (114.913), Mexico (60.480), India (58.546), the UK (41.433), Italy (35.441), France (30.528), and Spain (28.870). The pandemic affected seriously the Health system in Spain, Italy, the UK, the US and France, as well as other less developed countries. At a closer look, in the mid of the pandemic, the WHO (World Health Organization) was widely criticized by the lack of response to give a standardized plan of contingency, leading each nation to react differently to prevent the contagion. Doubtless, the industry of tourism and hospitality, as well as the global commerce slumped down before the COVID-19. This generated an unparalleled economic crisis worldwide. Today, scholars –in the constellations of tourism fields- divided in two clear-cut poles. Those worried for developing new methodological toolkits to understand tourism in a context of new normalcy (Wen et al. 2020; Miles & Shipway, 2020; Zenker & Kock, 2020; Verma & Gustaffsson, 2020), and those voices who enthusiastically envisaged the opportunities to create more resilient and sustainable destinations. De-growth tourism, for them, exhibits an interesting point of departure for the next decades (Gossling, Scott, & Hall, 2020; Gallego & Font 2020; Higgins-Desbiolles, 2020; Prayag, 2020; Galvani, Lew & Perez, 2020; Crossley, 2020). The fact is that one of the problems of these studies associate to the lack of an empirical basis to understand the dimension of the economic crisis. What seems to be more important, tourism-based research has systematically ignored the important role of rent-a-car industry (subsector) in a configuration of a resilient tourism industry. To fill this gap, the present chapter explores empirically the real economic and socio-cultural effects in a rent-a-car company which is geographically located in Argentina. As a substitute competitor of trains, buses or airplanes, rent-a-car organizations are a key-player of the tourist system. In the first section, we explore the effects of COVID19 in the tourism and hospitality industries. Secondly, we proffer a discussion on the importance of cars or automobile as alternative means of transports as well as its historical background in the inter-war period. In third we review the importance of adopting resilient recovery plans to face new virus outbreaks. Last but not least, we analyze the effects of the pandemic in a well-known rent-a-car company in Argentina.

At a closer look, the history of the rent-a-car industry goes in a similar direction. Although the specialized literature in rent-a-car subsector does not abound (Korstanje 2011), it is important to delineate the first steps of rental cars organization in the US. The historical roots of rental cars date us back to Germany (1906). The company Sixt Authofharen und selbsfahrer [Sixt Car Cruises and Self drivers] was established by the end of 1913. The model was rapidly adopted by Joe Saunders in Omaha, Nebraska by 1917. His innovation led to expanding to almost 50 cities in the next years importing what American historians dubbed as "Saunders system". The company was finally bought by John Hertz in 1923. Meanwhile, the UK Godfrey Davies (a young visionary man) borrows Saunders system to create a company which will become in Europcar. The end of WWII set the pace to new transport means which revolutionized the tourism industry while replacing the trolley and horse. Today, this subsector offers plenty of car classes which are allocated throughout the globe, in cases, at least as an ideal option, substituting mass transport forms as the commercial airlines, the train or buses.

INITIAL DISCUSSION

After the terrorist attacks that whipped the US in September of 2001, the morphology of tourism industry has changed forever. To this attack followed successive events in the most splendid European cities as Madrid, London, Paris, and Brussels (only to name a few). If this was not enough, one might speculate, other global risks as natural disaster, climate change, political turmoil and virus outbreaks forced to set a new agenda for policy-makers and authorities, according to a new global governance (Blake & Sinclair, 2003; Ritchie 2004; Santana 2004; Laws, Prideaux & Chon, 2007). The turn of the century has led us to a post-apocalyptic world, where nobody feels safe any-longer, starting a process of securitization where the psychological dimension of fear dominates (Bianchi, 2006). The days after 2001 were of great anguish, fear and anxiety. As a direct consequence of this turning point, scholars who passively witnessed how three commercial airplanes -esteemed as the bastions of capitalist society- were weaponized against the Twin Towers and the Pentagon. As a direct consequence of the major crisis the industry went through, the risk perception theory, which had more than four decades in the cognitive psychology, was widely adopted as a main paradigm in tourism research (Fuchs & Reichel 2006; Yuksel & Yuksel, 2007; Lepp & Gibson, 2008). By the emulation of potential scenarios to locate and eradicate potential risks, risk perception theory was originally moved in deepening the understanding of tourists´ motivations. The tourist´s mind, as well as their preferences, fears and aversion occupied a central position in the configuration of risk perception paradigms. Per scholars, this would help to protect the organic image of tourist destinations in long-run terms (Reisinger & Mavondo 2006; Floyd et al 2004). Risk perception theory –as a catch-all model- looked to encompass different fields and matters oscillating from terrorism (Floyd et al. 2004; Reisinger & Mavondo 2005; Seabra, Abrantes & Kastenholz, 2014; Wolff & Larsen 2014) to natural disasters (Matyas et al, 2011; Park & Reisinger, 2010; Jonas et al 2011), without mentioning virus outbreaks (McKercher & Chon, 2004; Monterrubio 2010), and local crime without mentioning political violence (Baker, Page & Meyer, 2003; George 2010). Although the theory preliminarily obtained promising results, the radicalization of some terrorist cells, accompanied with the rapid deterioration of ecology which created an unparalleled ecological crisis has led to scholar to calibrate new strategies to adapt the tourist destinations to much complex world. Instead of risk perception theory, post disaster and post-conflict approaches are based on the belief that the precautionary logic does not suffice to explain why some destinations fall or rise after a process of crisis. Hence, the figure of resilience plays a leading role tailoring the concept of adaptation to tourism research. In an ever-changing world, the notion of risk sets the pace to adaptation (Robinson & Jarvie 2008; Mair, Ritchie & Walters, 2016; Amujo & Otubanjo 2012; (Seraphin, Butcher & Korstanje 2017; Seraphin et al 2018; Seraphin, Korstanje & Gowreesunkar 2020). In a nutshell, risk perception theory was gradually substituted by far-reaching models that accept the risk as a quintessential feature of the tourist system. As Tarlow (2014) notably outlines, it is in vain to think a risk-zero society, while tourism industry should be prepared to enhance resilience to mitigate not only the negative aftermaths of external hazards but orchestrating sustainable policies for making tourist destinations safer.

EFFECTS OF COVID19 IN THE INDUSTRY OF TOURISM

The history of mankind and viruses are inextricably intertwined. Of course, tourism seems not to be an exception. Since 2001 different viruses have negatively impacted in the industry posing a real challenge for policy makers and other involving stakeholders. The question whether of tourists look for pleasurable experiences shifted to the needs of visiting secure destination.

Security and safety occupied a central position in the business talks as well as in the tourism management policies (Hall, Williams & Lew 2004; Brouder et al 2020). In 2002, a new virus known as Severe Acute respiratory syndrome (SARS) originated in Foshan, China threatened to be expanded to Western countries when it was contained by Chinese authorities. However, over 8.000 persons were infected in more than 30 countries and 770 deceased. In 2009, Mexico and the US witnessed an outbreak of Swine influenza (H1N1) paralyzing part of the international flights and global commerce worldwide. Some estimate numbers show that almost 284.000 persons died in the world because of H1N1. In 2012, a viral respiratory infection (Middle East respiratory syndrome MERS) caused mainly by MERS Coronavirus grinds the planet to a halt. Last but not least, the frightening Ebola virus disease arrives at the US in 2014 alerting all the health authorities in the Western hemisphere. In almost all cases, Governments adopted similar reactions which oscillated from the closure of airspace to stricter controls at borders. The tourism industry, which is centered on a high-mobile culture, was a fertile ground for the dissemination of viruses and different pathogens (McKercher & Chon 2004; Monterrubio 2010; Solarin 2015; Novelli et al. 2018). Also restrictions to mobilities were on the agenda of many governments. As Gossling, Scott & Hall (2020) accept, the current (unsustainable) forms of consumption marks surely the future of tourism and hospitality, in a planet characterized by over-crowded cities, a climate crisis and unsustainable conditions of life (Gossling, Scott & Hall, 2020:15)

Similar concerns accompany Higgins-Desbiolles´ paper entitled as Socialicing tourism for social and ecological justice. For her viewpoint, COVID19 brings the problem of sustainability into the foreground. The current ecological crisis lays the foundations towards the foundation of a new capitalism, most probably a more sustainable society where the global injustices of neoliberalism can be finally corrected (Sigala 2020; Carr 2020). Gretzel et al (2020) and Wen et al (2020) start –from different stances- a hot-debate respecting to the use of technology to forge new methodologies in the constellations of tourism research. Coronavirus disease calls attention to emerging practices of tourism ingrained in virtual consumption. It is safe to admit virtual or e-tourism are direct consequences of the economic crisis accelerated by COVID19. What is more important to discuss, the digital revolution allows a re-elaboration of transformative research. As earlier mentioned, despite their eloquence, the hot-released publications –with foci in COVID19- are abstract lucubration, probably based on the urgency of saying something in days of uncertainty, but lacking of an empirical basis. In fact, this happens because of two main reasons. In this vein, Francesc Romagosa (2020) calls the attention to reconsider the social effects of pandemics in western societies. Emotions as mistrust or fear have durable consequences not only for tourism but for society all. He toys with the belief that no-one knows with detail the future of the tourism industry or the long-lasting effects of COVID19 in all us. After all, COVID19 begs a more than interesting question: how do scientists study tourism in a world without tourists?

To respond this above-mentioned answer, we shall combine a method of triangulation (using quantitative and qualitative methods) to give an exploratory approach of how COVID19 and the current global crisis affect a rent-a-car company in Argentina.

THE ECONOMY OF RENTAL CAR MARKETS IN ARGENTINA

Because of confidentiality issues, the real name of the organization will be changed. We have been provided of statistic information vital for business and competition, but in any case we have facilitated to the costs or budget details. The statistic information was limited to volume of sales and inter-location businesses. The gathered information was complimented with a formal and informal interviews conducted from Jan to August 2020. In addition, the interviews were recorded and supported via Zoom and Skype. The company has more than 30 years of experience in the rent-a-car market and situates as a leading global organization. The main segments of renters are foreigner tourists and domestic tourists. The foreigner renters come from Brazil, Chile, the US, and Europe while domestic renters are city-dwellers from Buenos Aires, Cordoba and Rosario. Officially, 24 locations offer different car classes to different renters. The process of renting a car is very simple the class is previously reserved in order for the car to be picked up as specified. The rental length varies according to the driver´s needs and the vehicle can be dropped out at another than picked up location –often by paying a one way fee. Over the recent years, renting a car substituted as an alternative way to drive freely when the aero commercial industry does not work. For the sake of clarity, locations may be grouped in two groups: industrial and touristic locations. Industrial locations are primarily based on private corporations and factories while tourist locations focus on foreign or domestic tourists as main segments.

Given the advance of the pandemic, on 20 April of 2020 President Alberto Fernandez declared the state of emergency imposing a strict lockdown which closed different commercial activities, subsectors and industries. Although the lockdown remains even to date, it gradually evolved towards different facets. The government decided to bail out countless companies, above all the tourist sector, which was seriously compromised by the economic crisis generated by the pandemic. The sales of small size tourist companies slumped down considerably tenfold. This scenario leads Tourism ministry Matias Lammens to bid for financial aid programs to assist the tourist sector. With the airspace completely closed, hotels in the brink of collapse, and borders controlled by army forces, Argentina went through in the worse economic downturn of its history. In view of this mayhem, this chapter describes the turbulences, problems and limitations a rent-a-car company experienced during the pandemic. We try to validate or refute four types of different hypotheses.

1. H1. The pandemic accelerated a serious decline in the sales of the company.
2. H2. All the locations show a similar decline in their sales.
3. H3. In view of the absence of the aero commercial activity, the rent-a-car situated as an option to travel to other cities.

4. H4. Domestic drivers or renters replaced to foreign renters.

In the next section, we discuss the ebbs and flows of a well-famous rent-a-car organization as well as the negative impact of COVID19 and the restrictive measures of the government to intervene in the market. As a result, we combine qualitative methods (interviews conducted through digital platform) and quantitative ones (characterized by internal statistics we have been kindly authored to make public). Although we asked for the budget details, as well as the preliminary costs model but it was declined because of the revelation of these ciphers may compromise seriously the company. As stated, the obtained outcomes should be understood within the sample and universe they represent, and they cannot be extrapolated to other cases.

OUTCOMES AND DISCUSSIONS

It is important not to lose the sight of the fact that sales are not only reliable but credible indicators of business performance but gives a certain insight into the potential businesses in the short run. As discussed, in the tourism industry, which is a sensitive sector respecting to disrupting events, it is important to add, tourist often select safe avoiding unsafe destinations. Security and safety seem to be the tugs of the war of the industry.

Sales

As table 1 shows, sales have invariably collapsed because of COVID19. On January of 2019, the company amassed almost ARS 77.213.334 (including VAT and other taxes), an amount which notably increased to ARS 113.429.941 in February of the same year. In the low season, which means the months of April, May and June, the sales declined to ARS 51.706.987, ARS 43.775.670, and 38.024.031 respectively. In April of 2020 –next to the imposition to the lockdown- this company had a turnover of ARS 9.712.386. The level of sales keeps for May for ARS 9.341.356 but declines even more for June (ARS 6.473.256) and July (ARS 6.361.175). At a closer look, at the time of comparing April 2019 and April 2020, we understand the problem with clarity. In April 2019 the sales were ARS 51. 706.987 while in 2020 the sales declined to ARS 9.712.386. This authorizes us to say sales were down 81%. The same tendency can be observed in the subsequent months of May, June and July. In this period the company reduced its fleet size, selling more than 500 vehicles to pay wages and salaries. In the meantime, the rewarding program for sales was suspended until further notice. The number of closed rental agreement which exhibits the number of rental of the company was reduced from 5.905 in

Table 1. Indicators and Sales

Months	Sales	Closed Ra	Opened Ra	DBR days	Avg days	Driven kms	AVG kms
ene-19	77213334,92	6303	6232	34170,72	5,42	5443147	863,58
feb-19	113429941	7316	7655	36299,25	4,96	6044503	826,20
mar-19	74674390,76	4755	3995	23250,3	4,89	3969989	834,91
abr-19	51706987,16	5801	5905	23117,37	3,99	4072941	702,11
may-19	43775670	5081	5137	18991,77	3,74	3316364	652,70
jun-19	38024031,1	5171	5556	17460	3,38	3023765	584,75
jul-19	62345948,06	6156	6866	27305,67	4,44	4173966	678,03
ago-19	68362898,31	7006	7043	28481,35	4,07	4474323	638,64
sep-19	65957098,35	6644	6821	27349,1	4,12	4468094	672,50
oct-19	68548389,12	6906	7465	26892,18	3,89	4927580	713,52
nov-19	79355024,21	7596	8026	30426,85	4,01	5607464	738,21
dic-19	80572668,29	6981	7668	30221,7	4,33	5264876	754,17
ene-20	23306241	7328	7478	40092,46	5,47	6537841	892,17
feb-20	13474781,2	7316	7655	36300	4,96	6044503	826,20
mar-20	74713350,11	4755	3995	23252,2	4,89	3969989	834,91
abr-20	9712386	106	92	2822	26,62	291653	2751,44
may-20	9341356,04	119	123	1941,44	16,31	197950	1663,45
jun-20	6473256,14	183	186	2063,1	11,27	313081	1710,83
jul-20	6361175,08	120	139	1865,06	15,54	175010	1458,42

Source: self-elaboration, 2020

April 19 to 92 in April 2020 (98% of the total activity). The tendency replicates in the months of May, June and July.

What is more important, the average of days per RA (contract agreement) is notably increased during the pandemic because of two main reasons. On one hand, there are fewer rentals than in other months but at the same time, (on another) the rentals now are used for working and not for leisure prepuces. In April 2019 the average of rental days was 3.99 days per rental but in April 2020 it raised 26.62 days. The same happens with the average of driven mileages. This indicator is formed by the sum of all rentals and all driven mileages in a period of time. In April 2019 this amount was 702.11 mileages per RA while it radically changed in April 2020 to 2.751.44 per RA. These results confirm that renters are now using the vehicles to move to other states only for working. In view of this H1 and H3 are clearly confirmed.

Figure 1. Evolution of sales

At the time of catching a glimpse of the number of reservations created in the month the downward trend seems to be evidently clear. In January 2019, 8.661 new bookings were created, followed by the months of February (4.800), March (8.299), April (7.474), and May (8.036). Although we find a decline in February, respecting January, it was resulted from the economic crisis and the process of devaluation that whipped the presidency of Mauricio Macri in February of 2019. Quite aside from this little discrepancy, these numbers are radically changed for the months of April 2020 (333 new bookings), May (332) (For further details see Table 2).

The recollected evidence amply supports the hypothesis that not only the sales of this rent-a-car company slumped down because of the economic crisis ushered Argentina to adopt restrictive measures to stop the pandemic, but also confirms hypothesis 3 which infers that the cars are now rented by new professional segments mainly oriented to essential industries as factories, farming industry and other sectors unaffected by COVID19. With this information in mind, we have consulted to the marketing Director, Juan Carlos who says us:

"we were wrapped in a difficult position if you ask me the worse crisis the World has faced in its history or the worse I experienced. The first days were the saddest of my life. We do not know what to do. We were a company aimed for renting to foreigner tourists! Brazilians, Chileans, Americans who travelled to Bariloche, Iguazu and Calafate to enjoy our tourist destinations, now we were radically forced to swerve

and attend other segments as medicines, scientists, police, farmers who are limited to use the public transport. We discovered that after all renting a car is the most secure form of traveling!" (Juan Carlos, male 49 years old)

Table 2. Number of created bookings

Months	Created bookings
ene-19	8661
feb-19	4800
mar-19	8299
abr-19	7474
may-19	8036
jun-19	8960
jul-19	10074
ago-19	10156
sep-19	10862
oct-19	12008
nov-19	10901
dic-19	11187
ene-20	10151
feb-20	8599
mar-20	4917
abr-20	333
may-20	332
jun-20	398
jul-20	504

Source: self elaboration, 2020

The above mentioned excerpt reveals that renting a car still remains as a valid option for drivers who need to move inside Argentina, though it enthralls as a substitute transport mean by the lack of airplanes and trains. This suggests that the effects in locations, far from being homogenous, vary on their nature and segmentation. We have drawn to different groups: industrial and tourist locations. The former are grouped with locations where exist a great industrial manpower and infrastructure (i.e. Buenos Aires, Cordoba, Neuquen, Mar del Plata and Rosario). The latter, rather, is formed by locations based exclusively in leisure and tourist activities (i.e. Bariloche, Calafate, NOA [Northwestern Argentina & Iguazu and Mendoza).

Figure 2. Bookings
Source: self elaboration, 2020

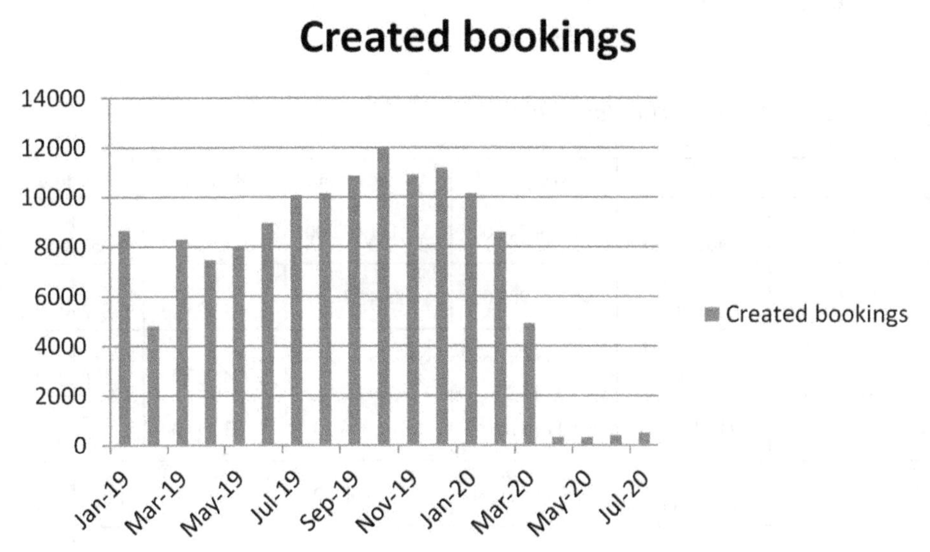

Sales Per Locations

Industrial Destinations

Per table 4, Buenos Aires city billed ARS 9.873.919 in April of 2019, but this amount declined to ARS 3.387.136 in April of 2020. The variation was 60%. In May and June, the variation goes from 55% and 61% respectively. Neuquen has not the same luck. This industrial location has sales for ARS 3.170.416 in April 2019 but it reduced strongly to April 2020 in ARS 240.293, the variation percentage is for 92% or near circa. Cordoba appears to offer a similar scenario. The tendency repeats for the months of May and June. Mar del Plata is another third example which evolves in its own dynamic. In April of 2019, Mar del Plata registers marks for rental services for ARS 703.398 which changes to ARS 520.201 in April 2020. The variation oscillates between only 26% and 28% in the months of April and May, but if we compare July 2019 to July 2020, the variation is % 81. Let´s explain readers that Mar del Plata is a hybridized destination which offers a product of sun & beach in the summer period, combining the low season with a fishing industry. To some extent, July meets with the Winter Recess where thousands of city-dwellers coming from different states of the country go to Mar del Plata for tourism and relax. Having said this, the economic consequences of the lockdown in the industrial destinations is far from being lineal or homogeneous. Locations as Buenos Aires city experience a nuanced decline while other locations –as the example of Cordoba shows- do not reach the same criterion.

Table 3. Sales in industrial destinations

Months	Buenos Aires	Neuquen	Mar del plata	Rosario	Cordoba
ene-19	$ 16.407.212,00	$ 1.959.542,00	$ 2.141.632,00	$ 1.384.666,00	$ 3.654.305,00
feb-19	$ 17.488.564,00	$ 5.128.987,00	$ 2.084.238,51	$ 2.231.075,00	$ 4.832.411,00
mar-19	$ 13.851.681,00	$ 3.573.132,00	$ 1.697.116,00	$ 2.734.960,00	$ 3.126.214,00
abr-19	$ 9.873.919,00	$ 3.170.416,00	$ 703.398,00	$ 793.294,00	$ 2.458.165,00
may-19	$ 10.645.311,00	$ 2.742.421,00	$ 554.998,00	$ 842.742,00	$ 1.959.542,00
jun-19	$ 9.127.561,00	$ 2.752.426,00	$ 538.918,00	$ 893.052,00	$ 1.590.277,00
jul-19	$ 11.687.592,00	$ 2.747.791,00	$ 524.104,00	$ 831.586,00	$ 2.280.718,00
ago-19	$ 9.361.832,00	$ 4.792.920,00	$ 684.662,00	$ 1.109.579,00	$ 2.093.109,00
sep-19	$ 11.703.226,00	$ 4.293.294,00	$ 535.901,00	$ 2.362.072,00	$ 2.651.467,00
oct-19	$ 10.232.142,00	$ 3.247.217,00	$ 2.595.859,00	$ 1.183.781,00	$ 2.595.859,00
nov-19	$ 13.446.148,00	$ 4.453.225,00	$ 862.631,00	$ 1.012.234,00	$ 2.844.833,00
dic-19	$ 16.032.321,00	$ 3.153.993,00	$ 973.857,00	$ 1.223.158,00	$ 3.605.012,00
ene-20	$ 24.248.628,00	$ 4.786.935,00	$ 2.235.770,00	$ 4.786.635,00	$ 6.116.465,00
feb-20	$ 17.488.564,00	$ 5.128.987,00	$ 2.084.228,00	$ 2.231.075,00	$ 4.832.411,00
mar-20	$ 13.854.487,00	$ 3.573.132,00	$ 1.697.116,00	$ 2.734.960,00	$ 3.126.214,00
abr-20	$ 3.387.136,00	$ 240.293,00	$ 520.201,00	$ 2.229.804,00	$ 1.305.821,00
may-20	$ 4.777.740,00	$ 259.904,00	$ 207.452,00	$ 712.471,00	$ 392.700,00
jun-20	$ 3.564.951,00	$ 120.261,00	$ 537.558,00	$ 694.125,00	$ 186.969,00
jul-20	$ 4.829.467,00	$ 131.026,00	$ 94.615,00	$ 238.695,00	$ 87.710,00

Source: self elaboration, 2020

Tourist Destinations

Per our inferences previously outlined, tourist locations are more sensitive to the lockdown tan industrial ones. In fact, it is evident when we glimpse the evolution of sales in Bariloche and Calafate, even this latter reduced the sales to zero, but this does not happen with NOA & Iguazu. The volume of sales in Bariloche for April 2019 was ARS 11.521.252, but going down in April 2020 to ARS 77.097, which represents a variation of 96%. Even in June, this variation goes to 99%. Similar results are obtained in the successive months. Contrariwise, NOA has sales for ARS 12.733.384 in April 2019 and ARS 1.400.900. Needless to say, the variation is for 88%. Mendoza, which is probably affected by the Chileans who cross annually the border, profited almost ARS 1.063.272 on April 19 and ARS 182.206 on April 20 consolidating a variation of 82% in the decline. With the benefits of hindsight, though tourist destinations are clearly more affected than industrial location no less true is that further investigation is needed in this direction since the results are not homogenous.

One of our consulted key informants, CEO Martin (male 62 years old) replied "*when the pandemic, we asked the government for a bail out, not credit, the government accessed to pay partly the wages of our staff, our intention is not to fire people, we are a family and in this epic challenge we will remain all together, we are not afraid of the situation, we passed for similar situations in the past, for example in 2001 when the domestic market here in Argentina collapsed. Months after this disaster, we received the flux of tourists coming from neighboring countries. We reconverted our mission and vision, we became a tourist company, and recycled as a rent-a-car leader in the tourist market. I feel now we have to forget tourism for a long time, and focus on domestic drivers!*.

One Way Fees

For the sake of clarity, one-way fees or drop off fees are charges held to the renters when the car is not delivered in the same location where it has been picked up. In normal conditions, one-way fees are encouraged in Argentina all but discouraged outside the country. This contrasts radically with the European market where cars can be picked up and returned in different countries of the European Union. The one-way fee denotes the demand of renters who often rent a car as the main form of transport when strikes in others subsectors as civil airlines or long-distance buses come into fruition. In April 2019 the company earned ARS 972.694 in one way fee. In April of 2020, the sales in the same concept are rising to ARS 1.323.000. This reflects that hypothesis 4 is confirmed. Renters take advantage of renting a car to replace other less secure forms of transport. In May 2019 the sales were for ARS

950.089 while in 2020 for ARS 712.662. June 19 shows sales for ARS 549.508 which increases to ARS 766.315 for June 20. These numbers support the idea that rent-a-car company situates as an alternative mode to boost local tourism in the post-Covid 19 contexts.

Table 4. Sales in tourist destinations

Months		Bariloche	Calafate	Mendoza	NOA e iguazu
ene-19		$ 29.799.384,00	$ 6.282.780,00	$ 4.424.763,00	$ 9.452.008,00
feb-19		$ 43.355.202,00	$ 13.102.181,00	$ 8.738.333,00	$ 14.310.851,00
mar-19		$ 22.226.856,00	$ 9.626.625,00	$ 6.641.901,00	$ 10.171.384,00
abr-19		$ 11.521.252,00	$ 4.663.143,00	$ 1.063.272,00	$ 12.733.894,00
may-19		$ 5.701.413,00	$ 2.553.804,00	$ 4.518.902,00	$ 13.716.809,00
jun-19		$ 7.620.628,00	$ 1.220.948,00	$ 3.508.111,00	$ 10.085.040,00
jul-19		$ 21.099.285,00	$ 1.395.359,00	$ 5.221.935,00	$ 15.868.679,00
ago-19		$ 22.487.297,00	$ 1.416.449,00	$ 5.614.311,00	$ 19.382.045,00
sep-19		$ 16.878.021,00	$ 2.359.275,00	$ 5.686.458,00	$ 16.878.021,00
oct-19		$ 12.969.476,00	$ 5.955.109,00	$ 6.902.404,00	$ 18.542.965,00
nov-19		$ 16.987.705,00	$ 8.519.779,00	$ 6.802.795,00	$ 19.250.664,00
dic-19		$ 23.570.766,00	$ 10.291.812,00	$ 6.632.215,00	$ 12.655.631,00
ene-20		$ 43.004.083,82	$ 12.564.524,00	$ 9.776.888,00	$ 16.115.603,00
feb-20		$ 43.357.149,00	$ 13.145.075,00	$ 8.738.333,00	$ 14.310.981,00
mar-20		$ 22.231.335,00	$ 9.651.286,00	$ 6.641.901,00	$ 10.176.398,00
abr-20		$ 350.897,00	$ -	$ 182.206,00	$ 1.400.990,00
may-20		$ 693.832,00	$ -	$ 35.939,00	$ 2.261.313,00
jun-20		$ 47.972,00	$ -	$ 266.334,00	$ 869.172,00
jul-20		$ 77.097,00	$ -	$ 106.709,00	$ 687.216,00

Source: self elaboration, 2020

To validate this, we interviewed mechanic Chief Staff (Marcelo, males, 42 years old) who claimed:

"this situation has good and bad things. People are worried, shocked, they do not know what to do to return to their homes. Thousands of Argentineans have been stranded abroad, or in other states. The lockdown prohibits the public circulation, a fundamental right as the free movement has been cancelled, suspended by the government to avoid the sickness dispersion. In this mayhem, we received a lot of

consult of young and elderly clients who needed a car to come back to home. The problem was that they drove thousands of mileage and sometimes the cars were not delivered in good conditions. In the months of May and June the situation normalized. Only those professional workers allowed by the government were renting cars. No foreign tourists anymore!"

Table 5. One way fees.

Months	Drop off sales
ene-19	$ 1.228.986,00
feb-19	$ 3.193.261,00
mar-19	$ 2.242.677,00
abr-19	$ 942.694,00
may-19	$ 950.089,00
jun-19	$ 549.508,00
jul-19	$ 1.009.384,00
ago-19	$ 1.259.363,00
sep-19	$ 1.154.542,00
oct-19	$ 1.840.775,00
nov-19	$ 3.188.153,00
dic-19	$ 2.371.178,00
ene-20	$ 3.714.028,00
feb-20	$ 3.193.121,00
mar-20	$ 2.242.677,00
abr-20	$ 1.323.600,00
may-20	$ 712.662,00
jun-20	$ 766.315,00
jul-20	$ 477.494,00

Source: self elaboration, 2020

Renters

The last table is self-explanatory, the number of foreign renters has resoundingly fallen. Three months were grouped to better understand the dilemma in this case. In January 2019, the percentage of foreigner renters was 51%, while in January 2020 it was 52%. In April 2019, which is part of low season, 41% of renters come from abroad while this percentage slumps to 32% in April 2020. Not surprisingly, in May

2019 we have 65% of foreigner renters while it was for 16% only in May 2020. The results evince that international demands is blocked and the rent-a-car company suffered serious financial losses for the lockdown associated to the pandemic.

Figure 3. Drop off sales
Source, self elaboration 2020

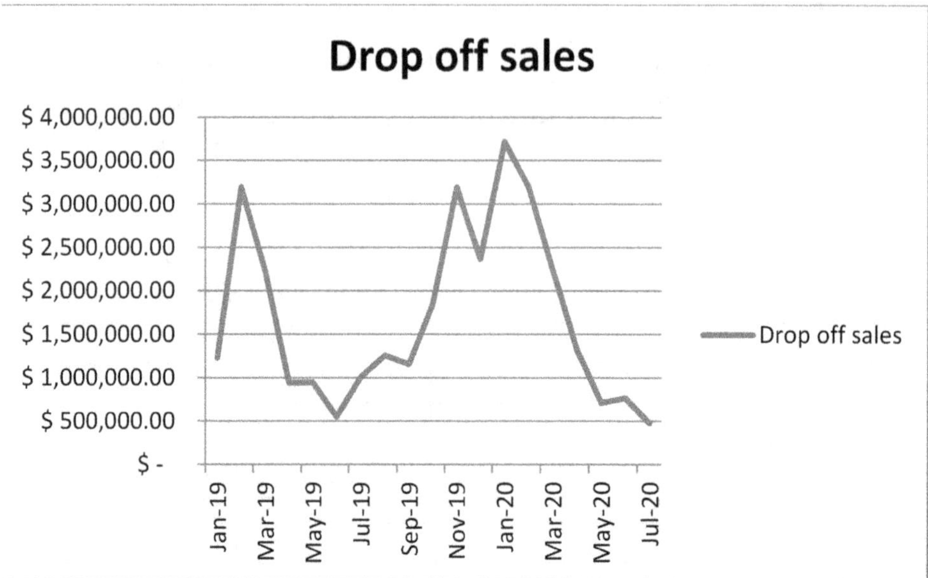

Table 6. Segmentation of renters

Months	Argentinians	% VAR	Foreigners	% VAR2	TOTAL
jan-19	3370	49%	3558	51%	6928
jan-20	3795	48%	4172	52%	7967
abr-19	3630	59%	2623	41%	6253
abr-20	122	68%	57	32%	179
may-19	1902	35%	3636	65%	5538
may-20	110	84%	22	16%	132

Source: self-elaboration, 2020

CONCLUSION

Metaphorically speaking, COVID19 not only interrogated furtherly the human omnipotence but also put the world on its knees. Its rapid dissemination in the modern means of transport escaped to all the sanitarian measures orchestrated in Asia. Only in months, COVID19 was wreaking havoc in Italy, Spain, and the US. Some additional months were needed for the Virus to arrive in Brazil, Ecuador, Chile and Argentina. The pandemic, in view of the lack of an effective vaccine, had a significant impact on the tourism and hospitality industries, resulting from travel-ban and the closure of borders. Academicians from the four corners of the world theorized on the effects and opportunities of the industry before this global hazard. Some voices claimed on the needs of adopting more sustainable forms of consumption while others remarked the urgency to create new methodological forms of research in a world without tourists. Still further, these studies lacked a robust empirical basis to understand the real effects of COVID in small-size companies. Though debatable to some extent, the present chapter provided with valuable information and evidence on the effects of the pandemic in a rent-a-car company, a subsector which was relegated in the agenda of academicians. The outcomes are not heterogeneous but confirm that not only the studied company was seriously affected by the lockdown in Argentina, but also that tourist locations are more prone to experience a rapid downturn in respect to industrial ones. What is more important, in the absence of firm commercial aviation industry, rent-a-car subsector presents as a promising option of economic recovery to boost local tourism. It is important to caution that these results cannot be extrapolated to other universe and should be limited only to the sample in question. This seems to be a much deeper issue which needs further investigation.

REFERENCES

Amujo, O. C., & Otubanjo, O. (2012). Leveraging rebranding of 'unattractive' nation brands to stimulate post-disaster tourism. *Tourist Studies*, *12*(1), 87–105. doi:10.1177/1468797612444196

Barker, M., Page, S. J., & Meyer, D. (2003). Urban visitor perceptions of safety during a special event. *Journal of Travel Research*, *41*(4), 355–361. doi:10.1177/0047287503041004004

Bianchi, R. (2006). Tourism and the globalisation of fear: Analysing the politics of risk and (in) security in global travel. *Tourism and Hospitality Research*, *7*(1), 64–74. doi:10.1057/palgrave.thr.6050028

Blake, A., & Sinclair, M. T. (2003). Tourism crisis management: US response to September 11. *Annals of Tourism Research, 30*(4), 813–832. doi:10.1016/S0160-7383(03)00056-2

Brouder, P., Teoh, S., Salazar, N. B., Mostafanezhad, M., Pung, J. M., Lapointe, D., Higgins Desbiolles, F., Haywood, M., Hall, C. M., & Clausen, H. B. (2020). Reflections and discussions: Tourism matters in the new normal post COVID-19. *Tourism Geographies*, *22*(3), 1–12. doi:10.1080/14616688.2020.1770325

Carr, A. (2020). COVID-19, indigenous peoples and tourism: A view from New Zealand. *Tourism Geographies*, 1–12.

Crossley, É. (2020). Ecological grief generates desire for environmental healing in tourism after COVID-19. *Tourism Geographies*, *22*(3), 1–10. doi:10.1080/14616688.2020.1759133

Floyd, M. F., & Pennington-Gray, L. (2004). Profiling risk perceptions of tourists. *Annals of Tourism Research*, *31*(4), 1051–1054. doi:10.1016/j.annals.2004.03.011

Fuchs, G., & Reichel, A. (2006). Tourist destination risk perception: The case of Israel. *Journal of Hospitality & Leisure Marketing*, *14*(2), 83–108. doi:10.1300/J150v14n02_06

Gallego, I., & Font, X. (2020). Changes in air passenger demand as a result of the COVID-19 crisis: Using Big Data to inform tourism policy. *Journal of Sustainable Tourism*, •••, 1–20. doi:10.1080/09669582.2020.1773476

Galvani, A., Lew, A. A., & Perez, M. S. (2020). COVID-19 is expanding global consciousness and the sustainability of travel and tourism. *Tourism Geographies*, *22*(3), 1–10. doi:10.1080/14616688.2020.1760924

George, R. (2010). Visitor perceptions of crime-safety and attitudes towards risk: The case of Table Mountain National Park, Cape Town. *Tourism Management*, *31*(6), 806–815. doi:10.1016/j.tourman.2009.08.011

Gössling, S., Scott, D., & Hall, C. M. (2020). Pandemics, tourism and global change: A rapid assessment of COVID-19. *Journal of Sustainable Tourism*, 1–20.

Gretzel, U., Fuchs, M., Baggio, R., Hoepken, W., Law, R., Neidhardt, J., ... Xiang, Z. (2020). e-Tourism beyond COVID-19: A call for transformative research. *Information Technology & Tourism*, 1.

Hall, C. M., Williams, A. M., & Lew, A. A. (2004). *Tourism: Conceptualizations, institutions, and issues. In A companion to tourism*. Blackwell Publishing.

Higgins-Desbiolles, F. (2020). Socialising tourism for social and ecological justice after COVID-19. *Tourism Geographies*, *22*(3), 1–14. doi:10.1080/14616688.2020.1757748

Jonas, A., Mansfeld, Y., Paz, S., & Potasman, I. (2011). Determinants of health risk perception among low-risk-taking tourists traveling to developing countries. *Journal of Travel Research*, *50*(1), 87–99. doi:10.1177/0047287509355323

Korstanje, M. E. (2011). Rent-a-car industry: A case study in Argentina. *Tourismos*, *6*(1), 1–15.

Korstanje, M. E. (2018). *The mobilities paradox: a critical analysis*. Edward Elgar Publishing. doi:10.4337/9781788113311

Laws, E., Prideaux, B., & Chon, K. S. (Eds.). (2007). *Crisis management in tourism*. Cabi. doi:10.1079/9781845930479.0000

Lepp, A., & Gibson, H. (2008). Sensation seeking and tourism: Tourist role, perception of risk and destination choice. *Tourism Management*, *29*(4), 740–750. doi:10.1016/j.tourman.2007.08.002

Mair, J., Ritchie, B. W., & Walters, G. (2016). Towards a research agenda for post-disaster and post-crisis recovery strategies for tourist destinations: A narrative review. *Current Issues in Tourism*, *19*(1), 1–26. doi:10.1080/13683500.2014.932758

Matyas, C., Srinivasan, S., Cahyanto, I., Thapa, B., Pennington-Gray, L., & Villegas, J. (2011). Risk perception and evacuation decisions of Florida tourists under hurricane threats: A stated preference analysis. *Natural Hazards*, *59*(2), 871–890. doi:10.100711069-011-9801-0

McKercher, B., & Chon, K. (2004). The over-reaction to SARS and the collapse of Asian tourism. *Annals of Tourism Research*, *31*(3), 716–719. doi:10.1016/j.annals.2003.11.002 PMID:32572281

Miles, L., & Shipway, R. (2020). Exploring the COVID-19 pandemic as a catalyst for stimulating future research agendas for managing crises and disasters at international sport events. *Event Management*, *24*(4), 537–552. doi:10.3727/152599519X15506259856688

Monterrubio, J. C. (2010). Short-term economic impacts of influenza A (H1N1) and government reaction on the Mexican tourism industry: An analysis of the media. *International Journal of Tourism Policy*, *3*(1), 1–15. doi:10.1504/IJTP.2010.031599

Novelli, M., Burgess, L. G., Jones, A., & Ritchie, B. W. (2018). 'No Ebola… still doomed'–The Ebola-induced tourism crisis. *Annals of Tourism Research, 70*, 76–87. doi:10.1016/j.annals.2018.03.006 PMID:32572288

Park, K., & Reisinger, Y. (2010). Differences in the perceived influence of natural disasters and travel risk on international travel. *Tourism Geographies, 12*(1), 1–24. doi:10.1080/14616680903493621

Prayag, G. (2020). Time for Reset? COVID-19 and Tourism Resilience. *Tourism Review International, 24*(2-3), 179–184. doi:10.3727/154427220X15926147793595

Reisinger, Y., & Mavondo, F. (2005). Travel anxiety and intentions to travel internationally: Implications of travel risk perception. *Journal of Travel Research, 43*(3), 212–225. doi:10.1177/0047287504272017

Reisinger, Y., & Mavondo, F. (2006). Cultural differences in travel risk perception. *Journal of Travel & Tourism Marketing, 20*(1), 13–31. doi:10.1300/J073v20n01_02

Ritchie, B. W. (2004). Chaos, crises and disasters: A strategic approach to crisis management in the tourism industry. *Tourism Management, 25*(6), 669–683. doi:10.1016/j.tourman.2003.09.004

Robinson, L., & Jarvie, J. K. (2008). Post-disaster community tourism recovery: The tsunami and Arugam Bay, Sri Lanka. *Disasters, 32*(4), 631–645. doi:10.1111/j.1467-7717.2008.01058.x PMID:18479472

Romagosa, F. (2020). The COVID-19 crisis: Opportunities for sustainable and proximity tourism. *Tourism Geographies, 22*(3), 1–5. doi:10.1080/14616688.2020.1763447

Santana, G. (2004). Crisis management and tourism: Beyond the rhetoric. *Journal of Travel & Tourism Marketing, 15*(4), 299–321. doi:10.1300/J073v15n04_05

Seabra, C., Abrantes, J. L., & Kastenholz, E. (2014). The influence of terrorism risk perception on purchase involvement and safety concern of international travellers. *Journal of Marketing Management, 30*(9-10), 874–903. doi:10.1080/0267257X.2014.934904

Séraphin, H., Butcher, J., & Korstanje, M. (2017). Challenging the negative images of Haiti at a pre-visit stage using visual online learning materials. *Journal of Policy Research in Tourism, Leisure & Events, 9*(2), 169–181. doi:10.1080/19407963.2016.1261146

Seraphin, H., Gowreesunkar, V., Roselé-Chim, P., Duplan, Y. J. J., & Korstanje, M. (2018). Tourism planning and innovation: The Caribbean under the spotlight. *Journal of Destination Marketing & Management*, *9*, 384–388. doi:10.1016/j.jdmm.2018.03.004

Séraphin, H., Korstanje, M., & Gowreesunkar, V. G. (Eds.). (2020). *Post-Disaster and Post-Conflict Tourism: Toward a New Management Approach*. CRC Press. doi:10.1201/9780429276224

Sigala, M. (2020). Tourism and COVID-19: Impacts and implications for advancing and resetting industry and research. *Journal of Business Research*, *117*, 312–321. Advance online publication. doi:10.1016/j.jbusres.2020.06.015 PMID:32546875

Solarin, S. A. (2015). September 11 attacks, H1N1 influenza, global financial crisis and tourist arrivals in Sarawak. *Anatolia*, *26*(2), 298–300. doi:10.1080/13032917.2014.991933

Tarlow, P. (2014). *Tourism security: strategies for effectively managing travel risk and safety*. Elsevier.

Verma, S., & Gustafsson, A. (2020). Investigating the emerging COVID-19 research trends in the field of business and management: A bibliometric analysis approach. *Journal of Business Research*, *118*, 253–261. Advance online publication. doi:10.1016/j.jbusres.2020.06.057 PMID:32834211

Wen, J., Wang, W., Kozak, M., Liu, X., & Hou, H. (2020). Many brains are better than one: The importance of interdisciplinary studies on COVID-19 in and beyond tourism. *Tourism Recreation Research*, 1–4. doi:10.1080/02508281.2020.1761120

Wolff, K., & Larsen, S. (2014). Can terrorism make us feel safer? Risk perceptions and worries before and after the July 22nd attacks. *Annals of Tourism Research*, *44*, 200–209. doi:10.1016/j.annals.2013.10.003

Yüksel, A., & Yüksel, F. (2007). Shopping risk perceptions: Effects on tourists' emotions, satisfaction and expressed loyalty intentions. *Tourism Management*, *28*(3), 703–713. doi:10.1016/j.tourman.2006.04.025

Zenker, S., & Kock, F. (2020). The coronavirus pandemic–A critical discussion of a tourism research agenda. *Tourism Management*, *81*, 104164. doi:10.1016/j.tourman.2020.104164 PMID:32518437

ADDITIONAL READING

Blake, A., & Sinclair, M. T. (2003). Tourism crisis management: US response to September 11. *Annals of Tourism Research, 30*(4), 813–832. doi:10.1016/S0160-7383(03)00056-2

Causevic, S., & Lynch, P. (2013). Political (in) stability and its influence on tourism development. *Tourism Management, 34*, 145–157. doi:10.1016/j.tourman.2012.04.006

Chew, E. Y. T., & Jahari, S. A. (2014). Destination image as a mediator between perceived risks and revisit intention: A case of post-disaster Japan. *Tourism Management, 40*, 382–393. doi:10.1016/j.tourman.2013.07.008

Hall, C. M., & Williams, A. (Eds.). (2013). *Tourism and migration: New relationships between production and consumption* (Vol. 65). Springer Science & Business Media.

Heilbroner, R. L. (2011). *The worldly philosophers: The lives, times and ideas of the great economic thinkers*. Simon and Schuster.

Hobbes, T. (1994). Leviathan: with selected variants from the Latin edition of 1668 (Vol. 8348). Cambridge: Hackett Publishing. (1668)

Hurlock, E. B. (1927). The use of group rivalry as an incentive. *Journal of Abnormal and Social Psychology, 22*(3), 278–290. doi:10.1037/h0071601

Korstanje, M. E., & George, B. P. (2012). Falklands/Malvinas: A re-examination of the relationship between sacralisation and tourism development. *Current Issues in Tourism, 15*(3), 153–165. doi:10.1080/13683500.2011.569535

Lambert, E. G., Pasupuleti, S., Cluse-Tolar, T., Jennings, M., & Baker, D. (2006). The impact of work-family conflict on social work and human service worker job satisfaction and organizational commitment: An exploratory study. *Administration in Social Work, 30*(3), 55–74. doi:10.1300/J147v30n03_05

Lash, S. M., & Urry, S. L. J. (1993). *Economies of signs and space* (Vol. 26). Sage.

Locke, J. (1988). *Locke: Two Treatises of Government Student Edition*. Cambridge University Press. doi:10.1017/CBO9780511810268

MacCannell, D. (1973). Staged authenticity: Arrangements of social space in tourist settings. *American Journal of Sociology, 79*(3), 589–603. doi:10.1086/225585

MacCannell, D. (1976). *The tourist: A new theory of the leisure class*. University of California Press.

KEY TERMS AND DEFINITIONS

Conflict: It is tension between two or more parts which needs from a solution. Sometimes conflict is confused or homologized to rivalry.

COVID-19: New virus outbreak originated in 2019 in the city of Wuhan China, and rapidly expanded to the world in form of a new pandemic.

Labor Relations: This refers to an academic field that often studies different inter-personal relations in working conditions.

Rent-a-Car: Sub industry within service and tourist sector that offers the renting of cars to clients and drivers.

Tourism Management: It consists in a net of techniques and disciplines oriented to keep the tourist system functioning.

Chapter 7
Short-Term Rental Development and Overtourism:
A Case of Lisbon, Portugal

Flavio Andrew Do Nascimento Santos
https://orcid.org/0000-0003-3771-4579
Universidade de Lisboa, Portugal

ABSTRACT

The boom of short-term rental (STR) intensifies the debate on overtourism because of some negative effects on destinations. Conversely, the STR was a way out in moments of crisis. Until now, only a few studies extend the analysis outside the limits of individual cities; that's why this case-study research was conducted by the analyses of Airbnb listings and the tourists' spatial distribution in Lisbon Metropolitan Area (LMA). For this purpose, this chapter uses two cartographic tools: 1) Airbnb listing from Inside Airbnb Project of Lisbon and 2) Geotaggers' World Atlas (map of sites that tourists took photos). Also, institutional Lisbon urban planning plans fed this study. Methodologically, combining the selected maps is a way to understand tourism spatial analysis by bringing together data on supply-side (rooms) and demand-side (distribution of tourists). The analysis demonstrates that a time-spatial distribution of visitors and the STR throughout the LMA could contribute to avoiding tourism congestion and proper distribution of economic benefits.

DOI: 10.4018/978-1-7998-7287-0.ch007

INTRODUCTION

The discussion on over-tourism and its consequences for local development has gain notoriety since some citizens started to question the excess of tourism activity and the post-pandemic situation of COVID-19. Different studies aimed to propose strategies to minimize the consequences and protect the cities against over-tourism, such as territorial decentralization (Martins, 2018), an increase of regulations, and public policies (DiNatale et al., 2018), or de-growing of tourism (Higgins-Desbiolles et al., 2019).

On the one hand, the boom of short-term rental (STR) – in coordination with the spread of new TIC – partially explains over-tourism and points out a debate on the process of gentrification in urban destinations, mainly global or world-class cities. On the other hand, the STR is assumed as an alternative for the economic crisis, and tourism is promised as a fast way to grow income for local economies. This situation creates a complex context in contemporary tourism: everyday life and temporary leisure are gradually bonded together within the city, leading to potential conflicts when space is under dispute (Condevaux, Djament-Tran, and Gravari-Barbas, 2016; Higgins-Desbiolles et al., 2019) analyzes that involve the spatial distribution of tourism elements is an interesting approach to understating the behavior, mobility, and current characterization of urban space at different levels (city, region, or country). Nevertheless, only a few studies extended the spatial analysis of STR beyond the limits of cities (Adamiak et al., 2019). This approach is also relevant having in mind that the tourism activities extrapolate institutional and legal zones limits, with the flows of the tourists, workers commuting, and regional policies.

In line with that, this viewpoint paper aims to grasp tourism spatial issues that go beyond the limits of the Lisbon city by overlapping two maps: a. STR listings from Airbnb and b. Places in the city where tourists are taking photos from the Geotaggers' World Atlas. Then, the analysis is to search for potential tourist places in the Lisbon Metropolitan Area (LMA) as a future alternative of over-tourism by the Strategic vision for urban planning tourism in Lisbon and the Strategic Tourism Plan for the Lisbon Region 2015-2019.

"OVER-TOURISM"

Over-tourism, as a concept in tourism literature, has received different influences from other concepts such as sustainability (Korstanje & George, 2020; Perkumienė & Pranskūnienė, 2019), tourism area life cycle, and carrying capacity (Koens et al., 2018; Postma and Schmuecker, 2017; Cheer et al., 2019; Panayiotopoulos and Pisano, 2019). According to Dodds & Butler (2019), the definition refers to an excessive number of tourists at a specific destination that can result in negative impacts of all types on the community involved. Moreover, Goodwin (2017) describes as destinations where hosts or guests, locals or visitors, feel that there are too many visitors and that the quality of life in the area or the quality of the experience has deteriorated unacceptably. In general, over-tourism refers to "the impact of tourism on a destination that excessively influences the perceived quality of life of citizens and/or quality of visitors' experiences in a negative way" (UNWTO, 2019).

Moreover, different reasons are employed to explain the increase of tourists' number, such as the access of the middle class to travel opportunities, the use of technology for transportation and accommodation, and the development of low-cost airlines and the sharing economy (Barata-Salgueiro, 2017; Koens et al., 2018). As a consequence, overtourism can generate different negatives effects and intensive processes, such as gentrification, the increase of the number of employees with no labor contract, tax and/or insurance evasion, and unfair competition (Jorge, 2017).

Furthermore, the fast-growing of tourism can transform the social and cultural local dynamics, resulting in criticism and movements of residents against tourism, as seen recently in Barcelona, Venice, Berlin, and Paris (Panayiotopoulos & Pisano, 2019; Seraphin et al., 2018; Séraphin et al., 2019). In this context, emerged the term 'turism-phobia', which has created a challenge to the coexistence of tourists and locals in the context of tourism development in urban environments (UNWTO, 2019).

Other authors suggest a solution for over-tourism based on the spatial-temporal distribution of the tourists (Koens et al., 2018; Postma and Schmuecker, 2017) since there are cities that can handle a high number of visitors, while others struggle with far fewer visitors. Also, it is important to remind that technology and smart solutions can help but not solve tourism congestion, and tourism congestion is not a tourism-only problem. One of these strategies is to promote the time-based dispersal of visitors within the city and beyond, not only in the attractions but with the accommodation for tourists, where the short-term rentals are included.

SHORT-TERM RENTALS AND TOURISM

An STR is a rented housing unit for less than 30 days, and it is conceptualized by non-institutionalized forms of accommodation while not broadly controlled by the authorities (DiNatale et al., 2018). Along with the popularization of the sharing economy or 'on-demand economy', the home-sharing market witnessed huge growth, and part of the housing stock units has been channelled to the STR market (Lima, 2019). Thereby, platforms such as Airbnb and Home Away offer opportunities for locals to share their goods with a monetary exchange (DiNatale et al., 2018), relying on the emerging "live like a local" trends as well as the promise of "authentic" experiences for travelers (Sarantakou and Terkenli, 2019) that made Airbnb as the world's most popular platform for STR (Maartje Roelofsen, 2018).

Regarding Airbnb, the company started in 2008 and it has facilitated over 400 million guest arrivals, with more than 5 million properties registered as "hosts" around the globe and a market value of 30 billion dollars. However, other companies and communities accuse the sharing companies of ditching their tax obligations and demand new legislation that creates minimum requirements for market entry and security rules. The response of these sharing platforms reinforces that the hosts are responsible for honoring the local taxes and the quality of the service, a reason why these platforms wouldn't need government intervention (Maartje Roelofsen, 2018). In this context, different studies demonstrated empirical evidence of the 'Airbnb-effect' in many popular European tourist destinations (see Gil and Sequera, 2018; Maartje Roelofsen, 2018), such as the increase of prices on housing and changing the local economy to a monoculture activity of tourism, gentrification, alienation of residents, overloaded infrastructure, pressures on the natural environment, threats to culture and heritage (See DiNatale et al., 2018; Sarantakou and Terkenli, 2019), that debate also had an intensification with the COVID-19 pandemic and the consequences for the cities.

Lastly, it is important to mention that some cities started to prohibit and regulate more strictly this type of accommodation, such as Berlin, where unlicensed lessees have been banned; in Lisbon, Barcelona, and Paris, new limitations or prohibitions also started to apply for new STR apartments (Lima, 2019) to achieve spatial dissipation and mitigate over-tourism withing the cities contexts.

STR in Lisbon

The process of growth of STRs in Lisbon occurred in a specific way, with influences of real estate speculation, economic crises that directly influenced the restructuring of its historical center. In the context of the 2008 crisis, Portugal bets on foreign capital and the attraction of residents (golden visas), stimulating the STR as a way of generating profits in the housing sector as an alternative to the long-term contract and consecutively higher payback than the average wage of Portuguese citizens. Many accommodations are shifting from the housing rental market to the STR, which influences the increase in housing shortages and the increase in rental values, and consequently, the exclusion of many families from market access.

In this context of the house owners shifting to STR market, real estate speculation and economic crises with accompanied the increase of tourists' flow, there was a Portuguese success in the editions of the World Travel Awards and some investments and promotional campaigns by the local government, making Lisbon highlighted in some of the main destinations in Europe (Barata-Salgueiro, 2017; Seixas et al.,

2019). However, Lisbon has an ambiguous scenario. The government that has leaded tourism development is now facing conflicts and social segregation, urging strategies to limit the number of tourists with taxes and limits on the STR market (Blanco-Romero et al., 2018). Also, the financial and economic crisis caused by COVID-19 helped the sense of tourism as an opportunity pos crisis in local economies changing austerity strategies in places such as Lisbon in Portugal, by local, regional and national administrations (Nofre et al., 2018).

Finally, territories of many LMA states have become the subject of operations for only financial reasons and not considering the social and economic needs of the community (Barata-Salgueiro, 2017; Tulumello, 2016). This type of appropriation is normally associated with the "business of the city" (Arantes et al., 2002), in which urbanism strategies can starts to act like a company whatever productivity e competitiveness is concerned.

METHODOLOGY

This viewpoint paper analyses maps and documents for indicating spatial possibilities to STR and tourist attractions in the Lisbon Metropolitan Area, that is made up of 18 cities: Alcochete, Almada, Amadora, Barreiro, Cascais, Lisboa, Loures, Mafra, Moita, Montijo, Odivelas, Oeiras, Palmela, Seixal, Sesimbra, Setúbal, Sintra, and Vila Franca de Xira.

The maps chosen are the Airbnb listing from Inside Airbnb Project of Lisbon and the Geotaggers' World Atlas that shows the number of pictures taken by tourists in Lisbon and their spatial distribution. Additionally, the Strategic vision for urban planning tourism in Lisbon (Câmara Municipal de Lisboa, 2018) and the Strategic Tourism Plan for the Lisbon Region 2015-2019 also have been taken into the analysis (Entidade Regional de Turismo da Região de Lisboa, 2019). Finally, the data have analyzed observing the wide spatial possibility of the Lisbon Metropolitan Area that could be an opportunity to STR.

The selection of maps and documents is due to their relevance to providing a broader and valuable spatial vision for the discussion. When analyzed together, they allow observing the fixation (supply side), and the flows (demand side) within the metropolitan area, providing an important indicator of tourists' concentration and STR listings in Lisbon.

ANALYSIS AND DISCUSSION

Regarding the Strategic Tourism Plan for the Lisbon Region (2015-2019)[1], it separates the LMA into subregions: Arrábida, Arco do Tejo, Cascais, Lisboa, and Sintra. For each one, specific strategies are set at a different phase of tourism development. It is important to mention that in some portions of this territory there are well-developed tourist attractions beyond Lisbon and are already positioned as international brands, such as Cascais-Estoril and Sintra. In other cities, such as Setúbal, Sesimbra, and Palmela, the tourist attractions are under development since there is some incipient kind of tourism. Mafra, Almada, Oeiras, Loures, Odivelas e Amadora are under the division of attractions to be developed sector.

Besides, there is an explicit objective of the dispersion of tourism throughout the metropolitan territory in both documents. However, some attractions such as the beaches of Caparica and the Cascais Line, or the other side of the Tagus River, do not follow this importance in the plan. Another example could be the number of micro areas that each area has. Lisbon has four micro areas, and other cities with huge potential like Oeiras and Almada got a smaller part in the division of the areas.

In this sense, the document reinforces the city-business analogy (Arantes et al. 2002): governmental interventions focus on the extension of the market and concentration of capital, since some neighborhoods in Lisbon got the same weight as some cities, although with additional potential to dispersion within the metropolitan territory.

This concentration also happens with the tourist behavior on the space, by looking at a map of Lisbon with the spatial distribution of taken pictures by tourists in 2010 (Figure 1).

Based on figure 1, is visible the concentration of tourists in the Metropolitan area of Lisbon, more specifically in the Baixa-Chiado, Alfama, Castelo, and Mouraria, Bairro Alto, Cais do Sodré and Santos, Marquês de Pombal, and Avenida da Liberdade. Belém and Parque das Nações are two separated points of interest. This map not only shows the concentration of these areas, but highlights areas of the Lisbon city that are almost with no tags, such as Beato, Penha de França, and Marvila. The same happens in the metropolitan region such as Oeiras, on the other side of the river, and Almada.

Although it is not possible to analyze STR in LMA with this map, it is important to reinforce the idea of over-tourism happening in Lisbon, where the tourists almost visit the same places and take similar pictures (Cheer et al., 2019; Koens et al., 2018; Panayiotopoulos and Pisano, 2019), even with a big space opportunity in the LMA. This concentration influences the local dynamics with social and cultural disruptions (Martins, 2018), and prompting some criticism from the sustainable

Figure 1. Geotag of pictures from tourists in Lisbon in 2010
Source: Geotaggers' World Atlas (2019)

tourism development looking for the local community, that suffer the pressure of this tourist congestion (Higgins-Desbiolles et al., 2019).

Regarding the STR, the following map, provided by Airbnb, reinforces the need to combine fixed spatial elements and some mobility in the STR market in LMA (Figure 2).

Unfortunately, the site does not map properties on the south bank of Tagus River even with rentals in that area, which is a limitation for the analysis. But it is important to note the same congestion and empty spaces, as shown in Figure 2, except by significant spots in the littoral area of Cascais.

Figure 2. Airbnb Listings of Lisbon
Source: Inside Airbnb Project (2019).

This argument is foreseen by one of the strategies UNWTO strategies to promote the time-based dispersal of visitors within the city and beyond, not only in the main tourist area but with the accommodation for tourists – STR is included. Based on the attractions and STR, to promote new itineraries combined with discounts and attractions can help to alleviate the congestion of tourists in the hot spots in space and time (UNWTO, 2019). In line with that, following the "off-the-beaten-track" tourism trend (Condevaux, Djament-Tran, and Gravari-Barbas, 2016), promote the discovery of areas far from the usual tourist centrality.

Lastly, the meaning and desire to "live like a local" must be reconsidered, since gentrification processes move places away from these specifics locations, so the demand for a "true" reality creates a dichotomous and illusory situation. Also, who would be the "real locals" residing in central areas of global cities like Barcelona? (Arias-Sans and Quaglieri, 2016).

CONCLUSION

Different studies suggest alternatives to minimize the consequences and protect cities from over-tourism, such as territorial deconcentration and increased regulations. This article adds the possibility of controlled expansion of the STRs beyond the limits of the city of Lisbon by widening the scope of tourism development towards the metropolitan region.

The analysis demonstrates that the concentration of listings can lead to a concentration of capital. Also, it shows some possibilities in the Lisbon city and the region such as Almada and Oeiras to avoid congestion. Beyond that, some LMA places that are apart from traditional tourism, such as The Oeiras Marine, a museum in Penha-de-França, the Panoramic Elevator of Boca do Vento and some sites of Tagus river aren´t in the strategic plan. Those are examples of places that are already existing tourist attractions and planning, and promotion could reduce the congestion in the LMA. At the same time, following the idea of the strategic plan and UNWTO (2019), new investments in other cities outside the congestion that exist today, such as Alcochete, Almada, Amadora, Loures, Mafra, Moita, Montijo, Odivelas, Oeiras, Palmela, Seixal, Sesimbra and Vila Franca de Xira.

Besides that, it is hard to assume that the aggregation of tourists is over-tourism or not since lots of spaces in the city and the region are underused. The suggestion to promote the space and time dispersal of visitors within the city and beyond can help this congestion but not solve the problem. It must be integrated with the city and the local attractions that are possible to control what time the tourists can visit, which could help to minimize the congestion of tourists within public transportation, public spaces, and other attractions that are not possible to control the number of tourists. This proposal can also help to avoid the inflation of prices in the services and promote a better-quality service in attractions and other services.

Finally, it is important to highlight that these issues cannot be tackled only by looking for tourist attractions and STRs, but all the region strategy and its actors (public policy, private companies, population). Future studies should try to cope with this assumption by employing different methodologies, such as to measure the real and possible tourist flows and other contexts in Portugal, such as Algarve and Oporto.

REFERENCES

Adamiak, C., Szyda, B., Dubownik, A., & Garcia-Alvarez, D. (2019). Airbnb Offer in Spain-Spatial Analysis of the Pattern and Determinants of Its Distribution. *ISPRS International Journal of Geo-Information*, *8*(3), 155. Advance online publication. doi:10.3390/ijgi8030155

Arantes, O. B. F., Vainer, C., & Maricato, E. (2002). *A cidade do pensamento único: desmanchando consensos*. Academic Press.

Barata-Salgueiro, T. (2017). Alojamentos turísticos em Lisboa. *Scripta Nova, 21*.

Câmara Municipal de Lisboa. (2018). *Visão Estratégica para o Ordenamento Urbanístico do Turismo em Lisboa*. https://www.am-lisboa.pt/documentos/1540997812O0jIl7ak1Wa23QC2.pdf

Campbell, M., McNair, H., Mackay, M., & Perkins, H. C. (2019). Disrupting the regional housing market: Airbnb in New Zealand. *Regional Studies, Regional Science*, *6*(1), 139–142. doi:10.1080/21681376.2019.1588156

Cheer, J. M., Milano, C., & Novelli, M. (2019). Tourism and community resilience in the Anthropocene: Accentuating temporal overtourism. *Journal of Sustainable Tourism*, *27*(4), 554–572. doi:10.1080/09669582.2019.1578363

Condevaux, A., Djament-Tran, G., & Gravari-Barbas, M. (2016). *El antes y el después del turismo. Evolución de los lugares y papel de los actores del turismo «fuera de lo común». Análisis bibliográfico. Via Tourism Review*. doi:10.4000/viatourism.414

DiNatale, S., Lewis, R., & Parker, R. (2018). Short-term rentals in small cities in Oregon: Impacts and regulations. *Land Use Policy*, *79*, 407–423. doi:10.1016/j.landusepol.2018.08.023

Dodds, R., & Butler, R. (2019). The phenomena of overtourism: A review. *International Journal of Tourism Cities*.

Entidade Regional de Turismo da Região de Lisboa. (2019). *Strategic tourism plan for the Lisboa region*. Author.

Gil, J., & Sequera, J. (2018). Expansión de la ciudad turística y nuevas resistencias. El caso de Airbnb en Madrid. *Empiria. Revista de Metodología de Ciencias Sociales*, *41*(41), 15–32. doi:10.5944/empiria.41.2018.22602

Goodwin, H. (2017). *The challenge of overtourism*. Responsible Tourism Partnership.

Higgins-Desbiolles, F., Carnicelli, S., Krolikowski, C., Wijesinghe, G., & Boluk, K. (2019). Degrowing tourism: Rethinking tourism. *Journal of Sustainable Tourism*, *0*(0), 1–19. doi:10.1080/09669582.2019.1601732

Jorge, C. G. (2017). *Economia partilhada e consumo colaborativo com quem? Como a presença do Airbnb afeta os preços dos imóveis residenciais em Lisboa e no Rio de Janeiro*. Academic Press.

Koens, K., Postma, A., & Papp, B. (2018). Is Overtourism Overused? Understanding the Impact of Tourism in a City Context. *Sustainability*, *10*(12), 4384. doi:10.3390u10124384

Korstanje, M. E., & George, B. P. (2020). Education as a Strategy to Tackle Over Tourism for Overtourism and Inclusive Sustainability in the Twenty-First Century. In *Overtourism* (pp. 341–359). Springer. doi:10.1007/978-3-030-42458-9_18

Lima, V. (2019). Towards an understanding of the regional impact of Airbnb in Ireland. *Regional Studies, Regional Science*, *6*(1), 78–91. doi:10.1080/21681376.2018.1562366

Martins, M. M. (2018). *Tourism Planning and Tourismphobia: An Analysis of the Strategic Tourism Plan of Barcelona 2010-2015*. Academic Press.

Nofre, J., Giordano, E., Eldridge, A., Martins, J. C., & Sequera, J. (2018). Tourism, nightlife and planning: challenges and opportunities for community liveability in La Barceloneta. *Tourism Geographies, 20*(3), 377–396. doi:10.1080/14616688.2017.1375972

Panayiotopoulos, A., & Pisano, C. (2019). Overtourism Dystopias and Socialist Utopias: Towards an Urban Armature for Dubrovnik. *Tourism Planning & Development*, *0*(0), 1–18. doi:10.1080/21568316.2019.1569123

Perkumienė, D., & Pranskūnienė, R. (2019). Overtourism: Between the Right to Travel and Residents' Rights. *Sustainability*, *11*(7), 2138. doi:10.3390u11072138

Postma, A., & Schmuecker, D. (2017). Understanding and overcoming negative impacts of tourism in city destinations: Conceptual model and strategic framework. *Journal of Tourism Futures*, *3*(2), 144–156. doi:10.1108/JTF-04-2017-0022

Roelofsen, M. (2018). Exploring the Socio-Spatial Inequalities of Airbnb in Sofia, Bulgaria. *Erdkunde*, *72*(4), 313–327. doi:10.3112/erdkunde.2018.04.04

Sarantakou, E., & Terkenli, T. S. (2019). Non-Institutionalized Forms of Tourism Accommodation and Overtourism Impacts on the Landscape: The Case of Santorini, Greece *. *Tourism Planning & Development*, *0*(0), 1–23. doi:10.1080/21568316.2019.1569122

Seraphin, H., Sheeran, P., & Pilato, M. (2018). Over-tourism and the fall of Venice as a destination. *Journal of Destination Marketing & Management*, *9*, 374–376. doi:10.1016/j.jdmm.2018.01.011

Séraphin, H., Zaman, M., Olver, S., Bourliataux-Lajoinie, S., & Dosquet, F. (2019). Destination branding and overtourism. *Journal of Hospitality and Tourism Management*, *38*, 1–4. doi:10.1016/j.jhtm.2018.11.003

Tulumello, S. (2016). Reconsidering neoliberal urban planning in times of crisis: Urban regeneration policy in a “dense” space in Lisbon. *Urban Geography*, *37*(1), 117–140. doi:10.1080/02723638.2015.1056605

UNWTO. (2019). ‘Overtourism’? Understanding and Managing Urban Tourism Growth beyond Perceptions Volume 2: Case Studies. doi:10.18111/9789284420643

ADDITIONAL READING

Armstrong, M. B., Ketz, J. E., & Owsen, D. (2003). Ethics education in accounting: Moving toward ethical motivation and ethical behavior. *Journal of Accounting Education*, *21*(1), 1–16. doi:10.1016/S0748-5751(02)00017-9

Bramwell, B., & Lane, B. (2011). Critical research on the governance of tourism and sustainability. *Journal of Sustainable Tourism*, *19*(4-5), 411–421. doi:10.1080/09669582.2011.580586

Bresson, G., & Logossah, K. (2011). Crowding-out effects of cruise tourism on stay-over tourism in the Caribbean: Non-parametric panel data evidence. *Tourism Economics*, *17*(1), 127–158. doi:10.5367/te.2011.0028

Cooper, C., & Shepherd, R. (1997). The relationship between tourism education and the tourism industry: Implications for tourism education. *Tourism Recreation Research*, *22*(1), 34–47. doi:10.1080/02508281.1997.11014784

De Kadt, E. (1979a). *Tourism: Passport toDevelopment. Perspectives on thesocial andcultural effects of tourism in developing countries*. World Bank Press.

de Kadt, E. (1979b). Social planning for tourism in the developing countries. *Annals of Tourism Research*, *6*(1), 36–48. doi:10.1016/0160-7383(79)90093-8

Inui, Y., Wheeler, D., & Lankford, S. (2006). Rethinking tourism education: What should schools teach. *Journal of Hospitality, Leisure, Sport and Tourism Education*, *5*(2), 25–35. doi:10.3794/johlste.52.122

Luthar, H. K., & Karri, R. (2005). Exposure to Ethics Education and the Perception of Linkage between Organizational Ethical Behavior and Business Outcomes. *Journal of Business Ethics*, *61*(4), 353–368. doi:10.100710551-005-1548-7

McKenzie-Mohr, D., Lee, N., Schultz, P. W., & Kotler, P. (2012). *Social marketing to protect the environment: what works*. Sage. doi:10.4135/9781483349466

McMichael, P. (2016). *Development and social change: A global perspective*. Sage Publications.

Wang, J., Ayres, H., & Huyton, J. (2010). Is tourism education meeting the needs of the tourism industry? An Australian case study. *Journal of Hospitality & Tourism Education*, *22*(1), 8–14. doi:10.1080/10963758.2010.10696964

KEY TERMS AND DEFINITIONS

Over Tourism: That is a term used to mean the perceived congestion or over-crowding of a city or certain tourist destination.

Short-Term Rent: It is aimed at describing the rental of self-contained services in short period of time.

Tourism Growth: It denotes the increase of fluxes, travels and profits associated to tourism consumption.

Tourism Phobia: Manifest expression of hostility against (foreigner) tourists because of real or imagined reasons.

ENDNOTE

1 Map available at http://www.ertlisboa.pt/fotos/editor2/lis_9970_04248_007_15.pdf. page 27.

Section 3

Chapter 8
COVID-19 and the End of Hospitality:
At Least as We Know It in the West

Maximiliano Emanuel Korstanje
https://orcid.org/0000-0002-5149-1669
University of Palermo, Argentina

Babu P. George
Christian Brothers University, USA

ABSTRACT

The turn of the century has brought many mega threats for the West, such as terrorism, natural disasters, and virus outbreaks including SARS, H1N1, Ebola, and now COVID-19. An invisible micro-organism suddenly paused our progress towards a globally interconnected flat world. We now realize that super-structures driving economic development cannot grow in specific directions without destroying themselves in certain other directions. The precautionary logic suggests the rational planning aided by our technological progress ought to alleviate most of these problems. The manner in which we deal with disasters like COVID-19, however, does not inspire confidence. Application of the precautionary logic did not avert a calamity, and recovery efforts are now guided by some crude forms of post-facto, post-cautionary logical thinking. Tourism as well as hospitality is now in crisis.

DOI: 10.4018/978-1-7998-7287-0.ch008

INTRODUCTION

The outbreak of a new virus in Wuhan, China, SARS-COv2, known as COVID19 has paralyzed not only the tourism industry but also the global commerce placing the health system of developed countries in the brink of collapse. Centered on a precautionary logic which is oriented to prevent risks, governments adopted the decision to close their airspaces, and borders while tightening the domestic controls. Lay-citizens were locked down or forced to keep the social distancing in the streets. As experts agree, the lack of a vaccine leads the world to live a type of new normality and of course, tourism is not an exemption (Higgins-Desbiolles, 2020; Romagosa, 2020; Gossling, Scott & Hall, 2020). Other voices called the attention to the urgency of thinking new methods of research in a world without tourists (Wen et al 2020). These studies focus on COVID19 as a foundational event which opens the doors to new opportunities and challenges for tourism research. Though eloquently, in essence, were believe rather that these studies overlook the fact that COVID19 seems to be part of a previously-established tendency which started after 9/11. This epoch was characterized by a tradition widely based on a much deeper process of securitization where the figure of the "Otherness" is neglected. We dubbed this process as the "end of hospitality", at least as we know it (Korstanje 2017; 2018). The goals of the paper are twofold. On one hand, we review conceptually the effects of COVID19 in the tourism and hospitality industries. On another, we revise the concept of hospitality and the philosophical problems of West to understand the "Non-Western Other". The present authors would like to see it as a continuum of events beginning with 9/11/ and the War on Terror; in our earlier works, we have dubbed this progression as the End of Western Hospitality. A general review of this tendency will be summed in the present paper. To some extent, terrorism mined the social trust introducing the idea nobody is safe any longer and anywhere. The figure of the non-Western Other was framed and demonized as a potential enemy of democracy, paving the ways for the rise of chauvinist and xenophobic expressions oriented to neglect the Foreigner. The attacks on Sept 11 not only closed the Western civilization itself but changed the cosmologies revolving around the "Non-Western Other". Anthropologically speaking, the archetype of the noble savage, which revived the curiosity of travelers for travel writing and the discovery of over-seas territories – mainly during the colonial period- sets the pace to the doctrine of living with the enemy inside (Korstanje 2007; 2018). Last but not least, one of the limitations of the present essay-review is the lack of an empirical basis to validate research hypotheses, but at a closer look, it is not aimed to be an empirical but philosophical paperwork. Rather, it discusses critically the continuum of COVID19 and the War on Terror while laying the foundations towards a new understanding of hospitality rite.

DEBATING HOSPITALITY

Over the years much has been debated and studied about hospitality (Lugosi 2014; Poulston 2015). Hospitality played a leading and historical role in the configuration of the Western mainstream cultural values (Morrison & O´Gorman, 2008; Bell, 2012; Molz 2012). Anthropologically speaking, the term hospitality has taken different meanings and connotations in the threshold of time. As Conrad Lashley (2015) puts it, it is remarkable to see how scholars divide hospitality from hospitableness. While the former refers to the offered shelter and food to newcomers or travelers, the latter denotes the possibility to engage with the "Other" relationally. Hospitableness begins with a human desire for accepting "Others" in a friendly relation. Beyond the spiritual domain, the term has been historically subject to great controversy and discussion which today seems to be far from been closed. Paul Lynch et al. (2011) argue convincingly theories dealing with hospitality can very well be grouped in two different families. Those works which discuss hospitality as a form of social control and those based on the gift-exchange process finely ingrained in economic production. The seminal book, *Of hospitality,* which is authored by Jacques Derrida, is a fundamental treatise in this area. Although Derrida was widely cited and well-received in the fields of tourism, his deep argumentation has not been correctly understood or at the least singled out. He ignites a rich debate revolving around the figure of the Xenos – the Stranger. Citing Plato, he strongly believes that the Other not only is educated in a strange language but also he interrogates furtherly the hosting culture. The philosophical dilemma of hospitality is given by the urgency to deal with the "stranger" (Xenos). The rite of hospitality inscribes in a bipolar logic where a "here-us" is counterpoised to "there-them". The border re-configures a liminoid space that separates the in from the out. The "Other", once intruded, is carefully scrutinized and subordinated to the law. As Derrida puts it, hospitality can be offered or rejected, but in whatever circumstances the guest is, the hosting states reserve the right to question: who are you, and what do you want?

Given the problem in these terms, as Derrida suggests, two types of hospitalities coexist. While the conditioned hospitality is offered only if the guest can give something in return, the absolute hospitality requests nothing in return. Commercial hospitality, which characterizes the hospitality industry, is granted only to those tourists who can pay for the services. Rather, the absolute hospitality seems to be a utopia because nobody knocks the doors of a home with nothing to offer, in so far as the state does not introduce a complete "unknown stranger" whose identity cannot be verified. When the borders of the state are unilaterally violated, hostility surfaces and the Stranger becomes an undesired guest (parasite). Having said this, Derrida says that the Stranger splits the world into two parts. What we know about our identity is not a legacy of the family, or the nation, but rather, what "aliens" understand from us. In this perspective, only outlanders know, see, and ask on our customs, escaping to the borders of ethnocentrism. While rejecting the alterity, we despise ourselves (Derrida 2000).

As the previous argument is given, the term hospitality derives from *hospitium (Lat.)*, which is formed by the formula ospes+pet (Proto-Iranian language- in English what belongs to the master). The ancient ritual of hospitality was originally practised by Romans, Celtics, and Germans, but it can be traced to ancient China and Africa as well. In this way, hospitality should be understood as an inter-tribal pact ensuring a rapid alliance in the warfare and exchange of citizens in peacetime (O´Gorman, 2007; Nichols 2011; Sanchez Moreno, 2011). Hospitality was often invoked in the ancient world in case of external invasions, and of course, some countless mythological stories and legends narrate what happens when the sacred law of hospitality is breached. As Nichols (2011) eloquently remarks, hospitality may very well equate to a principle of host-guest friendship where different groups understand each other. For this reason, hospitality and reciprocity are inextricably intertwined. In the cosmologies of ancient civilizations, natural disasters resulted from God´s rage when the law of hospitality was broken. They strongly believed that in the same way humans´ souls are protected in the afterlife by Gods, they should welcome foreign travelers who are in quest of shelter and food. However, this does not suffice to say that hospitality encompasses a universal nature. Not all cultures in the world practiced the rite of hospitality. In a seminal book entitled Lords of all the World, Anthony Pagden (1995) suggests that the law of hospitality was crucial to legitimate the conquest of the Americas. Per his viewpoint, neither the Treaty of Tordesillas nor the bulls of Alexander VI were enough to legitimate the authority of the Spanish King in the Americas. Authors like Voltaire, Rousseau, or Thomas Hobbes seriously attacked the authority of King over natives who do not profess the Catholic faith. Even the controversy aligned to a hot-debate within the circles of the Salamanca School. The philosophical dispute was finally closed when rumors and stories came from the new world, alerting that some natives not only do not recognize the sacred law of hospitality and free transit but also killed innocent Spanish travelers (hominem viatores). To some extent, since aborigines were unable to honor hospitality, which was a full-fledged part of the universal right, they were considered sub-humans and dispossessed from their lands. For Pagden, the ideological tergiversation of hospitality cemented the conquest of the Americas. As doctrinal rights, no less true is that hospitality and free transit accompanied the design of the nation-state from the modernity to date. This raises a more than pungent question why do some voices believe the modern hospitality is in crisis?

IS WESTERN HOSPITALITY IN CRISIS?

Needless to say the liberal society remarks on the needs of good-exchange and circulation as the preconditions towards social order (Korstanje 2018). From its inception, the modern nation-state not only stimulated lay-citizens to travel elsewhere but also the cartography to draw the lines and spirit of the new civilization. In the social imaginary of West, hence, free transit and hospitality occupied a central position. The national borders marked the cultural differentiation between us and them, or here and them under the auspices of a new discipline that homogenized various ethnicities into a common identity: *the nationhood* (Guidotti Hernandez 2011). As Roy C Wood (2019) noted, the radical hospitality which denotes the possibility anyone can receive hospitality without asking anything in return has set the pace to new commercial hospitality where money mediates between guests and hosts. In ancient times, mankind practiced pure hospitality, a type of tribal hospitality which was gradually corrupted by the advance of industrialization. The class struggle evinces not only the progress of history but the gap between exploiters (capital owners) the exploited (proletariat). Today´s hospitality successfully fills this gap (Wood, 2019). This begs a more than a pungent question, is hospitality being commoditized by global capitalism?

In quest of answers that help to answer the above-formulated questions, Tom Selwyn (2019) speaks to us of a much deeper climate of hostility against the *Non-Western Other* recently gestated in the West. He explores the cases of Brexit, the fire in Grenfell Tower, and Windrush Scandal event that forced mass deportation of Caribbean migrants. Selwyn argues convincingly that the UK is involved in a sentiment of anti-hospitality, which resulted from the triumph of efficiency over other cultural values. There is a structural hostility against everything or everyone who is not profitable or proactive in the wealth amassing. Considered as human leftovers, migrants and asylum seekers are labeled as potential enemies of the state, objects of suspicion that should be carefully controlled. Complementarily, George Ritzer (2019) coins the term McDonaldization to describe how humanist values have been replaced by the needs of enhancing efficiency and forecasting, two values which are in contradiction to the genuine hospitality. The urgencies to adopt standardized protocols in the tourism and hospitality industries had led invariably towards a climate of depersonalization, where the "Other" remains unrecognized, at least for what he can pay. Paradoxically, while much attention is focused on the tourists, less we know of them. Ritzer (2019), who toys with the idea of "inhospitable hospitality," overtly says that host-guest interaction is certainly based on an alienated force where the borders of intimacy cannot be crossed. It is important not to lose sight of the fact that workers and housekeeping staff at hotels are systematically subject to working exploitation, which ranges from excessive working hours and low-paid salaries, without mentioning to a climate of precaritization monopolized by men. Feminists have exerted a radical criticism on the role of women in the hospitality industry (Martin 1998; Knox, 2008; 2011 Eringa 2019; Rowson, 2019). Karney & Semonovitch (2011) acknowledge that the encounter with the alterity is given in a liminoid space, a type of threshold, where uncertainty prevails. We live in a world fraught of strangers, but the guest is the only one who asks to enter our homes. The anxieties revolving around this encounter can be very well compared to the anxiety of being out-of-home. Once this Stranger founds a definitive home, he or she becomes in a friend or a rival, as authors hold.

In a recently published book, Maximiliano Korstanje (2017) has claimed "the end of hospitality, at least as we know it. The western civilization launched the adventure to colonize the world, indexing over-seas territories that were orchestrated as factories that provided slaves, goods, and commodities. West introduced the figure of the "Other" –or the "non-Western Other"- as an ideological condition of a so-called cultural superiority –conserved by Europeanness- over the tribal organizations. Not only the aborigines were the object of curiosity and fear, alimenting a set of literary genres as travel writing or captivity novels, but geography divided the world in two: here-us, and there-them. Hospitality acts as a mechanism of subordination that marked the generosity of white lords by the ever-increasing migration force coming from former colonies (a period that anthropologists know as decolonization process). Of course, needless to say, this order suffered radical transformations in the threshold of time but was until 9/11 the European paternalism and Western hospitality imploded. The archetype of the noble savage, a point that was originally featured in colonialism, sets the pace to the idea of the "undesired guest". The 9/11 and the "War on Terror", aligned to a culture of fear, closed not only borders, as well as accelerating travel-ban for Muslim migrants, but also aggravated in a xenophobic discourse articulated against the "foreigner". It will come as no surprise that movements as anti-tourism, or tourist-phobia, Islamophobia, Brexit, and now the lockdown post-COVID-19 are results of "the decline of hospitality". Last but not least, Daniel Innerarity (2017) alerts on the ontological impossibility that suggests a zero-risk society. He evokes the metaphor of the Stranger who asks for hospitality. He may be accepted or rejected, but what is more important seems to be he interrogates furtherly the proper culture. The host is henceforth equated to the risk. Societies, which are obsessed with security and safety, are doomed to be mined from within. The real hospitality, like the risk, should be given without asking anything in exchange. When the Stranger is neglected, society withers away.

THE TOURIST CITY IN THE AFTERMATH OF COVID-19

In 1999, Judd & Fainstein publish their book *The tourist city*. In this work, they call attention to the role of a new (tourist) city urbanized to attract foreign visitors. As places of play, these new cities are systematically devoted to tourism and leisure practices. Editors enumerate cities as Las Vegas, Chicago, New York, or Boston as hosting destinations designed to absorb an international tourism demand into a daily urban lifestyle (Judd & Fainstein 1999). Also, the tourist city is a historic-based place where traditions, customs, and the remnants of the pastime are culturally recycled and commoditized as a form of tourist attraction. In these types of new places, heritage consumption occupies a central position. As Ashworth & Tunbridge remark "*history has become heritage, heritage has become an urban resource, and this resource supplies a major history-heritage industry, which shapes not merely the form but the functioning and purpose of the commodified city* (Ashworth & Tunbridge, 2000: 2); a tourist city -in terms of MacCannell (1992)- that not only revitalizes the psychological frustrations of capitalism but also serves as a totem for the modern culture. Whether the totem is the touchstone of tribal order from where emanates the chiefdom´s authority, tourism is for the modern city (MacCannell 1976), where social ties have deteriorated. The host-guest encounter evolves in an empty ground where the genuine relationship succumbs before cultural cannibalism (MacCannell 1992). The local "Other" is enslaved to the taste of an international demand of first-world tourists externally-designed and unilaterally imposed to be internalized by the periphery (Hottola 2014; Tzanelli 2018). For some voices, the tourist city is a continuation of the colonial city where the center-periphery dependency is enlarged (Palmer 1994). The notion of consumed heritage appears to be adjusted to a biased interpretation of social facts, where the "Non-Western Other" is systematically silenced and exploited as a commodity (Comaroff & Comaroff, 2009; Korstanje 2012). Echoing Paul Virilio (1989) and Marc Augé (1996), one might speculate that one of the troublesome aspects of tourist city is the lack of walls, which differentiated it from the ancient (walled) city. For Virilio, the ancient city was fortified to be protected from external attacks. With the advance of modernity, which resulted from the technological breakthroughs, mobilities accelerated not only human relations but changed the global geography flatting the earth –like a screen- where events are covered, packaged and disseminated by the media in real-time.

It is noteworthy that the old philosophical dilemmas revolving around the geographical borders between here and there have been blurred. The velocity of modern transport creates an excess of time which is filled with media entertainment and tourism consumption. From the same premise starts French ethnologist Marc Augé, who considers post-modernity reproduces a culture of the present where tradition and customs are destroyed. He coins the term *Non-place* to refer to spaces of anonymity lacked any identity and tradition. Tourist destinations, airports, shop malls, and transport hubs are clear examples of these non-places. Per Augé, even the logic of ethnography should be contemplated again simply because the differentiation between selfhood and alterity has certainly been reversed. There is nothing like the "Other" who inspired the first ethnographers to adventure to visit overseas territories. Nowadays, the modern urban lifestyle marks a new pace where *The Non-Western Other* has been cannibalized and transformed into a modern consumer (Augé 1992; 1996; 1995). The tourist trip is an adventure that never starts in reality. In consonance with this, Zygmunt Bauman (2017) explores the paradoxes and complexities of the mobility-based cultures. At a first glimpse, a privileged group is legally encouraged to travel worldwide, whereas the major part of humanity is strictly restricted to the soil. In *Tourists and Vagabonds,* Bauman eloquently argues that the modern political citizen feels pleasure in being there, but the vagabond has no such luck. Vagabonds are trapped in the immobility where there is no access to the cultural capital tourism confers. As a sign of status, by traveling, we paradoxically deny the nature of the travels. We move from here to arrive there (to reach a destination). In touring, there is no point of arrival because there is no point of departure. As he cites,

In the tourist life, the length of stay in any place is hardly ever planned; neither is the next destination. The point of tourist life is to be on the move, not to arrive; unlike in the case of their predecessors, the pilgrims, the tourists' successive stopovers are not stations on the road, since there is no goal beckoning at the end of life travels which could make them into stations. If the successive addresses add up into an itinerary, it happens only retrospectively, when logic is discovered or imputed which did not guide the wanderer at the time of his wandering. When still on the move, no image of the future state is at hand to fill the present experience with meaning; each successive present, like the works of contemporary art, must explain itself in its own terms and provide its own key to read out its sense. (Bauman, 2017: 13).

To some extent, Bauman does not focus on the function of hospitality in his text, but he lays some foundations to understand the complex interconnection of state and mobilities. It is unfortunate that the specialized literature historically divided the fields of hospitality in commercial and non-commercial hospitality overlooking its anthropological nature. What does change with COVID-19?

COVID-19: YET ANOTHER POINTER TO THE END OF HOSPITALITY?

Returning to the problem of Covid-19 for a moment, the number of victims in the world is appalling. By the end of August 2020, there were more than 26 million people were infected and 863.000 deceased. The US is the country with more casualties (189.941), followed by Brazil (122.941), India (67.000), Mexico (65.000), the UK (41.514,)Peru (29.000), Italy (35.497), France (30.000) and Spain (29.194) only to name a few. To the material losses and the unparalleled economic downturn this virus outbreaks accelerated, it adds the cancellation of global commerce and tourism worldwide.

Argentina –in a precautionary logic- adopted restrictive measures to contain the advance of COVID-19. To avoid the effects of the virus in Spain, Italy, and the US, a set of different restrictive measures and steps were unilaterally adopted by President Alberto Fernandez. Argentina is the best example of how the lockdown stopped not only the commercial activity but also the industry of tourism and hospitality, a tendency replicated worldwide.

The nations react differently to this pandemic, but basically, we can note two groups. Those nations which moved by the needs of protecting their industries do not adopt a strict quarantine, and those nations which implementing restrictive measures to impede the domestic mobilities face serious economic harms. To mitigate the negative effects in the economy, President Alberto Fernandez disposed of a set of measures and programs to support the payment of wages to workers, as well as the temporal cancelation of classes. Only basic services such as medical systems, drugstores, food companies, security forces, and bus or caps drivers were allowed to work. The full suspension of activities was followed by the closure of the hospitality industry, which was hired to host sick patients or persons who need to keep in quarantine. Those tourists, who come from highly infected countries such as Europe, the US, or Brazil, were forced to live two weeks in isolation. Some of them living in Buenos Aires city were sent to hotels, while those who lived in the metropolitan areas (Buenosairean Conurbano) were delivered to their homes. There were suspected cases where hosts escaped from the hotels placing their health in risks. In other circumstances, they lied at the borders or at airports about the quarantine addresses to violate the isolation. As a consequence of this, some Argentinean citizens who respected the quarantine echoed a sentiment of hostility against tourists, which accelerated the number of denounces to stop the quarantine breakers. As a result, more than 2.000 persons were detained by the security forces in recent days. Another secondary effect was the repatriation of almost 20.000 Argentinean tourists stranded abroad. The army and air-forces, as well as the commercial aviation, played a leading role in repatriating tourists to Buenos Aires in the first two weeks of the pandemic outbreak. To avoid a spill-over effect, President Fernandez made the polemic decision to cancel the repatriations leaving almost 10.000 Argentinean citizens in the world. Under the lemma stay (at) home, journalism and Press emphasized the importance of respecting the quarantine. Rumors about the closure of the border pressed many Argentineans to return the country even when they were suspected to be infected. The figure of the tourist (tourist-gaze), which historically was admired, set the pace to a new phenomenon: the wicked-gaze (or undesired-guest). How may we define this neologism in objective terms?

Originally, Urry (2002) defines the tourist gaze as the interplay of expectations, narratives and cosmologies amalgamated to maximize the self-pleasure through heritage consumption (host´s commoditization), the *wicked-gaze* can be defined as an anti-force resulted from a process of global re-feudalization where the "Other" is undesired. If classic ethnographers witnessed a world where the Other was imagined, romanticized, and rejected, now it is time to discuss the position of undesired-Other. Keeping back to Urry, the tourist gaze may be explained as the urgency to be in contact with exotic cultures (to dispossess and commoditize them) and aggressively promoted by media and marketing. The tourist-gaze seems to be externally-elaborated and imposed unilaterally to local cultures and peoples who are often commercialized as embellished products. Locals often negotiate and internalize the stereotypes fabricated by the Global North. The quest of authenticity rests on the needs of reconstructing the own identity internally fragmented –if not deteriorated- by capitalist exploitation. The reconstruction of heritage and ethnicity is of paramount importance since locals look to meet tourists´ expectancies through reviving local (lost or invented) traditions. As Urry (2001) eloquently reminded, the tourist-gaze coexists and potentiates a much deeper process of high mobility based on the globalization as well as digital technologies breakthrough. Instead, the *wicked-gaze* goes in the opposite direction. The industry of tourism offers a contrasting landscape, connoting the principle of conditioned hospitality. No stranger is welcomed if he is not paying the accommodation. In the days of COVID-19 this dialectics, which was well-formulated and described by Derrida, subverts to a new logic where hotels are recycled and refurbished as hospitals. Foreign tourists who often are seen as ambassadors of progress and prosperity are transformed in *undesired guests* or potential carriers of sickness. The tourist gaze, at least as the metaphor was imagined by John Urry (2002), sets the pace analogically to "the wicked gaze".

It certainly entails a feudalization of the world where an anti-tourist sentiment surfaces. Before the state of emergency, the mainstream cultural values of global society, such as mobility and personal contact, are temporarily suspended. The free transit, which cemented the authority of the nation-state is replaced by the quarantine, impeding the inter-personal fluid contact. As a result, tourists are suspected as potential enemies who silently carry the virus and may potentially infect others.

Hospitality and friendship do not apply for foreign tourists any-longer because they were re-labeled as *an undesired guest.* Echoing Derrida, the *undesired guest* is portrayed as a parasite, an organism that predates the hosting body (society). In the same way, tourists are considered dangerous agents of infection, illness, individualism, and predation. Here much can be said, above all, when tourists break the quarantine voluntarily. In a nutshell, the wicked-gaze is supported by the end of mobilities as a new issue that marked the government´s agenda just after Covid-19. This virus, which is far from being apocalyptic, endorses a previous tendency to closure that the West experienced just after 9/11. To some extent, 9/11 and COVID-19 are inextricably interlined. Terrorism and 9/11 opened the doors to a culture of fear where the precautionary principle arrived to come. The old tensions of the Cold war not only disappeared but also coalesced in a new culture where the enemy lives within. The enemy is no longer the communist, but a citizen who looks like us assisted in the same universities and listened to the same music. He is waiting for the time to attack! The fear culture revives long-dormant xenophobic expression where "The Non-Western alterity" has no place, no choice to exist. Such a trend aims at neglecting the alterity is a direct consequence of 9/11 and the War on Terror. Emulating the metaphor of the enemy living within, the terrorist operates in the darkness of clandestine life, but he or she looks like us, behave like us, and consume like us. They even can be a neighbor or what is worse, a friend. This culture of fear fed back a state of paranoia and anxiety that paved the ways for the triumph of radical discourses oriented to demonize the *"Non-Western Other", an Other who now lives in our society.* Covid-19 (or SARS-COV2) seems to reinforce such a tendency, re-locating all citizens in equal conditions, all we are potential killers (terrorists) because the illness, the evilness lies inside us.

If the triumph of Occident was based not only on its commercial and military expansion but also in the imposition of the sacred-law of hospitality (to domesticate natives, what is clear is that this law is wounded to death. Terrorism has initiated a sentiment of anti-hospitality, which can be expressed in the supremacist discourse or the hate against foreigners. Doubtless, we are seeing how West is being eroded from inside, through the decline of the sacred law of hospitality. There is an *undesired Other* epitomized in the form of a so-called terrorist, a migrant, and today a *wicked-guest,* which means a carrier of contagion. The wall promised by Donald Trump in the US-Mexico frontier, the hate against Islam community, or Tourist-phobia are part of the same trend: the closure of West to what cannot be controlled. The quarantine emulates the precautionary logic because it is not imposed by a real threat that looms us but because of a potential risk that does not take a room in reality. The world of ancient Greeks, so to speak their homes were protected by walls, but now, these walls do not exist anymore. The globe has been flattened, virtualized in an immobile climate of exploitation, where citizens´ bodies are cannibalized. The virus does not recognize classes, ages, nor nationalities and moves through bodies. Not surprisingly, the idea of transmission occupied a vital position in the medical discourse. "Being infected" means a sentence of death, a pretext to be physically isolated in the quarantine, because the infected person is a potential killer. This metaphor has a sense only in the future, neither in the present nor in the past. Because of Coronavirus disease, foreign tourists –above all those who come from infected countries- are being carefully monitored, jailed, and deported to protect public health worldwide. The hotels as remarkable emblems of commercial hospitality are transformed in hospitals (non-commercial hospitality). Let me pause here for a moment; as discussed in earlier sections, Jacques Derrida notably observed two types of hospitalities: conditional and unconditional. While the former is given only to those who can pay for it (in this case, the tourists), the latter is ensured without asking nothing in return (migrants). As stated, the renting logic which is the touchstone of commercial hospitality has been temporarily suspended.

CONCLUSION

It is almost evident that COVID-19 would accelerate the lingering moral crisis in Western civilization. It may not be the end of hospitality, but it undeniably is going to be the end of hospitality that we are familiarized. Will there be the traditional core values of hospitality, in its new iteration? We have to wait and watch. If we believe in the idea of progress from generation to generation, we must be optimistic. However, short term signals may not be exciting for many. Doubtless, tourism is mutating towards new –probably unknown- forms. This essay-review discussed critically the effects of COVID19 as a continuation of the securitization process ignited by 9/11. We hold that like a stranger who asks for hospitality and enters the home without permission, COVID-19 directly confronts the Western civilization and its problems; it forces the West to understand the *"non-Western Other"*. The present conceptual work discussed the urgency to manipulate hospitality to impose the hegemony of Europe in the colonial process, a so-called superiority, which was accompanied by the economic exploitation of overseas colonies. As Anthony Pagden (1995) clearly explained, the western rationality abused from an ideological meaning of hospitality to expand and dispossess aborigines from their lands. It is safe to say, Europe successfully colonized the world according to previous technological transformations, as well as dogmatist discourse associated with free-transit and hospitality. Today, experts agree that COVID-19 is the epicenter of new normality. This paper, on the contrary, proves that far from being a foundational event, COVId-19 affirms a precedent trend originated in 9/11, which announced the "end of hospitality" epitomized by the "neglect of the Non-Western Other". It is important not to lose sight that 9/11 represented a traumatic event that installed a fear culture, where the enemy lives within. Both 9/11 and COVID19 paradoxically reaffirm the logic of living with the enemy within. Like the terrorists who can attack anytime, COVID-19 instills panic because all we are potential terrorists (killers), who, unless isolated, are biological weapons. In this context, the future of tourism and hospitality remain uncertain, but what is more important, like a guest the virus interrogates the West as never before. Last but not least, this essay review is in essence theoretical and critical but the main elements derived from the argumentation should be empirically contrasted or validated in future approaches.

REFERENCES

Ashworth, G. J., & Tunbridge, J. E. (2000). *The tourist-historic city*. Routledge. doi:10.4324/9780080519470

Augé, M. (1992). *Non-lieux. Introduction à une anthropologie de la submodernité*. Le Seuil.

Augé, M. (1995). *Non-lieux*. Verso.

Augé, M. (1996). Paris and the ethnography of the contemporary world. In M. Sheringham (Ed.), *Parisian Fields* (pp. 175–181). Reaktion Books.

Bauman, Z. (2017). Tourists and vagabonds: Or, living in postmodern times. In Identity and social change. Routledge.

Bell, D. (2012). Hospitality is society. *Hospitality & Society*, *1*(2), 137–152. doi:10.1386/hosp.1.2.137_1

Comaroff, J. L., & Comaroff, J. (2009). *Ethnicity, Inc*. University of Chicago Press. doi:10.7208/chicago/9780226114736.001.0001

Derrida, J. & Dufourmantelle. (2000). *Of Hospitality*. Stanford University Press.

Eringa, K. (2019). Ladies and Gentlemen serving ladies and Gentlemen. In B. Rowson & C. Lashley (Eds.), *Experiencing hospitality* (pp. 229–246). Nova Science Publishers.

George, S. K. (2009). Hospitality as openness to the other: Levinas, Derrida and the Indian hospitality ethos. *Journal of Human Values*, *15*(1), 29–47. doi:10.1177/097168580901500103

Gössling, S., Scott, D., & Hall, C. M. (2020). Pandemics, tourism and global change: A rapid assessment of COVID-19. *Journal of Sustainable Tourism*, 1–20.

Higgins-Desbiolles, F. (2020). Socialising tourism for social and ecological justice after COVID-19. *Tourism Geographies*, *22*(3), 1–14. doi:10.1080/14616688.2020.1757748

Hottola, P. (2014). Somewhat empty meeting grounds: Travelers in South India. *Annals of Tourism Research*, *44*, 270–282. doi:10.1016/j.annals.2013.10.007

Innerarity, D. (2017). *Ethics of hospitality*. Taylor & Francis. doi:10.4324/9781315618241

Judd, D. R. S., & Fainstein, S. S. (Eds.). (1999). *The tourist city*. Yale University Press.

Karney, R., & Semonovitch, K. (2011). At the threshold: foreigners, strangers and Others. In Phenomenologies of the Strangers. Fordham University Press. doi:10.5422/fordham/9780823234615.003.0001

Knox, A. (2008). Gender desegregation and equal employment opportunities in Australian luxury hotels: Are we there yet? *Asia Pacific Journal of Human Resources*, *46*(2), 153–172. doi:10.1177/1038411108091756.

Knox, A. (2011). Upstairs, downstairs: An analysis of low paid work in Australian hotels. *Labour & Industry*, *21*(3), 573–594. doi:10.1080/10301763.2011.10669421

Korstanje, M. (2012). Reconsidering cultural tourism: An anthropologist's perspective. *Journal of Heritage Tourism*, *7*(2), 179–184. doi:10.1080/1743873X.2011.639883

Korstanje, M. E. (2017). *Terrorism, Tourism and the End of Hospitality in the 'West*. Springer.

Korstanje, M. E. (2018). *The mobilities paradox: a critical analysis*. Edward Elgar Publishing. doi:10.4337/9781788113311

Lashley, C. (2015). Hospitality and Hospitableness. *Research in Hospitality Management*, *5*(1), 1–7. doi:10.1080/22243534.2015.11828322

Lashley, C. (2019). Towards a Theoretical understanding of hospitality. In B. Rowson & C. Lashley (Eds.), *Experiencing hospitality* (pp. 1–24). Nova Science Publishers.

Lugosi, P. (2014). Hospitality and organizations: Enchantment, entrenchment and reconfiguration. *Hospitality & Society*, *4*(1), 75–92. doi:10.1386/hosp.4.1.75_7

Lynch, P., Molz, G. J., Mcinthosh, A., Lugosi, P., & Lashley, C. (2011). Theorizing hospitality. *Hospitality & Society*, *1*(1), 3–24. doi:10.1386/hosp.1.1.3_2

MacCannell, D. (1976). *The tourist: A new theory of the leisure class*. University of California Press.

MacCannell, D. (1992). *Empty meeting grounds: The tourist papers*. Psychology Press.

Martin, R. J. (1998). *Professional management of housekeeping operations*. John Wiley and Sons.

Morrison, A., & O'Gorman, K. (2008). Hospitality studies and hospitality management: A symbiotic relationship. *International Journal of Hospitality Management*, *27*(2), 214–221. doi:10.1016/j.ijhm.2007.07.028

Nichols, J. (2011). *Hospitality among the Romans. In The Oxford Handbook of Social Relations in the Roman World*. Oxford University Press.

O'Gorman, K. (2007a). Dimensions of hospitality: exploring ancient and classical origins. In *Hospitality: A social lens* (pp. 31–46). Routledge. doi:10.1016/B978-0-08-045093-3.50005-9

O'Gorman, K. D. (2005). Modern Hospitality: Lessons from the past. *Journal of Hospitality and Tourism Management*, *12*(2), 141–151.

O'Gorman, K. D. (2006). Jacques Derrida's philosophy of hospitality. *Hospitality Review*, *8*(4), 50–57.

O'Gorman, K. D. (2007b). Discovering commercial hospitality in ancient Rome. *Hospitality Review*, *9*(2), 44–52.

O'Gorman, K. D. (2007c). The hospitality phenomenon: Philosophical enlightenment? *International Journal of Culture, Tourism and Hospitality Research*, *1*(3), 189–202. doi:10.1108/17506180710817729

Pagden, A. (1995). *Lords of all the World: Ideologies of Empire in Spain, Britain and France c. 1500-c. 1800*. Yale University Press.

Palmer, C. A. (1994). Tourism and colonialism: The experience of the Bahamas. *Annals of Tourism Research*, *21*(4), 792–811. doi:10.1016/0160-7383(94)90084-1

Poulston, J. (2015). Expressive labour and the gift of hospitality. *Hospitality & Society*, *5*(2-3), 145–165. doi:10.1386/hosp.5.2-3.145_1

Ritzer, G. (2019). Inhospitable hospitality? In B. Rowson & C. Lashley (Eds.), *Experiencing hospitality* (pp. 73–90). Nova Science Publishers.

Romagosa, F. (2020). The COVID-19 crisis: Opportunities for sustainable and proximity tourism. *Tourism Geographies*, 1–5.

Rowson, B. (2019). Working in hospitality: flexible working and the Gig Economy. In B. Rowson & C. Lashley (Eds.), *Experiencing hospitality* (pp. 135–156). Nova Science Publishers.

Sánchez-Moreno, E. (2001). Cross-cultural Links in Ancient Iberia: Socio-economic Anatomy of Hospitality. *Oxford Journal of Archaeology, 20*(4), 391–414. doi:10.1111/1468-0092.00144

Selwyn, T. (2019). Hostility and hospitality: connecting Brexit, Grenfell, Windrush. In B. Rowson & C. Lashley (Eds.), *Experiencing hospitality* (pp. 51–72). Nova Science Publishers.

Tzanelli, R. (2018). *Cinematic tourist mobilities and the plight of development: On atmospheres, affects, and environments*. Routledge. doi:10.4324/9780429424427

Urry, J. (1992). The tourist gaze "revisited". *The American Behavioral Scientist, 36*(2), 172–186. doi:10.1177/0002764292036002005

Urry, J. (2002). *The tourist gaze*. Sage.

Virilio, P. (1989). *War and cinema. The Logistics of Perception*. Patrick Camille.

Wen, J., Wang, W., Kozak, M., Liu, X., & Hou, H. (2020). Many brains are better than one: The importance of interdisciplinary studies on COVID-19 in and beyond tourism. *Tourism Recreation Research*, 1–4. doi:10.1080/02508281.2020.1761120

Wood, C. R. (2019). One Cheer for Marxism: hospitality as a bourgeois phenomenon. In B. Rowson & C. Lashley (Eds.), *Experiencing hospitality* (pp. 25–50). Nova Science Publishers.

ADDITIONAL READING

Berking, H. (1999). *Sociology of giving*. Sage.

Cohen, E. (1996). *Sociology of tourism: approaches, issues and findings*. Routledge.

Costa, N. (2013). The applied sociology of tourism. The up skills of the facilitator in the Italian hospitality industry. *Advances in Applied Sociology, 3*(01), 1–12. doi:10.4236/aasoci.2013.31001

Everingham, P., & Chassagne, N. (2020). Post COVID-19 ecological and social reset: Moving away from capitalist growth models towards tourism as Buen Vivir. *Tourism Geographies*, 1–12. doi:10.1080/14616688.2020.1713879

Gibson, S. (2016). *Mobilizing hospitality: The ethics of social relations in a mobile world*. Routledge. doi:10.4324/9781315595795

Ikkala, T., & Lampinen, A. (2014, February). Defining the price of hospitality: networked hospitality exchange via Airbnb. In *Proceedings of the companion publication of the 17th ACM conference on Computer supported cooperative work & social computing* (pp. 173-176). 10.1145/2556420.2556506

Korstanje, M., & Seraphin, H. (2017). Revisiting the sociology of consumption in tourism. In *The Routledge Handbook of Consumer Behaviour in Hospitality and Tourism* (pp. 2–16). Routledge.

Lashley, C., & Morrison, A. (Eds.). (2013). *In search of hospitality*. Routledge. doi:10.4324/9781315042817

Lynch, P. A. (2005). Sociological impressionism in a hospitality context. *Annals of Tourism Research, 32*(3), 527–548. doi:10.1016/j.annals.2004.09.005

Morrison, A., & O'Mahony, G. B. (2002). Hospitality: A liberal introduction. *Journal of Hospitality and Tourism Management, 9*(2), 189–198.

Sheller, M. (2020). Reconstructing tourism in the Caribbean: Connecting pandemic recovery, climate resilience and sustainable tourism through mobility justice. *Journal of Sustainable Tourism*, 1–14. doi:10.1080/09669582.2020.1791141

Slattery, P. (2002). Finding the hospitality industry. *Journal of Hospitality, Leisure, Sport and Tourism Education, 1*(1), 19–28. doi:10.3794/johlste.11.7

KEY TERMS AND DEFINITIONS

COVID-19: New virus outbreak known as Coronavirus desease, originated in Wuhan China in 2019.

Hospitality: Ancient ritual performed to protect and venerate strangers.

Lockdown: Strict steps and protocols organized to limit the free transit in societies.

Sustainability: Discipline oriented to study and mitigate the negative impacts of communities in the environment.

Tourism: Service sector oriented to given services and meet demand of tourists.

Chapter 9
Digital Labour, Pandemic COVID-19, and Emotions

Adrian Scribano
https://orcid.org/0000-0002-0523-8056
CONICET, University of Buenos Aires, Argentina

Florencia Chahbenderian
Center of Research on Consumption, Sensibilities and Creativity (CICSEC), University of Palermo, Argentina

ABSTRACT

This chapter seeks to outline in a preliminary way the consequences of the pandemic in work in general and especially in digital work in its connection with emotions and the politics of sensibilities. Based on public and private reports and the opinion of experts, some traces are presented here that allow us to reconstruct some changes in the politics of sensibilities that have occurred due to the socio-labour pandemic impact. In this sense, the following argumentative strategy has been developed: 1) the theoretical perspective on the connection between digital and political work of sensibilities is outlined, 2) some of the main consequences of the pandemic at work are synthesized, and 3) brief final openings are given to connect the described scenario and the modifications of the politics of sensibilities.

INTRODUCTION

Digital labour is one of the pillars of society 4.0 and on a planetary scale it is part of the axes of transformation which accelerates the social structuration of the 21st century. The beginning of the century marked the expansion of the virtual/mobile/digital world, which implied substantial transformation in the fields of Artificial

DOI: 10.4018/978-1-7998-7287-0.ch009

intelligence, economy, society, Gig Data as well as models of construction and analysis of narratives, the developments of Fintech companies, unicorns, Startups, platform work and social media. Everyday life is increasingly a matter of mobile phones, digital devices, social networks and the Internet of Things (Castells, 1989). In such a context, COVID19 outbreak expands generating not only millionaire losses but also radical transformation in labor management, production and good-exchange processes. The present chapter seeks to discuss preliminary the consequences of pandemic in working conditions as well as the digital work as part inherently linked to emotionalities and the politics of sensibilities. Methodologically speaking, we focus on private and public documents, reports and experts´ reviews which help us to reconstruct the narratives revolving around COVID19 and the new normality. In this vein, our goals are threefold: a) to explore the theoretical perspective on the connection between digital and political work of sensibilities, b) to expand the current understanding on main consequences of the Pandemic at work and c) to offer a snapshot on the politics of sensibilities.

The pandemic has brought an increase in delivery work, greater precariousness and uncertainty regarding the future of these and other jobs. Renting industry has occupied a central position in the configuration of the new trade and businesses in the post pandemic days. The multiplication of works as well as the demand does not entail in a rapid gratification for workers. In fact, the workforce was subject to ceaseless exploitation as long as the pandemic. Sebastian Blanco in his Article of last 20th July titled "COVID-19 Means More Packages, and a New Game: Delivery-Driver Tag" reproduces a Wall Street Journal paper on a curious competition between UPS and FedEx drivers expressing one of the axes of the delivery work in the Pandemic: there are more packages to distribute. An interesting aspect of delivery work is constituted by "traditional" companies such as UPS or FedEx, whose delivery drivers have been overworked, these being one of the gears of the device that keeps the world running during closures related to COVID-19 and orders to stay at home. Once people recognized they could shop online rather than in stores, delivery numbers increased radically, starting with what most business-minded people would see as a positive: a 10 percent increase in the first quarter of 2020. More packages, more work, greater "commitment" so as not to lose the job.

The future of Europe seems to be also uncertain as Valeria Pulignano has argued: "The coronavirus crisis has highlighted how the welfare state of the future must include the growing mass of precarious labour, especially among youth" (Pulignano, 2020, p. 1). Pulignano describes how the International Labor Organization (ILO) –at the end of May- demanded rapid and large-scale political actions to act in advance on lasting damage from the COVID-19 pandemic, especially among young people. The international organization fears multiple shocks will operate that will lead to a 'lockdown generation'. Young people were already living in precarious conditions in terms of social and human rights (particularly in participation and collective bargaining) and little or no social protection (without adequate unemployment and health benefits). In the European context, it is easy to see that the changes that have been taking place in the market, work and daily life of workers have suffered a drastic transformation on COVID-19 presence.

According to Esther Lynch (2020), as well as in the welfare state, it was intended to protect workers from the risks and "volatility" of the labor market in the post-COVID-19 times, the reduction of working time and greater autonomy should be on the agenda.

As it is easy to detect on a planetary scale, COVID-19 has radically transformed workplaces, turning offices into empty helmets and turning homes into offices. This is complemented by the demands of hygiene and distancing requirements in sectors ranging from culture and catering to manufacturing and distribution.

Greater flexibility or autonomy must not mean greater insecurity. Research confirms that social protection and income security increase, rather than reducing, platform workers' autonomy, and their interests must also be included in post-virus recovery plans. In Belgium, the Smart cooperative, set up to support freelance workers, offers a model of democratic management in which all members take part in decision-making, increasing their collective capability. (Lynch, 2020, p. 6)

In this mayhem, it is important not to lose the sight of the fact that the Pandemic operates as a magnifying glass that increases the visibility of previous problems in terms of "new economies", material asymmetries as well as previous encrusted economic problems while enhancing new "sensibilities of platform" which allow to the rise of young people economic recovery facet. The COVID19 potentiates old problems unresolved by late capitalism.

THEORETICAL PERSPECTIVE: SOCIETY 4.0, DIGITAL LABOUR AND POLITICS OF SENSIBILITIES

In order to understand what we mentioned in the introductory section, we must articulate the schematic diagnosis with the following conceptual instruments regarding our approach to a sociology of bodies/emotions (Scribano, 2017, 2019). Social agents know and grasp the world through their bodies. Perceptions, sensations and emotions build a tripod that allows us to understand where sensibilities are founded. Thus, a set of impressions impact in the ways subjects "exchange" with the socio-environmental context. Such impressions of objects, phenomenon, processes and other agents structure the perceptions that subjects accumulate and reproduce.

Perception, from this perspective, constitutes a naturalized way of organizing the set of impressions that are given in an agent.

This weaving of impressions configures the sensations that "produce" what can be called the internal and external world: social, subjective and "natural" worlds. Such configurations are formed in a dialectic tension between impressions, perceptions and their results, that give sensations the "meaning" of a surplus or excess. At the same time, organic and social senses also enable what seems unique and unrepeatable as are individual sensations and elaborate the "un-perceived work" of incorporating social elements turned into emotions. Consequently, the policy of bodies (i.e., the strategies that a society accepts in order to offer a response to the social availability of individuals) acts as a vehicle towards in the instruction manual of power. These strategies are tied and 'strengthened' by the policies of emotions that tend to regulate the construction of social sensibility.

The forms of sociability and experience are strained and twisted as if contained in a Moebius strip along with the sensibilities that arise from regulatory devices and the aforementioned mechanisms. The need to distinguish and link the possible relations between sociability, experience and social sensibilities becomes crucial at this point. Sociability is a way of expressing the means by which agents live and coexist interactively. Experience is a way of expressing how the world is phenomenologically perceived while being in physical proximity with others, as a result of experiencing the dialogue between the individual body, the social body, and the subjective body, on the one hand; and the natural appropriation of bodily and social energies.

As has already been said, the politics of sensibilities are understood as the set of cognitive-affective social practices tending to the production, management and reproduction of horizons of action, disposition and cognition (Scribano, 2017, p. 244). These horizons refer to: 1) the organization of daily life (day-to-day, vigil/sleep, food/abstinence, etc.), 2) information to sort preferences and values (adequate/inadequate, acceptable/unacceptable, bearable/unbearable), and 3) parameters for time/space management (displacement/location, walls/bridges; enjoyment). Having said this, it is possible to understand how the digitalization of the world coexists with the emotionalization of the processes of domination and of everyday life. We are facing a social system that is globalized by producing / buying / selling emotions in and through the media, social networks and the Internet. In this sense, it is probable to understand what is possible to call the emergence of "sensibilities of platform" (Scribano, 2019).

We live in a virtual / digitally connected world shaped by the technological transformations of the last 10 years (Hearn, 2010; Graham & Dutton, 2014). Internet and mobile telephony are two vectors that set the stage for three strong changes in the politics of sensibilities: a) the organization of the day / night unlinked of the experience of the subjects that experience it, b) the modification of the sensations of classification, and c) valuations on world modifications. Each society has a preponderant way of managing labour and this constitutes a central axis of the politics of sensibilities. The 4.0 society implies the massification of digital labour. A "sensibilities of platform" emerges in this 4.0 society that is immediate in three senses: a) in the vehicle the action resides (it is the feeling of always being "on line"), b) it is a society that "is during use", "between", "in passing", and c) is pure presentification (here / now). Much of digital work has the same characteristics and, in this direction, the political economy of morality consecrates this way of "feeling the world". The sense of the immediate appears to be functional to the connections between the digitalization of society and the consolidation processes of normalized societies in the immediate enjoyment through consumption. The ephemeral of enjoyment resembles what many authors associate to digital work as disruptive or creative destruction. The immediate is similar with "on demand" platform strategy. Lastly "in the course", "in this action becoming permanently", in this idea of the immediate and ephemeral, we should interpolate the world with silence. An act of listening where one feels the other in a different way. Silence is the starting point of dialogue as a matrix of knowledge and life become personal interaction.

PANDEMIC COVID-19 IMPACT AND FUTURE EXPECTATIONS

According to report EUROFOUND (2020a), the expected economic and labor impact of the pandemic will be more serious than that of the global financial crisis of 2008-2009:

1. As the ILO model estimates, global working hours in the second quarter of 2020 are expected to be 10.5% less than in the fourth quarter of 2019 (equivalent to 305 million full-time jobs worldwide); 2. the above will be experienced with somewhat more impacts in the main developed economies, including the European Union (EU); 3. the EU GDP growth projections for 2020 have been revised from + 1.5% to -7.5% as expected in spring 2020; and 4. the projections differ greatly in their severity from fall and the nature of the subsequent recovery according to the countries.

Report EUROFOUND (2020a) has pointed out, among others, the following aspects of state aid in the face of the pandemic: a) Initiatives to support companies took mainly in the form of non-reimbursable grants for self-employed, micro and small businesses (37%); b) about 70% of measures to protect employment were linked to reduced working hours. It is not clear how long the support schemes will remain especially at low cost to the employer, although in some countries the application periods have already been extended, and c) another feature of income support was targeted at groups not previously covered (such as the self-employed and workers with temporary contracts), demonstrating the possibility of finding solutions (at least temporary) long-standing political debates versus impending difficulties for groups often more directly impacted in the context of the economic crisis.

In this scenario "The Future of Jobs Report 2020", World Economic Forum (2020) is very clear:

The COVID-19 pandemic-induced lockdowns and related global recession of 2020 have created a highly uncertain outlook for the labour market and accelerated the arrival of the future of work. The Future of Jobs Report 2020 aims to shed light on: 1) the pandemic-related disruptions thus far in 2020, contextualized within a longer history of economic cycles, and 2) the expected outlook for technology adoption jobs and skills in the next five years. (World Economic Forum [WEF], 2020, p. 5)

The following reproduces the axes emphasized by the Report in its executive summary.

1. The pace of technology adoption is expected to remain unabated and may accelerate in some areas. The adoption of cloud computing, big data and e-commerce remain high priorities for business leaders, following a trend established in previous years. However, there has also been a significant rise in interest for encryption, non-humanoid robots and artificial intelligence. (WEF, 2020, p. 5)

The Pandemic accelerates the necessary discussion about the meaning, rights and social place of intelligent non-human individuals in the constitution of society where "sensibilities of platform" will increasingly be created by such individuals but designed and experienced by human beings.

2. Automation, in tandem with the COVID-19 recession, is creating a 'double-disruption' scenario for workers. In addition to the current disruption from the pandemic-induced lockdowns and economic contraction, technological adoption by companies will transform tasks, jobs and skills by 2025. (WEF, 2020, p. 5)

In the context opened by the expansion of digital labour produced in the last ten years (Scholz, 2013), the post COVID-19 work structure demands a special attention to efforts for the emotional regulation of workers (OECD, 2015) who must incorporate new skills where emotions allow to "keep working together" tasks, jobs and skills.

3. Although the number of jobs destroyed will be surpassed by the number of 'jobs of tomorrow' created, in contrast to previous years, job creation is slowing while job destruction accelerates. (…) we estimate that by 2025, 85 million jobs may be displaced by a shift in the division of labour between humans and machines, while 97 million new roles may emerge that are more adapted to the new division of labour between humans, machines and algorithms. (WEF, 2020, p. 5)

The crosses between intelligent jobs, intelligent machines and workers trained in their creation and supervision generate transformations in the politics of sensibilities that will emerge after the pandemic focused on "adaptation", "recreation", elaboration of emotional skills to "support" modifications, changes and uncertainty conditioned by connection machines, devices and workers.

4. Skills gaps continue to be high as in-demand skills across jobs change in the next five years. The top skills and skill groups which employers see as rising in prominence in the lead up to 2025 include groups such as critical thinking and analysis as well as problem-solving, and skills in self-management such as active learning, resilience, stress tolerance and flexibility. (WEF, 2020, p. 5)

Emotions are the material for suturing/closing cracks between required skills and possessed abilities. "Pro-activity", the ability to manage stress, the management of thresholds for acceptance of the different and the arrangement for change are developed as a set of pre-conditions for the work of the future. Employment policies become politics of sensibilities.

5. The future of work has already arrived for a large majority of the online white-collar workforce. Eighty-four percent of employers are set to rapidly digitalize working processes, including a significant expansion of remote work—with the potential to move 44% of their workforce to operate remotely. (WEF, 2020, p. 6)

The digitization of work involves the consolidation of a remote action with consequences in diverse and plural times/spaces. This reconstructs the parameters of the definition of the situation (*sensu* Thomas), the connection between perception and sensation and the management of time. It is this traits that point in the direction of how the "new" work will change social relations in general through an important modification of the senses: seeing, listening, touching, etc.

6. In the absence of proactive efforts, inequality is likely to be exacerbated by the dual impact of technology and the pandemic recession. Jobs held by lower wage workers, women and younger worker were more deeply impacted in the first phase of the economic contraction. (WEF, 2020, p. 6)

The Pandemic has made it possible to look more closely at the deficits in labour management systems, health and transport, including wage inequality, income gap and the serious problems of access to work are some of the axes that have become apparent and which have far since increased and deepened.

7. Online learning and training is on the rise but looks different for those in employment and those who are unemployed. There has been a four-fold increase in the numbers of individuals seeking out opportunities for learning online through their own initiative, a five-fold increase in employer provision of online learning opportunities to their workers and a nine-fold enrolment increase for learners accessing online learning through government programs. (WEF, 2020, p. 6)

Living in a virtual/mobile/digital world does not directly mean in personal terms that all the people have access to devices, connectivity, and their abilities to manage. As the pandemic deepens the worker's dependence on this "world", the inequalities and needs of those who "must be converted" are becoming more severe.

8. The window of opportunity to reskill and upskill workers has become shorter in the newly constrained labour market. This applies to workers who are likely to stay in their roles as well as those who risk losing their roles due to rising recession-related unemployment and can no longer expect to retrain at work. (WEF, 2020, p. 6)

There is clearly a shadow cone regarding the volume, density, and scope of re-workouts in demand new skills: there is little time to learn is a threatening face of new emotional precariousness. Added are the uncertainty of the tenure of the position, the need to transform emotional skills and the decrease of jobs with the "old" skills as an experience horizon of workers.

9. Despite the current economic downturn, the large majority of employers recognize the value of human capital investment. An average of 66% of

> employers surveyed expect to get a return on investment in upskilling and reskilling within one year. (WEF, 2020, p. 6)

As opposed to point (6), the results of the study we are analyzing point out in the direction of employers' awareness of investing in the conversion of "human capital" so it can be noted that, in addition to the already explicit digitization, it is quite possible that the training and conversion of work skills and competencies resulting in another turn of commoditization of the skilled sensibilities.

> 10. Companies need to invest in better metrics of human and social capital through adoption of environmental, social and governance (ESG) metrics and matched with renewed measures of human capital accounting. A significant number of business leaders understand that reskilling employees, particularly in industry coalitions and in public-private collaborations, is both cost-effective and has significant mid- to long-term dividends—not only for their enterprise but also for the benefit of society more broadly. Companies hope to internally redeploy nearly 50% of workers displaced by technological automation and augmentation, as opposed to making wider use of layoffs and automation-based labour savings as a core workforce strategy. (WEF, 2020, p. 6)

In the context that has been presented, the emphasis on the needs of new metrics is interesting, because these assessments connect governance, ecology and social impact, and companies for reasons of own and social benefit plan to re-attract half of the staff in need of skills breakdown.

> 11. The public sector needs to provide stronger support for reskilling and upskilling for at-risk or displaced workers. Currently, only 21% of businesses report being able to make use of public funds to support their employees through reskilling and upskilling. The public sector will need to create incentives for investments in the markets and jobs of tomorrow; provide stronger safety nets for displaced workers in the midst of job transitions; and to decisively tackle long-delayed improvements to education and training systems. Additionally, it will be important for governments to consider the longer-term labour market implications of maintaining, withdrawing or partly continuing the strong COVID-19 crisis support they are providing to support wages and maintain jobs in most advanced economies. (WEF, 2020, p. 6)

Direct state intervention to ensure market continuity that emerged and globalized during the Pandemic has arrived to stay. Employers expect the state to be a relevant player in adapting workers to the new working conditions imposed by the "new" skills and the necessary processes of conversion and improvement of them. The State "should" ensure labour management processes by subsidizing employers in the training of workers.

The Pandemic has consolidated and increased two features of the impacts of Revolution 4.0 on social structuring processes: the increase in digital work and the global expansion of platform work.

SOME NEW OPENINGS

The impact of COVID-19 will affect the constitution of society in different ways, but especially work, some of the obvious and in which the inquiries and the scholars of the problem seem to coincide can be synthesized as follows:

1. The growing participation of work at home in the various spheres of the productive system (Cherry, 2011).
2. The massive use of artificial intelligence to design, create and expand marketable objects, processes and individuals (Fisher & Fuchs, 2015).
3. The growing importance of social networks as media and producers of "real effects" (Papacharissi, 2009; Mollett et al., 2011).
4. The globalization and massification of the platform economy as an instrument for generating wealth and also precariousness (Graham et al., 2017; Srnicek, 2017; Armano et al., 2017).
5. The naturalization of transfer services such as Uber, Cabify, etc. as "public" transport.
6. The unnoticed acceptance that delivery jobs are a fundamental gear of the market (Blanco, 2020).
7. The "incorporation" of the migrant's place as a distribution worker and its impact on the "impossibility" of forming trade unions (Fuchs & Sandoval, 2015).
8. The expansion of the management of emotions as a basic skill of the worker (OECD, 2015; Hearn, 2010).
9. The consecration of new gender inequalities produced by working from home, at home and at home through digital / mobile / virtual means (EUROFOUND, 2020b).
10. The redefinition and increase of precariousness and flexibility in employment contracts and the security regimes associated with them (Huws, 2015; Meil & Kirov, 2017).

In terms of changes in Politics of Sensibilities (Scribano, 2017) in light of the impact of the Pandemic on work, it is possible to sustain:

Table 1. Politics of sensibilities and COVID-19 labor modification

Politics of Sensibilities Features	COVID-19 Labor Modification
Organization of daily life	Labor-in-house "a continuous/nonstop job" Daily -Night indifference
Information to sort preferences and values	Fear of losing the job / anguish
Parameters for time/space management	Locked up / depressed / no contact with others

Source: Own elaboration.

The Pandemic has impacted not only work but especially what we experience when working, emotions (which allow us to map/know the world) have been modified and with them what we consider to be near or far, risky or safe, threatening or friendly.

To work is to inhabit the world in a particular way, as work has changed this involved a change in the politics of sensibilities and with them the social structuration processes.

REFERENCES

Armano, E., Murgia, A., & Teli, M. (2017). Plataform capitalism e confini del lavoro negli spazi digitali [Platform capitalism and the boundaries of work in digital spaces]. *Mimesis*.

Blanco, S. (2020, July 20). *COVID-19 Means More Packages, and a New Game: Delivery-Driver Tag*. https://www.caranddriver.com/news/a33366841/delivery-driver-tag-game-coronavirus/

Castells, M. (1989). *The informational city: Information technology, economic restructuring, and the urban-regional process*. Blackwell.

Cherry, M. (2011). A taxonomy of virtual work. *Georgia Law Review (Athens, Ga.)*, *45*(4), 954–1009.

EUROFOUND. (2020a). *Labour market change. COVID-19: Policy responses across Europe*. Publications Office of the European Union.

EUROFOUND. (2020b). *Living, working and COVID-19*. Publications Office of the European Union.

Fisher, E., & Fuchs, C. (2015). *Reconsidering Value and Labour in the Digital Age*. Palgrave- Macmillan. doi:10.1057/9781137478573

Graham, M., Hjorth, I., & Lehdonvirta, V. (2017). Digital labour and development: Impacts of global digital labour platforms and the gig economy on worker livelihoods. *Transfer: European Review of Labour and Research*, *23*(2), 135–162. doi:10.1177/1024258916687250 PMID:28781494

Hearn, A. (2010). Structuring feeling: Web 2.0, online ranking and rating, and the digital "reputation "economy". *Ephemera*, *10*(3/4), 421–438.

Huws, U. (2015). *A review on the future of work: Online labour exchanges, or 'crowdsourcing': Implications for occupational safety and health*. European Agency for Safety and Health at Work.

Lynch, E. (2020, September 24). Making work fit for workers after Covid-19. *Social Europe*. https://www.socialeurope.eu/making-work-fit-for-workers-after-covid-19

Meil, P., & Kirov, V. (2017). *Policy Implications of Virtual Work*. Palgrave – Macmillan. doi:10.1007/978-3-319-52057-5

Mollett, A., Moran, D., & Dunleavy, P. (2011). *Using Twitter in university research, teaching and impact activities. Impact of social sciences: maximizing the impact of academic research*. LSE Public Policy Group.

OECD. (2015). *Skills for Social Progress: The Power of Social and Emotional Skills*. OECD Publishing., doi:10.1787/9789264226159-

Papacharissi, Z. (2009). The virtual geographies of social networks: A comparative analysis of Facebook, Linkedln and ASmallWorld. *New Media & Society*, *11*(1-2), 199–220. doi:10.1177/1461444808099577

Pulignano, V. (2020, September 9). Including the precariat. *Social Europe*. https://www.socialeurope.eu/including-the-precariat

Scholz, T. (Ed.). (2013). *Digital Labor. The Internet as Playground and Factory*. Routledge.

Scribano, A. (2017). *Normalization, Enjoyment and Bodies/Emotions: Argentines Sensibilities*. Nova Science Publications.

Scribano, A. (2019). Introduction: Politics of Sensibilities, Society 4.0 and Digital Labour. In A. Scribano & P. Lisdero (Eds.), Digital Labour, Society and Politics of Sensibilities (pp. 1-19). Palgrave Macmillan.

Srnicek, N. (2017). Platform capitalism. *Polity*.

World Economic Forum. (2020). *The Future of Jobs Report 2020*. World Economic Forum. www.weforum.org

KEY TERMS AND DEFINITIONS

COVID-19: A new virus outbreak located originally in Wuhan china at the end of 2019. The virus spreads worldwide constituting one of the worse pandemics of the century.

Digital Labor: It exhibits an emergent form of labor marked by the production of value through interaction with digital technologies and TICs.

Politics of Sensibilities: The term signals to a set of policies, strategies and actions oriented to enhance the emotional perception of environment.

Technology: It represents a technique or sum of skills given to the production and exchange of goods or at least to the maximization of goals.

Virtual Work: It refers to the application of forces and movements into a mechanical virtual system.

Chapter 10
Emotions and Digital Delivery Platforms:
An Approach to the Configuration of Sensibilities During the Isolation Caused by the COVID-19 Pandemic

Maria Victoria Mairano
Center of Research on Consumption, Sensibilities and Creativity (CICSEC), University of Palermo, Argentina

ABSTRACT

From the global spread of the infectious disease COVID-19, in Argentina as in other states worldwide, health measures, social emergency, economic and public order measures were taken. One of the main and earliest measures of social order in the face of this disease was the delimitation of a period of population isolation, known as preventive and obligatory social isolation. The compulsory social isolation generated unprecedented growth in the demand for services to the platform economies in Argentina in general and in Buenos Aires in particular, causing the platform delivery activity to be conceived as an essential activity. The purpose of the writing is to explore the configuration of a certain politics of sensibilities that is used as a reproduction transport by digital delivery platforms in the city of Buenos Aires, during the isolation that the COVID-19 pandemic led to. From a process of digital ethnography, the main web pages and applications for smartphones of the firms are registered to problematize the information built from the notions of platform and politics of sensibilities.

DOI: 10.4018/978-1-7998-7287-0.ch010

INTRODUCTION

The virus outbreak, which is known by experts as SARS-COV-2, showed the lack of shared protocols to prevent the dissemination of pandemics worldwide. Each government adopted different steps and measures to stop the mass-contagion which oscillate from strict lockdowns to the closure of airspaces and borders as never before. It is safe to say that COVID-19 negatively affected global trade as well as many service subsectors. Thousands of tourists and travelers were stranded at airports while administrations coordinated desperately their citizens' repatriation (Korstanje 2020). Having said this, in Argentina the state of emergency was originally declared by President Alberto Fernandez on 20 March of 2020. This sanitary emergency, doubtless to say, was accompanied by a social economic and public crisis, as well as serious social maladies as the rise of poverty, unemployment and inflation (only to name a few). The imposition of a strict lockdown (which lasted roughly 321 days) was an earlier measure that facilitated the preparation of the health system as well as delaying what experts dubbed as the COVID-19 pandemic peak (Li & Linton 2021). This quarantine was known as Preventive and Compulsory Social isolation. Meanwhile these restrictive measures as well as travel bans generated paradoxically unprecedented growth in the demand for food services to the platform economies countrywide, but more precisely in Argentina. In this way, food and digital service subsectors were esteemed as an essential activity to the Argentinean economy. At the same time, nobilities and travels were strictly banned. The lemma "stay at home", which was imposed by the authorities under the auspices of the global pandemic, culturally shaped new experiences revolving around digital consumption. The present chapter aims to explore the configuration of a certain politics of sensibilities that digital delivery platforms have as a reproduction transport in the city of Buenos Aires, during the isolation to which the Covid19 Pandemic led. Based on digital ethnography this book chapter explores the content of the main web pages and applications for smart-phones of the firms such as Rappy, Orders Now, Uber Eats and Glovo. In so doing, we center our analysis on the society 4.0 model with rise of the new politics of sensibilities and platform sensibilities adjoined to the information constructed from the notions of platform sensitivity and the politics of sensibilities. In this chapter we place the problem of digital technologies, labor precaritization and the new normality into the critical lens of scrutiny.

SOCIETY 4.0, DELIVERY PLATFORMS AND PANDEMIC

The 21st century brought with it a set of digital transformations that constitute the so-called era of society 4.0 of revolution 4.0. The concept of Society 4.0 refers to the economic and social processes that were structured from the so-called "Fourth Industrial Revolution", around the global massification of new information technologies. Among the main elements of Society 4.0 are the appearance of Big Data and the handling of large amounts of information about people at the mercy of companies; and the emergence of an Economy of Orders, which promoted new forms of labor through digital platforms

As the previous backdrop, the new millennium evinces the predatory expansion of capitalism on a planetary scale (see Schumpeter), and the consequent manifestation of a series of changes and transformations in social processes on a world scale; among them: the large-scale increase in the use of the Internet and mobile devices, digital work and the new political economy of morality. In that way, the notion of "digital capitalism" expresses that the social changes that have been brewing show continuities regarding the basic relationships of economic exploitation, cultural alienation, and political domination (Van den Ecker and Sevignani, 2020).

According to We Are Social & Hootsuite (2020), more and more people are spending more time doing their things online. As of January 2020, the number of people around the world using the Internet grew to 4.54 million, an increase of 7 per cent (298 million new users) compared to January 2019. On the other hand, globally, more than 5.19 billion people now use mobile phones, with a 124 million (2.4 per cent) increase in the number of users during 2019.

At the end of December of 2019 the first cases of infected people who have developed severe symptoms of the virus take place in Wuhan -China. Originally suspected to be originated in a Wholesale Seafood supermarket the preliminary investigations suggest that the COVID-19 is a new Coronavirous for what humanity has neither treatment nor vaccine. Hence, at the end of January 2020, the W.H.O. declares the Coronavirus an international public health emergency and names it the following month COVID-19. The following months, as we already know, were caused by a global pandemic that caused important transformations in the daily life of the population. As Scribano (2020) puts it, this devastating global pandemic not only speaks to us of a much deeper economic downturn but also denotes some practices mainly-enrooted in inequality, dehumanization, and discrimination proper of the capitalist system. In the context of isolation where that immediate consumption was interrupted, and with it, enjoyment, digital delivery platforms will fill much of that void and respond to the wishes of the population. In this sense, people forced to stay at home, cell phones and other digital devices, were consolidated as the main vehicle for education, work, shopping, ordering food, sending money, among others. If we return to the We are reports social & Hootsuite (2020), we can observe that throughout the planet, we are using mobile applications in almost all aspects of our lives, from interacting with our friends, family; go shopping; manage our finances until we find love for applications like Tinder. According to information from GlobalWebIndex, as of January 2021, 89% of users between 16 and 64 years old have used mobile phones for chat applications and social networks, 65% for video applications, 47% for online games, and 66% have done it for shopping or shopping applications. In this pandemic context, the fear of becoming infected and infecting others, especially at the beginning of isolation when it was reported that the virus remained for a long time on surfaces, was a very strong boost to a certain culture of touch and click. As a result, cash is effectively replaced by online mobile payments, as well as old restaurant menus replaced by menu access links, to name a couple of examples. In this way, we affirm following Scribano and Lisdero (2019) that currently: "Being able to touch", more than a skill, is a condition of cognitive/affective possibility of being in the world" (p. 35).

However, according to Global WebIndex (2020), these transformations in consumption and online shopping worldwide had already been brewing before the Covid-19 breakdown. "In reality, most Internet users were shopping online before the outbreak. So when these new users are added to the existing online shopper base before the pandemic, the growth is not as substantial as many might assume. This method indicates that the increase in the total online shopper base so far due to the lockdown is only 6%. Ultimately, it is clear that COVID-19 has driven predominantly user demand for online purchases existing" (GlobalWebIndex, 2020: 12).

At a closer look, per a report issued by the Argentine Chamber of Electronic Commerce, in the first 6 months of 2020, e-Commerce in our country increased 106% in turnover compared to the same period of 2019, being food and beverages the best-selling product, followed by units for the home, furniture, and garden; tools and objects for construction; clothing and sportswear respectively. On the other hand, in the same sense as the world statistics, the report makes it clear that in Argentina, 9 out of 10 people had already bought online at some point, and 1 in 10 did so for the first time in this context of a pandemic. Thus, if we refer to the technical note of the International Labor Organization (2020) regarding delivery in a pandemic in the City of Buenos Aires, the opportunities offered by this business model took on a special dimension in the context of a pandemic since many of businesses have seen these platforms as the only solution to continue marketing their products.

As Richard Sennett (1998) eloquently noted, we witness the start of a new division of labor which is characterized by the narrative of flexibility while becoming a device to soften the hard effects of exploitation over human beings. The argument of labor flexibility impacts the subjectivity and character of the subjects; two attributes that are intimately related to our emotional experience. In this sense, when we talk about digital delivery platforms, we cannot avoid referring to the work and working conditions of those people who are in charge of making deliveries throughout the city. This could be obvious if it weren't that companies like Amazon are working so that in some offices people are replaced by new technologies, as is the case with drones. Meanwhile, the work of platform workers becomes a necessary vector for the materialization of digital consumption. It should be mentioned that the platform worker is considered an independent worker and is registered under the mon tax regime, which brings with it certain basic precaritization such as the lack of health insurance, vacations, among others. Consequently, the success of these platforms during the quarantine, while the government insisted on the imperative "stay home", can only be understood from the work of thousands of workers, despite contextual circumstances. Furthermore, concerns about the lack of safety and hygiene elements, flexibility, and increased job insecurity, led to some protests at the international level, expressed in the form of strikes and mobilizations of delivery men, under the slogan #Idonotdistribute.

SENSIBILITIES AROUND DIGITAL CONSUMPTION

As early mentioned, consumption is a social organizer (Baudrillard, 1969), and digital consumption itself is one of the main protagonists of the 21st-century society: a society of "hyperconsumption" (Lipovetsky, 2007). Instead, consumption has the characteristic of permeating the production and reproduction of life, of social agents, as a way of being and being with others (Dettano and Lava, 2014). In this sense, as described by Lipovetsky (2007), in hyper-consumption societies, the consumer is on the lookout for emotional experiences and in constant search of greater well-being, in such a way that the 5 senses are put into play in the search for sensations by and through the acquisition of objects/services. In short, Dettano and Lava (2014) highlight that the added enjoyment and satisfaction that the acquisition of products brings with it can only be understood from the commoditization of sensibilities that, "in these societies, there are many incentives to hedonism, to the commercialization of ways of life, pleasures, and tastes. Experiences as experiences, drive hyper-consumption practices" (Dettano and Lava, 2014: 29).

In order to understand the structuring process of hyper-consumption societies, one might imagine the social order of hyper-consumption is inextricably intertwined with a regime of sensitivity. Each action oriented to acquire (consume) objects and of course their usage, are associated with a daily and massive doing closely linked to certain ways of feeling such as pleasure, enjoyment, resignation, happiness, among others (Dettano, 2018). Henceforth, we consider the approach to consumption practices from the fellow's emotions as potential. Following Boragnio (2020), emotions are consequences of the sensations that will allow people to feel (himself) and are linked to social interaction while in them subjectivity and social reality are inter-linked. For Scribano (2015), any act of consumption obliges us to keep on consuming. This happens simply because the existence of sensitivity opens the doors to moments of immediate enjoyment which re-structure the social agency. The human agent is actively encouraged to suppress negative feelings while avoiding conflict for the system to perpetuate itself. To put the same in other terms, it is at the intersection/convergence between industry 4.0 and the globalization of digital consumption where new properties of the politics of sensibilities are developed (Scribano, 2019). In consonance with Scribano, digital consumption constitutes a set of cognitive-affective social practices that tend to produce, manage and reproduce horizons of action, disposition, and cognition. These horizons refer to 1) the organization of daily life (daily routines, wakefulness / sleep, food / abstinence, etc.); 2) to the information to order preferences and values (adequate / inadequate; acceptable / unacceptable; bearable / unbearable), and (3) the parameters for time / space management (displacement / location; walls / bridges; enjoyment) (Scribano, 2019: 7). Whatever the case may be, we mean to the politics of digital sensibilities as the promise of instant consumption without conflicts, taking for granted the thousands of people "behind the scenes" who make those sensations possible" (Scribano, 2019: 3).

In line with Scribano´s assertion, it is from the "immediate" that some of the connections emerge between the digitization of society and the processes of consolidation of normalized societies in immediate enjoyment through consumption ... The immediate is similar to a strategy platform "on-demand" (p.15 / 17). In this context, three important changes are manifested in the politics of current sensibilities: a) the organization of the day/night unrelated to the experience of the subjects who they experience it; b) the modification of the classification sensations and c) valuations on world modifications (see furtherly on Scribano, 2019).

It is difficult to resist the impression that the process of digitalization –of the surrounding world- coexists with the use of emotion to exploit "the Other" which is taken as usual in daily life. Not surprisingly, society is facing a new unparalleled process that combines production, buying/selling through the lens of emotions. In so doing, the internet, media and social networks occupy a central position not only mediating between citizens and their new institutions (in a post-COVID-19 context) but creating specific sensibilities which are orchestrated through the appearance of digital platforms. We coin the term here, platform sensibilities to denote the relationship of cognitive-affective social practices and consumption. This happens because sensibilities –broadly speaking- are cognitive-affective social practices that are formed through other social practices (De Sena, 2020). While platform sensibilities, in particular, are practices that occur in and through social networks as vehicles for the production and reproduction of a certain capitalist Neo-Colonial Religion (Scribano, 2017). Still further, platform sensibilities are characterized by being immediate in three senses: (a) in the vehicle in which the action resides (it is the feeling of always being "online"), (b) it is a society that "is during use", "between", "in passing" and (c) is pure presesentification (here / now) (Scribano, 2019: 15).

METHODOLOGY

From the massification of the Internet and information technologies in the daily life of the population, the use of research strategies that include the Internet as a tool for social research becomes essential. On this occasion, a proposal was chosen as a methodological qualitative approach, based on a process of virtual ethnography. Virtual/digital ethnography is an inquiry strategy in which the researcher immerses himself/herself in the virtual world to understand the meanings that are constructed there from the published content and the interaction between users. In it, a variety of support techniques are assumed, such as the observation of virtual space; the registry of publications, interviews and digital surveys, discourse analysis, among many others (Domínguez Figaredo, 2007; Hine, 2004). In short, digital ethnography helps to achieve an enriched sense of the meanings that technology acquires in the cultures that host it or that are formed thanks to it (Hine, 2004). Therefore, in this writing the main options were recorded, services and products offered by and through the web pages and digital applications of each delivery company. An analysis of those records was then carried out based on the notions of platform sensibilities and new sensibilities politics. As well, it was deepened in the measures that each one of them adopted from the pandemic and the sensibilities that can be manifested in each platform. The data that we were able to build from the ethnographic work is explained below.

DELIVERY PLATFORMS IN TIMES OF PANDEMIC

The current phase of capitalism, we have touched in early sections, is marked by its predatory expansion, including, of course, also competitors for attracting customers in the consumer market. Thus, between the start of isolation in March 2020 and November of the same year, of the 4 delivery platforms that we were analyzing, only 2 continue to operate in our country, Pedidos Ya and Rappi. Glovo was absorbed by Pedidos Ya while UberEats decided to stop working and focus on the successful mobility platform, to which it had sought to associate the delivery platform when it offered the customer to order "Your favourite food, at the speed of Uber". In a world epitomized by the speed, less than two years were enough for the company to assess that the results obtained were not as expected and thus decide to withdraw thanking the "UberEats community in Argentina for their support".

Figure 1. Picture from La Nacion Newspaper, August 19, 2020.

Let´s start our explanation with the study case of Pedidos ya, "Pedidos Ya" platform, from its nomination, the application readily shows what one of its main values will be and how closely related it is to the society we have characterized: immediacy. Before going into the description of the structure of the web page (https://www.pedidosya.com.ar/) we must point out that the above reappears when the first thing the client reads when entering the site is: " Fly with your online delivery! "Below that legend, the center of the page is occupied by the search engine where the customer must fill in their address and the "restaurant or food", they choose. At the bottom of the page, the way to operate is explained in 3 simple steps, which every customer must know when entering the page: 1. Choose your food 2. Place your order and 3. I received your food.

By going down, designed so that without wasting time the client enters what they want and where they want to receive it, 2 phrases appear for those who are not so determined and must somehow be seduced. First "The best restaurants" and below

6 logos of fast food places, ice cream parlors, sushi, supermarkets, etc. that change every time one enters the page. Then, a section directed towards: "Our community" where opinions of equally changing users are expressed.

If we continue our exploration of the platform, the legend "Delivery that satisfies your senses" will appear where the customer is explained that the love for food is shared by the company and the operation of the platform is reinforced: "Enter your address, choose the restaurant, select your favorite food and that's it. "In case there are still doubts, the customer is shown 3 classifications: Top cities, Top neighborhoods, and Top foods, and in each one the 6 that lead the order ranking.

In addition to the options to register and enter, the customer is offered the online help button, where 6 points appear: Coupons and promotions, Are you coming from Glovo?, Online payments, My Account, Safety and hygiene, and Other queries. The second has to do with what we mentioned at the beginning and seeks to be an aid to the "transition" from one platform to another. The option "Safety and hygiene" responds to the precautions that the company raises concerning the pandemic.

Taking into consideration the mobile application of Orders Now, it offers 7 options: restaurants, markets, drinks, kiosks, cafe and deli, shipping, stores, as well as offers the possibility of repeating your last order and shows you the places where you ordered previously. On the other hand, there are several options to choose from that are presented at the beginning: a) a section of suggestions for you where some restaurant promos are presented in your area (recommended by location), b) a section of unbeatable prices where they have presented the cheapest dishes concerning your area of residence, c) a sector for purchases in markets, d) a section that depending on the time slot in which you open the application, restaurants are displayed for lunch, breakfast, etc., e) options of places where you can pay online, f) an option of restaurants selected essentially to discover and finally, two sections that refer one to popular restaurants and the other to exclusive restaurants.

Regarding payments, Pedidos Ya already offers promotions that are generally for days or for purchases with credit cards from some specific banks that work with the app. You receive notifications such as: "we have a ball of promos", "ask 80% off in the second unit, activate ice cream mode ".On the other hand, the section with restaurant options where you can pay online has a legend with the description:" forget about cash, pay for your food online ", which could be put in tension with the need to add health care according to the measures promoted by the pandemic and effectively consolidate this culture of touch or click from payments and purchases from e-commerce.

Rappi as main study case gives an interesting imprint. At the time we delve into the website, we can highlight that the first thing one reads at the beginning is a search engine with the legend "Find what you need", followed by hashtags such as # ice cream; #pizza: #empanadas; #burgers. In this sense, certain types of food-related to a certain moment of pleasure are prioritized. In the center of the page, there are 3 options: restaurants, supermarkets, and pharmacies, as well as 3 indications to finish convincing the client: 1) I received your product without leaving your home, 2) a shopper selects your products with love and 3) if you don't like the condition of a product, you don't pay for it. The company offers free shipping options on purchases greater than a certain amount if you pay with a credit card; premium support and exclusive offers 24/7 for prime users, and gifts of a certain amount of money once a month in surprise sections. At the bottom of the page, you can find a message for customers who refer to the reasons why you should use Rappi as an application to order what you need: "With an increasingly busy routine, sometimes there is little time to think about the menu of the week or the dish of the day. Rappi brings together the best restaurants in your city! Find everything from quick meals to healthy alternatives. Receive your order quickly and rest assured of our guarantee of quality in delivery".

Instead, from the application a search engine is slid that asks "What do you want today?", Along with the addresses commonly used to select. Then, several options are presented to choose what you want to consume: restaurants, markets, Rappi shopping, pharmacies, kiosk, drinks, foodie boxes, pets, Rappi Travel, Rappi cash, games, and messaging services. The options of Rappi Games, live events, and Rappi Travel are grouped under the section dedicated to entertainment. There is also the possibility that you can customize your Rappi, that is, the option "made to measure", where they ask for personal data to "recommend what you better in Rappi "according to your preferences".

By regards to the means of payment and discounts, the Rappi platform offers the options of paying with Rappi and/or money in the account, options that are presented in balance format. This section allows you to observe the balance that one has in the account and a History of the transactions that were carried out from the application. From these options, one can send money, collect and deposit money. What is more important, some coupons are presented in the application as available and expired coupons, so that the consumer already knows which coupons they can or cannot use at that time.

As previously noted, according to We Are Social & Hootsuite (2020), people are using the applications in almost every aspect of our lives, from shopping, ordering food, managing our finances, buying medicines, sending money, entertaining, etc. That is why the firms that are behind these platforms offer customers the possibility of carrying out each of these daily practices through their applications. Because of this, we can highlight that the two platforms that we analyze offer the possibility of shopping; send and receive money; order food/pharmacy supplies/items and food for pets; attend live events; travel, among others. In this way, it is important to bring up that shopping has been one of the main activities carried out through mobile phones, chosen by 66% of users, together with online games, which represent the choice of 47% of users (GlobalWebIndex, 2020).

Stepping back to what the users ask for consumers, it is important to consider the report: "Commerce Flagship Report on the latest trends in Commerce", published by GlobalWebIndex (2020) where it is presented that 46% of Internet users want brands to be eco-friendly, 44% want them to take into account the opinion of consumers, 44% to be socially responsible, 37% to simplify your life and 30% to offer personalized products or specially designed for the user, and the list goes on. Following these results, delivery platforms offer the possibility of personalizing your order, offer you products made especially for each user, organize your finances, and provide all kinds of services to make life easier for users, in short: "they do things for you". It is noteworthy that they constantly notify the user about the easy use of the application, their speed, and effectiveness, and in short, they dedicate a section for the community, to receive opinions, suggestions, and/or criticisms from users, to show a certain interest in consumer's feedback. The fact is that we were able to register that both present a question at the beginning towards the client that manifests as "What do you want to ask?" and "What do you want today?" These questions give off meanings that refer to consumption as an organizer of life but are also linked to the enjoyment of the act of consuming itself. The platform thus becomes a device that has the function of enabling the customer to choose what to consume daily, continuously offering different products and services. In this sense, returning to Lipovetsky (2007), an endless search for emotional experiences and greater well-being is reproduced by and through these platforms based on the efforts to continue consuming. This hyper-consumption process cannot be understood if we do not take into account the commoditization of sensibilities that are produced from the Internet as the main vehicle for their reproduction. In such a way that it becomes interesting to investigate the sensibilities that are put into play in the delivery platforms when referring to the consumer. From the companies, the commercialization of lifestyles, tastes, pleasures, experiences, and sensations is encouraged. that these can emerge from this consumption putting the axis in certain imperatives of enjoyment and happiness. In the case of Pedidos-Ya, a: "Delivery that satisfies your senses" is offered in explicit words within the app. a section with selected restaurants to "discover", along with a description with the message: "suggestions to enjoy new experiences" and another section with "suggestions for you" where products or restaurants that match previous orders are presented. This is due to the impressive action of Artificial Intelligence on these platforms, which they analyze from the work of an algorithm. Consumers´ tastes, preferences, desires, etc. On the other hand, concerning Rappi, they offer the possibility of "personalizing your Rappi'', in the sense of "making it to your measure" so that you can, worth the redundancy, enjoy the moment of consumption in a personalized and exclusive way. Online, the need for consumers to acquire certain objects/services instantaneously is a key vector in the manifestation of platform sensibilities (citing Scribano 2019). These sensibilities, as we have already said, are organized around immediacy and manifest themselves in the vehicle of being always online where the only thing that matters is the presentification (the here and now that resides in the action). The latter will be guarantors of digital consumption mediated by a certain immediate enjoyment, which acts as a way to avoid social conflict.

In a nutshell, the digital platforms adopted some measures to contribute to safety and health measures. In this sense, based on ethnographic work, we can highlight the options and discounts related to online payments that are offered from the platforms to avoid contagion through cash and the possibility that deliverymen left orders at home doors, preventing close contact. On the other hand, if we refer to the International Work Organization's report (2020), workers were able to access courses and information on the use of the chinstrap and alcohol gel and certain recommendations for social distancing. However, in the words of the delivery drivers themselves, in the most drastic months of the spread of the virus, they suffered the constant fear of catching it and infecting others, as contact with customers continued, as well as denouncing the lack of bathrooms to be able to constantly sanitize your hands.

FINAL APPROACHES

The present book chapter aims to discuss critically the constellations of COVID-19 and its effects on digital society. The functionality of delivery platforms and their implications in the City of Buenos Aires have been placed under the critical lens of scrutiny. We base our insights on the sociology of bodies/emotions that puts in tension the current digitalization context and the times of a pandemic along with the world, from the bodies/emotions of users/consumers Considering that, in line with Scribano (2020), despite the practices of inequality, dehumanization, and discrimination that are accentuated in the pandemic context, society relies on conspicuous consumption that seeks sensory satisfaction through enjoyment and the living of new experiences, conditioning the margins of emotion/action of the subjects. We are facing an emotionalization regime of domination from our bodies.

Likewise, it was possible to observe how digital consumption through platforms is constituted as an ordering practice of daily life, and the feeling of enjoyment through the immediacy that it promotes guarantees the social order, mitigating the conflict. In this way is corroborated the existence of a system of sensibilities that assumes as a vehicle of reproduction of the digital distribution platforms, based on the imperatives of well-being-happiness-enjoyment-satisfaction that permeate the experiences of the daily events of society and helps the process of normalization.

Advances regarding information technologies, artificial intelligence, digital work, and the economy of commissions have arrived in the global south, and some effects of these processes are already manifesting in the transformations of social relations, digital work, the new politics of sensibilities, among others. As can be seen, the transformations of the world 4.0 that happen to us are not limited to the sustained increase in production, the processing of immense databases, artificial intelligence, and advances in technologies such as drones, robots, androids, etcetera; rather, these imply reconfigurations in the capitalist modes of appropriation and domination that sustain their essence in the colonization of the internal planet of human beings (sensu Melucci).

With the benefits of hindsight, future research is posed on vexed-questions which remains overlooked in the specialized literature, here some questions turn to our attention as how does the current capitalist sensibility regime manifest itself in the experiences of platform workers? What does it mean to be a delivery worker in the 21st century? What continuities and ruptures can we think of in digital work based on the pandemics that are increasing us?

These questions will be continued in future approaches.

REFERENCES

Baudrillard, J. (2009). *Consumer society. Its myths, its structures*. University of Jaén. Available at https://revistaselectronicas.ujaen.es/index.php/rae

Boragnio, A. (2020) Taste and Eating practices: between the body and the emotions. *Sapiens Research Scientific Bulletin*, *10*(2), 46-52. Recovered from https://www.srg.com.co/bcsr/index.php/bcsr/article/view/399

Dettano, A. (2019). Reading consumption from social emotions. Some routes and possible perspectives. *Text*, *1*, 1–10.

Dettano, A. & Lava, M. P. (2014). Establishing links between the consumer society, sensibilities and social policies from the global south. *Sapiens Research Scientific Bulletin*, *4*(2), 27-32.

Elias, N. (2009). *The process of civilization*. Fund for Economic Culture.

GLOBALWEBINDEX. (2020). *Commerce Flagship Report on the latest trends in Commerce*. Retrieved from https://blog.globalwebindex.com/?_ga=2.240951939.108077076.1614084071-293189393.1614084071

Hine, C. (2004). Virtual ethnography. New Technologies and Society Collection. Barcelona: Editorial UOC.

International Work Organization. (2020). *Delivery in a pandemic: work on digital delivery platforms in Argentina, technical note*. Recovered from: https://www.ilo.org/wcmsp5/groups/public/---americas/---ro-lima/---ilo-buenos_aires/documents/publication/wcms_765155.pdf

Korstanje, M. E. (2020). Passage from the Tourist Gaze to the Wicked Gaze: A Case Study on COVID-19 with Special Reference to Argentina. In *International Case Studies in the Management of Disasters*. Emerald Publishing Limited. doi:10.1108/978-1-83982-186-820201012

Li, S., & Linton, O. (2021). When will the Covid-19 pandemic peak? *Journal of Econometrics*, *220*(1), 130–157. doi:10.1016/j.jeconom.2020.07.049 PMID:33519027

Lipovesky, G. (2007). *Paradoxical happiness. Essay on society of overconsumption*. Anagrama Editorial.

Sena, D. E. A. (2020). Spinning the web of sensibilities in receiving households and not of social programs. In Social policies and emotions: survivals around state interventions. Buenos Aires: Estudios Sociológicos Editora.

Sennett, R. (1998). *The corrosion of character: The personal consequences of work in the new capitalism*. W. W. Norton & Company.

Sribano, A. (2010). First you have to know how to suffer ...!!! Towards a sociology of "waiting" as a mechanism of social support. In A. Scribano & P. Lisdero (Eds.), *Sensibilities at stake: multiple views from the social studies of the body and emotions* (pp. 169–194). CEA-CONICET E-book.

Sribano, A. (2015). *Enjoy it! An approach to the political economy of morality from consumption*. The Aleph.

Sribano, A. (2017) Neo-Colonial Religion as Current Form of the Political Economy of Morality. In Normalization, Enjoyment and Bodies/Emotions. Argentine Sensibilities. Nova Science Publishers.

Sribano, A. (2019) Trust in society 4.0. In Confidence and Politics of Sensibilities. Buenos Aires: Estudios Sociológicos Editora.

Sribano, A. (2019) Introduction: Politics of Sensibilities, Society 4.0 and Digital Labor. In Digital Labor, Society and Politics of Sensibilities. Palgrave Macmillan.

Sribano, A. (2020). The war of curves: pandemic, sensibilities, and social structuring. *Simbiótica*, *7*(1).

Sribano, A., & Lisdero, P. (2019). Digital gaze and visual experience. In Digital Labor, Society and Politics of Sensibilities. Palgrave Macmillan.

Van den Ecker, M., & Sevignani, S. (2020). Media and Communication in Digital Capitalism: Critical Perspectives. *Global Dialogue,* 10(2). Available at: HTTPS: // globaldialogue.isa-sociology.org/

We Are Social & Hootsuite. (2020). *Digital 2020. Global Digital Overview.* Retrieved from https: //wearesocial.com/digital-2020

ADDITIONAL READING

Crary, J. (1989). Spectacle, attention, counter-memory. *October, 50*, 97-107.

Crary, J. (2013). *24/7: Late capitalism and the ends of sleep*. Verso Books.

Illouz, E. (Ed.). (2017). *Emotions as commodities: Capitalism, consumption and authenticity*. Routledge. doi:10.4324/9781315210742

Luna-Zamora, R. (2010). The sociology of emotions as a disciplinary field. Interactions and social structures. In A. Scribano & P. Lisdero (Eds.), Sensibilites at stake: Multiple views from the social studies of bodies and emotions. Academic Press.

Ogle, V. (2019). Time, temporality and the history of capitalism. *Past & Present, 243*(1), 312–327. doi:10.1093/pastj/gtz014

Pace, J. (2018). The concept of digital capitalism. *Communication Theory*, *28*(3), 254–269. doi:10.1093/ct/qtx009

Rossi, U. (2017). *Cities in global capitalism*. John Wiley & Sons.

Schumpeter, J. (1942). Capitalism. *Socialism and Democracy.*

KEY TERMS AND DEFINITIONS

Digital Consumption: Social organizer's practices in 21st century society. This practice implies the production and reproduction of life, ways of experiencing, being in the world and being with others.

Digital Ethnography: Qualitative method developed with the advances of the internet.

Platform Sensibilities: Cognitive-affective social practices that occur in and through social networks as vehicles for the production and reproduction of a capitalist regime. They are characterized by being immediate in different senses.

Politics of Sensibilities: Set of cognitive-affective social practices that tend to produce, manage, and reproduce horizons of action, disposition, and cognition.

Society 4.0: Economic and social processes around the global massification of new information technologies in the 21st century.

Chapter 11
Metamorphosis of Labour in Digital Societies:
Platform Workers (Deliveries) and the Pandemic

Pedro Lisdero
CIECS-CONICET, National University of Córdoba, Argentina & National University of Villa Maria, Argentina & CIES, Argentina & University of Palermo, Argentina

ABSTRACT

In a global context of social metamorphosis, it is important to understand how and why the reconfiguration of work experiences comes about in relation to the modifications produced by the digitalisation of society. All areas of people's lives are colonised by the logic of the digital, and the different work experiences are affected. This chapter aims to explore the connections between these two critical dimensions of the social structuration process in Latin America, which have reached a superlative role in the context of the COVID-19 pandemic. In order to do that, it considers "digital labor" and particularly the work of deliveries by platforms as a paradigmatic experience that condenses the tendencies mentioned. The selected argumentative strategy proposes to contextualize the expansion of "digital labor" in the region by drawing from the analysis of secondary data, and from primary data generated through virtual ethnography oriented to capture the experiences of workers (deliveries by platforms).

DOI: 10.4018/978-1-7998-7287-0.ch011

INTRODUCTION[1]

Countless studies and applied research describe in-depth the transformation of the world of work; at least over the last twenty years. These works should not ignore the important role played by the convergence of the global and the local. Therefore, there is nothing like the isolated process in the configuration of work experience worldwide which requires further attention. Having said this, it is important to expand the current understanding of how work experiences are previously moulded by technological breakthroughs or much deeper modifications accelerated by the digitalisation of society. The digital society brings together the expansion of digital labour, with a wide-spread process of globalisation based mainly on digital consumption: the spheres of human dimension are widely colonised by the logic of the digital in which case individual behaviour (experiences) are not exceptions. The present chapter book aims to explore the intersection of digital technologies with the re-structuration of labour in Latin America; a point that takes a superlative role in the Post COVID19 context. The re-structuration of the work is gradually accompanied by the digitalisation of all human relationships. Digital labour is defined as the process that organizes work according to the delivery of platforms, emotions, experiences and tendencies according to a specific goal.

At a first glimpse, the selected argumentative strategy proposes to remark some conceptual observations while framing the expansion of digital labour in the region. In so doing, the drawing of analysis of secondary data generated through virtual ethnography is of vital importance to describe workers´ experiences. What is equally important, we look to bring together objective and subjective elements in the comprehension of a global phenomenon, from a singular perspective that incorporates the contributions that can be reconstituted from those who live these processes in a post-COVID-19 Latin America.

METAMORPHOSIS OF WORK AND DIGITALISATION: TOWARDS A FRAMEWORK FOR UNDERSTANDING DIGITAL LABOUR

At the start of a new millennium, complex societies demand reductionist viewpoints revolving around the understanding each society has about itself. What we call here the "metamorphosis" of the "world of work" and the "digitalisation" of societies constitutes two of the social processes that, undoubtedly, comprise key elements of the experience of living in the 21st century. If capitalist modernity was successful in the configuration of a global "integrated" system during the 19th and 20th centuries, it was –among others– under the condition that some more or less widespread ways of managing the availability of subjects and their productive energies be diffused. Beyond the material symmetries and cultural diversities that plagued the tensions among regions, the modern and Western notion of work associates with a set of practices that permeate day-to-day life.

The so-called "centrality of work" (Castel 1996) in Western societies, characterised in a historical context specific to the development of capitalism in the 20th century, is just the tip of the iceberg or the expression of some fundamental tendencies for these social formations, in which labour activities hold a certain unavoidable reference as the organiser of most dimensions in the lives of the subjects. However, the sense of ontological security which relates to a universal meaning of labour faces an unparalleled crisis in the second half of the last century: the decline of salary society (Castel 1996) gives workers they are stranded or adrift exposed helplessly to global risks (which are proper of risk society (Beck, 2000). Of course, this reveals the precaritization of all certainties as well as the precarious existence of work and life (Cingolani, 2014; Korstanje 2015). All these problems coexist with previous transformations connected to a new configuration of society more oriented to digital technologies which reconnect human relations. A different aspect of human emotions is being systematically digitalized and transformed because of the new capitalism. Hence, since the labour starts to adopt *other* forms and meanings, digital technologies permeate at the same time all the needs of the subjects, interposing themselves as "obligatory" mediators in their interactions. The scope of these transformations disrupts then essential categories in the understanding that the individuals have of themselves and their environment; in the same way, it re-configures the structuring of the times and spaces that characterise their experiences. The modern dichotomies that gave meaning to the organisation and definition of everyday situations, such as the division between work and leisure, between the company/factory and home, the public and the private, etc., begin to lose meaning, and the meaning of work changes faced with the expansion of phenomena such as home-working, teleworking, the overlapping between the spheres of "consumption" and "production" ("prosumer"), working on platforms, etc.

These above-noted series of practices are in some way paradigmatic of the transformations underway since they condense the impact of the aforementioned tendencies. An example of this is so-called "digital labour", understood -at least in an introductory way- as a series of openings depending on the expansion of ICT practices involving a set of "productive" relations concocted in and from digital platforms that "enhance" the "collaborative" features of interactions. The notion of "digital labour" itself has revitalised discussions around critical communication studies, but it has also been relevant to inquiries on the metamorphosis of work relationships, and even in studies of everyday life in the context of the digitalisation of societies. To begin to understand the scope of the current transformations, and to delimit the relevance of focusing on "digital labour" as a paradigmatic practice, it is necessary to introduce a series of discussions as a starting point revolving around the digitalization of the reciprocity.

"Digitalisation" and "Digital Labour"

As already stated, the digitalisation of societies seems to be a process of broad scope, which equates to a consolidation of the historical development of technologies that converge and multiply their effects on the types of social relationships. Machlup (1962) toys with the idea of the information society as the precondition to stress a new emerging social order where an increasing number of subjects are employed for information management tasks. These new jobs entail the creation of new roles based on wealth creation as well as knowledge production –mainly marked by the health system (Drucker, 1969; Bell 1973). In consonance with this, Castells (1997) amply shows that the technological phenomenon is in constant change. Regarding this, the report on "Digitalisation, trade and development" (UNCTAD 2017) by the United Nations Conference on Trade and Development states in its opening words: "The world is at the dawn of the next technological revolution. It will be multifaceted and its implications transformational (...) It will disrupt existing practices, expose incumbents to competition, change skills requirements of workers and result in job losses in some countries and sectors." (UNCTAD 2017, V)

With the benefits of hindsight, the bits come as the "materiality" of a paradigm that is born in a specific subsystem but that colonises the diverse areas of human vitality, and poses questions regarding its impact on the social formation. Originally Shannon (1948) conceives the idea of bit, a binary digit, as a peculiar way of representing information, triggering possibilities of processing whose development and magnification multiply the potential for gathering, translation, and reproduction of information. It is easy to imagine what the revolution of computerisation (an increase in the capacity to process and store information) added to this tendency, and later, the thrust that hyper-connectivity implied after the expansion of the "network of networks".

Stepping back to the same line of inquiry, for example at the societies of the 21st century whose initial tendency is materialised today in a series of technologies that bolster the digital revolution, and that includes among other relevant landmarks the development of advanced robotics (more sophisticated, agile and flexible robots), Artificial Intelligence (understood as the capability of machines to imitate human intelligence), the Internet of Things (the extension of connectivity to objects and devices, enabled –among other factors– by the reduction of costs and the extension of sensors), Cloud Computing (flexibility of access, data storage and computing resources, enabled as a result of massively enhanced processing power, data storage and higher transmission speeds); Big Data (the possibility of aggregation of large amounts of data in the Cloud); three-dimensional printing; digital payment systems; and interoperable technology systems and platforms. (UNCTAD 2017)

The truly deep-rooted way in which this tendency is expressed in society, associated with the complexity of social processes that converge in the bit, find its greatest historical development in today's societies from the qualitative and quantitative leap implied by high-speed broadband access to increasingly powerful computing and storage capacity, as well as drastically reduced costs of ICT equipment and data management. This has affected in an unprecedented (and increasing) way the most relevant activities of people in the 21st century, such as trading, education, the bureaucratic processes associated with "digital citizenship", and of course, labour.

At this point then, it is necessary to contextualise and historicise the relationship between labour-technology and capitalism, in order to understand how digitalisation is articulated with the processes of metamorphosis of labour. Thus, one of the characteristic features of the global transformations of the "world of work" is related to the reconfiguration of a set of flexible processes aimed at the expropriation and commodification of the cognitive and affective corporal energies of workers (Scribano and Lisdero 2019; Lisdero 2013). This seems to be a transversal phenomenon, which not only affects the "old" and new "occupations" but also constitutes a central element of the structuring processes of social relations. The forms from which Western modernity was accustomed to commodify the vital forces seem to find a new point of redefinition, as digitalisation of societies expands.

What is equally important, one might point out how the complex group of studies about "digital labour" has contributed to generating new questions on the characteristics and the reach of the transformations underway[2]. Beyond the important contributions that different perspectives make about the complexity of digital labour, it is interesting to note that the need to resolve the different discussions outlined is inextricably linked to the concern to redefine the broader structuration process in which the work experiences in question are inscribed ("cognitive capitalism", "platform capitalism", "sharing economy", "prosumer capitalism", among others). It is in this sense the perspective proposed here starting from the discussion about the body/emotions linked to digital labour.

This perspective seeks to establish the mediations between the vitality of bodies and emotions as an object of exploitation. It tries to inquire about the redefinition of corporality associated with the surface where digital devices/technologies are deployed, seeking the connection between these elements and the processes of accumulation and reproduction of the capitalist structures of 21st century societies.

In this sense it is interesting to note that informational labour is usually associated with the "use of the brain", so that beyond the possible combinations with digital technologies or the non-digital, this always intervenes in the process. It is perhaps at this point that it is possible to begin to rethink the definition of digital labour, questioning this naturalised relationship between brain and information. Thus, by complexing the questions and the understanding of the uses of the body beyond the Cartesian split body/mind, what is proposed here is to put as a centre of reflection the sensibilities[3] constructed as conditions and result of the interaction between body-working conditions and the expansion of digital technologies in society.

Rethinking Work in the Capitalist Context: A Perspective from the Sociology of Sensibilities

As we have been mentioning, work has been a central element in understanding the forms of social relationships. As modern capitalist society expands, the daily life of subjects finds in work an organiser of the times, spaces, and areas in which it develops. Consequently, it is not surprising that through the global processes that are associated with the "digitalisation of societies", not only is the "world of work" put into question but also more broadly the connections between "what subjects do" and "the ways in which they are related" (even beyond the "productive" areas of their lives).

Looking back at the transformations of work, a wide variety of studies from diverse disciplines since around the 1970s point out a series of transformations that affect the everyday life of work relations. Indeed, among the descriptions offered about the transformations of the "world of work", it might be easy to find a variety of perspectives unable to reach a consensus on the characteristics and consequences of these changes, or even on the limits and scope of the analytical units needed to account for them. This could be read as a sign of the high complexity of the phenomenon that goes beyond the different theoretical and epistemic focus of these perspectives (De la Garza 2000). However, a second glance reveals that the reflections about work activities are associated with a variable and heterogeneous set of problematics that arise questions about a global process of transformation, and that different authors approach as "risk society" (Beck 2000), and "late modernity" (1993), "post-industrialism" (Bell 1973), "The Information Age" (Castels 1997), among others.

In this sense, the transformations in the "world of work" call for a reconsideration of, among other things, the processes in the sphere of production of commodities in our societies, and particularly in their relation to the constitution of "the-body-of-those-who-work". This latter perspective, and the relationship between these elements (i.e. the constitution of bodies and the processes of the production of commodities), is already present in Marx's critique of capitalist society (Haber and Renault 2007; Scribano 2012). The body is thus constituted in tension with the dynamic processes implicating domination and resistance; they are neither matter infinitely malleable by norms, nor simple vessels of social interiorisations.

Thus, looking back at the relationship between the body and capitalism, it is constituted as an "indicator" of the recent history of this system since the dynamics of these social formations can be reconstructed from the forms and tensions acquired by the metabolic process from which the corporal energies are expropriated, based on the reproduction of capital (Lisdero 2013). It can be said then that the history of human work is the history of the expropriation of corporal energies. The political economy of capitalism reinvents itself hand-in-hand with the technological development centred on maximisation of the increased rates of corporal energies. Ever more parts of the human are reduced to the reproductive sphere of capitalism: emotions, affections, communicative competences, and so on.

Long gone are the days of the "end of work" ideas fashionable in the 1980s and 1990s; no one today disputes the centrality of work in today's global framework. Thus, the fundamental question today is what are the limits, experiences, possibilities, and contradictions of the new grammar generated by the "world of work" in its process of transformation. The widening scope of the exercise of the accumulation of corporal energies extends to new territories of human and natural being.

This is the right place to bring to the fore, in relation to the questions raised by these scenarios, the contributions of a sociology of bodies/emotions as central components for comprehending the sensibilities. In this sense, a quick look at these contributions accounts for a wide and diverse field of study, including the works of Le Breton and Turner, theorists from the second half of the twentieth century such as Erving Goffman (1989) or Norbert Elías (2015), or ideas by Pierre Bourdieu (1999) and Anthony Giddens (2003), among others. As a disciplinary field, some authors place the beginnings of the sociology of bodies and emotions in the work of Brian Turner (Gremilion 2005), while others consider Thomas Scheff, Arlie Hochschild, and Theodore Kemper as the real pioneers of the discipline (Bericat Alastuey 2000).

Indeed, from the perspective proposed here, the classics of sociology already raised questions about these objects of study, which played a relevant role in their thinking. In this sense, a more or less explicit concern of social theory becomes evident in a problematizing of bodies and emotions in relation to the social processes which constitute the modern social order. The emergence of the state —and a logic of violence as a defence of sovereignty and vigilance as control of difference— "imposes" a research agenda about forms of managing linked to the corporal. The new geometries of bodies emerging with the ordering of social relations required a closer look into disrupted and unproductive bodies as threats to order. This is the context for the establishment of certain connections at the time of the birth and reproduction of capitalist social relations, between what has been described as an act of expropriation of bodily energies, and the processes of management of deviant individuals through a scientific intervention upon bodies.

According to the developments made up to now, it is not difficult to imagine the possible links, or certain concurrent problems, between this way of understanding the processes of capitalist re-structuration of work and the "digitalisation of society" described above. The expansion of digital life to the most diverse areas of interaction, paradigmatically expressed in "digital labour", leads us to rethink the ways in which digital mediations re-invent the productive characteristics of bodies, among them emotions (new skills), are articulated with renewed ways of organising the productive processes, re-structure the ways of managing the margins and its control/disciplining, among other relevant dimensions.

Yet moving even further, if this framework for understanding "digital labour" constitutes a first epistemic shift to be able to comprehend the global transformations underway, a second shift in this sense would be the possibility to think the "whole from the parts", that is, to be able to contribute to a global characterisation from the unique view reflected in the ways in which these processes are expressed on the "margins": such is the case of Latin America.

In this sense, it is relevant to understand that the territorialities configured during this stage of the development of capitalism make the world map complex with new geo-political coordinates of power. Harvey (2004) observes in this regard that the collapse of spatial barriers does not lead to a loss of the meaning of space; thus, the labour transformations, despite having a global effect, do not have an impact at local level in the same way all over the world.

Seen from Latin America, González Casanova (1969) early on points out these kinds of territorial consequences for dominated countries: "The development of imperialism and colonialism transfers the impoverishment original of working classes to the dominated countries, and it weighs on the set of colonial and semi-colonial countries, and on the groups and social classes that suffer colonial exploitation" (1969-2006: 233). Coming back to this postulate, below is a general description of some edges of the phenomena conceptualised in and from Latin America.

WORK AND DIGITALISATION IN LATIN AMERICA: FROM PRECARIOUSNESS TO THE GAP

Based on the available statistical information, it is possible to describe some significant features of the process of "labour metamorphosis" and "digitisation" from the following relevant characteristics:

Precariousness: Re-Configuration of Productive Territories

In Latin America, labour statistics account for this territorialisation of the tendencies (although it must be noted there is some heterogeneity within the region). While the employment-to-population ratio (the percentage of the working-age population that is employed) is 57.3%, and thus getting closer to the global tendencies, other indicators available emphasise the structuration of risk and precariousness as extended characteristics of the work experience. Thus, unemployment (the percentage of people in the labour market who are not working) is greater than the global average, increasing in the region to 8.4%, and labour informality is more than double that for developed countries. This precarious panorama becomes more noticeable in specific subregions; likewise, significant vectors associated to sectors particularly affected by these processes open up, such as youth (those between 14 and 24 years of age) and women. In this regard, informal employment among youth is 62.6%, unemployment is nearly 20% (triple that of the adult population) and women's labour force participation continues to rise in a steady but slow process of closing gaps (it still shows 20 points of difference) (OIL 2018, 32)

This general panorama presented so far coincides with some of the trends for the region characterised from a heterogeneous and broad field of social studies about work (Antunes, et. Al 2005, Antunes 2005, Neffa 2003, De la Garza, 2000). In general, most of these investigations account for a strong re-structuration process that begins during the 1970s, marked by the advance of the precariousness of the labour experience, and that is linked to other relevant processes such as:

- The transformations in the composition of the working class. This tendency registers a heterogenisation, greater complexity and fragmentation of the-subjects-who-live-from-work; marked by phenomena such as deproletarianisation of traditional industrial work; sub-proletarianisation as a consequence of the different forms of part-time work, precarious, outsourced; the subcontracted related to informal economy and the service sector. (Antunes 2005, Antunes and Braga, 2009)
- The gradual "feminization of work" as a significant phenomenon of the new labour scenarios. (Peres and Hilbert 2009)
- Trasformations in the organisation of work, or of management processes. There is a qualitative expansion and transformation of new models of rationalisation of the productive processes, endowed with a strong discipline and linked to intensive work. Some of the characteristics observed in the different studies can be summarised in the following: flexibility of production, the appearance of a participative and multipurpose worker, the spread of teamwork, and the

transfer of responsibilities for elaboration and quality control of production, among others (Antunes 2005; Neffa 1999).

- Transformations in the workers' rights, whose characteristics can be summarised in deregulation and relaxation of the regulations that guaranteed the workers' rights. (Novick 2010).

Summing up, then, we can highlight some of the different elements presented briefly with the idea of the "pendulum" to illustrate the processes of structuration of Latin American labour realities, which oscillates on the one hand between the informal, precarious pole, far from the protections of social risks, where, besides, the vectors that configure inequalities are multiplied. On the other hand, those jobs-occupations for which, in part, the salary equation between work and social protection is detected, are not detached from the general tendencies of precariousness of life that the society assumes. In this way, Latin American societies have inequality as one of their outstanding features, where the Gini Index -which takes values between 0 (to represent the absence of inequality) and 1 (to represent the maximum inequality)- reaches an average value of 0.4675. (Peres and Hilbert 2009). This process of precariousness is associated with the logics of risk and uncertainty as outstanding common features:

(...) precarious labour is a means used by employers to transfer the risks and responsibilities to the workers. It is labour that is done in the formal and informal economy and that is characterised by variable levels and degrees of objective (legal situation) and subjective (sensation) of uncertainty and insecurity singularities. While a precarious job may have various facets, it is usually defined by the uncertainty that it entails as regards the duration of the job, the presence of several possible employers, an undercover or ambiguous work relation, the inability to enjoy social protection and the benefits that are usually associated with a job, a low salary and remarkable legal as well as practical obstacles to becoming a member of a trade union and negotiate collectively. (ILO 2012: 32)

The risks of "becoming unemployed", or falling into the multiple and iterative commercial and service activities necessary to "ignite" the urban mega-concentrations, constitute a "structural feature" of Latin American societies, associated with the destabilization that workers experience in order to plan their lives, to bad health conditions, to the inequalities due to age and gender in labour situations, to the discouragement of taking part in trade unions or, in general, in processes of societal cooperation. The "feeling of helplessness and fear" (ILO 2012: 46) take a central place in the experience of workers.

Digital Gap: The Body as a Territory of Digitalisation

At this point it is relevant to move forward by clarifying certain issues regarding the specificities adopted by the digital gap for Latin America, since its impact on digital labour is associated with the productive possibilities of the bodies as a territory or substratum of four basic IT operations (acquisition, storage, transmission and computing).

In this direction, it is curious how at the same time, digital gaps remain and new ones are emerging (UNCTAD 2017). Reports by the "Economic Commission for Latin America and the Caribbean" (CEPAL 2003[a] in Peres and Hilbert 2009, 47-48) postulate a double sense of the regional gap. First, there is an international gap, in which while several studies show tendencies to improve the access -for example to the Internet-, relevant differences regarding quality of the connections -in this case- compared to the OECD countries are emphasised.

On the other hand, the "internal gap" is associated with other economic and social inequalities (income, education, gender, ethnic group, and geographic location) that act as factors that explain the grouping and differences of the tendencies presented. A relevant issue in this sense, appears by distinguishing between "access and connectivity" and "effective use of digital tools". Thus, for example, the spread of cell phones seemed to close the access gap in comparison to the still restrictive access to a land line. However, the data that illustrate the "use" of ICTs for the region confirm that it is associated mainly with information searches and communication, staying away thus far from being used extensively to make online transactions. This example is just an aspect of the qualitative revolution of the gaps. It overlaps in the region with other pre-existing inequalities. In this way, Peres and Hilbert observe that in order to explain the differences in the uses of ICTs, factors such as income and educational inequalities become relevant (Peres and Hilbert 2009, 60).

Re-writing the global geometry in the bodies of the workers according to their digital knowledge, re-invents their productive capacities in a basic sense: it creates dispositions regarding the ways of relating to the environment, to others and to themselves. Thus, the incubation environment of digital skills in developed countries contrasts to the social landscapes characterised by inequality in the region, configuring a hybrid "social body" where characteristics of the "cyborgs" and "slaves" coincide at the same time (Dyer-Witheford 2015). The polarisation assumed by the labour force at a global level is expressed in paradoxical ways in the region: not only does information labour grow at the same time as precarious manual workers in industrial and service sectors grow, but besides, there emerge "hybridations" linking, for example, a subsistence worker with the forms and elements that characterise digital life.

In this context, the characteristics that digital labour acquires intensify the tendency to heterogenisation of those-who-live-to-work (Antunes 2005). The new proletarian condition that transforms and permeates "silently" the occupational structure, reconfiguring the workers' bodies and daily routines, from the "voluntary imposition" of digital mediations, and with them, new forms of control, of mechanisms from which the emergence of new precarious identities is consented in the production chains (Antunes and Braga 2009), among other relevant effects.

THE EXPERIENCE OF WORKING WITH BITS: CORPOREALITY AND DISPOSITIONS

If the data presented so far shows an image of the social structures that configure the conditions and expansion of digital labour in Latin America, it is also necessary to question the experience of the subjects themselves, who are the protagonists of these realities, in order to be able complement the framework for understanding these trends. In other words, exploring the workers' experiences implies transcending the mere characterisation of the material conditions for digital production, or even the description of "digital workers" that can be drawn from there, in order to construct a view that allows us to gather greater information about how the singularities (hybrid practices) are expressed in these territories. The experiences of the subjects themselves enable and inform us about the mediations that configure living and working in the territories of "precariousness" and the "digital gap". With this objective in mind, some fragments of records of virtual ethnography that have digital workers as the protagonists[4] are shared in this section. In this sense, an analytical axis opens up faced with the chance to reflect about the body as substratum of the transformations underway and it is connected to the question about the set of dispositions that compromise digital workers. Jobs such as deliverymen working for digital platforms have spread over recent years in Latin America, and are a clear example of this set of dispositions. Exploring digital communities such as Facebook groups, where these subjects exchange their opinions, it is possible to find the shared sensation that "to work it is only necessary to have a bike and to be eager". One of the leading companies in the sector promotes the search for work as a deliveryman in the following way:

Deliverymen. Work only the number of hours you want. Be your own boss. Flexible timetable, competitive income and the chance to know your city working outdoors. Register and be one of our collaborators in less than 24hs. (https://glovoapp.com/)

Beyond the skills required by the labour market crossed by the digitalisation process, the capacities to "be productive" (at work and in life) are inscribed within the frame of the accepted ways that society has in order to administer and manage the energies of their bodies (including those which will become "digital labour"). This "politics of the bodies" (Scribano, 2019) presupposes specific and diverse biographical paths, but mainly implies a singular state of the distributions of the social energies available to be metabolized from the digital "machines". Thus, the productivity of a multiplicity of activities and situations finds a "tailored" mediation enabled by the capacity that digital media have to identify, define and process the labour demand/offer in a very tight period of time, and to match in a synchronised way the subjects' disposition with the companies' offer.

The workers' experience confirms that managing timing is precisely the key to the meaning of the action, and the nucleus of the value associated to the interaction between ICTs –body– and labour. Here follows a transcription of a fragment of a discussion held by a group of workers in a Facebook community ("Glovers Argentina (deliverymen for Glovo)"):

(Worker 1) Germán doesn't have medical insurance, or Labour Risk Insurance; he doesn't have paid holidays or a bonus. He doesn't contribute to his retirement plan. Germán believes he is helping the country to move forward by pedalling and carrying a rucksack with the logo of a company that denies any employment relationship with him. Germán is a dumb-ass, don't be like German.

(Worker 2) (…) ... if we were registered employees, we would earn ARS18000 per month... they even make a discount for the retirement plan.......go and ask today's elderly people if the pension is good... Medical insurance: we have it. Holidays: we can take them whenever we want and not when a company says so ... We earn between ARS 35 and 60 thousand and we don't want trade unions... Even if it hurts them, we don't want to be registered employees (…)

(…)

(Worker 4) it is called working as a freelancer or independently. Obviously if you don't work, you won't be paid. The more you work, the more you'll earn. Also, at least in my case, I do other things to have more income, even when I'm sick at home" [the worker posts a link to access a platform to work as a transcriber of audio files to text] (May 29, 2019)

The translation of vitality to "productive digital energy" is a process that starts before being materialized in a piece of software, or mediatised by a digital sensor. It is not only the wonderful capacity that the digital panopticon possesses to connect offer and demand that is the basis of production of value of these digital chains. The information contained in the bit, in the algorithm that enables this singularity for the despotic cooperation chain of capital, is first and foremost the energy of those bodies made available to be processed by that algorithm.

The process itself constitutes a specific form of social body, and as such, it is the result of social and historical relations that are embodied as special dispositions for action. If twenty years ago, losing your job in Argentina meant a risk of being excluded, not only from the labour market but also from social life, "losing your job" in the digitalised society, as it is evidenced in the argument, is just an anecdote, even an opportunity to "flow" in the multiple opportunities that digital labour offers.

Hello, I lost my job. Can you help me find someone who can advise me to work with glovo? I have a bike. (May 23, 2019)

The feelings of rejection from legally regulated, traditional work, and the prerogatives that were historically associated with it (paid holidays, a bonus, and social security) do not constitute a desirable horizon for these subjects, but on the contrary, they come as a solid embodied conviction of what the subjects feel is more convenient for them; a conviction on which precisely the beginning of the value chain of these companies is supported.

In this direction, the most diverse experiences of digital workers account for how the ICTs "constitute an extension of their own body", that is, they work because they rely on the social support that was historically constructed so that these tools are effective as a social relation of the production of digital connection. Even though the tools look different (it is not the same to work a Headset in a Call Centre as to work with an app on a cell phone as a deliveryman, or on a computer at home transcribing interviews), and the digital devices materialise as "external" to the individuals (a cell phone, a GPS, etc.), the digital dispositions constitute true body marks, performative landmarks of vitality, that contribute to constructing the necessary mediation between ICTs and productive processes.

The construction of value, and the appraisal processes associated with it, then take on a more extended character: the intimacy of the mechanisms that operate as a cog necessary for the functioning of the chain of digital production increases the flexibility of the sensitive terminals that are processed by the wonderful capacity of the sensors to catch the creative forces of this society. Although "labour informality" and "unequal distribution access" to digital skills constitute global tendencies, inhabiting the Latin American "gap" supposes "re-inventing oneself" as productive beyond the renewed unequal conditions. The feeling of "doing it on my own", being an "entrepreneur", being "autonomous" (which means more than a hiring condition), "defending myself" (rejecting the affiliation options), are all components of an accepted way of seeing oneself (identity), the context (naturalization of the digital labour conditions) and "others" (who are lost and uniformed behind the bit: the colleagues, the State, etc.). In the region where digitalisation came to add another vector to inequalities, the body is the testimony of the sedimentations that these processes produce, and it is the place where each new vector that glorifies social distances is inscribed (with the "other jobs", with the "other territories").

COVID-19 PANDEMIC: IMAGES AND QUESTIONS

In 2002, the rapid spread of COVID-19 in Latin America was accompanied by a series of measures taken by the various governments, which sought - among other consequences - to reduce the mobility of people and slow down the spread of the virus. In the face of the successive "lock downs", delivery workers played a key role in the life of the cities: in many places they were the ones who made possible the provision of food and other important elements in the moments of greatest "confinement" of the population.

Although it is not the aim here to provide a detailed description of the impact of the pandemic on the activity, it is interesting to extract at least two "images" from the virtual ethnographic register that allow us to observe some "messages"[5] about the structuring processes of digital work in our societies.

a- "Neither heroes nor heroines": a message about the fragility of bodies and the limits of systemic compatibility linked to the re-production of work "in the cities".

In the Argentinean context, the moment of greatest restrictions on the mobility of the population coincided with the popularisation of a collective action whereby various individuals, at certain times and coordinated by social networks, carried out collective applause to recognise the work of doctors in "the fight against the pandemic". Within the framework of these actions, which are repeated in various parts of the world, a discourse is structured that assumes a war metaphor ("combat"), and proposes an emotional reward for those "heroes" who "put their bodies" on the "front line of combat". In this context, some groups of delivery workers publicly denounce the precariousness and the risk they take, making certain demands linked to the claim for protective elements (alcohol gel, etc.), but also for monetary "compensation", disputing the meaning of the logic of war by "denying the heroic":

"Neither heroes nor heroines" (Communiqué App Sindical)

"Platform workers are among those exempted from lock down from the coronavirus. If we don't go out on the streets to work, we don't earn a penny and for most of us this is the only source of income." (Twitter AppSyndical 23 March, 2020)

The first "message" that can be extracted refers directly to what has been developed in the previous sections: the successive processes of precariousness of those sectors that constitute "the real motor of cities": the millions of people who live from work (Antunes, 2005), who go beyond the traditional categories of "informal", and who have suffered "in the flesh" the successive downward trends in both working conditions and living conditions. To deny the idea of the "hero", and to recognise the extortion that "if I don't go out on the streets I don't get paid" (a situation that is often disguised in the charitable garb that usually accompanies the categories of "self-employed" or "entrepreneur") is at the same time to show that the limit of the re-production of this "logic" of work is in the body itself.

A paradoxical question emerges at this point when we recognise that the protest reveals the tip of the iceberg of a problem built on the historical tendencies that have been revealed up to this point. The COVID pandemic does not significantly affect working conditions in the sector, but rather dramatically reveals the precariousness in which these people carry out their work. However, it is paradoxical to reflect that, at the same time, this situation seems to "prophesy" about the re-productive limits that "we can expect" for "those who give their blood" in future work contexts increasingly affected by digitalisation. In this last sense, we could ask: are we facing a new predatory phase of the productive energies of our societies?

b- "Indispensable mechanisms": the necessary movement so that nobody moves.

The second image that we would like to highlight here arises from an expressive element that the protagonists of the aforementioned protest put into play, and from which we could recover the premise that "the form is the message". In this sense, it is interesting to focus on the image that accompanies the abovementioned publication (see Image 1): an empty city, and a young platform delivery worker at the centre of the scene...

In the context of the Pandemic, the frenzy of the "daily movements" necessary to make the city run stops: workers stop going to the factories, employees in ministries and all offices migrate to "teleworking", housewives stay at home, and so on. Despite all this, the flow of commodity circulation does not stop, and the previously "invisible" subjects (perhaps the representatives of the millions of informal, unrecognised workers) remain at the centre of the scene: they become "essential". This is precisely the category with which the "Decree of Necessity and Urgency"

Figure 1. Deliveries as an "essential" activity
Source: (Twitter AppSindical 23 March, 2020)

(DNU) that dictates the "Preventive and Obligatory Isolation" (lockdown) enables a group of workers to continue their activities.

It is possible to interpret here a second "message" linked to the social proximities and distances on which our societies are structured. Against any representation of the modern city, invaded by the massive flows of daily interaction (subjects going to work, to school, to the shops), the times and spaces that the pandemic shows how the "essential" is (pornographically) the circulation of merchandise. At the same time, it shows that public spaces (far from being empty) are charged by dense digital flows, which become central in the re-structuring of the meanings of practices: workers are thus expressions of the zeros and ones of the digital flow that construct the new grammars of actions. Once again: here the pandemic shows nothing new (deliveries could not have embodied an essential activity, could not have played the role of "connectors" in an "enclosed society" if that society had not been traversed by the processes of structuring digital life that has been unfolding especially since this new century). However, this is also a question for the structuring processes to come, in terms of to what extent can social life be captured by the logic of the digital? What are the limits of the "digital situations" of interaction, what is the range of possibilities for the reconversion of "the public" within the framework of digital geometrics and grammars of action?

The questions raised by the images that have emerged from the pandemic require not only a rethinking of the confluent tendencies addressed here but above all a re-examination of the theoretical tools from which the complex social reality can be made comprehensible.

CONCLUSION: METAMORPHOSIS OF LABOUR IN DIGITAL SOCIETY. A THEORETICAL PROPOSAL

If, as it has been proposed, the history of Western modernity can be written then as the continuous effort to reinvent how the vital energies of the bodies transmute in capitalist social relations (accumulation), and the "digitalisation of societies" is strongly connected to the expansion of the market's ability to integrate "new skills" in a global system of productive cooperation as it has never been seen before, it is not trivial to outline a framework for comprehending the convergence of these processes based on a question about broader continuity/social changes.

In a germinal way, we can then define the "*metamorphosis of labour in digital societies*" from three relevant axes: firstly, recovering the idea of *structuration processes* by Giddens (2003) as a frame from which to examine the relationship between continuity and change at the moment of analysing the tendencies underway. From this perspective, the logic of structuration of digital life does not constitute a global metaphysical presence or a state of suggestion of individual effects. It cannot be reduced to the characterisation of the material conditions supported by digital infrastructure either, or to the mere subjectivity linked to the development of digital jobs. In a state of tension with these elements, the "digitalisation of society" can be understood as a *logic of structuration* of a series of social practices that take place in a specific context, which must be taken into account at the moment of understanding this process as an undetermined whole.

It is within this frame, understanding the constitution of digital societies implies re-thinking the successive industrial revolutions as historical processes that precede and that configure the current conditions as "structural properties" (Giddens 2003), that they turn out to be effective in the configuration of certain "inertias" of the practices in situated and specific contexts. Thus, the overwhelming presence of this logic in today's societies is related to the structuration of global times/spaces, which can be thought of as the probability of occurrence of many of the practices described in this research paper, and that cross in different ways modern borders to define the distances between leisure and work, between productive and unproductive, between material and immaterial, and between "developed" and "developing" territories.

Reducing this structuration logic, as well as "digital labour", to the conditions of these specific practices, to the use of digital devices, or the result of the production of information (or to any stage of its treatment) constitutes a simplification that is largely anchored in epistemological obstacles to understanding the scope of the qualitative transformations of societies. Precisely, the second issue to recover from the notion of "metamorphosis of labour in digital societies" has to do with the difficulty of adopting dynamic concepts to understand social change. There is certain recurrence between the theories that -without approaching the intention of knowledge about what many times appears as a fragmentary puzzle of experiences- link different aspects of "digitalisation" ("digital labour", "digital economy", etc.) with the emergence-rising of "new social formations" ("Information Society", "Knowledge Society", "Post-Fordism", etc.). What is proposed is to recover the idea of metamorphosis/mutation (Castel 1996) to think about in what sense we are faced with a capitalist society where despite the "collapse" of the social forms that constructed the certainties of everyday life, certain logics are still preserved, specifically, the re-invention of the mechanisms (in this case digital ones) from which the energies of the subjects are metabolized in re-productive social relations.

Last but not least, the third key point for understanding this structuration logic has to do with the expansion of a politics of sensibilities. Understanding the correct ways of being and feeling of the subjects that are the protagonists of digital labour in the different global strata are the keystone for understanding its expansion and effectiveness. The subtraction of vitality from bodies is linked to a form of the political economy of morality (Scribano 2012) founded on competence, which becomes a moral law regulating practices framed in a set of relations based on the sale of the workforce, under conditions such that the-subjects-who-work (Antunes 2005) are driven to the limits of their corporal reproduction in developing countries, as happens with millions of workers in Latin America.

REFERENCES

Antunes, R. (2005). *Os sentidos do trabalho: ensaio sobre a afirmação e a negação do trabalho*. Boitempo.

Antunes, R., & Braga, R. (2009). *Infoproletários. Degradaçao real do trabalho virtual*. Boitempo.

Beck, U. (2000). *Un nuevo mundo feliz. Precariedad del trabajo en la era de la globalización*. Paidós.

Bell, D. (1973). *The Coming of Post-industrial Society: A Venture of Social Forecasting*. Basic Books.

Bericat Alastuey, E. (2000). La Sociología de la emoción y la emoción en la Sociología. *Papers*, *62*, 145–176. doi:10.5565/rev/papers/v62n0.1070

Bourdieu, P. (1999). *Meditaciones pascalianas*. Anagrama.

Castel, R. (1996). *La metamorfosis de la cuestión social. Una crónica del salariado*. Paidos.

Castells, M. (1997). The Information Age: Economy, Society, and Culture. In *The Rise of the Network Society*. Blackwell Publishers Inc.

Cingolani, P. (2014). La idea de precariedad en la sociología francesa. *RELACES*, *16*, 48–55.

De la Garza, E. (2000). *Tratado latinoamericano de sociología del trabajo*. Fondo de Cultura Económica.

De Sena, A., & Lidero, P. (2015). Etnografía Virtual: aportes para su discusión y diseño. In A. De Sena (Ed.), *Caminos cualitativos. Aportes para la investigación en ciencias sociales* (pp. 71–100). CICCUS / Imago Mundi.

Drucker, P. (1969). *The Age of Discontinuity: Guidelines to our Changing Society*. Harper & Row.

Dyer-Witheford, N. (2015). *Cyber-proletariat. Global Labour in the Digital Vortex*. Pluto Press. doi:10.2307/j.ctt183p1zg

Elías, N. (1993). *El proceso de la civilización*. Fondo de Cultura Económico.

Giddens, A. (1993). *Consecuencias de la Modernidad*. Alinaza.

Giddens, A. (2003). *La Constitución de la Sociedad*. Amorrortu.

Goffman, E. (1989). *La presentación de la persona en la vida cotidiana*. Amorrortu.

González Casanova, P. (2006). *Sociología de la Explotación*. CLACSO. (Original work published 1969)

Gremilion, H. (2005). The cultural politics of body size. *Annual Review of Anthropology*.

Haber, S., & Renault, E. (2007). Un Análisis Marxista de los cuerpos? In S. Haber (Ed.), *Cuerpos dominados, cuerpos en ruptura*. Nueva Visión.

Harvey, D. (2004). *El nuevo imperialismo*. Akal.

International Labour Organization – ILO. (2012). *From precarious work to decent work. Policies and regulations to combat precarious employment.* International Labour Organization.

International Telecommunication Union - ITU. (2018). *Measuring the Information Society Report. 2018* (Vol. 1). International Telecommunication Union.

Korstanje, M. E. (2015). *A difficult World: examining the roots of capitalism.* Nova Science publisher.

Lisdero, P. (2013). La guerra silenciosa en el mundo de los Calls Centers. *Papeles del CEIC*, *80*, 1–31.

Machlup, F. (1962). *The Production and Distribution of Knowledge in the United States*. Princeton University Press.

Neffa, J. C. (2003). *El Trabajo Humano. Contribuciones al estudio de una valor que permanece*. Lumen Hvmanitas.

Novick, M. (2010). Trabajo y contextos en el desarrollo productivo argentino. In *Convivir con la incertidumbre. Aproximaciones a la flexibilización y precarización del trabajo en la Argentina.* CICCUS.

Peres, W., & Hilbert, M. (Eds.). (2009). *La sociedad de la información en América Latina y el Caribe. Desarrollo de las tecnologías para el desarrollo. Santiango de Chile: Comisión Económica para América Latina y el Caribe*. CEPAL.

Scribano, A. (2012). Sociología de los cuerpos/emociones. RELACES-Revista Latinoamericana de Estudios sobre Cuerpos. *Emociones y Sociedad*, *10*, 93–113.

Scribano, A. (2019). Introduction: Politics of Sensibilities, Society 4.0 and Digital Labour. In *Scribano, A. and Lisdero, P. (2019) Digital Labour, Society and the Politics of Sensibilities. Gewerbestrasse* (pp. 1–17). Palgrave – MacMillan., doi:10.1007/978-3-030-12306-2

Scribano, A., & Lisdero, P. (2019). *Digital Labour, Society and the Politics of Sensibilities. Gewerbestrasse*. Palgrave – MacMillan., doi:10.1007/978-3-030-12306-2

Shannon, C. (1948). *A mathematical theory of communication. Bell System Technical Journal*, 27 . doi:10.1002/j.1538-7305.1948.tb01338.x

United Nations Conference on Trade and Development – UNCTAD. (2017). *Information Economy Report 2017. Digitalization, Trade and Development*. Geneva: United Nations.

KEY TERMS AND DEFINITIONS

COVID-19: A new virus (known as SARSCOv2) originated in Wuhan, China. This virus rapidly expanded to the four continents constituting as one of the worst pandemics of the 21st century.

Digital Society: The term signals to a society mainly marked by the monopoly and distribution of digital technologies.

Division of Labour: It is a process known as the division of skills, specialization and roles to optimize the economic system and labour market. The notion of specialization is a homologous term.

Economy: Is an area of the production, distribution and exchange that often administers or deals with scarce goods.

Work Precaritization: It denotes the precarious existence of some groups or individuals who are systematically exploited by a unilaterally imposed system or by a selective group of persons. The term associates to job unemployment or political instability.

ENDNOTES

1 A preliminary version of some parts of this work was discussed in the framework of the 2019 Area Studies Forum at Tsinghua University, China, 10-12 July 2019.

2 An extended version of this analysis can be read in Scribano and Lisdero, 2019.

3 A sociology of sensibilities is proposed as a particular approach to a sociology of bodies / emotions: social agents know the world through their bodies. Perceptions, sensations and emotions build a tripod that allows us to understand where the sensibilities are founded and how they are associated with socially constructed forms of the "politics of bodies" (the strategies that a society accepts in order to offer a response to the social availability of individuals), and the "politics of emotions" (the coorect way of felling). Both politics of body and politics of emotions contribute to think the regulation and make bearable the conditions under which social order is produced and reproduced. (Scribano, 2019, 14-15)

4 About the definition of Virtual Ethnography can be seen De Sena and Lisdero (2015). Other publications based on the analysis of virtual ethnography records related to the use made of the technique are available in Scribano and Lisdero, 2019. The records presented are the result of a virtual ethnography work that has been carried out since March 2019, which is part of several research

projects funded by the National University of Rafaela, the National University of Villa María, and the National Council for Scientific and Technical Research (Consejo Nacional de Investigaciones Científicas y Técnicas). Although these investigations have particular objectives, they all involve the possibility of recording the activity of workers and their organisations in various social networks. Here we present some fragments of discussions drawn mainly from Facebook and Twitter.

5 We use here the idea of "messages" as used by Melucci (1994) in the analysis of collective action: that is, we seek to interpret the meanings of action as communicating the processes by which society is re-constructed.

Compilation of References

Adamiak, C., Szyda, B., Dubownik, A., & Garcia-Alvarez, D. (2019). Airbnb Offer in Spain-Spatial Analysis of the Pattern and Determinants of Its Distribution. *ISPRS International Journal of Geo-Information, 8*(3), 155. Advance online publication. doi:10.3390/ijgi8030155

Ahuja, R., & Lyons, R. C. (2017). *The Silent Treatment: LGBT Discrimination in the Sharing Economy*. Trinity College.

Airbnb. (2014). *New Study: Airbnb Community Contributes C$54.6 million to Montreal Economy.* https://www.airbnb.com.tr/press/news/new-study-airbnb-community-contributes-c-54-6-million-to-montreal-economy

Airbnb. (2020). *$250M to support hosts impacted by cancellations.* https://www.airbnb.com.au/resources/hostinghomes/a/250m-to-support-hosts-impacted-by-cancellations-165

Akay, B. (2014). *Impact of Competition Determinants in Car Rental Sector on Operation Performance: A Research in Tourism Destinations* (PhD thesis). Sakarya University Institute of Social Sciences, Turkey.

Akbar, Y. H., & Tracogna, A. (2018). The sharing economy and the future of the hotel industry: Transaction cost theory and platform economics. *Intenatioal. Journal of Hospitality Managament, 71*, 91–101. doi:10.1016/j.ijhm.2017.12.004

Amujo, O. C., & Otubanjo, O. (2012). Leveraging rebranding of 'unattractive' nation brands to stimulate post-disaster tourism. *Tourist Studies, 12*(1), 87–105. doi:10.1177/1468797612444196

Antunes, R. (2005). *Os sentidos do trabalho: ensaio sobre a afirmação e a negação do trabalho.* Boitempo.

Antunes, R., & Braga, R. (2009). *Infoproletários. Degradaçao real do trabalho virtual.* Boitempo.

Arantes, O. B. F., Vainer, C., & Maricato, E. (2002). *A cidade do pensamento único: desmanchando consensos*. Academic Press.

Aristábal García, D. M. (2020). Estudios sociales sobre el consumo. Trayectorias disciplinares de un campo de estudio en construcción [Social Studies on Consumption: disciplinary routes in a field on underway construction]. *Revista de Estudios Sociales, 71*(71), 87–99. doi:10.7440/res71.2020.07

Armano, E., Murgia, A., & Teli, M. (2017). Plataform capitalism e confini del lavoro negli spazi digitali [Platform capitalism and the boundaries of work in digital spaces]. *Mimesis*.

Armstrong, A., & Stedman, R. C. (2013). Culture clash and second home ownership in the U.S. northern forest. *Rural Sociology*, *78*(3), 318–345. doi:10.1111/ruso.12010

Asgary, A., Rezvani, M. R., & Mehregan, N. (2011). Local residents' preferences for second home tourism development policies: A choice experiment analysis. *Tourismos*, *6*, 31–51.

Ashworth, G. J., & Tunbridge, J. E. (2000). *The tourist-historic city*. Routledge. doi:10.4324/9780080519470

Augé, M. (1992). *Non-lieux. Introduction à une anthropologie de la submodernité*. Le Seuil.

Augé, M. (1995). *Non-lieux*. Verso.

Augé, M. (1996). Paris and the ethnography of the contemporary world. In M. Sheringham (Ed.), *Parisian Fields* (pp. 175–181). Reaktion Books.

Aurélien, A., Daudigeosb, T., & Pinksec, J. (2017). Promises and paradoxes of the sharing economy: An organizing framework. *Technological Forecasting and Social Change*, *125*, 1–10. doi:10.1016/j.techfore.2017.07.006

Avis Budget Group. (2017). *Avis Budget Group, 2016 Annual Report.* Retrieved from https://www.annualreports.com/HostedData/AnnualReportArchive/a/NYSE_CAR_2016.pdf

Barata-Salgueiro, T. (2017). Alojamentos turísticos em Lisboa. *Scripta Nova, 21*.

Bardhi, F., & Eckhardt, G. M. (2012). Access-Based Consumption: The Case of Car Sharing. *The Journal of Consumer Research*, *39*(4), 881–898. doi:10.1086/666376

Barke, M. (2007). Second homes in Spain: An analysis of change at the provincal level 1981-2001. *Geography (Sheffield, England)*, *9*(3), 195–207. doi:10.1080/00167487.2007.12094200

Barker, M., Page, S. J., & Meyer, D. (2003). Urban visitor perceptions of safety during a special event. *Journal of Travel Research*, *41*(4), 355–361. doi:10.1177/0047287503041004004

Batool, M., Ghulam, H., Hayat, H. M., Naeem, M. Z., Ejaz, A., Imran, Z. A., Spulbar, C., Birau, R., & Tiberiu, T. H. (2020). *How COVID-19 has shaken the sharing economy? An analysis using Google trends data.* Economic Research-Ekonomska Istraživanja. doi:10.1080/1331677X.2020.1863830

Baudrillard, J. (2009). *Consumer society. Its myths, its structures*. University of Jaén. Available at https://revistaselectronicas.ujaen.es/index.php/rae

Bauman, Z. (2017). Tourists and vagabonds: Or, living in postmodern times. In Identity and social change. Routledge.

Bauwens, M., & Kostakis, V. (2014). From the Communism of Capital to Capital for the Commons: Towards an Open Co-operativism. *tripleC: Communication, Capitalism & Critique. Journal for a Global Sustainable Information Society*, *12*(1), 356–361.

Bayburs, Ö. K. (2020, July 13). Turizmde doğa dostu proje: Hobbit evleri [An environmentally friendly project in tourism: Hobbit Homes]. *Turizm Günlüğü.* https://www.turizmgunlugu.com

Beck, U. (2000). *Un nuevo mundo feliz. Precariedad del trabajo en la era de la globalización.* Paidós.

Bell, D. (1973). *The Coming of Post-industrial Society: A Venture of Social Forecasting*. Basic Books.

Bell, D. (2012). Hospitality is society. *Hospitality & Society*, *1*(2), 137–152. doi:10.1386/hosp.1.2.137_1

Bennett, B. K., & Bradbury, M. E. (2003). Capitalizing non-cancelable operating leases. *Journal of International Financial Management & Accounting*, *14*(2), 101–114. doi:10.1111/1467-646X.00091

Bericat Alastuey, E. (2000). La Sociología de la emoción y la emoción en la Sociología. *Papers*, *62*, 145–176. doi:10.5565/rev/papers/v62n0.1070

Bestor, A. (2013). *What you should know about renting a car in Europe in 2013.* Retrieved from www.gemut.com

Bianchi, R. (2006). Tourism and the globalisation of fear: Analysing the politics of risk and (in) security in global travel. *Tourism and Hospitality Research*, *7*(1), 64–74. doi:10.1057/palgrave.thr.6050028

Bieger, T., Beritelli, P., & Weinert, R. (2007). Understanding second home owners who do not rent: Insights on the proprietors of self-catered accommodation. *International Journal of Hospitality Management*, *26*(2), 263–276. doi:10.1016/j.ijhm.2006.10.011

Blake, A., & Sinclair, M. T. (2003). Tourism crisis management: US response to September 11. *Annals of Tourism Research*, *30*(4), 813–832. doi:10.1016/S0160-7383(03)00056-2

Blanco, S. (2020, July 20). *COVID-19 Means More Packages, and a New Game: Delivery-Driver Tag*. https://www.caranddriver.com/news/a33366841/delivery-driver-tag-game-coronavirus/

Böcker, L., & Meelen, T. (2017). Sharing for people, planet or profit? Analysing motivations for intended sharing economy participation. *Environmental Innovation and Societal Transitions*, *23*, 28–39. doi:10.1016/j.eist.2016.09.004

Bocock, R. (2008). *Consumption.* Routledge. doi:10.4324/9780203131091

Bonoma, V. T. (1984). *Managing marketing: text, cases and readings*. Macmillan Inc.

Boragnio, A. (2018). Disposable commensality: strategies for the selection of meals in the office. *Eureka: Social and Humanities*, *5*(2018), 16-28.

Boragnio, A. (2020) Taste and Eating practices: between the body and the emotions. *Sapiens Research Scientific Bulletin, 10*(2), 46-52. Recovered from https://www.srg.com.co/bcsr/index.php/bcsr/article/view/399

Boragnio, A. (2020c). Las emociones del comer cotidiano: mujeres entre el asco, la culpa y la vergüenza [The emotions of everyday eating: women between disgust, guilt and shame]. *Polis, Revista Latinoamericana, 55*, 56-70. https://www.polis.ulagos.cl/index.php/polis/article/view/1444/2613

Boragnio, A. (Ed.). (2020b). Etnografía virtual: un acercamiento a las sensibilidades desde el siglo XXI [Virtual ethnography: an approach to sensitivities from the 21st century]. In *Documentos del trabajo del CIES*. Buenos Aires: Estudios Sociológicos Editora. http://estudiosociologicos.org/portal/etnografia-virtual-un-acercamiento-a-las-sensibilidades-desde-el-siglo-xxi/

Boragnio, A., & Sordini, V. (2019). Gustos y prácticas alimentarias de mujeres empleadas de oficinas públicas y mujeres destinatarias de programas alimentarios en Argentina [Food tastes and practices of women employees of public offices and women recipients of food programs in Argentina]. *Aposta. Revista de Ciencias Sociales, 81*, 69-86.

Boragnio, A. (2020a). Producción de subjetividades en el autocuidado alimentario cotidiano [Production of subjectivities in daily food self-care]. In R. Del Monaco & M. E. Epele (Eds.), *Tecnologías y Técnicas en Investigaciones Socioantropológicas de la Salud*. Estudios Sociológicos Editora.

Boragnio, A. (2021). Sensibilities of eating inside: Emotions and Food Practices in a time of pandemic. In *Emotionality of COVID19. Now and After: The War Against a Virus. Nova Scientia.*

Botsman, R., & Rogers, R. (2010). *What's mine is yours: The rise of collaborative consumption*. HarperBusiness.

Bourdieu, P. (1979). *La Distinction. Critique sociale du jugement*. Les Éditions de Minuit.

Bourdieu, P. (1999). *Meditaciones pascalianas*. Anagrama.

Bremser, K., Alonso-Almeida, M. M., & Llach, J. (2018). Strategic alternatives for tourism companies to overcome times of crisis. *Service Business, 12*(2), 229–251. doi:10.100711628-017-0344-7

Brouder, P., Teoh, S., Salazar, N. B., Mostafanezhad, M., Pung, J. M., Lapointe, D., Higgins Desbiolles, F., Haywood, M., Hall, C. M., & Clausen, H. B. (2020). Reflections and discussions: Tourism matters in the new normal post COVID-19. *Tourism Geographies, 22*(3), 1–12. doi:10.1080/14616688.2020.1770325

Bruera, M. (2006). *La Argentina Fermentada. Vino, alimentación y cultura* [The Argentina Fermented. Wine, food and culture]. Paidós.

Buhalis, D., Andreu, L., & Gnoth, J. (2020). The dark side of the sharing economy: Balancing value co-creation and value co-destruction. *Psychology and Marketing, 37*(5), 689–704. doi:10.1002/mar.21344

Business Wire. (2013). *Global Car Rental Market Report: 2013.* Retrieved from ww.researchandmarkets.com

Caerols Mateo, R., Tapia Frade, A., & Carretero Soto, A. (2013). Instagram, la imagen como soporte de discurso comunicativo participado [Instagram, the image as a support for participated communicative discourse]. *Revista de Comunicación Vivat Academia, 15*(124), 68-78.

Câmara Municipal de Lisboa. (2018). *Visão Estratégica para o Ordenamento Urbanístico do Turismo em Lisboa.* https://www.am-lisboa.pt/documentos/1540997812O0jII7ak1Wa23QC2.pdf

Campbell, M., McNair, H., Mackay, M., & Perkins, H. C. (2019). Disrupting the regional housing market: Airbnb in New Zealand. *Regional Studies, Regional Science, 6*(1), 139–142. doi:10.1080/21681376.2019.1588156

Car Rental Business. (2008). *Global strategic business report global industry analysts.* Retrieved from www.researchandmarkets.com/reports

Carr, A. (2020). COVID-19, indigenous peoples and tourism: A view from New Zealand. *Tourism Geographies*, 1–12.

Carter, L. Barger, T. & Kuczynski, I. (1996). *Leasing in emerging markets.* World Bank IFC Lessons of Experience Series 3.

Castells, M. (1989). *The informational city: Information technology, economic restructuring, and the urban-regional process.* Blackwell.

Castells, M. (1997). The Information Age: Economy, Society, and Culture. In *The Rise of the Network Society.* Blackwell Publishers Inc.

Castel, R. (1996). *La metamorfosis de la cuestión social. Una crónica del salariado.* Paidos.

Cengizoğlu, F. P., & Özyılmaz, H. (2016). Adapting the secondary houses to the primary houses: Mersin sample. *Planning (Chicago, Ill.), 26*, 219–233. doi:10.14744/planlama.2016.83702

Ceylan, S., & Somuncu, M. (2020). Using for recreational aims of second homes in tourism areas: Case of Pelitköy (Burhaniye/Balıkesir). *Turkish Journal of Geographical Sciences, 18*, 28–56.

Chang, C. L., McAleer, M., & Ramos, V. (2020). A charter for sustainable tourism after COVID-19. *Sustainability, 12*(9), 3671. doi:10.3390u12093671

Cheer, J. M., Milano, C., & Novelli, M. (2019). Tourism and community resilience in the Anthropocene: Accentuating temporal overtourism. *Journal of Sustainable Tourism, 27*(4), 554–572. doi:10.1080/09669582.2019.1578363

Chen, G., Cheng, M., Deborah Edward, D., & Xu, L. (2021). COVID-19 pandemic exposes the vulnerability of the sharing economy: A novel accounting framework. *Journal of Sustainable Tourism*, 1–18. doi:10.1080/09669582.2020.1868484

Cherry, M. (2011). A taxonomy of virtual work. *Georgia Law Review (Athens, Ga.), 45*(4), 954–1009.

Cingolani, P. (2014). La idea de precariedad en la sociología francesa. *RELACES*, *16*, 48–55.

Cockayne, D. G. (2016). Sharing and neoliberal discourse: The economic function of sharing in the digital on-demand economy. *Geoforum*, *77*, 73–82. doi:10.1016/j.geoforum.2016.10.005

Comaroff, J. L., & Comaroff, J. (2009). *Ethnicity, Inc.* University of Chicago Press. doi:10.7208/chicago/9780226114736.001.0001

Condevaux, A., Djament-Tran, G., & Gravari-Barbas, M. (2016). *El antes y el después del turismo. Evolución de los lugares y papel de los actores del turismo «fuera de lo común». Análisis bibliográfico. Via Tourism Review*. doi:10.4000/viatourism.414

Contino, R. M. (2002). *The complete equipment-leasing handbook*. AMACOM American Management Association.

Coppock, J. T. (1977). *Second homes.: Curse or blessing?* Pergamon Press.

Crossley, É. (2020). Ecological grief generates desire for environmental healing in tourism after COVID-19. *Tourism Geographies*, *22*(3), 1–10. doi:10.1080/14616688.2020.1759133

Culture and Tourism Ministry. (2019). *Torism statistics*. Ministry of Culture and Tourism General Directorate of Investment and Enterprises.

Czarnecki, A., & Frenkel, I. (2014). Counting the invisible second home in polish statistical data collections. *Journal of Policy Research in Tourism, Leisure & Events*. Advance online publication. doi:10.1080/19407963.2014.935784

Dalir, S., Mahamadaminov, A., & Olya, H. G. T. (2020). *Airbnb and taxation: Developing a seasonal tax system. Tourism Economics*. . doi:10.1177/1354816620904894

De la Garza, E. (2000). *Tratado latinoamericano de sociología del trabajo*. Fondo de Cultura Económica.

De Sena, A., & Lidero, P. (2015). Etnografía Virtual: aportes para su discusión y diseño. In A. De Sena (Ed.), *Caminos cualitativos. Aportes para la investigación en ciencias sociales* (pp. 71–100). CICCUS / Imago Mundi.

De Sena, A., & Lisdero, P. (2015). Etnografía virtual: Aportes para su discusión y diseño [Virtual Ethnography: Contributions for its discussion and design]. In *Caminos cualitativos. Aportes para la investigación en ciencias sociales*. CICCUS.

De Sena, A., & Scribano, A. (2020). *Social Policies and Emotions. A look from the global South*. Palgrave Macmillan. doi:10.1007/978-3-030-34739-0

Deller, S. C., Marcouiller, D. W., & Green, G. P. (1997). Recreational housing and local governmentfinance. *Annals of Tourism Research*, *24*(3), 687–705. doi:10.1016/S0160-7383(97)00025-X

Derrida, J. & Dufourmantelle. (2000). *Of Hospitality*. Stanford University Press.

Dettano, A. & Lava, M. P. (2014). Establishing links between the consumer society, sensibilities and social policies from the global south. *Sapiens Research Scientific Bulletin*, *4*(2), 27-32.

Dettano, A. (2020). Introducción. Contorneando los relieves del consumo: una topografía posible del Siglo XXI [Introduction. Contouring the reliefs of consumption: a possible topography of the 21st century]. In Topografías del consumo. Ciudad Autónoma de Buenos Aires: Estudios Sociológicos Editora.

Dettano, A. (2019). Leyendo al consumo desde las emociones sociales. Algunos recorridos y perspectivas posibles [Reading consumption from social emotions. Some possible routes and perspectives]. *Antropología Experimental*, (19), 2019.

Dettano, A. (2019). Reading consumption from social emotions. Some routes and possible perspectives. *Text*, *1*, 1–10.

Dias, J. A., Correia, A., & Lopez, F. J. M. (2015). The meaning of rental second homes and places: The owners' perspectives. *Tourism Geographies*, *17*(2), 244–261. doi:10.1080/14616688.2014.959992

DIGITAL 2020. (2020). *Global Digital Overview: essential insights into how people around the world use the internet, mobile devices, social medirá, and ecommerce*. Author.

Dijist, M., Lanzendorf, M., Barendregt, A., & Smit, L. (2005). Second homes in Germany and the Netherlands: Ownership and travel impact explained. *Tijdschrift voor Economische en Sociale Geografie*, *96*(2), 139–152. doi:10.1111/j.1467-9663.2005.00446.x

DiNatale, S., Lewis, R., & Parker, R. (2018). Short-term rentals in small cities in Oregon: Impacts and regulations. *Land Use Policy*, *79*, 407–423. doi:10.1016/j.landusepol.2018.08.023

Dodds, R., & Butler, R. (2019). The phenomena of overtourism: A review. *International Journal of Tourism Cities*.

Domínguez Figaredo, D. (2007). Sobre la intención de la etnografía virtual [About the intention of virtual ethnography]. *Revista Electrónica Teoría de la Educación. Educación y Cultura en la Sociedad de la Información*, *8*(1).

Drucker, P. (1969). *The Age of Discontinuity: Guidelines to our Changing Society*. Harper & Row.

Duke, J. C., Hsieh, S. J., & Su, Y. (2009). Operating and synthetic leases: Exploiting financial benefits in the post-enron era. *Advances in Accounting, Incorporating. Advances in International Accounting*, *25*(1), 28–39. doi:10.1016/j.adiac.2009.03.001

Dyer-Witheford, N. (2015). *Cyber-proletariat. Global Labour in the Digital Vortex*. Pluto Press. doi:10.2307/j.ctt183p1zg

Edelman, B. G., Luca, M., & Svirsky, D. (2016). *Racial discrimination in the sharing economy: Evidence from a field experiment.* Harvard Business School Working Paper 16-069. Retrieved from https://papers.ssrn.com/abstract=2701902

Ekiz, E. H., Bavik, A., & Arasli, H. (2009). RENTQUAL: A new measurement scale for car rental services. *Tourism An International Interdisciplinary Journal*, *57*(2), 135–153.

El Comercio. (2020). https://www.cace.org.ar/noticias-el-comercio-electronico-crecio-84-en-abril

Elías, N. (1993). *El proceso de la civilización*. Fondo de Cultura Económico.

Elias, N. (2009). *The process of civilization*. Fund for Economic Culture.

Emekli, G. (2014). Importance of tourism geography for researching second homes and the development of second homes in Turkey. *Aegean Geographical Journal*, *23*, 25–42.

Enderson, J. C. (2007). *Tourism crisis: causes, consequences and management*. Elsevier Publishing. doi:10.4324/9780080466033

Entidade Regional de Turismo da Região de Lisboa. (2019). *Strategic tourism plan for the Lisboa region*. Author.

Eringa, K. (2019). Ladies and Gentlemen serving ladies and Gentlemen. In B. Rowson & C. Lashley (Eds.), *Experiencing hospitality* (pp. 229–246). Nova Science Publishers.

EUROFOUND. (2020a). *Labour market change. COVID-19: Policy responses across Europe*. Publications Office of the European Union.

EUROFOUND. (2020b). *Living, working and COVID-19*. Publications Office of the European Union.

European Commission. (2016). *The use of collaborative platforms*. Flash Eurobarometer 438.

Ezzell, J. R., & Vora, P. P. (2001). Leasing versus purchasing: Direct evidence on a corporation's motivations for leasing and consequences of leasing. *The Quarterly Review of Economics and Finance*, *41*(1), 33–47. doi:10.1016/S1062-9769(00)00060-0

Faracce Macia, C. (2020). Políticas sociales y consumo en la Sociedad 4.0 [Social policies and consumption in Society 4.0]. In A. Dettano (Ed.), *Topografías del consumo*. Estudios Sociológicos Editora.

Fesharaki, P. (1996). *Rural geography*. Islamic Azad University Press.

Fink, A., & Reiners, T. (2006). Modeling and solving the short-term car rental logistics problem. *Logistics and Transportation Review*, *42*(4), 272–292. doi:10.1016/j.tre.2004.10.003

Fisher, E., & Fuchs, C. (2015). *Reconsidering Value and Labour in the Digital Age*. Palgrave-Macmillan. doi:10.1057/9781137478573

Fleischer, A., & Tchetchik, A. (2015). Does rural tourism benefit from agriculture*? Tourism Management*, *26*(4), 493–528. doi:10.1016/j.tourman.2003.10.003

Floyd, M. F., & Pennington-Gray, L. (2004). Profiling risk perceptions of tourists. *Annals of Tourism Research*, *31*(4), 1051–1054. doi:10.1016/j.annals.2004.03.011

Fuchs, G., & Reichel, A. (2006). Tourist destination risk perception: The case of Israel. *Journal of Hospitality & Leisure Marketing*, *14*(2), 83–108. doi:10.1300/J150v14n02_06

Gallego, I., & Font, X. (2020). Changes in air passenger demand as a result of the COVID-19 crisis: Using Big Data to inform tourism policy. *Journal of Sustainable Tourism*, •••, 1–20. do i:10.1080/09669582.2020.1773476

Gallent, N., Mace, A., & Tewdwr-Jones, M. (2005). *Second homes: European perspectives and UK policies*. Publishing Limited.

Galvani, A., Lew, A. A., & Perez, M. S. (2020). COVID-19 is expanding global consciousness and the sustainability of travel and tourism. *Tourism Geographies*, *22*(3), 1–10. doi:10.1080/1 4616688.2020.1760924

Ganapatia, S., & Reddick, C. G. (2018). Prospects and challenges of sharing economy for the public sector. *Government Information Quarterly*, *35*(1), 77–87. doi:10.1016/j.giq.2018.01.001

Gandini, A. (2016). *The reputation economy: Understanding knowledge work in digital society*. Palgrave Macmillan. doi:10.1057/978-1-137-56107-7

Gençler, G. (2012). *Beyaz Filo Oto Kiralama A.Ş. 01.01.2012-30.09.2012 Faaliyet Raporu*. Retrieved from www.beyazfilo.com

George, R. (2010). Visitor perceptions of crime-safety and attitudes towards risk: The case of Table Mountain National Park, Cape Town. *Tourism Management*, *31*(6), 806–815. doi:10.1016/j.tourman.2009.08.011

George, S. K. (2009). Hospitality as openness to the other: Levinas, Derrida and the Indian hospitality ethos. *Journal of Human Values*, *15*(1), 29–47. doi:10.1177/097168580901500103

Geraghty, M. K., & Johnson, E. (1997). Revenue Management Saves National Car Rental. *Interfaces*, *27*(1), 107–128. doi:10.1287/inte.27.1.107

Gezer, Ö., & Çiçek, B. (2011). Binek Oto Kiralamalarında Vergi Uygulamaları. *Mali Çözüm Dergisi*, *11*(4), 161–176.

Giddens, A. (1993). *Consecuencias de la Modernidad*. Alinaza.

Giddens, A. (2003). *La Constitución de la Sociedad*. Amorrortu.

Gil, J., & Sequera, J. (2018). Expansión de la ciudad turística y nuevas resistencias. El caso de Airbnb en Madrid. *Empiria. Revista de Metodología de Ciencias Sociales*, *41*(41), 15–32. doi:10.5944/empiria.41.2018.22602

Glaesser, D. (2003). *Crisis management in the tourism industry*. Butterworth-Heinemann Publications.

GLOBALWEBINDEX. (2020). *Commerce Flagship Report on the latest trends in Commerce*. Retrieved from https://blog.globalwebindex.com/?_ga=2.240951939.108077076.1614084071-293189393.1614084071

Goffman, E. (1989). *La presentación de la persona en la vida cotidiana*. Amorrortu.

González Casanova, P. (2006). *Sociología de la Explotación*. CLACSO. (Original work published 1969)

Goodwin, H. (2017). *The challenge of overtourism*. Responsible Tourism Partnership.

Gossling, S., & Michael Hall, C. (2019). Sharing versus collaborative economy: How to align ICT developments and the SDGs in tourism? *Journal of Sustainable Tourism*, *27*(1), 74–96. doi:10.1080/09669582.2018.1560455

Gössling, S., Scott, D., & Hall, C. M. (2020). Pandemics, tourism and global change: A rapid assessment of COVID-19. *Journal of Sustainable Tourism*, *29*(1), 1–20. doi:10.1080/09669582.2020.1758708

Graham, M., Hjorth, I., & Lehdonvirta, V. (2017). Digital labour and development: Impacts of global digital labour platforms and the gig economy on worker livelihoods. *Transfer: European Review of Labour and Research*, *23*(2), 135–162. doi:10.1177/1024258916687250 PMID:28781494

GreenwoodB.WattalS. (2015). *Show Me The Way To Go Home: An Empirical Investigation of Ride Sharing and Alcohol Related Motor Vehicle Homicide*. Fox School of Business Research Paper 15-054. http://ssrn.com/abstract=2557612 doi:10.2139srn.2557612

Gremilion, H. (2005). The cultural politics of body size. *Annual Review of Anthropology*.

Gretzel, U., Fuchs, M., Baggio, R., Hoepken, W., Law, R., Neidhardt, J., ... Xiang, Z. (2020). e-Tourism beyond COVID-19: A call for transformative research. *Information Technology & Tourism*, 1.

Guttentag, D. A., & Smith, S. L. J. (2017). Assessing Airbnb as a disruptive innovation relative to hotels: Substitution and comparative performance expectations. *International Journal of Hospitality Management*, *64*, 1–10. doi:10.1016/j.ijhm.2017.02.003

Haber, S., & Renault, E. (2007). Un Análisis Marxista de los cuerpos? In S. Haber (Ed.), *Cuerpos dominados, cuerpos en ruptura*. Nueva Visión.

Hall, C. M. & Muller, D. (2004). *Tourism, Mobility and Second homes: Between elite landscape and common ground.* Channel View.

Hall, C. M. (2014). Second home tourism: An International review. *Tourism Review International*, *18*(3), 115–135. Advance online publication. doi:10.3727/154427214X14101901317039

Hall, C. M., Williams, A. M., & Lew, A. A. (2004). *Tourism: Conceptualizations, institutions, and issues. In A companion to tourism*. Blackwell Publishing.

Hao, F., Xiao, Q., & Chon, K. (2020). COVID-19 and China's hotel industry: Impacts, a disaster management framework, and post-pandemic agenda. *International Journal of Hospitality Management*, *90*, 102636. doi:10.1016/j.ijhm.2020.102636 PMID:32834356

Harvey, D. (2004). *El nuevo imperialismo*. Akal.

Hearn, A. (2010). Structuring feeling: Web 2.0, online ranking and rating, and the digital "reputation "economy". *Ephemera, 10*(3/4), 421–438.

Higgins-Desbiolles, F. (2020). Socialising tourism for social and ecological justice after COVID-19. *Tourism Geographies, 22*(3), 1–14. doi:10.1080/14616688.2020.1757748

Higgins-Desbiolles, F., Carnicelli, S., Krolikowski, C., Wijesinghe, G., & Boluk, K. (2019). Degrowing tourism: Rethinking tourism. *Journal of Sustainable Tourism, 0*(0), 1–19. doi:10.1080/09669582.2019.1601732

Hiltunen, M. J., Pitkanen, K., Vepsalainen, M., & Hall, C. M. (2013). Second home tourism in finland: current trends and eco-social impacts. In Z. Roca (Ed.), *Second homes in Europe: from lifestyle to policy ıssues* (pp. 165–198). Ashgate.

Hine, C. (2004). Etnografía virtual [Virtual Ethnography]. In Colección Nuevas Tecnologías y Sociedad. Barcelona: Editorial UOC.

Hine, C. (2004). Virtual ethnography. New Technologies and Society Collection. Barcelona: Editorial UOC.

Hoggart, K., & Buller, H. (1995). British home owners and housing change in rural France. *Housing Studies, 10*(2), 179–198. doi:10.1080/02673039508720816

Hong, S., & Lee, S. S. (2018). Adaptive governance and decentralization: Evidence from regulation of the sharing economy in multi-level governance. *Government Information Quarterly, 35*(2), 299–305. doi:10.1016/j.giq.2017.08.002

Hossain, M. (2021). The effect of the Covid-19 on sharing economy activities. *Journal of Cleaner Production, 280*, 124782. doi:10.1016/j.jclepro.2020.124782 PMID:33106734

Hottola, P. (2014). Somewhat empty meeting grounds: Travelers in South India. *Annals of Tourism Research, 44*, 270–282. doi:10.1016/j.annals.2013.10.007

Huws, U. (2015). *A review on the future of work: Online labour exchanges, or 'crowdsourcing': Implications for occupational safety and health*. European Agency for Safety and Health at Work.

İçöz, O. (2003). *Travel agencies and tour operators management.* Turhan Publisher.

IFC. (2005). *Leasing in development: lessons from emerging economies*. International Finance Corporation.

IFC. (2006). *Leasing handbook, international finance corporation.* World Bank Group.

INDEC. (2020a). https://www.indec.gob.ar/uploads/informesdeprensa/super_04_20FDF3CFC833.pdf

INDEC. (2020b). https://www.indec.gob.ar/uploads/informesdeprensa/super_05_202A09BABB1B.pdf

INDEC. (2020c). https://www.indec.gob.ar/uploads/informesdeprensa/super_09_20DDB84A2C4B.pdf

Innerarity, D. (2017). *Ethics of hospitality*. Taylor & Francis. doi:10.4324/9781315618241

International Labour Organization – ILO. (2012). *From precarious work to decent work. Policies and regulations to combat precarious employment*. International Labour Organization.

International Telecommunication Union - ITU. (2018). *Measuring the Information Society Report. 2018* (Vol. 1). International Telecommunication Union.

International Work Organization. (2020). *Delivery in a pandemic: work on digital delivery platforms in Argentina, technical note*. Recovered from: https://www.ilo.org/wcmsp5/groups/public/---americas/---ro-lima/---ilo-buenos_aires/documents/publication/wcms_765155.pdf

ISOC. (2009). www.isoc.org

Jaakson, R. (1986). Second-home domestic tourism. *Annals of Tourism Research*, *13*(3), 367–391. doi:10.1016/0160-7383(86)90026-5

Jamal, T., & Budke, C. (2020). Tourism in a world with pandemics. *Journal of Tourism Futures*, *6*(2), 181–188.

Jang, S., Tang, C., & Chen, M. (2008). Financing behaviors of hotel companies. *International Journal of Hospitality Management*, *27*, 478–487. doi:10.1016/j.ijhm.2007.08.010

Jonas, A., Mansfeld, Y., Paz, S., & Potasman, I. (2011). Determinants of health risk perception among low-risk-taking tourists traveling to developing countries. *Journal of Travel Research*, *50*(1), 87–99. doi:10.1177/0047287509355323

Jorge, C. G. (2017). *Economia partilhada e consumo colaborativo com quem? Como a presença do Airbnb afeta os preços dos imóveis residenciais em Lisboa e no Rio de Janeiro*. Academic Press.

Judd, D. R. S., & Fainstein, S. S. (Eds.). (1999). *The tourist city*. Yale University Press.

Kadıoğlu, Y. (1990). *Use of second homes in domestic and international tourism* (Unpublished master's thesis). B. Ü, İstanbul.

Kaiser, B. (2003). Life worlds of EU immigrants in Turkey. In E. Zeybekoğlu & B. Johanson (Eds.), Migration and Labour in Europe: views from Turkey and Sweden. Academic Press.

Kalyankar, M. D., & Patil, P. (2020). Impact of Covid-19 pandemic on the tourism sector. *UGC Care Journal*, *31*, 611–617.

KANTAR. CACE. (2020). https://cace.org.ar/uploads/estudios/estudiomidterm-2020.pdf

Karney, R., & Semonovitch, K. (2011). At the threshold: foreigners, strangers and Others. In Phenomenologies of the Strangers. Fordham University Press. doi:10.5422/fordham/9780823234615.003.0001

Kesenci, Ç. A. (2010). *Araç kiralama sektörünün gelişimi ve ülke ekonomilerine etkileri. In Tüm Oto Kiralama Kuruluşları Derneği*. TOKKDER.

Keshavarznia, N., Sarvar, R., & Mahdavi, M. (2013). Environmental Impact of Second Home Development on Damash Village in Gilan Province Iran. *International Journal of Engineering and Advanced Technology*, *3*, 181–184.

Kısa, P. (1998). *Facade, mass and outdoor formation in second residential architecture* (Unpublished master's thesis). Trakya University, Edirne.

Kisi, N. (2015). The Reflections of Sharing Economy in the Transportation Sector: Uber Sample. *Journal of International Management and Social Researches*, *5*(10), 57–68.

Knox, A. (2008). Gender desegregation and equal employment opportunities in Australian luxury hotels: Are we there yet? *Asia Pacific Journal of Human Resources*, *46*(2), 153–172. doi:10.1177/1038411108091756.

Knox, A. (2011). Upstairs, downstairs: An analysis of low paid work in Australian hotels. *Labour & Industry*, *21*(3), 573–594. doi:10.1080/10301763.2011.10669421

Koens, K., Postma, A., & Papp, B. (2018). Is Overtourism Overused? Understanding the Impact of Tourism in a City Context. *Sustainability*, *10*(12), 4384. doi:10.3390u10124384

Koh, J. H., & Jang, S. (2009). Determinants of using operating lease in the hotel industry. *International Journal of Hospitality Management*, *28*(4), 638–640. doi:10.1016/j.ijhm.2009.03.002

Komppula, R., Reijonenen, H., & Timonen, T. (2008). Vacation home owners' willingness to lease through an intermediary: a case study in two finnish ski resorts. In P. Keller & T. Bieger (Eds.), *Real estate and destination development in tourism* (pp. 285–300). Erich Schmidt Verlag.

Koopman, C., Mitchell, M. D., & Thierer, A. D. (2015). The sharing economy and consumer protection regulation: The case for policy change. *The Journal of Business, Entrepreneurship & The Law*, *8*(2).

Korstanje, M. (2012). Reconsidering cultural tourism: An anthropologist's perspective. *Journal of Heritage Tourism*, *7*(2), 179–184. doi:10.1080/1743873X.2011.639883

Korstanje, M. E. (2011). Rent-a-car industry: A case study in Argentina. *Tourismos*, *6*(1), 1–15.

Korstanje, M. E. (2015). *A difficult World: examining the roots of capitalism*. Nova Science publisher.

Korstanje, M. E. (2017). *Mobilities Paradox: a critical analysis*. Edward Elgar.

Korstanje, M. E. (2017). *Terrorism, Tourism and the End of Hospitality in the'West*. Springer.

Korstanje, M. E. (2018). *The mobilities paradox: a critical analysis*. Edward Elgar Publishing. doi:10.4337/9781788113311

Korstanje, M. E. (2020). Passage from the Tourist Gaze to the Wicked Gaze: A Case Study on COVID-19 with Special Reference to Argentina. In *International Case Studies in the Management of Disasters*. Emerald Publishing Limited. doi:10.1108/978-1-83982-186-820201012

Korstanje, M. E., & George, B. P. (2020). Education as a Strategy to Tackle Over Tourism for Overtourism and Inclusive Sustainability in the Twenty-First Century. In *Overtourism* (pp. 341–359). Springer. doi:10.1007/978-3-030-42458-9_18

Kozak, M., & Duman, T. (2011). Reviving second homes in tourism sectör: The case of Muğla-Datça Province. *Journal of Doğuş University*, *12*, 226–242.

Lapointe, D. (2020). Reconnecting tourism after COVID-19: The paradox of alterity in tourism areas. *Tourism Geographies*, *22*(3), 633–638. doi:10.1080/14616688.2020.1762115

Larsson, L., & Müller, D. K. (2019). Coping with second home tourism: Responses and strategies of private and public service providers in western Sweden. *Current Issues in Tourism*, *22*(16), 1958–1974. doi:10.1080/13683500.2017.1411339

Lashley, C. (2015). Hospitality and Hospitableness. *Research in Hospitality Management*, *5*(1), 1–7. doi:10.1080/22243534.2015.11828322

Lashley, C. (2019). Towards a Theoretical understanding of hospitality. In B. Rowson & C. Lashley (Eds.), *Experiencing hospitality* (pp. 1–24). Nova Science Publishers.

Lava, M. (2012) Des-mitificando el dicho popular: "sobre el gusto no hay nada escrito" [Demystifying the popular saying: "about taste there is nothing written"]. In Las tramas del sentir. Ensayos desde una sociología de los cuerpos y las emociones. Buenos Aires: Estudios Sociológicos Editora.

Laws, E., Prideaux, B., & Chon, K. S. (Eds.). (2007). *Crisis management in tourism*. Cabi. doi:10.1079/9781845930479.0000

Lepp, A., & Gibson, H. (2008). Sensation seeking and tourism: Tourist role, perception of risk and destination choice. *Tourism Management*, *29*(4), 740–750. doi:10.1016/j.tourman.2007.08.002

Li, Z., Hong, Y., & Zhang, Z. (2016). Do ride-sharing services affect traffic congestion? An empirical study of Uber entry. SSRN *Electronic Journal*. Retrieved from https://ssrn.com/abstract=2838043

Lima, V. (2019). Towards an understanding of the regional impact of Airbnb in Ireland. *Regional Studies, Regional Science*, *6*(1), 78–91. doi:10.1080/21681376.2018.1562366

Lipkina, O. (2013). Motives for Russian second home ownership in Finland. *Scandinavian Journal of Hospitality and Tourism*, *13*(4), 299–316. doi:10.1080/15022250.2013.863039

Lipovesky, G. (2007). *Paradoxical happiness. Essay on society of overconsumption*. Anagrama Editorial.

Li, S., & Linton, O. (2021). When will the Covid-19 pandemic peak? *Journal of Econometrics*, *220*(1), 130–157. doi:10.1016/j.jeconom.2020.07.049 PMID:33519027

Lisdero, P. (2013). La guerra silenciosa en el mundo de los Calls Centers. *Papeles del CEIC*, *80*, 1–31.

Li, Z., & Tao, F. (2010). On determining optimal fleet size and vehicle transfer policy for a car rental company. *Computers & Operations Research Journal*, *37*(2), 341–350.

Ljungdahl, S. (1938). Sommar-Stockholm. *Ymer*, *58*, 218–242.

Lugosi, P. (2014). Hospitality and organizations: Enchantment, entrenchment and reconfiguration. *Hospitality & Society*, *4*(1), 75–92. doi:10.1386/hosp.4.1.75_7

Lynch, E. (2020, September 24). Making work fit for workers after Covid-19. *Social Europe*. https://www.socialeurope.eu/making-work-fit-for-workers-after-covid-19

Lynch, P., Molz, G. J., Mcinthosh, A., Lugosi, P., & Lashley, C. (2011). Theorizing hospitality. *Hospitality & Society*, *1*(1), 3–24. doi:10.1386/hosp.1.1.3_2

MacCannell, D. (1976). *The tourist: A new theory of the leisure class*. University of California Press.

MacCannell, D. (1992). *Empty meeting grounds: The tourist papers*. Psychology Press.

Machlup, F. (1962). *The Production and Distribution of Knowledge in the United States*. Princeton University Press.

Mair, J., Ritchie, B. W., & Walters, G. (2016). Towards a research agenda for post-disaster and post-crisis recovery strategies for tourist destinations: A narrative review. *Current Issues in Tourism*, *19*(1), 1–26. doi:10.1080/13683500.2014.932758

Manisa, K. (2007). *İkinci konutların turizm sektöründe yeniden kullanılabilmesine ilişkin bir model önerisi* [A model proposal for reuse of second homes in the tourism sector] (Unpublished Doctoral Thesis). Yıldız Tecnical University, İstanbul.

Mao, C., Ding, C., & Lee, H. (2010). Post-SARS tourist arrival recovery patterns: An analysis based on a catastrophe theory. *Tourism Management*, *31*(6), 855–861. doi:10.1016/j.tourman.2009.09.003 PMID:32287733

Marjavaara, R., & Müller, D. K. (2007). The development of second homes assessed property values in Sweden 1991-20021. *Scandinavian Journal of Hospitality and Tourism*, *7*(3), 202–222. doi:10.1080/15022250601160305

Martin, R. J. (1998). *Professional management of housekeeping operations*. John Wiley and Sons.

Martins, M. M. (2018). *Tourism Planning and Tourismphobia: An Analysis of the Strategic Tourism Plan of Barcelona 2010-2015*. Academic Press.

Maswera, T., Dawson, R., & Edwards, J. (2008). E-commerce adoption of travel and tourism organizations South Africa, Kenya, Zimbabwe and Uganda. *Telematics and Informatics*, *25*(3), 187–200.

Matteucci, X., Lund-Durlacher, D., & Beyer, M. (2008). The socio-economic and environmental impact of second home tourism: the sounth pacific coast of nicaragua example. In P. Keller & T. Bieger (Eds.), *Real estate and destination development in tourism* (pp. 149–164). Erich Schmidt Verlag.

Matyas, C., Srinivasan, S., Cahyanto, I., Thapa, B., Pennington-Gray, L., & Villegas, J. (2011). Risk perception and evacuation decisions of Florida tourists under hurricane threats: A stated preference analysis. *Natural Hazards*, *59*(2), 871–890. doi:10.100711069-011-9801-0

Mayes, D. G., & Nicholas, C. S. (1988). *The Economic Impact of Leasing*. Macmillan Press. doi:10.1007/978-1-349-09523-0

McKercher, B., & Chon, K. (2004). The over-reaction to SARS and the collapse of Asian tourism. *Annals of Tourism Research*, *31*(3), 716–719. doi:10.1016/j.annals.2003.11.002 PMID:32572281

Meil, P., & Kirov, V. (2017). *Policy Implications of Virtual Work*. Palgrave – Macmillan. doi:10.1007/978-3-319-52057-5

Mercado de Trabajo. (2020). https://www.indec.gob.ar/uploads/informesdeprensa/mercado_trabajo_eph_2trim20929E519161.pdf

Miles, L., & Shipway, R. (2020). Exploring the COVID-19 pandemic as a catalyst for stimulating future research agendas for managing crises and disasters at international sport events. *Event Management*, *24*(4), 537–552. doi:10.3727/152599519X15506259856688

Milli Eğitim Bakanlığı (MEB). (2006). *Konaklama ve Seyahat Hizmetleri Rezervasyon Sistemleri*. Mesleki Eğitim ve Öğretim Sisteminin Güçlendirilmesi Projesi.

Minifie, J., & Wiltshire, T. (2016). *Peer-to-peer pressure: policy for the sharing economy. Report*. Grattan Institute.

Mirani, S. Z., & Farahani, B. M. (2015). Second homes tourism and sustainable rural developmen in all around the world. *International Journal of Leisure and Tourism Marketing*, *4*(3/4), 176–188. doi:10.1504/IJLTM.2015.072076

Mollett, A., Moran, D., & Dunleavy, P. (2011). *Using Twitter in university research, teaching and impact activities. Impact of social sciences: maximizing the impact of academic research*. LSE Public Policy Group.

Molz, J. G. (2013). Social Networking Technologies and the Moral Economy of Alternative Tourism: The Case of Couchsurfing.org. *Annals of Tourism Research*, *43*, 210–230. doi:10.1016/j.annals.2013.08.001

Monterrubio, J. C. (2010). Short-term economic impacts of influenza A (H1N1) and government reaction on the Mexican tourism industry: An analysis of the media. *International Journal of Tourism Policy*, *3*(1), 1–15. doi:10.1504/IJTP.2010.031599

Morrison, A., & O'Gorman, K. (2008). Hospitality studies and hospitality management: A symbiotic relationship. *International Journal of Hospitality Management*, *27*(2), 214–221. doi:10.1016/j.ijhm.2007.07.028

Müller, D. K. (1999). *German second home owners in the Swedish countryside: on the internationalization of the leisure space* (Unpublished Doctoral Thesis). Umea University, Sweden.

Müller, D. K., Hall, C. M., & Keen, D. (2004). Second home tourism impact, planning and management. In C. M. Hall & D. K. Müller (Eds.), *Tourism, mobility and second homes: between elite landscape and common ground* (pp. 15–35). Channel View Publications. doi:10.21832/9781873150825-004

Müller, D. K., & Hoogendoom, G. (2013). Second homes: Curse of blessing? A review 36 years later. *Scandinavian Journal of Hospitality and Tourism*, *13*(4), 353–369. doi:10.1080/15022250.2013.860306

Neffa, J. C. (2003). *El Trabajo Humano. Contribuciones al estudio de una valor que permanece.* Lumen Hvmanitas.

Nichols, J. (2011). *Hospitality among the Romans. In The Oxford Handbook of Social Relations in the Roman World.* Oxford University Press.

Nofre, J., Giordano, E., Eldridge, A., Martins, J. C., & Sequera, J. (2018). Tourism, nightlife and planning: challenges and opportunities for community liveability in La Barceloneta. *Tourism Geographies*, *20*(3), 377–396. doi:10.1080/14616688.2017.1375972

Novelli, M., Burgess, L. G., Jones, A., & Ritchie, B. W. (2018). 'No Ebola… still doomed'– The Ebola-induced tourism crisis. *Annals of Tourism Research*, *70*, 76–87. doi:10.1016/j.annals.2018.03.006 PMID:32572288

Novick, M. (2010). Trabajo y contextos en el desarrollo productivo argentino. In *Convivir con la incertidumbre. Aproximaciones a la flexibilización y precarización del trabajo en la Argentina.* CICCUS.

O'Gorman, K. (2007a). Dimensions of hospitality: exploring ancient and classical origins. In *Hospitality: A social lens* (pp. 31–46). Routledge. doi:10.1016/B978-0-08-045093-3.50005-9

O'Gorman, K. D. (2005). Modern Hospitality: Lessons from the past. *Journal of Hospitality and Tourism Management*, *12*(2), 141–151.

O'Gorman, K. D. (2006). Jacques Derrida's philosophy of hospitality. *Hospitality Review*, *8*(4), 50–57.

O'Gorman, K. D. (2007b). Discovering commercial hospitality in ancient Rome. *Hospitality Review*, *9*(2), 44–52.

O'Gorman, K. D. (2007c). The hospitality phenomenon: Philosophical enlightenment? *International Journal of Culture, Tourism and Hospitality Research*, *1*(3), 189–202. doi:10.1108/17506180710817729

OECD. (2015). *Skills for Social Progress: The Power of Social and Emotional Skills*. OECD Publishing., doi:10.1787/9789264226159-

OECD. (2016). *OECD Tourism Trends and Policies 2016*. OECD Publishing. doi:10.1787/tour-2016-

OECD. (2020). *OECD Tourism Trends and Policies 2020*. OECD Publishing. doi:10.1787/6b47b985-

Okuyucu, A. (2016). *İkinci konutların ekonomik ve sosyo-kültürel etkileri konusunda bir araştırma: Yalova-Çınarcık Örneği* [A research on economic and socio-cultural effect of second homes. The case of Yalova-Çınarcık] (Unpublished Doctoral Thesis). Ankara University, Ankara.

Oliveria, J. A., Roca, M. N. O., & Roca, Z. (2015). Economic effects of second homes: A case study in Portugal. *Economia e Sociologia*, *8*(3), 183–196. doi:10.14254/2071-789X.2015/8-3/14

Operti, F., & Mesquita Moreira, M. (2020). Impacto del coronavirus en el comercio y la integración: ¿qué hacer? [Impact of the coronavirus on trade and integration: What to do?]. *Banco Interamericano de Desarrollo*. Disponible en: https://blogs.iadb.org/integracioncomercio/es/coronavirus-comercio-integracion/

Özdemir, K. (2020, July 13). Erzincan dumanlı yaylası izole piknik imkanı sunuyor [Erzincan Dumanlı Plateau offers isolated picnic opportunities]. *Anadolu Ajansı*. https://www.aa.com.tr/tr

Özsoy, T. (2015). Use of secondary housing approach in marketing of Turkish tourism. *The Journal of KAU IIBF*, *6*, 1–18.

Pachon, E. J. (2000). *Strategic and tactical fleet planning for the car rental industry*. University of Miami.

Pagden, A. (1995). *Lords of all the World: Ideologies of Empire in Spain, Britain and France c. 1500-c. 1800*. Yale University Press.

Palmer, C. A. (1994). Tourism and colonialism: The experience of the Bahamas. *Annals of Tourism Research*, *21*(4), 792–811. doi:10.1016/0160-7383(94)90084-1

Palmer-Tous, T., Riera-Font, A., & Rossello-Nadal, J. (2007). Taxing tourism: The case of rental cars in Mallorca. *Tourism Management*, *28*, 271–279.

Panayiotopoulos, A., & Pisano, C. (2019). Overtourism Dystopias and Socialist Utopias: Towards an Urban Armature for Dubrovnik. *Tourism Planning & Development*, *0*(0), 1–18. doi:10.1080/21568316.2019.1569123

Papacharissi, Z. (2009). The virtual geographies of social networks: A comparative analysis of Facebook, Linkedln and ASmallWorld. *New Media & Society*, *11*(1-2), 199–220. doi:10.1177/1461444808099577

Park, K., & Reisinger, Y. (2010). Differences in the perceived influence of natural disasters and travel risk on international travel. *Tourism Geographies, 12*(1), 1–24. doi:10.1080/14616680903493621

Peres, W., & Hilbert, M. (Eds.). (2009). *La sociedad de la información en América Latina y el Caribe. Desarrollo de las tecnologías para el desarrollo. Santiango de Chile: Comisión Económica para América Latina y el Caribe*. CEPAL.

Perkumienė, D., & Pranskūnienė, R. (2019). Overtourism: Between the Right to Travel and Residents' Rights. *Sustainability, 11*(7), 2138. doi:10.3390u11072138

Phillips, M. (1998). Investigations of the British rural middle class: Part 2, fragmentation, identity, morality and contestation. *Journal of Rural Studies, 14*(4), 427–443. doi:10.1016/S0743-0167(98)00031-X

Postma, A., & Schmuecker, D. (2017). Understanding and overcoming negative impacts of tourism in city destinations: Conceptual model and strategic framework. *Journal of Tourism Futures, 3*(2), 144–156. doi:10.1108/JTF-04-2017-0022

Poulston, J. (2015). Expressive labour and the gift of hospitality. *Hospitality & Society, 5*(2-3), 145–165. doi:10.1386/hosp.5.2-3.145_1

Pran, N. S. (2008). *Successful tourism: tourism practices* (Vol. 2). Sterling Publisher.

Prayag, G. (2020). Time for Reset? COVID-19 and Tourism Resilience. *Tourism Review International, 24*(2-3), 179–184. doi:10.3727/154427220X15926147793595

Pulignano, V. (2020, September 9). Including the precariat. *Social Europe*. https://www.socialeurope.eu/including-the-precariat

Raskop, R. R. (1994). *Is the public being taken for a ride? The car rental industry: its policies, practices and the public interest*. Golden Gate University.

Rauch, D., & Schleicher, D. (2015). *Like Uber, But for Local Governmental Policy: The Future of Local Regulation of the 'Sharing Economy'*. George Mason Law & Economics Research Paper 15-01. doi:10.2139srn.2549919

Reisinger, Y., & Mavondo, F. (2005). Travel anxiety and intentions to travel internationally: Implications of travel risk perception. *Journal of Travel Research, 43*(3), 212–225. doi:10.1177/0047287504272017

Reisinger, Y., & Mavondo, F. (2006). Cultural differences in travel risk perception. *Journal of Travel & Tourism Marketing, 20*(1), 13–31. doi:10.1300/J073v20n01_02

Renee, L. G. (2009). *The Motor Vehicle Leasing & Rental Industry: Trends and Prospects*. Industry and Trade Administration.

Republic of Turkey Ministry of Development. (2013). *Eleventh development plan*. Ministry of Development.

Research & Markets. (2019). *Middle East Car Rental Market - Growth, Trends, and Forecast (2020 - 2025).* Retrieved from https://www.researchandmarkets.com /reports/4987210/middle-east-car-rental-market-growth-trends#pos

Rezvani, M. (2003). Analyzing the process of establishment and developmen of second homes in rural areas of North of tehran province. *Geographical research Quarterly*, *45*, 59-73.

Riebsame, W., Gosnell, H., & Theobold, D. (1996). Land use and landscape chane in the Colorado mountains 1: Theory, scale and pattern. *Mountain Research and Development*, *16*(4), 395–405. doi:10.2307/3673989

Ritchie, B. (2008). Tourism disaster planning and management: From response and recovery to reduction and readiness. *Current Issues in Tourism*, *11*(4), 315–348. doi:10.1080/13683500802140372

Ritchie, B. W. (2004). Chaos, crises and disasters: A strategic approach to crisis management in the tourism industry. *Tourism Management*, *25*(6), 669–683. doi:10.1016/j.tourman.2003.09.004

Ritzer, G. (2019). Inhospitable hospitality? In B. Rowson & C. Lashley (Eds.), *Experiencing hospitality* (pp. 73–90). Nova Science Publishers.

Robinson, L., & Jarvie, J. K. (2008). Post-disaster community tourism recovery: The tsunami and Arugam Bay, Sri Lanka. *Disasters*, *32*(4), 631–645. doi:10.1111/j.1467-7717.2008.01058.x PMID:18479472

Roelofsen, M. (2018). Exploring the Socio-Spatial Inequalities of Airbnb in Sofia, Bulgaria. *Erdkunde*, *72*(4), 313–327. doi:10.3112/erdkunde.2018.04.04

Roland Berger Gmb, H. (2018). *Trends in the truck & trailer market.* Retrieved from https://www.rolandberger.com/fr/Insights/Publications/Trends-in-the-truck-trailer-market.html

Romagosa, F. (2020). The COVID-19 crisis: Opportunities for sustainable and proximity tourism. *Tourism Geographies*, *22*(3), 1–5. doi:10.1080/14616688.2020.1763447

Rowson, B. (2019). Working in hospitality: flexible working and the Gig Economy. In B. Rowson & C. Lashley (Eds.), *Experiencing hospitality* (pp. 135–156). Nova Science Publishers.

Şahbaz, Y. (2020, July 28). Bungalovlara 'pandemi' ilgisi ['Pandemic' interest in bungalows]. *Anadolu Ajansı.* https://www.aa.com.tr/tr

Salehinasab, Z. (2005). *Tourism of second homes and their impacts on rural areas* (Unpublished Master's Thesis). Tehran University.

Sánchez-Moreno, E. (2001). Cross-cultural Links in Ancient Iberia: Socio-economic Anatomy of Hospitality. *Oxford Journal of Archaeology*, *20*(4), 391–414. doi:10.1111/1468-0092.00144

Sansür, L. (2020, July 19). Ünlü tatil beldelerinde kiralık villa furyası [The rush of rental villas in famous holiday resorts]. *Sözcü Newspaper.* https://www.sozcu.com.tr

Santana, G. (2004). Crisis management and tourism: Beyond the rhetoric. *Journal of Travel & Tourism Marketing, 15*(4), 299–321. doi:10.1300/J073v15n04_05

Sarantakou, E., & Terkenli, T. S. (2019). Non-Institutionalized Forms of Tourism Accommodation and Overtourism Impacts on the Landscape: The Case of Santorini, Greece *. *Tourism Planning & Development, 0*(0), 1–23. doi:10.1080/21568316.2019.1569122

Scholz, T. (Ed.). (2013). *Digital Labor. The Internet as Playground and Factory*. Routledge.

Scribano, A. (2013). Una aproximación conceptual a la moral del disfrute: normalización, consumo y espectáculo [A conceptual approach to the morality of enjoyment: normalization, consumption and spectacle]. *RBSE – Revista Brasileira de Sociologia da Emoção, 12*(36), 738-750. http://www.cchla.ufpb.br/rbse/Index.html

Scribano, A. (2015). *¡Disfrútalo! Una aproximación a la economía política de la moral desde el consumo* [Enjoy it! An approach to the political economy of morality from consumption]. Ciudad Autónoma de Buenos Aires: Elaleph.com.

Scribano, A. (2019). Introduction: Politics of Sensibilities, Society 4.0 and Digital Labour. In A. Scribano & P. Lisdero (Eds.), Digital Labour, Society and Politics of Sensibilities (pp. 1-19). Palgrave Macmillan.

Scribano, A. (2012). Sociología de los cuerpos/emociones [Sociology of bodies/emotions]. *Revista Latinoamericana de Estudios sobre Cuerpos, Emociones y Sociedad, 4*(10), 93–113.

Scribano, A. (2012). Sociología de los cuerpos/emociones. RELACES-Revista Latinoamericana de Estudios sobre Cuerpos. *Emociones y Sociedad, 10*, 93–113.

Scribano, A. (2017). *Normalization, enjoyment and bodies/emotions: Argentine sensibilities*. Nova Science Publishers.

Scribano, A. (2017). *Normalization, Enjoyment and Bodies/Emotions: Argentines Sensibilities*. Nova Science Publications.

Scribano, A. (2017, August). "Instaimagen: mirar tocando para sentir" [Instaimagen: look by touching to feel]. *RBSE Revista Brasileira de Sociología da Emoção, 16*(47), 45–55.

Scribano, A. (2020). Consumo digital y sensibilidades de plataforma: algunas pistas para su análisis [Digital consumption and platform sensitivities: some clues for analysis]. In A. Dettano (Ed.), *Topografías del consumo*. Estudios Sociológicos Editora.

Scribano, A., & Lisdero, P. (2019). *Digital labor, Society and Politics of Sensibilities*. Palgrave Macmillan. doi:10.1007/978-3-030-12306-2

Seabra, C., Abrantes, J. L., & Kastenholz, E. (2014). The influence of terrorism risk perception on purchase involvement and safety concern of international travellers. *Journal of Marketing Management, 30*(9-10), 874–903. doi:10.1080/0267257X.2014.934904

Seay, S., & Narsing, A. (2013). Transitioning to a lean paradigm: A model for sustainability in the leasing and rental ındustries. *Academy of Strategic Management Journal*, *12*(1), 113–124.

Selwyn, T. (2019). Hostility and hospitality: connecting Brexit, Grenfell, Windrush. In B. Rowson & C. Lashley (Eds.), *Experiencing hospitality* (pp. 51–72). Nova Science Publishers.

Sena, D. E. A. (2020). Spinning the web of sensibilities in receiving households and not of social programs. In Social policies and emotions: survivals around state interventions. Buenos Aires: Estudios Sociológicos Editora.

Sennett, R. (1998). *The corrosion of character: The personal consequences of work in the new capitalism*. W. W. Norton & Company.

Séraphin, H., Butcher, J., & Korstanje, M. (2017). Challenging the negative images of Haiti at a pre-visit stage using visual online learning materials. *Journal of Policy Research in Tourism, Leisure & Events*, *9*(2), 169–181. doi:10.1080/19407963.2016.1261146

Seraphin, H., Gowreesunkar, V., Roselé-Chim, P., Duplan, Y. J. J., & Korstanje, M. (2018). Tourism planning and innovation: The Caribbean under the spotlight. *Journal of Destination Marketing & Management*, *9*, 384–388. doi:10.1016/j.jdmm.2018.03.004

Séraphin, H., Korstanje, M., & Gowreesunkar, V. G. (Eds.). (2020). *Post-Disaster and Post-Conflict Tourism: Toward a New Management Approach*. CRC Press. doi:10.1201/9780429276224

Seraphin, H., Sheeran, P., & Pilato, M. (2018). Over-tourism and the fall of Venice as a destination. *Journal of Destination Marketing & Management*, *9*, 374–376. doi:10.1016/j.jdmm.2018.01.011

Séraphin, H., Zaman, M., Olver, S., Bourliataux-Lajoinie, S., & Dosquet, F. (2019). Destination branding and overtourism. *Journal of Hospitality and Tourism Management*, *38*, 1–4. doi:10.1016/j.jhtm.2018.11.003

Shah, P. (2019). *Car Rental Market Research Report: P&S Intelligence*. Retrieved from https://www.researchgate.net/publication/337324851_Car_Rental_Market_Global_Industry_Analysis_and_Forecast_to_2024

Shaheen, S., Sperling, D., & Wagner, C. (1999). A Short History of Carsharing in the 90's. *The Journal of World Transport Policy and Practice*, *5*(3), 18–40.

Shannon, C. (1948). *A mathematical theory of communication. Bell System Technical Journal* , 27 . doi:10.1002/j.1538-7305.1948.tb01338.x

Sigala, M. (2020). Tourism and COVID-19: Impacts and implications for advancing and resetting industry and research. *Journal of Business Research*, *117*, 312–321. Advance online publication. doi:10.1016/j.jbusres.2020.06.015 PMID:32546875

Solarin, S. A. (2015). September 11 attacks, H1N1 influenza, global financial crisis and tourist arrivals in Sarawak. *Anatolia*, *26*(2), 298–300. doi:10.1080/13032917.2014.991933

South, A. T. R. (2019). *State of tourism report 2017/18.* Retrieved from https://www.tourism.gov.za/AboutNDT/Publications/State%20of%20Tourism%20Report%20(STR)%202017-18.pdf

South, A. T. R. (2020). *State of tourism 2018/19 report,* Retrieved from https://www.tourism.gov.za/AboutNDT/Publications/State%20of%20Tourism%20Report%202018-19.pdf

Southan, J. (2011). Trend driven: what's in store for car rental? *Business Traveler.* Retrieved from http://go.galegroup.com/ps/i.do?

Sribano, A. (2017) Neo-Colonial Religion as Current Form of the Political Economy of Morality. In Normalization, Enjoyment and Bodies/Emotions. Argentine Sensibilities. Nova Science Publishers.

Sribano, A. (2019) Introduction: Politics of Sensibilities, Society 4.0 and Digital Labor. In Digital Labor, Society and Politics of Sensibilities. Palgrave Macmillan.

Sribano, A. (2019) Trust in society 4.0. In Confidence and Politics of Sensibilities. Buenos Aires: Estudios Sociológicos Editora.

Sribano, A. (2020). The war of curves: pandemic, sensibilities, and social structuring. *Simbiótica, 7*(1).

Sribano, A., & Lisdero, P. (2019). Digital gaze and visual experience. In Digital Labor, Society and Politics of Sensibilities. Palgrave Macmillan.

Sribano, A. (2010). First you have to know how to suffer ...!!! Towards a sociology of "waiting" as a mechanism of social support. In A. Scribano & P. Lisdero (Eds.), *Sensibilities at stake: multiple views from the social studies of the body and emotions* (pp. 169–194). CEA-CONICET E-book.

Sribano, A. (2015). *Enjoy it! An approach to the political economy of morality from consumption.* The Aleph.

Srineck, N. (2016). *Platform Capitalism.* Polity Press.

Srnicek, N. (2017). Platform capitalism. *Polity.*

Stemler, A. (2017). Feedback loop failure: Implications for the self-regulation of the sharing economy. *Minnesota Journal of Law, Science & Technology, 18*(2), 673–712.

Stettler, S., & Danielli, G. (2008). Image, truth and illusion in tourism promotion: the problem of he rapid spread of second homes in Switzerland and planning strategies. In P. Keller & T. Bieger (Eds.), *Real estate and destination development in tourism* (pp. 249–268). Erich Schmidt Verlag.

Struyk, R. J., & Angelici, K. (1996). The Russian dacha phenomenon. *Housing Studies, 11*(2), 233–250. doi:10.1080/02673039608720854

Sundararajan, A. (2016). *The sharing economy: The end of employment and the rise of crowdbased capitalism.* MIT Press.

Sund, T. (1948). Sommer-Bergen. Avisenes adresseforandringer som vitnesbyrd om bergensernes landopphold sommeren 1947. *Norsk Geografisk Tidsskrift*, *12*(2), 92–103. doi:10.1080/00291954808551651

Tarlow, P. (2014). *Tourism security: strategies for effectively managing travel risk and safety.* Elsevier.

Taylor, S. J., & Bogdan, R. (1987). *Introducción a los métodos cualitativos de investigación* [Introduction to qualitative research methods]. Editorial Paidós.

Teodorescu, C. D. (2014). The leasing-evolutions and trends. *Economic Insights - Trends and Challenges*, *3*(2), 85–92.

TOKKDER. (2020). *Operational Leasing Sector Report Presentation – 2020.* Retrieved from https://tokkder.org/tokkder-dergi/3139

Tongxia, L., Rahimie, K., & Qaiser, M. (2016). The determinants of leasing decisions: An empirical analysis from Chinese listed SMEs. *Managerial Finance*, *42*(8), 763–790. doi:10.1108/MF-06-2015-0166

Tsamis, A., Gibson, G., Felix Kirsch, F., & Lohr, E. (2016). *Ex-post evaluation of Directive 2006/1/EC.* Retrieved from https://ec.europa.eu/transport /sites/transport/files/facts-fundings/evaluations/doc/2016-ex-post-evaluation-of directive -2006-1-ec-final-report.pdf

Tulumello, S. (2016). Reconsidering neoliberal urban planning in times of crisis: Urban regeneration policy in a "dense" space in Lisbon. *Urban Geography*, *37*(1), 117–140. doi:10.1080/02723638.2015.1056605

Turizm Dosyası. (2020, May 22). Kiralık villa aramaları 4 kat arttı [Rental vılla calls ıncreased four tımes]. *Turizm Dosyası.* http://www.turizmdosyasi.com

Turizm Günlüğü. (2020, May 27). İşte pandemide nefes aldıracak 19 ekoturizm rotası [Here are nineteen ecotourism routes that will breathe in the pandemic]. *Turizm Günlüğü.* https://www.turizmgunlugu.com

Turizm, G. M. (2020, November 9). Bodrum'da Tarihi Nüfus Artışı Koronavirüs Kaçışları Sürüyor [Historical population increase coronavirus escape continues in Bodrum]. *Turizm GM.* https://www.turizmgm.com

Turizmin Sesi. (2020, May 8). Koronavirüs salgını temassız tatil devrini başlattı [Coronavirus epidemic started the contactless holiday era]. *Turizmin Sesi.* https://www.turizminsesi.com

Turkey Republic Health Ministry. (2020, December 12). *Covid-19 General Situation.* https://covid19.saglik.gov.tr

Tutu, J. (2011). *International tourism marketing -promoting BRC budget car rental and tour, Ethiopia* (Master's thesis). School of Tourism and Hospitality Management.

Tyya, N. T. (2007). *Hospitality & tourism industry employers.* Vault Inc.

Tzanelli, R. (2018). *Cinematic tourist mobilities and the plight of development: On atmospheres, affects, and environments*. Routledge. doi:10.4324/9780429424427

United Nations Conference on Trade and Development – UNCTAD. (2017). *Information Economy Report 2017. Digitalization, Trade and Development*. Geneva: United Nations.

UNWTO. (2019). 'Overtourism'? Understanding and Managing Urban Tourism Growth beyond Perceptions Volume 2: Case Studies. doi:10.18111/9789284420643

UNWTO. (2019). *International Tourism Highlights, 2019 Edition,* Retrieved from https://www.e-unwto.org/doi/pdf/10.18111/9789284421152

UNWTO. (2020). *2020: worst year in tourism history with 1 billion fewer international arrivals.* Retrieved from https://www.unwto.org/taxonomy/term/347

Urry, J. (1992). The tourist gaze "revisited". *The American Behavioral Scientist*, *36*(2), 172–186. doi:10.1177/0002764292036002005

Urry, J. (2002). *The tourist gaze*. Sage.

Vagner, J., Müller, D. K., & Fialova, D. (2011). Second home tourism in light of the historical political and socia geographical development of Czechia and Sweden. *Geografie (Utrecht)*, *116*(2), 191–210. doi:10.37040/geografie2011116020191

Van den Ecker, M., & Sevignani, S. (2020). Media and Communication in Digital Capitalism: Critical Perspectives. *Global Dialogue,* 10(2). Available at: HTTPS: //globaldialogue.isa-sociology.org/

Vasiliou, D., & Ipirotis, N. (2008). *Financial management (theory and practice)*. Rosili Publishing, Chapman and Hall/CRC.

Velvin, J., Kvikstad, T. M., Drag, E., & Krogh, E. (2013). The impact of second home tourism on local economic development in rural areas in Norwey. *Tourism Economics*, *19*(3), 689–705. doi:10.5367/te.2013.0216

Verma, S., & Gustafsson, A. (2020). Investigating the emerging COVID-19 research trends in the field of business and management: A bibliometric analysis approach. *Journal of Business Research*, *118*, 253–261. Advance online publication. doi:10.1016/j.jbusres.2020.06.057 PMID:32834211

Virilio, P. (1989). *War and cinema. The Logistics of Perception*. Patrick Camille.

Vujovic, S., Arsic, L., & Premovic, J. (2018). Financing in tourism: basic models of financing the accommodation offer. *J Hotel Bus Manage*, *7*(2), 185.

Wachsmuth, D., & Weisler, A. (2018). Airbnb and the rent gap: Gentrification through the sharing economy. *Environment and Planning A. Economy and Space*, *0*(0), 1–24.

Walter, F. (2010). *Einführung in die fremden verkehrs ökonomie* (10th ed.). Oldenburg Verlag.

Wang, C. C. (2012). Transport equipment rental & leasing. Taiwan industry reports. *Ref. Code*, *19786*, 1–19.

Warde, A. (2016). *Consumption: A sociological analysis*. Springer.

We Are Social & Hootsuite. (2020). *Digital 2020. Global Digital Overview*. Retrieved from https: //wearesocial.com/digital-2020

Wen, J., Wang, W., Kozak, M., Liu, X., & Hou, H. (2020). Many brains are better than one: The importance of interdisciplinary studies on COVID-19 in and beyond tourism. *Tourism Recreation Research*, 1–4. doi:10.1080/02508281.2020.1761120

Whittaker, C. (2008). Hotel operator motives in UK sale and leaseback/managementback transactions. *International Journal of Hospitality Management*, *27*(4), 641–648. doi:10.1016/j.ijhm.2007.07.031

William, J. C., & Richard, C. G. (1995). Evolutionary change in product management: Experiences in the car rental ındustry. *Interfaces*, *25*(5), 84–104.

Wolff, K., & Larsen, S. (2014). Can terrorism make us feel safer? Risk perceptions and worries before and after the July 22nd attacks. *Annals of Tourism Research*, *44*, 200–209. doi:10.1016/j.annals.2013.10.003

Wood, C. R. (2019). One Cheer for Marxism: hospitality as a bourgeois phenomenon. In B. Rowson & C. Lashley (Eds.), *Experiencing hospitality* (pp. 25–50). Nova Science Publishers.

World Economic Forum. (2020). *The Future of Jobs Report 2020*. World Economic Forum. www.weforum.org

World Health Organizations. (2020, December 12). *Covid-19 Number at Glance*. www.who.int/covid-19/information

World Tourism Organisation. (2020). *COVID-19: Putting People First*. Author.

Yang, Y., Jin, W., & Hao, X. (2008). Car rental logistics problem: A review of literature. *IEEE International Conference on Service Operations and Logistics, and Informatics,* 2815–2819.

Yirik, Ş., Uslu, A., & Küçük, F. (2015). Yerleşik Yabancıların Türkiye'ye İlişkin Sosyo Kültürel Algılarının Demografik Özelliklerine Göre İncelenmesi [Analysis of foreign residents' socio-cultural perceptions of Turkey according to their demographic characteristics]. *Journal of Bartın İİBF,* 263-282.

Yirik, Ş., & Baltacı, F. (2016). Investigating the demographic particulars of aliens who setted in Antalya within the scope of second residence and the reasons for their choice. *Journal of Academic Researches*, *68*, 137–156.

Yüksel, A., & Yüksel, F. (2007). Shopping risk perceptions: Effects on tourists' emotions, satisfaction and expressed loyalty intentions. *Tourism Management*, *28*(3), 703–713. doi:10.1016/j.tourman.2006.04.025

Zenker, S., & Kock, F. (2020). The coronavirus pandemic–A critical discussion of a tourism research agenda. *Tourism Management*, *81*, 104164. doi:10.1016/j.tourman.2020.104164 PMID:32518437

Zervas, G. & Byers J. W. (2017) The Rise of the Sharing Economy: Estimating the Impact of Airbnb on the Hotel Industry. *Journal of Marketing Research, 54*(5).

Zhang, M., Xie, Y., Huang, L., & Zhen, H. (2014). Service quality evaluation of car rental industry in China. *International Journal of Quality & Reliability Management*, *31*(1), 82–102.

Zoğal, V., & Emekli, G. (2020). The changing meanings of second homes during Covid-19 Pandemic in Turkey. *International Journal of Geography and Geography Education*, *42*, 168–181.

Related References

To continue our tradition of advancing information science and technology research, we have compiled a list of recommended IGI Global readings. These references will provide additional information and guidance to further enrich your knowledge and assist you with your own research and future publications.

Abtahi, M. S., Behboudi, L., & Hasanabad, H. M. (2017). Factors Affecting Internet Advertising Adoption in Ad Agencies. *International Journal of Innovation in the Digital Economy*, *8*(4), 18–29. doi:10.4018/IJIDE.2017100102

Agrawal, S. (2017). The Impact of Emerging Technologies and Social Media on Different Business(es): Marketing and Management. In O. Rishi & A. Sharma (Eds.), *Maximizing Business Performance and Efficiency Through Intelligent Systems* (pp. 37–49). Hershey, PA: IGI Global. doi:10.4018/978-1-5225-2234-8.ch002

Alnoukari, M., Razouk, R., & Hanano, A. (2016). BSC-SI: A Framework for Integrating Strategic Intelligence in Corporate Strategic Management. *International Journal of Social and Organizational Dynamics in IT*, *5*(2), 1–14. doi:10.4018/IJSODIT.2016070101

Alnoukari, M., Razouk, R., & Hanano, A. (2016). BSC-SI, A Framework for Integrating Strategic Intelligence in Corporate Strategic Management. *International Journal of Strategic Information Technology and Applications*, *7*(1), 32–44. doi:10.4018/IJSITA.2016010103

Altındağ, E. (2016). Current Approaches in Change Management. In A. Goksoy (Ed.), *Organizational Change Management Strategies in Modern Business* (pp. 24–51). Hershey, PA: IGI Global. doi:10.4018/978-1-4666-9533-7.ch002

Alvarez-Dionisi, L. E., Turner, R., & Mittra, M. (2016). Global Project Management Trends. *International Journal of Information Technology Project Management, 7*(3), 54–73. doi:10.4018/IJITPM.2016070104

Anantharaman, R. N., Rajeswari, K. S., Angusamy, A., & Kuppusamy, J. (2017). Role of Self-Efficacy and Collective Efficacy as Moderators of Occupational Stress Among Software Development Professionals. *International Journal of Human Capital and Information Technology Professionals, 8*(2), 45–58. doi:10.4018/IJHCITP.2017040103

Aninze, F., El-Gohary, H., & Hussain, J. (2018). The Role of Microfinance to Empower Women: The Case of Developing Countries. *International Journal of Customer Relationship Marketing and Management, 9*(1), 54–78. doi:10.4018/IJCRMM.2018010104

Arsenijević, O. M., Orčić, D., & Kastratović, E. (2017). Development of an Optimization Tool for Intangibles in SMEs: A Case Study from Serbia with a Pilot Research in the Prestige by Milka Company. In M. Vemić (Ed.), *Optimal Management Strategies in Small and Medium Enterprises* (pp. 320–347). Hershey, PA: IGI Global. doi:10.4018/978-1-5225-1949-2.ch015

Aryanto, V. D., Wismantoro, Y., & Widyatmoko, K. (2018). Implementing Eco-Innovation by Utilizing the Internet to Enhance Firm's Marketing Performance: Study of Green Batik Small and Medium Enterprises in Indonesia. *International Journal of E-Business Research, 14*(1), 21–36. doi:10.4018/IJEBR.2018010102

Atiku, S. O., & Fields, Z. (2017). Multicultural Orientations for 21st Century Global Leadership. In N. Baporikar (Ed.), *Management Education for Global Leadership* (pp. 28–51). Hershey, PA: IGI Global. doi:10.4018/978-1-5225-1013-0.ch002

Atiku, S. O., & Fields, Z. (2018). Organisational Learning Dimensions and Talent Retention Strategies for the Service Industries. In N. Baporikar (Ed.), *Global Practices in Knowledge Management for Societal and Organizational Development* (pp. 358–381). Hershey, PA: IGI Global. doi:10.4018/978-1-5225-3009-1.ch017

Ávila, L., & Teixeira, L. (2018). The Main Concepts Behind the Dematerialization of Business Processes. In M. Khosrow-Pour, D.B.A. (Ed.), Encyclopedia of Information Science and Technology, Fourth Edition (pp. 888-898). Hershey, PA: IGI Global. doi:10.4018/978-1-5225-2255-3.ch076

Bartens, Y., Chunpir, H. I., Schulte, F., & Voß, S. (2017). Business/IT Alignment in Two-Sided Markets: A COBIT 5 Analysis for Media Streaming Business Models. In S. De Haes & W. Van Grembergen (Eds.), *Strategic IT Governance and Alignment in Business Settings* (pp. 82–111). Hershey, PA: IGI Global. doi:10.4018/978-1-5225-0861-8.ch004

Bashayreh, A. M. (2018). Organizational Culture and Organizational Performance. In W. Lee & F. Sabetzadeh (Eds.), *Contemporary Knowledge and Systems Science* (pp. 50–69). Hershey, PA: IGI Global. doi:10.4018/978-1-5225-5655-8.ch003

Bedford, D. A. (2018). Sustainable Knowledge Management Strategies: Aligning Business Capabilities and Knowledge Management Goals. In N. Baporikar (Ed.), *Global Practices in Knowledge Management for Societal and Organizational Development* (pp. 46–73). Hershey, PA: IGI Global. doi:10.4018/978-1-5225-3009-1.ch003

Benmoussa, F., Nakara, W. A., & Jaouen, A. (2016). The Use of Social Media by SMEs in the Tourism Industry. In I. Lee (Ed.), *Encyclopedia of E-Commerce Development, Implementation, and Management* (pp. 2159–2170). Hershey, PA: IGI Global. doi:10.4018/978-1-4666-9787-4.ch155

Berger, R. (2016). Indigenous Management and Bottom of Pyramid Countries: The Role of National Institutions. In U. Aung & P. Ordoñez de Pablos (Eds.), *Managerial Strategies and Practice in the Asian Business Sector* (pp. 107–123). Hershey, PA: IGI Global. doi:10.4018/978-1-4666-9758-4.ch007

Bharwani, S., & Musunuri, D. (2018). Reflection as a Process From Theory to Practice. In M. Khosrow-Pour, D.B.A. (Ed.), Encyclopedia of Information Science and Technology, Fourth Edition (pp. 1529-1539). Hershey, PA: IGI Global. doi:10.4018/978-1-5225-2255-3.ch132

Bhatt, G. D., Wang, Z., & Rodger, J. A. (2017). Information Systems Capabilities and Their Effects on Competitive Advantages: A Study of Chinese Companies. *Information Resources Management Journal, 30*(3), 41–57. doi:10.4018/IRMJ.2017070103

Bhushan, M., & Yadav, A. (2017). Concept of Cloud Computing in ESB. In R. Bhadoria, N. Chaudhari, G. Tomar, & S. Singh (Eds.), *Exploring Enterprise Service Bus in the Service-Oriented Architecture Paradigm* (pp. 116–127). Hershey, PA: IGI Global. doi:10.4018/978-1-5225-2157-0.ch008

Bhushan, S. (2017). System Dynamics Base-Model of Humanitarian Supply Chain (HSCM) in Disaster Prone Eco-Communities of India: A Discussion on Simulation and Scenario Results. *International Journal of System Dynamics Applications, 6*(3), 20–37. doi:10.4018/IJSDA.2017070102

Biswas, A., & De, A. K. (2017). On Development of a Fuzzy Stochastic Programming Model with Its Application to Business Management. In S. Trivedi, S. Dey, A. Kumar, & T. Panda (Eds.), *Handbook of Research on Advanced Data Mining Techniques and Applications for Business Intelligence* (pp. 353–378). Hershey, PA: IGI Global. doi:10.4018/978-1-5225-2031-3.ch021

Bücker, J., & Ernste, K. (2018). Use of Brand Heroes in Strategic Reputation Management: The Case of Bacardi, Adidas, and Daimler. In A. Erdemir (Ed.), *Reputation Management Techniques in Public Relations* (pp. 126–150). Hershey, PA: IGI Global. doi:10.4018/978-1-5225-3619-2.ch007

Bureš, V. (2018). Industry 4.0 From the Systems Engineering Perspective: Alternative Holistic Framework Development. In R. Brunet-Thornton & F. Martinez (Eds.), *Analyzing the Impacts of Industry 4.0 in Modern Business Environments* (pp. 199–223). Hershey, PA: IGI Global. doi:10.4018/978-1-5225-3468-6.ch011

Buzady, Z. (2017). Resolving the Magic Cube of Effective Case Teaching: Benchmarking Case Teaching Practices in Emerging Markets – Insights from the Central European University Business School, Hungary. In D. Latusek (Ed.), *Case Studies as a Teaching Tool in Management Education* (pp. 79–103). Hershey, PA: IGI Global. doi:10.4018/978-1-5225-0770-3.ch005

Campatelli, G., Richter, A., & Stocker, A. (2016). Participative Knowledge Management to Empower Manufacturing Workers. *International Journal of Knowledge Management, 12*(4), 37–50. doi:10.4018/IJKM.2016100103

Căpusneanu, S., & Topor, D. I. (2018). Business Ethics and Cost Management in SMEs: Theories of Business Ethics and Cost Management Ethos. In I. Oncioiu (Ed.), *Ethics and Decision-Making for Sustainable Business Practices* (pp. 109–127). Hershey, PA: IGI Global. doi:10.4018/978-1-5225-3773-1.ch007

Carneiro, A. (2016). Maturity in Health Organization Information Systems: Metrics and Privacy Perspectives. *International Journal of Privacy and Health Information Management, 4*(2), 1–18. doi:10.4018/IJPHIM.2016070101

Chan, R. L., Mo, P. L., & Moon, K. K. (2018). Strategic and Tactical Measures in Managing Enterprise Risks: A Study of the Textile and Apparel Industry. In K. Strang, M. Korstanje, & N. Vajjhala (Eds.), *Research, Practices, and Innovations in Global Risk and Contingency Management* (pp. 1–19). Hershey, PA: IGI Global. doi:10.4018/978-1-5225-4754-9.ch001

Chandan, H. C. (2016). Motivations and Challenges of Female Entrepreneurship in Developed and Developing Economies. In N. Baporikar (Ed.), *Handbook of Research on Entrepreneurship in the Contemporary Knowledge-Based Global Economy* (pp. 260–286). Hershey, PA: IGI Global. doi:10.4018/978-1-4666-8798-1.ch012

Charlier, S. D., Burke-Smalley, L. A., & Fisher, S. L. (2018). Undergraduate Programs in the U.S: A Contextual and Content-Based Analysis. In J. Mendy (Ed.), *Teaching Human Resources and Organizational Behavior at the College Level* (pp. 26–57). Hershey, PA: IGI Global. doi:10.4018/978-1-5225-2820-3.ch002

Chaudhuri, S. (2016). Application of Web-Based Geographical Information System (GIS) in E-Business. In U. Panwar, R. Kumar, & N. Ray (Eds.), *Handbook of Research on Promotional Strategies and Consumer Influence in the Service Sector* (pp. 389–405). Hershey, PA: IGI Global. doi:10.4018/978-1-5225-0143-5.ch023

Choudhuri, P. S. (2016). An Empirical Study on the Quality of Services Offered by the Private Life Insurers in Burdwan. In U. Panwar, R. Kumar, & N. Ray (Eds.), *Handbook of Research on Promotional Strategies and Consumer Influence in the Service Sector* (pp. 31–55). Hershey, PA: IGI Global. doi:10.4018/978-1-5225-0143-5.ch002

Dahlberg, T., Kivijärvi, H., & Saarinen, T. (2017). IT Investment Consistency and Other Factors Influencing the Success of IT Performance. In S. De Haes & W. Van Grembergen (Eds.), *Strategic IT Governance and Alignment in Business Settings* (pp. 176–208). Hershey, PA: IGI Global. doi:10.4018/978-1-5225-0861-8.ch007

Damnjanović, A. M. (2017). Knowledge Management Optimization through IT and E-Business Utilization: A Qualitative Study on Serbian SMEs. In M. Vemić (Ed.), *Optimal Management Strategies in Small and Medium Enterprises* (pp. 249–267). Hershey, PA: IGI Global. doi:10.4018/978-1-5225-1949-2.ch012

Daneshpour, H. (2017). Integrating Sustainable Development into Project Portfolio Management through Application of Open Innovation. In M. Vemić (Ed.), *Optimal Management Strategies in Small and Medium Enterprises* (pp. 370–387). Hershey, PA: IGI Global. doi:10.4018/978-1-5225-1949-2.ch017

Daniel, A. D., & Reis de Castro, V. (2018). Entrepreneurship Education: How to Measure the Impact on Nascent Entrepreneurs. In A. Carrizo Moreira, J. Guilherme Leitão Dantas, & F. Manuel Valente (Eds.), *Nascent Entrepreneurship and Successful New Venture Creation* (pp. 85–110). Hershey, PA: IGI Global. doi:10.4018/978-1-5225-2936-1.ch004

David, F., van der Sijde, P., & van den Besselaar, P. (2016). Enterpreneurial Incentives, Obstacles, and Management in University-Business Co-Operation: The Case of Indonesia. In J. Saiz-Álvarez (Ed.), *Handbook of Research on Social Entrepreneurship and Solidarity Economics* (pp. 499–518). Hershey, PA: IGI Global. doi:10.4018/978-1-5225-0097-1.ch024

David, R., Swami, B. N., & Tangirala, S. (2018). Ethics Impact on Knowledge Management in Organizational Development: A Case Study. In N. Baporikar (Ed.), *Global Practices in Knowledge Management for Societal and Organizational Development* (pp. 19–45). Hershey, PA: IGI Global. doi:10.4018/978-1-5225-3009-1.ch002

Delias, P., & Lakiotaki, K. (2018). Discovering Process Horizontal Boundaries to Facilitate Process Comprehension. *International Journal of Operations Research and Information Systems, 9*(2), 1–31. doi:10.4018/IJORIS.2018040101

Denholm, J., & Lee-Davies, L. (2018). Success Factors for Games in Business and Project Management. In *Enhancing Education and Training Initiatives Through Serious Games* (pp. 34–68). Hershey, PA: IGI Global. doi:10.4018/978-1-5225-3689-5.ch002

Deshpande, M. (2017). Best Practices in Management Institutions for Global Leadership: Policy Aspects. In N. Baporikar (Ed.), *Management Education for Global Leadership* (pp. 1–27). Hershey, PA: IGI Global. doi:10.4018/978-1-5225-1013-0.ch001

Deshpande, M. (2018). Policy Perspectives for SMEs Knowledge Management. In N. Baporikar (Ed.), *Knowledge Integration Strategies for Entrepreneurship and Sustainability* (pp. 23–46). Hershey, PA: IGI Global. doi:10.4018/978-1-5225-5115-7.ch002

Dezdar, S. (2017). ERP Implementation Projects in Asian Countries: A Comparative Study on Iran and China. *International Journal of Information Technology Project Management, 8*(3), 52–68. doi:10.4018/IJITPM.2017070104

Domingos, D., Martinho, R., & Varajão, J. (2016). Controlled Flexibility in Healthcare Processes: A BPMN-Extension Approach. In M. Cruz-Cunha, I. Miranda, R. Martinho, & R. Rijo (Eds.), *Encyclopedia of E-Health and Telemedicine* (pp. 521–535). Hershey, PA: IGI Global. doi:10.4018/978-1-4666-9978-6.ch040

Domingos, D., Respício, A., & Martinho, R. (2017). Reliability of IoT-Aware BPMN Healthcare Processes. In C. Reis & M. Maximiano (Eds.), *Internet of Things and Advanced Application in Healthcare* (pp. 214–248). Hershey, PA: IGI Global. doi:10.4018/978-1-5225-1820-4.ch008

Dosumu, O., Hussain, J., & El-Gohary, H. (2017). An Exploratory Study of the Impact of Government Policies on the Development of Small and Medium Enterprises in Developing Countries: The Case of Nigeria. *International Journal of Customer Relationship Marketing and Management, 8*(4), 51–62. doi:10.4018/IJCRMM.2017100104

Durst, S., Bruns, G., & Edvardsson, I. R. (2017). Retaining Knowledge in Smaller Building and Construction Firms. *International Journal of Knowledge and Systems Science, 8*(3), 1–12. doi:10.4018/IJKSS.2017070101

Edvardsson, I. R., & Durst, S. (2017). Outsourcing, Knowledge, and Learning: A Critical Review. *International Journal of Knowledge-Based Organizations, 7*(2), 13–26. doi:10.4018/IJKBO.2017040102

Edwards, J. S. (2018). Integrating Knowledge Management and Business Processes. In M. Khosrow-Pour, D.B.A. (Ed.), Encyclopedia of Information Science and Technology, Fourth Edition (pp. 5046-5055). Hershey, PA: IGI Global. doi:10.4018/978-1-5225-2255-3.ch437

Ejiogu, A. O. (2018). Economics of Farm Management. In *Agricultural Finance and Opportunities for Investment and Expansion* (pp. 56–72). Hershey, PA: IGI Global. doi:10.4018/978-1-5225-3059-6.ch003

Ekanem, I., & Abiade, G. E. (2018). Factors Influencing the Use of E-Commerce by Small Enterprises in Nigeria. *International Journal of ICT Research in Africa and the Middle East, 7*(1), 37–53. doi:10.4018/IJICTRAME.2018010103

Ekanem, I., & Alrossais, L. A. (2017). Succession Challenges Facing Family Businesses in Saudi Arabia. In P. Zgheib (Ed.), *Entrepreneurship and Business Innovation in the Middle East* (pp. 122–146). Hershey, PA: IGI Global. doi:10.4018/978-1-5225-2066-5.ch007

El Faquih, L., & Fredj, M. (2017). Ontology-Based Framework for Quality in Configurable Process Models. *Journal of Electronic Commerce in Organizations, 15*(2), 48–60. doi:10.4018/JECO.2017040104

El-Gohary, H., & El-Gohary, Z. (2016). An Attempt to Explore Electronic Marketing Adoption and Implementation Aspects in Developing Countries: The Case of Egypt. *International Journal of Customer Relationship Marketing and Management, 7*(4), 1–26. doi:10.4018/IJCRMM.2016100101

Entico, G. J. (2016). Knowledge Management and the Medical Health Librarians: A Perception Study. In J. Yap, M. Perez, M. Ayson, & G. Entico (Eds.), *Special Library Administration, Standardization and Technological Integration* (pp. 52–77). Hershey, PA: IGI Global. doi:10.4018/978-1-4666-9542-9.ch003

Faisal, M. N., & Talib, F. (2017). Building Ambidextrous Supply Chains in SMEs: How to Tackle the Barriers? *International Journal of Information Systems and Supply Chain Management, 10*(4), 80–100. doi:10.4018/IJISSCM.2017100105

Fernandes, T. M., Gomes, J., & Romão, M. (2017). Investments in E-Government: A Benefit Management Case Study. *International Journal of Electronic Government Research, 13*(3), 1–17. doi:10.4018/IJEGR.2017070101

Fouda, F. A. (2016). A Suggested Curriculum in Career Education to Develop Business Secondary Schools Students' Career Knowledge Management Domains and Professional Thinking. *International Journal of Technology Diffusion, 7*(2), 42–62. doi:10.4018/IJTD.2016040103

Gallardo-Vázquez, D., & Pajuelo-Moreno, M. L. (2016). How Spanish Universities are Promoting Entrepreneurship through Your Own Lines of Teaching and Research? In L. Carvalho (Ed.), *Handbook of Research on Entrepreneurial Success and its Impact on Regional Development* (pp. 431–454). Hershey, PA: IGI Global. doi:10.4018/978-1-4666-9567-2.ch019

Gao, S. S., Oreal, S., & Zhang, J. (2018). Contemporary Financial Risk Management Perceptions and Practices of Small-Sized Chinese Businesses. In I. Management Association (Ed.), Global Business Expansion: Concepts, Methodologies, Tools, and Applications (pp. 917-931). Hershey, PA: IGI Global. doi:10.4018/978-1-5225-5481-3.ch041

Garg, R., & Berning, S. C. (2017). Indigenous Chinese Management Philosophies: Key Concepts and Relevance for Modern Chinese Firms. In B. Christiansen & G. Koc (Eds.), *Transcontinental Strategies for Industrial Development and Economic Growth* (pp. 43–57). Hershey, PA: IGI Global. doi:10.4018/978-1-5225-2160-0.ch003

Gencer, Y. G. (2017). Supply Chain Management in Retailing Business. In U. Akkucuk (Ed.), *Ethics and Sustainability in Global Supply Chain Management* (pp. 197–210). Hershey, PA: IGI Global. doi:10.4018/978-1-5225-2036-8.ch011

Giacosa, E. (2016). Innovation in Luxury Fashion Businesses as a Means for the Regional Development. In L. Carvalho (Ed.), *Handbook of Research on Entrepreneurial Success and its Impact on Regional Development* (pp. 206–222). Hershey, PA: IGI Global. doi:10.4018/978-1-4666-9567-2.ch010

Giacosa, E. (2018). The Increasing of the Regional Development Thanks to the Luxury Business Innovation. In L. Carvalho (Ed.), *Handbook of Research on Entrepreneurial Ecosystems and Social Dynamics in a Globalized World* (pp. 260–273). Hershey, PA: IGI Global. doi:10.4018/978-1-5225-3525-6.ch011

Gianni, M., & Gotzamani, K. (2016). Integrated Management Systems and Information Management Systems: Common Threads. In P. Papajorgji, F. Pinet, A. Guimarães, & J. Papathanasiou (Eds.), *Automated Enterprise Systems for Maximizing Business Performance* (pp. 195–214). Hershey, PA: IGI Global. doi:10.4018/978-1-4666-8841-4.ch011

Gianni, M., Gotzamani, K., & Linden, I. (2016). How a BI-wise Responsible Integrated Management System May Support Food Traceability. *International Journal of Decision Support System Technology*, *8*(2), 1–17. doi:10.4018/IJDSST.2016040101

Glykas, M., & George, J. (2017). Quality and Process Management Systems in the UAE Maritime Industry. *International Journal of Productivity Management and Assessment Technologies*, *5*(1), 20–39. doi:10.4018/IJPMAT.2017010102

Glykas, M., Valiris, G., Kokkinaki, A., & Koutsoukou, Z. (2018). Banking Business Process Management Implementation. *International Journal of Productivity Management and Assessment Technologies*, *6*(1), 50–69. doi:10.4018/IJPMAT.2018010104

Gomes, J., & Romão, M. (2017). The Balanced Scorecard: Keeping Updated and Aligned with Today's Business Trends. *International Journal of Productivity Management and Assessment Technologies*, *5*(2), 1–15. doi:10.4018/IJPMAT.2017070101

Gomes, J., & Romão, M. (2017). Aligning Information Systems and Technology with Benefit Management and Balanced Scorecard. In S. De Haes & W. Van Grembergen (Eds.), *Strategic IT Governance and Alignment in Business Settings* (pp. 112–131). Hershey, PA: IGI Global. doi:10.4018/978-1-5225-0861-8.ch005

Grefen, P., & Turetken, O. (2017). Advanced Business Process Management in Networked E-Business Scenarios. *International Journal of E-Business Research*, *13*(4), 70–104. doi:10.4018/IJEBR.2017100105

Haider, A., & Saetang, S. (2017). Strategic IT Alignment in Service Sector. In S. Rozenes & Y. Cohen (Eds.), *Handbook of Research on Strategic Alliances and Value Co-Creation in the Service Industry* (pp. 231–258). Hershey, PA: IGI Global. doi:10.4018/978-1-5225-2084-9.ch012

Haider, A., & Tang, S. S. (2016). Maximising Value Through IT and Business Alignment: A Case of IT Governance Institutionalisation at a Thai Bank. *International Journal of Technology Diffusion*, *7*(3), 33–58. doi:10.4018/IJTD.2016070104

Hajilari, A. B., Ghadaksaz, M., & Fasghandis, G. S. (2017). Assessing Organizational Readiness for Implementing ERP System Using Fuzzy Expert System Approach. *International Journal of Enterprise Information Systems*, *13*(1), 67–85. doi:10.4018/IJEIS.2017010105

Haldorai, A., Ramu, A., & Murugan, S. (2018). Social Aware Cognitive Radio Networks: Effectiveness of Social Networks as a Strategic Tool for Organizational Business Management. In H. Bansal, G. Shrivastava, G. Nguyen, & L. Stanciu (Eds.), *Social Network Analytics for Contemporary Business Organizations* (pp. 188–202). Hershey, PA: IGI Global. doi:10.4018/978-1-5225-5097-6.ch010

Hall, O. P. Jr. (2017). Social Media Driven Management Education. *International Journal of Knowledge-Based Organizations*, *7*(2), 43–59. doi:10.4018/IJKBO.2017040104

Hanifah, H., Halim, H. A., Ahmad, N. H., & Vafaei-Zadeh, A. (2017). Innovation Culture as a Mediator Between Specific Human Capital and Innovation Performance Among Bumiputera SMEs in Malaysia. In N. Ahmad, T. Ramayah, H. Halim, & S. Rahman (Eds.), *Handbook of Research on Small and Medium Enterprises in Developing Countries* (pp. 261–279). Hershey, PA: IGI Global. doi:10.4018/978-1-5225-2165-5.ch012

Hartlieb, S., & Silvius, G. (2017). Handling Uncertainty in Project Management and Business Development: Similarities and Differences. In Y. Raydugin (Ed.), *Handbook of Research on Leveraging Risk and Uncertainties for Effective Project Management* (pp. 337–362). Hershey, PA: IGI Global. doi:10.4018/978-1-5225-1790-0.ch016

Hass, K. B. (2017). Living on the Edge: Managing Project Complexity. In Y. Raydugin (Ed.), *Handbook of Research on Leveraging Risk and Uncertainties for Effective Project Management* (pp. 177–201). Hershey, PA: IGI Global. doi:10.4018/978-1-5225-1790-0.ch009

Hassan, A., & Privitera, D. S. (2016). Google AdSense as a Mobile Technology in Education. In J. Holland (Ed.), *Wearable Technology and Mobile Innovations for Next-Generation Education* (pp. 200–223). Hershey, PA: IGI Global. doi:10.4018/978-1-5225-0069-8.ch011

Hassan, A., & Rahimi, R. (2016). Consuming "Innovation" in Tourism: Augmented Reality as an Innovation Tool in Digital Tourism Marketing. In N. Pappas & I. Bregoli (Eds.), *Global Dynamics in Travel, Tourism, and Hospitality* (pp. 130–147). Hershey, PA: IGI Global. doi:10.4018/978-1-5225-0201-2.ch008

Hawking, P., & Carmine Sellitto, C. (2017). Developing an Effective Strategy for Organizational Business Intelligence. In M. Tavana (Ed.), *Enterprise Information Systems and the Digitalization of Business Functions* (pp. 222–237). Hershey, PA: IGI Global. doi:10.4018/978-1-5225-2382-6.ch010

Hawking, P., & Sellitto, C. (2017). A Fast-Moving Consumer Goods Company and Business Intelligence Strategy Development. *International Journal of Enterprise Information Systems*, *13*(2), 22–33. doi:10.4018/IJEIS.2017040102

Hawking, P., & Sellitto, C. (2017). Business Intelligence Strategy: Two Case Studies. *International Journal of Business Intelligence Research*, *8*(2), 17–30. doi:10.4018/IJBIR.2017070102

Haynes, J. D., Arockiasamy, S., Al Rashdi, M., & Al Rashdi, S. (2016). Business and E Business Strategies for Coopetition and Thematic Management as a Sustained Basis for Ethics and Social Responsibility in Emerging Markets. In M. Al-Shammari & H. Masri (Eds.), *Ethical and Social Perspectives on Global Business Interaction in Emerging Markets* (pp. 25–39). Hershey, PA: IGI Global. doi:10.4018/978-1-4666-9864-2.ch002

Hee, W. J., Jalleh, G., Lai, H., & Lin, C. (2017). E-Commerce and IT Projects: Evaluation and Management Issues in Australian and Taiwanese Hospitals. *International Journal of Public Health Management and Ethics*, *2*(1), 69–90. doi:10.4018/IJPHME.2017010104

Hernandez, A. A. (2018). Exploring the Factors to Green IT Adoption of SMEs in the Philippines. *Journal of Cases on Information Technology*, *20*(2), 49–66. doi:10.4018/JCIT.2018040104

Hernandez, A. A., & Ona, S. E. (2016). Green IT Adoption: Lessons from the Philippines Business Process Outsourcing Industry. *International Journal of Social Ecology and Sustainable Development*, *7*(1), 1–34. doi:10.4018/IJSESD.2016010101

Hollman, A., Bickford, S., & Hollman, T. (2017). Cyber InSecurity: A Post-Mortem Attempt to Assess Cyber Problems from IT and Business Management Perspectives. *Journal of Cases on Information Technology*, *19*(3), 42–70. doi:10.4018/JCIT.2017070104

Igbinakhase, I. (2017). Responsible and Sustainable Management Practices in Developing and Developed Business Environments. In Z. Fields (Ed.), *Collective Creativity for Responsible and Sustainable Business Practice* (pp. 180–207). Hershey, PA: IGI Global. doi:10.4018/978-1-5225-1823-5.ch010

Ilahi, L., Ghannouchi, S. A., & Martinho, R. (2016). A Business Process Management Approach to Home Healthcare Processes: On the Gap between Intention and Reality. In M. Cruz-Cunha, I. Miranda, R. Martinho, & R. Rijo (Eds.), *Encyclopedia of E-Health and Telemedicine* (pp. 439–457). Hershey, PA: IGI Global. doi:10.4018/978-1-4666-9978-6.ch035

Iwata, J. J., & Hoskins, R. G. (2017). Managing Indigenous Knowledge in Tanzania: A Business Perspective. In P. Jain & N. Mnjama (Eds.), *Managing Knowledge Resources and Records in Modern Organizations* (pp. 198–214). Hershey, PA: IGI Global. doi:10.4018/978-1-5225-1965-2.ch012

Jabeen, F., Ahmad, S. Z., & Alkaabi, S. (2016). The Internationalization Decision-Making of United Arab Emirates Family Businesses. In N. Zakaria, A. Abdul-Talib, & N. Osman (Eds.), *Handbook of Research on Impacts of International Business and Political Affairs on the Global Economy* (pp. 1–22). Hershey, PA: IGI Global. doi:10.4018/978-1-4666-9806-2.ch001

Jain, P. (2017). Ethical and Legal Issues in Knowledge Management Life-Cycle in Business. In P. Jain & N. Mnjama (Eds.), *Managing Knowledge Resources and Records in Modern Organizations* (pp. 82–101). Hershey, PA: IGI Global. doi:10.4018/978-1-5225-1965-2.ch006

Jamali, D., Abdallah, H., & Matar, F. (2016). Opportunities and Challenges for CSR Mainstreaming in Business Schools. *International Journal of Technology and Educational Marketing*, *6*(2), 1–29. doi:10.4018/IJTEM.2016070101

James, S., & Hauli, E. (2017). Holistic Management Education at Tanzanian Rural Development Planning Institute. In N. Baporikar (Ed.), *Management Education for Global Leadership* (pp. 112–136). Hershey, PA: IGI Global. doi:10.4018/978-1-5225-1013-0.ch006

Janošková, M., Csikósová, A., & Čulková, K. (2018). Measurement of Company Performance as Part of Its Strategic Management. In R. Leon (Ed.), *Managerial Strategies for Business Sustainability During Turbulent Times* (pp. 309–335). Hershey, PA: IGI Global. doi:10.4018/978-1-5225-2716-9.ch017

Jean-Vasile, A., & Alecu, A. (2017). Theoretical and Practical Approaches in Understanding the Influences of Cost-Productivity-Profit Trinomial in Contemporary Enterprises. In A. Jean Vasile & D. Nicolò (Eds.), *Sustainable Entrepreneurship and Investments in the Green Economy* (pp. 28–62). Hershey, PA: IGI Global. doi:10.4018/978-1-5225-2075-7.ch002

Jha, D. G. (2016). Preparing for Information Technology Driven Changes. In S. Tiwari & L. Nafees (Eds.), *Innovative Management Education Pedagogies for Preparing Next-Generation Leaders* (pp. 258–274). Hershey, PA: IGI Global. doi:10.4018/978-1-4666-9691-4.ch015

Joia, L. A., & Correia, J. C. (2018). CIO Competencies From the IT Professional Perspective: Insights From Brazil. *Journal of Global Information Management*, *26*(2), 74–103. doi:10.4018/JGIM.2018040104

Juma, A., & Mzera, N. (2017). Knowledge Management and Records Management and Competitive Advantage in Business. In P. Jain & N. Mnjama (Eds.), *Managing Knowledge Resources and Records in Modern Organizations* (pp. 15–28). Hershey, PA: IGI Global. doi:10.4018/978-1-5225-1965-2.ch002

K., I., & A, V. (2018). Monitoring and Auditing in the Cloud. In K. Munir (Ed.), *Cloud Computing Technologies for Green Enterprises* (pp. 318-350). Hershey, PA: IGI Global. doi:10.4018/978-1-5225-3038-1.ch013

Kabra, G., Ghosh, V., & Ramesh, A. (2018). Enterprise Integrated Business Process Management and Business Intelligence Framework for Business Process Sustainability. In A. Paul, D. Bhattacharyya, & S. Anand (Eds.), *Green Initiatives for Business Sustainability and Value Creation* (pp. 228–238). Hershey, PA: IGI Global. doi:10.4018/978-1-5225-2662-9.ch010

Kaoud, M. (2017). Investigation of Customer Knowledge Management: A Case Study Research. *International Journal of Service Science, Management, Engineering, and Technology*, *8*(2), 12–22. doi:10.4018/IJSSMET.2017040102

Kara, M. E., & Fırat, S. Ü. (2016). Sustainability, Risk, and Business Intelligence in Supply Chains. In M. Erdoğdu, T. Arun, & I. Ahmad (Eds.), *Handbook of Research on Green Economic Development Initiatives and Strategies* (pp. 501–538). Hershey, PA: IGI Global. doi:10.4018/978-1-5225-0440-5.ch022

Katuu, S. (2018). A Comparative Assessment of Enterprise Content Management Maturity Models. In N. Gwangwava & M. Mutingi (Eds.), *E-Manufacturing and E-Service Strategies in Contemporary Organizations* (pp. 93–118). Hershey, PA: IGI Global. doi:10.4018/978-1-5225-3628-4.ch005

Khan, M. A. (2016). MNEs Management Strategies in Developing Countries: Establishing the Context. In M. Khan (Ed.), *Multinational Enterprise Management Strategies in Developing Countries* (pp. 1–33). Hershey, PA: IGI Global. doi:10.4018/978-1-5225-0276-0.ch001

Khan, M. A. (2016). Operational Approaches in Organizational Structure: A Case for MNEs in Developing Countries. In M. Khan (Ed.), *Multinational Enterprise Management Strategies in Developing Countries* (pp. 129–151). Hershey, PA: IGI Global. doi:10.4018/978-1-5225-0276-0.ch007

Kinnunen, S., Ylä-Kujala, A., Marttonen-Arola, S., Kärri, T., & Baglee, D. (2018). Internet of Things in Asset Management: Insights from Industrial Professionals and Academia. *International Journal of Service Science, Management, Engineering, and Technology*, *9*(2), 104–119. doi:10.4018/IJSSMET.2018040105

Klein, A. Z., Sabino de Freitas, A., Machado, L., Freitas, J. C. Jr, Graziola, P. G. Jr, & Schlemmer, E. (2017). Virtual Worlds Applications for Management Education. In L. Tomei (Ed.), *Exploring the New Era of Technology-Infused Education* (pp. 279–299). Hershey, PA: IGI Global. doi:10.4018/978-1-5225-1709-2.ch017

Kożuch, B., & Jabłoński, A. (2017). Adopting the Concept of Business Models in Public Management. In M. Lewandowski & B. Kożuch (Eds.), *Public Sector Entrepreneurship and the Integration of Innovative Business Models* (pp. 10–46). Hershey, PA: IGI Global. doi:10.4018/978-1-5225-2215-7.ch002

Kumar, J., Adhikary, A., & Jha, A. (2017). Small Active Investors' Perceptions and Preferences Towards Tax Saving Mutual Fund Schemes in Eastern India: An Empirical Note. *International Journal of Asian Business and Information Management*, *8*(2), 35–45. doi:10.4018/IJABIM.2017040103

Lassoued, Y., Bouzguenda, L., & Mahmoud, T. (2016). Context-Aware Business Process Versions Management. *International Journal of e-Collaboration*, *12*(3), 7–33. doi:10.4018/IJeC.2016070102

Lavassani, K. M., & Movahedi, B. (2017). Applications Driven Information Systems: Beyond Networks toward Business Ecosystems. *International Journal of Innovation in the Digital Economy*, *8*(1), 61–75. doi:10.4018/IJIDE.2017010104

Lazzareschi, V. H., & Brito, M. S. (2017). Strategic Information Management: Proposal of Business Project Model. In G. Jamil, A. Soares, & C. Pessoa (Eds.), *Handbook of Research on Information Management for Effective Logistics and Supply Chains* (pp. 59–88). Hershey, PA: IGI Global. doi:10.4018/978-1-5225-0973-8.ch004

Lederer, M., Kurz, M., & Lazarov, P. (2017). Usage and Suitability of Methods for Strategic Business Process Initiatives: A Multi Case Study Research. *International Journal of Productivity Management and Assessment Technologies, 5*(1), 40–51. doi:10.4018/IJPMAT.2017010103

Lee, I. (2017). A Social Enterprise Business Model and a Case Study of Pacific Community Ventures (PCV). In V. Potocan, M. Üngan, & Z. Nedelko (Eds.), *Handbook of Research on Managerial Solutions in Non-Profit Organizations* (pp. 182–204). Hershey, PA: IGI Global. doi:10.4018/978-1-5225-0731-4.ch009

Lee, L. J., & Leu, J. (2016). Exploring the Effectiveness of IT Application and Value Method in the Innovation Performance of Enterprise. *International Journal of Enterprise Information Systems, 12*(2), 47–65. doi:10.4018/IJEIS.2016040104

Lee, Y. (2016). Alignment Effect of Entrepreneurial Orientation and Marketing Orientation on Firm Performance. *International Journal of Customer Relationship Marketing and Management, 7*(4), 58–69. doi:10.4018/IJCRMM.2016100104

Leon, L. A., Seal, K. C., Przasnyski, Z. H., & Wiedenman, I. (2017). Skills and Competencies Required for Jobs in Business Analytics: A Content Analysis of Job Advertisements Using Text Mining. *International Journal of Business Intelligence Research, 8*(1), 1–25. doi:10.4018/IJBIR.2017010101

Leu, J., Lee, L. J., & Krischke, A. (2016). Value Engineering-Based Method for Implementing the ISO14001 System in the Green Supply Chains. *International Journal of Strategic Decision Sciences, 7*(4), 1–20. doi:10.4018/IJSDS.2016100101

Levy, C. L., & Elias, N. I. (2017). SOHO Users' Perceptions of Reliability and Continuity of Cloud-Based Services. In M. Moore (Ed.), *Cybersecurity Breaches and Issues Surrounding Online Threat Protection* (pp. 248–287). Hershey, PA: IGI Global. doi:10.4018/978-1-5225-1941-6.ch011

Levy, M. (2018). Change Management Serving Knowledge Management and Organizational Development: Reflections and Review. In N. Baporikar (Ed.), *Global Practices in Knowledge Management for Societal and Organizational Development* (pp. 256–270). Hershey, PA: IGI Global. doi:10.4018/978-1-5225-3009-1.ch012

Lewandowski, M. (2017). Public Organizations and Business Model Innovation: The Role of Public Service Design. In M. Lewandowski & B. Kożuch (Eds.), *Public Sector Entrepreneurship and the Integration of Innovative Business Models* (pp. 47–72). Hershey, PA: IGI Global. doi:10.4018/978-1-5225-2215-7.ch003

Lhannaoui, H., Kabbaj, M. I., & Bakkoury, Z. (2017). A Survey of Risk-Aware Business Process Modelling. *International Journal of Risk and Contingency Management*, *6*(3), 14–26. doi:10.4018/IJRCM.2017070102

Li, J., Sun, W., Jiang, W., Yang, H., & Zhang, L. (2017). How the Nature of Exogenous Shocks and Crises Impact Company Performance?: The Effects of Industry Characteristics. *International Journal of Risk and Contingency Management*, *6*(4), 40–55. doi:10.4018/IJRCM.2017100103

Lu, C., & Liu, S. (2016). Cultural Tourism O2O Business Model Innovation-A Case Study of CTrip. *Journal of Electronic Commerce in Organizations*, *14*(2), 16–31. doi:10.4018/JECO.2016040102

Machen, B., Hosseini, M. R., Wood, A., & Bakhshi, J. (2016). An Investigation into using SAP-PS as a Multidimensional Project Control System (MPCS). *International Journal of Enterprise Information Systems*, *12*(2), 66–81. doi:10.4018/IJEIS.2016040105

Malega, P. (2017). Small and Medium Enterprises in the Slovak Republic: Status and Competitiveness of SMEs in the Global Markets and Possibilities of Optimization. In M. Vemić (Ed.), *Optimal Management Strategies in Small and Medium Enterprises* (pp. 102–124). Hershey, PA: IGI Global. doi:10.4018/978-1-5225-1949-2.ch006

Malewska, K. M. (2017). Intuition in Decision-Making on the Example of a Non-Profit Organization. In V. Potocan, M. Üngan, & Z. Nedelko (Eds.), *Handbook of Research on Managerial Solutions in Non-Profit Organizations* (pp. 378–399). Hershey, PA: IGI Global. doi:10.4018/978-1-5225-0731-4.ch018

Maroofi, F. (2017). Entrepreneurial Orientation and Organizational Learning Ability Analysis for Innovation and Firm Performance. In N. Baporikar (Ed.), *Innovation and Shifting Perspectives in Management Education* (pp. 144–165). Hershey, PA: IGI Global. doi:10.4018/978-1-5225-1019-2.ch007

Martins, P. V., & Zacarias, M. (2017). A Web-based Tool for Business Process Improvement. *International Journal of Web Portals*, *9*(2), 68–84. doi:10.4018/IJWP.2017070104

Matthies, B., & Coners, A. (2017). Exploring the Conceptual Nature of e-Business Projects. *Journal of Electronic Commerce in Organizations*, *15*(3), 33–63. doi:10.4018/JECO.2017070103

McKee, J. (2018). Architecture as a Tool to Solve Business Planning Problems. In M. Khosrow-Pour, D.B.A. (Ed.), Encyclopedia of Information Science and Technology, Fourth Edition (pp. 573-586). Hershey, PA: IGI Global. doi:10.4018/978-1-5225-2255-3.ch050

McMurray, A. J., Cross, J., & Caponecchia, C. (2018). The Risk Management Profession in Australia: Business Continuity Plan Practices. In N. Bajgoric (Ed.), *Always-On Enterprise Information Systems for Modern Organizations* (pp. 112–129). Hershey, PA: IGI Global. doi:10.4018/978-1-5225-3704-5.ch006

Meddah, I. H., & Belkadi, K. (2018). Mining Patterns Using Business Process Management. In R. Hamou (Ed.), *Handbook of Research on Biomimicry in Information Retrieval and Knowledge Management* (pp. 78–89). Hershey, PA: IGI Global. doi:10.4018/978-1-5225-3004-6.ch005

Mendes, L. (2017). TQM and Knowledge Management: An Integrated Approach Towards Tacit Knowledge Management. In D. Jaziri-Bouagina & G. Jamil (Eds.), *Handbook of Research on Tacit Knowledge Management for Organizational Success* (pp. 236–263). Hershey, PA: IGI Global. doi:10.4018/978-1-5225-2394-9.ch009

Mnjama, N. M. (2017). Preservation of Recorded Information in Public and Private Sector Organizations. In P. Jain & N. Mnjama (Eds.), *Managing Knowledge Resources and Records in Modern Organizations* (pp. 149–167). Hershey, PA: IGI Global. doi:10.4018/978-1-5225-1965-2.ch009

Mokoqama, M., & Fields, Z. (2017). Principles of Responsible Management Education (PRME): Call for Responsible Management Education. In Z. Fields (Ed.), *Collective Creativity for Responsible and Sustainable Business Practice* (pp. 229–241). Hershey, PA: IGI Global. doi:10.4018/978-1-5225-1823-5.ch012

Muniapan, B. (2017). Philosophy and Management: The Relevance of Vedanta in Management. In P. Ordóñez de Pablos (Ed.), *Managerial Strategies and Solutions for Business Success in Asia* (pp. 124–139). Hershey, PA: IGI Global. doi:10.4018/978-1-5225-1886-0.ch007

Muniapan, B., Gregory, M. L., & Ling, L. A. (2016). Marketing Education in Sarawak: Looking at It from the Employers' Viewpoint. In B. Smith & A. Porath (Eds.), *Global Perspectives on Contemporary Marketing Education* (pp. 112–130). Hershey, PA: IGI Global. doi:10.4018/978-1-4666-9784-3.ch008

Murad, S. E., & Dowaji, S. (2017). Using Value-Based Approach for Managing Cloud-Based Services. In A. Turuk, B. Sahoo, & S. Addya (Eds.), *Resource Management and Efficiency in Cloud Computing Environments* (pp. 33–60). Hershey, PA: IGI Global. doi:10.4018/978-1-5225-1721-4.ch002

Mutahar, A. M., Daud, N. M., Thurasamy, R., Isaac, O., & Abdulsalam, R. (2018). The Mediating of Perceived Usefulness and Perceived Ease of Use: The Case of Mobile Banking in Yemen. *International Journal of Technology Diffusion*, *9*(2), 21–40. doi:10.4018/IJTD.2018040102

Naidoo, V. (2017). E-Learning and Management Education at African Universities. In N. Baporikar (Ed.), *Management Education for Global Leadership* (pp. 181–201). Hershey, PA: IGI Global. doi:10.4018/978-1-5225-1013-0.ch009

Naidoo, V., & Igbinakhase, I. (2018). Opportunities and Challenges of Knowledge Retention in SMEs. In N. Baporikar (Ed.), *Knowledge Integration Strategies for Entrepreneurship and Sustainability* (pp. 70–94). Hershey, PA: IGI Global. doi:10.4018/978-1-5225-5115-7.ch004

Nayak, S., & Prabhu, N. (2017). Paradigm Shift in Management Education: Need for a Cross Functional Perspective. In N. Baporikar (Ed.), *Management Education for Global Leadership* (pp. 241–255). Hershey, PA: IGI Global. doi:10.4018/978-1-5225-1013-0.ch012

Ndede-Amadi, A. A. (2016). Student Interest in the IS Specialization as Predictor of the Success Potential of New Information Systems Programmes within the Schools of Business in Kenyan Public Universities. *International Journal of Information Systems and Social Change*, *7*(2), 63–79. doi:10.4018/IJISSC.2016040104

Nedelko, Z., & Potocan, V. (2016). Management Practices for Processes Optimization: Case of Slovenia. In G. Alor-Hernández, C. Sánchez-Ramírez, & J. García-Alcaraz (Eds.), *Handbook of Research on Managerial Strategies for Achieving Optimal Performance in Industrial Processes* (pp. 545–561). Hershey, PA: IGI Global. doi:10.4018/978-1-5225-0130-5.ch025

Nedelko, Z., & Potocan, V. (2017). Management Solutions in Non-Profit Organizations: Case of Slovenia. In V. Potocan, M. Ünğan, & Z. Nedelko (Eds.), *Handbook of Research on Managerial Solutions in Non-Profit Organizations* (pp. 1–22). Hershey, PA: IGI Global. doi:10.4018/978-1-5225-0731-4.ch001

Nedelko, Z., & Potocan, V. (2017). Priority of Management Tools Utilization among Managers: International Comparison. In V. Wang (Ed.), *Encyclopedia of Strategic Leadership and Management* (pp. 1083–1094). Hershey, PA: IGI Global. doi:10.4018/978-1-5225-1049-9.ch075

Nedelko, Z., Raudeliūnienė, J., & Črešnar, R. (2018). Knowledge Dynamics in Supply Chain Management. In N. Baporikar (Ed.), *Knowledge Integration Strategies for Entrepreneurship and Sustainability* (pp. 150–166). Hershey, PA: IGI Global. doi:10.4018/978-1-5225-5115-7.ch008

Nguyen, H. T., & Hipsher, S. A. (2018). Innovation and Creativity Used by Private Sector Firms in a Resources-Constrained Environment. In S. Hipsher (Ed.), *Examining the Private Sector's Role in Wealth Creation and Poverty Reduction* (pp. 219–238). Hershey, PA: IGI Global. doi:10.4018/978-1-5225-3117-3.ch010

Nycz, M., & Pólkowski, Z. (2016). Business Intelligence as a Modern IT Supporting Management of Local Government Units in Poland. *International Journal of Knowledge and Systems Science, 7*(4), 1–18. doi:10.4018/IJKSS.2016100101

Obaji, N. O., Senin, A. A., & Olugu, M. U. (2016). Supportive Government Policy as a Mechanism for Business Incubation Performance in Nigeria. *International Journal of Information Systems and Social Change, 7*(4), 52–66. doi:10.4018/IJISSC.2016100103

Obicci, P. A. (2017). Risk Sharing in a Partnership. In *Risk Management Strategies in Public-Private Partnerships* (pp. 115–152). Hershey, PA: IGI Global. doi:10.4018/978-1-5225-2503-5.ch004

Obidallah, W. J., & Raahemi, B. (2017). Managing Changes in Service Oriented Virtual Organizations: A Structural and Procedural Framework to Facilitate the Process of Change. *Journal of Electronic Commerce in Organizations, 15*(1), 59–83. doi:10.4018/JECO.2017010104

Ojasalo, J., & Ojasalo, K. (2016). Service Logic Business Model Canvas for Lean Development of SMEs and Start-Ups. In N. Baporikar (Ed.), *Handbook of Research on Entrepreneurship in the Contemporary Knowledge-Based Global Economy* (pp. 217–243). Hershey, PA: IGI Global. doi:10.4018/978-1-4666-8798-1.ch010

Ojo, O. (2017). Impact of Innovation on the Entrepreneurial Success in Selected Business Enterprises in South-West Nigeria. *International Journal of Innovation in the Digital Economy, 8*(2), 29–38. doi:10.4018/IJIDE.2017040103

Okdinawati, L., Simatupang, T. M., & Sunitiyoso, Y. (2017). Multi-Agent Reinforcement Learning for Value Co-Creation of Collaborative Transportation Management (CTM). *International Journal of Information Systems and Supply Chain Management, 10*(3), 84–95. doi:10.4018/IJISSCM.2017070105

Ortner, E., Mevius, M., Wiedmann, P., & Kurz, F. (2016). Design of Interactional Decision Support Applications for E-Participation in Smart Cities. *International Journal of Electronic Government Research, 12*(2), 18–38. doi:10.4018/IJEGR.2016040102

Pal, K. (2018). Building High Quality Big Data-Based Applications in Supply Chains. In A. Kumar & S. Saurav (Eds.), *Supply Chain Management Strategies and Risk Assessment in Retail Environments* (pp. 1–24). Hershey, PA: IGI Global. doi:10.4018/978-1-5225-3056-5.ch001

Palos-Sanchez, P. R., & Correia, M. B. (2018). Perspectives of the Adoption of Cloud Computing in the Tourism Sector. In J. Rodrigues, C. Ramos, P. Cardoso, & C. Henriques (Eds.), *Handbook of Research on Technological Developments for Cultural Heritage and eTourism Applications* (pp. 377–400). Hershey, PA: IGI Global. doi:10.4018/978-1-5225-2927-9.ch018

Parry, V. K., & Lind, M. L. (2016). Alignment of Business Strategy and Information Technology Considering Information Technology Governance, Project Portfolio Control, and Risk Management. *International Journal of Information Technology Project Management, 7*(4), 21–37. doi:10.4018/IJITPM.2016100102

Pashkova, N., Trujillo-Barrera, A., Apostolakis, G., Van Dijk, G., Drakos, P. D., & Baourakis, G. (2016). Business Management Models of Microfinance Institutions (MFIs) in Africa: A Study into Their Enabling Environments. *International Journal of Food and Beverage Manufacturing and Business Models, 1*(2), 63–82. doi:10.4018/IJFBMBM.2016070105

Patiño, B. E. (2017). New Generation Management by Convergence and Individual Identity: A Systemic and Human-Oriented Approach. In N. Baporikar (Ed.), *Innovation and Shifting Perspectives in Management Education* (pp. 119–143). Hershey, PA: IGI Global. doi:10.4018/978-1-5225-1019-2.ch006

Pawliczek, A., & Rössler, M. (2017). Knowledge of Management Tools and Systems in SMEs: Knowledge Transfer in Management. In A. Bencsik (Ed.), *Knowledge Management Initiatives and Strategies in Small and Medium Enterprises* (pp. 180–203). Hershey, PA: IGI Global. doi:10.4018/978-1-5225-1642-2.ch009

Pejic-Bach, M., Omazic, M. A., Aleksic, A., & Zoroja, J. (2018). Knowledge-Based Decision Making: A Multi-Case Analysis. In R. Leon (Ed.), *Managerial Strategies for Business Sustainability During Turbulent Times* (pp. 160–184). Hershey, PA: IGI Global. doi:10.4018/978-1-5225-2716-9.ch009

Perano, M., Hysa, X., & Calabrese, M. (2018). Strategic Planning, Cultural Context, and Business Continuity Management: Business Cases in the City of Shkoder. In A. Presenza & L. Sheehan (Eds.), *Geopolitics and Strategic Management in the Global Economy* (pp. 57–77). Hershey, PA: IGI Global. doi:10.4018/978-1-5225-2673-5.ch004

Pereira, R., Mira da Silva, M., & Lapão, L. V. (2017). IT Governance Maturity Patterns in Portuguese Healthcare. In S. De Haes & W. Van Grembergen (Eds.), *Strategic IT Governance and Alignment in Business Settings* (pp. 24–52). Hershey, PA: IGI Global. doi:10.4018/978-1-5225-0861-8.ch002

Perez-Uribe, R., & Ocampo-Guzman, D. (2016). Conflict within Colombian Family Owned SMEs: An Explosive Blend between Feelings and Business. In J. Saiz-Álvarez (Ed.), *Handbook of Research on Social Entrepreneurship and Solidarity Economics* (pp. 329–354). Hershey, PA: IGI Global. doi:10.4018/978-1-5225-0097-1.ch017

Pérez-Uribe, R. I., Torres, D. A., Jurado, S. P., & Prada, D. M. (2018). Cloud Tools for the Development of Project Management in SMEs. In R. Perez-Uribe, C. Salcedo-Perez, & D. Ocampo-Guzman (Eds.), *Handbook of Research on Intrapreneurship and Organizational Sustainability in SMEs* (pp. 95–120). Hershey, PA: IGI Global. doi:10.4018/978-1-5225-3543-0.ch005

Petrisor, I., & Cozmiuc, D. (2017). Global Supply Chain Management Organization at Siemens in the Advent of Industry 4.0. In L. Saglietto & C. Cezanne (Eds.), *Global Intermediation and Logistics Service Providers* (pp. 123–142). Hershey, PA: IGI Global. doi:10.4018/978-1-5225-2133-4.ch007

Pierce, J. M., Velliaris, D. M., & Edwards, J. (2017). A Living Case Study: A Journey Not a Destination. In N. Silton (Ed.), *Exploring the Benefits of Creativity in Education, Media, and the Arts* (pp. 158–178). Hershey, PA: IGI Global. doi:10.4018/978-1-5225-0504-4.ch008

Radosavljevic, M., & Andjelkovic, A. (2017). Multi-Criteria Decision Making Approach for Choosing Business Process for the Improvement: Upgrading of the Six Sigma Methodology. In J. Stanković, P. Delias, S. Marinković, & S. Rochhia (Eds.), *Tools and Techniques for Economic Decision Analysis* (pp. 225–247). Hershey, PA: IGI Global. doi:10.4018/978-1-5225-0959-2.ch011

Radovic, V. M. (2017). Corporate Sustainability and Responsibility and Disaster Risk Reduction: A Serbian Overview. In M. Camilleri (Ed.), *CSR 2.0 and the New Era of Corporate Citizenship* (pp. 147–164). Hershey, PA: IGI Global. doi:10.4018/978-1-5225-1842-6.ch008

Raghunath, K. M., Devi, S. L., & Patro, C. S. (2018). Impact of Risk Assessment Models on Risk Factors: A Holistic Outlook. In K. Strang, M. Korstanje, & N. Vajjhala (Eds.), *Research, Practices, and Innovations in Global Risk and Contingency Management* (pp. 134–153). Hershey, PA: IGI Global. doi:10.4018/978-1-5225-4754-9.ch008

Raman, A., & Goyal, D. P. (2017). Extending IMPLEMENT Framework for Enterprise Information Systems Implementation to Information System Innovation. In M. Tavana (Ed.), *Enterprise Information Systems and the Digitalization of Business Functions* (pp. 137–177). Hershey, PA: IGI Global. doi:10.4018/978-1-5225-2382-6.ch007

Rao, Y., & Zhang, Y. (2017). The Construction and Development of Academic Library Digital Special Subject Databases. In L. Ruan, Q. Zhu, & Y. Ye (Eds.), *Academic Library Development and Administration in China* (pp. 163–183). Hershey, PA: IGI Global. doi:10.4018/978-1-5225-0550-1.ch010

Ravasan, A. Z., Mohammadi, M. M., & Hamidi, H. (2018). An Investigation Into the Critical Success Factors of Implementing Information Technology Service Management Frameworks. In K. Jakobs (Ed.), *Corporate and Global Standardization Initiatives in Contemporary Society* (pp. 200–218). Hershey, PA: IGI Global. doi:10.4018/978-1-5225-5320-5.ch009

Renna, P., Izzo, C., & Romaniello, T. (2016). The Business Process Management Systems to Support Continuous Improvements. In W. Nuninger & J. Châtelet (Eds.), *Handbook of Research on Quality Assurance and Value Management in Higher Education* (pp. 237–256). Hershey, PA: IGI Global. doi:10.4018/978-1-5225-0024-7.ch009

Rezaie, S., Mirabedini, S. J., & Abtahi, A. (2018). Designing a Model for Implementation of Business Intelligence in the Banking Industry. *International Journal of Enterprise Information Systems, 14*(1), 77–103. doi:10.4018/IJEIS.2018010105

Riccò, R. (2016). Diversity Management: Bringing Equality, Equity, and Inclusion in the Workplace. In J. Prescott (Ed.), *Handbook of Research on Race, Gender, and the Fight for Equality* (pp. 335–359). Hershey, PA: IGI Global. doi:10.4018/978-1-5225-0047-6.ch015

Romano, L., Grimaldi, R., & Colasuonno, F. S. (2017). Demand Management as a Success Factor in Project Portfolio Management. In L. Romano (Ed.), *Project Portfolio Management Strategies for Effective Organizational Operations* (pp. 202–219). Hershey, PA: IGI Global. doi:10.4018/978-1-5225-2151-8.ch008

Rostek, K. B. (2016). Risk Management: Role and Importance in Business Organization. In D. Jakóbczak (Ed.), *Analyzing Risk through Probabilistic Modeling in Operations Research* (pp. 149–178). Hershey, PA: IGI Global. doi:10.4018/978-1-4666-9458-3.ch007

Rouhani, S., & Savoji, S. R. (2016). A Success Assessment Model for BI Tools Implementation: An Empirical Study of Banking Industry. *International Journal of Business Intelligence Research, 7*(1), 25–44. doi:10.4018/IJBIR.2016010103

Ruan, Z. (2016). A Corpus-Based Functional Analysis of Complex Nominal Groups in Written Business Discourse: The Case of "Business". *International Journal of Computer-Assisted Language Learning and Teaching*, *6*(2), 74–90. doi:10.4018/IJCALLT.2016040105

Ruhi, U. (2018). Towards an Interdisciplinary Socio-Technical Definition of Virtual Communities. In M. Khosrow-Pour, D.B.A. (Ed.), Encyclopedia of Information Science and Technology, Fourth Edition (pp. 4278-4295). Hershey, PA: IGI Global. doi:10.4018/978-1-5225-2255-3.ch371

Ryan, J., Doster, B., Daily, S., & Lewis, C. (2016). A Case Study Perspective for Balanced Perioperative Workflow Achievement through Data-Driven Process Improvement. *International Journal of Healthcare Information Systems and Informatics*, *11*(3), 19–41. doi:10.4018/IJHISI.2016070102

Safari, M. R., & Jiang, Q. (2018). The Theory and Practice of IT Governance Maturity and Strategies Alignment: Evidence From Banking Industry. *Journal of Global Information Management*, *26*(2), 127–146. doi:10.4018/JGIM.2018040106

Sahoo, J., Pati, B., & Mohanty, B. (2017). Knowledge Management as an Academic Discipline: An Assessment. In B. Gunjal (Ed.), *Managing Knowledge and Scholarly Assets in Academic Libraries* (pp. 99–126). Hershey, PA: IGI Global. doi:10.4018/978-1-5225-1741-2.ch005

Saini, D. (2017). Relevance of Teaching Values and Ethics in Management Education. In N. Baporikar (Ed.), *Management Education for Global Leadership* (pp. 90–111). Hershey, PA: IGI Global. doi:10.4018/978-1-5225-1013-0.ch005

Sambhanthan, A. (2017). Assessing and Benchmarking Sustainability in Organisations: An Integrated Conceptual Model. *International Journal of Systems and Service-Oriented Engineering*, *7*(4), 22–43. doi:10.4018/IJSSOE.2017100102

Sambhanthan, A., & Potdar, V. (2017). A Study of the Parameters Impacting Sustainability in Information Technology Organizations. *International Journal of Knowledge-Based Organizations*, *7*(3), 27–39. doi:10.4018/IJKBO.2017070103

Sánchez-Fernández, M. D., & Manríquez, M. R. (2018). The Entrepreneurial Spirit Based on Social Values: The Digital Generation. In P. Isaias & L. Carvalho (Eds.), *User Innovation and the Entrepreneurship Phenomenon in the Digital Economy* (pp. 173–193). Hershey, PA: IGI Global. doi:10.4018/978-1-5225-2826-5.ch009

Sanchez-Ruiz, L., & Blanco, B. (2017). Process Management for SMEs: Barriers, Enablers, and Benefits. In M. Vemić (Ed.), *Optimal Management Strategies in Small and Medium Enterprises* (pp. 293–319). Hershey, PA: IGI Global. doi:10.4018/978-1-5225-1949-2.ch014

Sanz, L. F., Gómez-Pérez, J., & Castillo-Martinez, A. (2018). Analysis of the European ICT Competence Frameworks. In V. Ahuja & S. Rathore (Eds.), *Multidisciplinary Perspectives on Human Capital and Information Technology Professionals* (pp. 225–245). Hershey, PA: IGI Global. doi:10.4018/978-1-5225-5297-0.ch012

Sarvepalli, A., & Godin, J. (2017). Business Process Management in the Classroom. *Journal of Cases on Information Technology, 19*(2), 17–28. doi:10.4018/JCIT.2017040102

Satpathy, B., & Muniapan, B. (2016). Ancient Wisdom for Transformational Leadership and Its Insights from the Bhagavad-Gita. In U. Aung & P. Ordoñez de Pablos (Eds.), *Managerial Strategies and Practice in the Asian Business Sector* (pp. 1–10). Hershey, PA: IGI Global. doi:10.4018/978-1-4666-9758-4.ch001

Saygili, E. E., Ozturkoglu, Y., & Kocakulah, M. C. (2017). End Users' Perceptions of Critical Success Factors in ERP Applications. *International Journal of Enterprise Information Systems, 13*(4), 58–75. doi:10.4018/IJEIS.2017100104

Saygili, E. E., & Saygili, A. T. (2017). Contemporary Issues in Enterprise Information Systems: A Critical Review of CSFs in ERP Implementations. In M. Tavana (Ed.), *Enterprise Information Systems and the Digitalization of Business Functions* (pp. 120–136). Hershey, PA: IGI Global. doi:10.4018/978-1-5225-2382-6.ch006

Seidenstricker, S., & Antonino, A. (2018). Business Model Innovation-Oriented Technology Management for Emergent Technologies. In M. Khosrow-Pour, D.B.A. (Ed.), Encyclopedia of Information Science and Technology, Fourth Edition (pp. 4560-4569). Hershey, PA: IGI Global. doi:10.4018/978-1-5225-2255-3.ch396

Senaratne, S., & Gunarathne, A. D. (2017). Excellence Perspective for Management Education from a Global Accountants' Hub in Asia. In N. Baporikar (Ed.), *Management Education for Global Leadership* (pp. 158–180). Hershey, PA: IGI Global. doi:10.4018/978-1-5225-1013-0.ch008

Sensuse, D. I., & Cahyaningsih, E. (2018). Knowledge Management Models: A Summative Review. *International Journal of Information Systems in the Service Sector, 10*(1), 71–100. doi:10.4018/IJISSS.2018010105

Sensuse, D. I., Wibowo, W. C., & Cahyaningsih, E. (2016). Indonesian Government Knowledge Management Model: A Theoretical Model. *Information Resources Management Journal, 29*(1), 91–108. doi:10.4018/irmj.2016010106

Seth, M., Goyal, D., & Kiran, R. (2017). Diminution of Impediments in Implementation of Supply Chain Management Information System for Enhancing its Effectiveness in Indian Automobile Industry. *Journal of Global Information Management, 25*(3), 1–20. doi:10.4018/JGIM.2017070101

Seyal, A. H., & Rahman, M. N. (2017). Investigating Impact of Inter-Organizational Factors in Measuring ERP Systems Success: Bruneian Perspectives. In M. Tavana (Ed.), *Enterprise Information Systems and the Digitalization of Business Functions* (pp. 178–204). Hershey, PA: IGI Global. doi:10.4018/978-1-5225-2382-6.ch008

Shaikh, A. A., & Karjaluoto, H. (2016). On Some Misconceptions Concerning Digital Banking and Alternative Delivery Channels. *International Journal of E-Business Research, 12*(3), 1–16. doi:10.4018/IJEBR.2016070101

Shams, S. M. (2016). Stakeholder Relationship Management in Online Business and Competitive Value Propositions: Evidence from the Sports Industry. *International Journal of Online Marketing, 6*(2), 1–17. doi:10.4018/IJOM.2016040101

Shamsuzzoha, A. (2016). Management of Risk and Resilience within Collaborative Business Network. In R. Addo-Tenkorang, J. Kantola, P. Helo, & A. Shamsuzzoha (Eds.), *Supply Chain Strategies and the Engineer-to-Order Approach* (pp. 143–159). Hershey, PA: IGI Global. doi:10.4018/978-1-5225-0021-6.ch008

Shaqrah, A. A. (2018). Analyzing Business Intelligence Systems Based on 7s Model of McKinsey. *International Journal of Business Intelligence Research, 9*(1), 53–63. doi:10.4018/IJBIR.2018010104

Sharma, A. J. (2017). Enhancing Sustainability through Experiential Learning in Management Education. In N. Baporikar (Ed.), *Management Education for Global Leadership* (pp. 256–274). Hershey, PA: IGI Global. doi:10.4018/978-1-5225-1013-0.ch013

Shetty, K. P. (2017). Responsible Global Leadership: Ethical Challenges in Management Education. In N. Baporikar (Ed.), *Innovation and Shifting Perspectives in Management Education* (pp. 194–223). Hershey, PA: IGI Global. doi:10.4018/978-1-5225-1019-2.ch009

Sinthupundaja, J., & Kohda, Y. (2017). Effects of Corporate Social Responsibility and Creating Shared Value on Sustainability. *International Journal of Sustainable Entrepreneurship and Corporate Social Responsibility*, *2*(1), 27–38. doi:10.4018/IJSECSR.2017010103

Škarica, I., & Hrgović, A. V. (2018). Implementation of Total Quality Management Principles in Public Health Institutes in the Republic of Croatia. *International Journal of Productivity Management and Assessment Technologies*, *6*(1), 1–16. doi:10.4018/IJPMAT.2018010101

Smuts, H., Kotzé, P., Van der Merwe, A., & Loock, M. (2017). Framework for Managing Shared Knowledge in an Information Systems Outsourcing Context. *International Journal of Knowledge Management*, *13*(4), 1–30. doi:10.4018/IJKM.2017100101

Soares, E. R., & Zaidan, F. H. (2016). Information Architecture and Business Modeling in Modern Organizations of Information Technology: Professional Career Plan in Organizations IT. In G. Jamil, J. Poças Rascão, F. Ribeiro, & A. Malheiro da Silva (Eds.), *Handbook of Research on Information Architecture and Management in Modern Organizations* (pp. 439–457). Hershey, PA: IGI Global. doi:10.4018/978-1-4666-8637-3.ch020

Sousa, M. J., Cruz, R., Dias, I., & Caracol, C. (2017). Information Management Systems in the Supply Chain. In G. Jamil, A. Soares, & C. Pessoa (Eds.), *Handbook of Research on Information Management for Effective Logistics and Supply Chains* (pp. 469–485). Hershey, PA: IGI Global. doi:10.4018/978-1-5225-0973-8.ch025

Spremic, M., Turulja, L., & Bajgoric, N. (2018). Two Approaches in Assessing Business Continuity Management Attitudes in the Organizational Context. In N. Bajgoric (Ed.), *Always-On Enterprise Information Systems for Modern Organizations* (pp. 159–183). Hershey, PA: IGI Global. doi:10.4018/978-1-5225-3704-5.ch008

Steenkamp, A. L. (2018). Some Insights in Computer Science and Information Technology. In *Examining the Changing Role of Supervision in Doctoral Research Projects: Emerging Research and Opportunities* (pp. 113–133). Hershey, PA: IGI Global. doi:10.4018/978-1-5225-2610-0.ch005

Studdard, N., Dawson, M., Burton, S. L., Jackson, N., Leonard, B., Quisenberry, W., & Rahim, E. (2016). Nurturing Social Entrepreneurship and Building Social Entrepreneurial Self-Efficacy: Focusing on Primary and Secondary Schooling to Develop Future Social Entrepreneurs. In Z. Fields (Ed.), *Incorporating Business Models and Strategies into Social Entrepreneurship* (pp. 154–175). Hershey, PA: IGI Global. doi:10.4018/978-1-4666-8748-6.ch010

Sun, Z. (2016). A Framework for Developing Management Intelligent Systems. *International Journal of Systems and Service-Oriented Engineering*, *6*(1), 37–53. doi:10.4018/IJSSOE.2016010103

Swami, B., & Mphele, G. T. (2016). Problems Preventing Growth of Small Entrepreneurs: A Case Study of a Few Small Entrepreneurs in Botswana Sub-Urban Areas. In N. Baporikar (Ed.), *Handbook of Research on Entrepreneurship in the Contemporary Knowledge-Based Global Economy* (pp. 479–508). Hershey, PA: IGI Global. doi:10.4018/978-1-4666-8798-1.ch020

Tabach, A., & Croteau, A. (2017). Configurations of Information Technology Governance Practices and Business Unit Performance. *International Journal of IT/Business Alignment and Governance*, *8*(2), 1–27. doi:10.4018/IJITBAG.2017070101

Talaue, G. M., & Iqbal, T. (2017). Assessment of e-Business Mode of Selected Private Universities in the Philippines and Pakistan. *International Journal of Online Marketing*, *7*(4), 63–77. doi:10.4018/IJOM.2017100105

Tam, G. C. (2017). Project Manager Sustainability Competence. In *Managerial Strategies and Green Solutions for Project Sustainability* (pp. 178–207). Hershey, PA: IGI Global. doi:10.4018/978-1-5225-2371-0.ch008

Tambo, T. (2018). Fashion Retail Innovation: About Context, Antecedents, and Outcome in Technological Change Projects. In I. Management Association (Ed.), Fashion and Textiles: Breakthroughs in Research and Practice (pp. 233-260). Hershey, PA: IGI Global. doi:10.4018/978-1-5225-3432-7.ch010

Tambo, T., & Mikkelsen, O. E. (2016). Fashion Supply Chain Optimization: Linking Make-to-Order Purchasing and B2B E-Commerce. In S. Joshi & R. Joshi (Eds.), *Designing and Implementing Global Supply Chain Management* (pp. 1–21). Hershey, PA: IGI Global. doi:10.4018/978-1-4666-9720-1.ch001

Tandon, K. (2016). Innovative Andragogy: The Paradigm Shift to Heutagogy. In S. Tiwari & L. Nafees (Eds.), *Innovative Management Education Pedagogies for Preparing Next-Generation Leaders* (pp. 238–257). Hershey, PA: IGI Global. doi:10.4018/978-1-4666-9691-4.ch014

Tantau, A. D., & Frăţilă, L. C. (2018). Information and Management System for Renewable Energy Business. In *Entrepreneurship and Business Development in the Renewable Energy Sector* (pp. 200–244). Hershey, PA: IGI Global. doi:10.4018/978-1-5225-3625-3.ch006

Teixeira, N., Pardal, P. N., & Rafael, B. G. (2018). Internationalization, Financial Performance, and Organizational Challenges: A Success Case in Portugal. In L. Carvalho (Ed.), *Handbook of Research on Entrepreneurial Ecosystems and Social Dynamics in a Globalized World* (pp. 379–423). Hershey, PA: IGI Global. doi:10.4018/978-1-5225-3525-6.ch017

Trad, A., & Kalpić, D. (2016). The E-Business Transformation Framework for E-Commerce Architecture-Modeling Projects. In I. Lee (Ed.), *Encyclopedia of E-Commerce Development, Implementation, and Management* (pp. 733–753). Hershey, PA: IGI Global. doi:10.4018/978-1-4666-9787-4.ch052

Trad, A., & Kalpić, D. (2016). The E-Business Transformation Framework for E-Commerce Control and Monitoring Pattern. In I. Lee (Ed.), *Encyclopedia of E-Commerce Development, Implementation, and Management* (pp. 754–777). Hershey, PA: IGI Global. doi:10.4018/978-1-4666-9787-4.ch053

Trad, A., & Kalpić, D. (2018). The Business Transformation Framework, Agile Project and Change Management. In M. Khosrow-Pour, D.B.A. (Ed.), Encyclopedia of Information Science and Technology, Fourth Edition (pp. 620-635). Hershey, PA: IGI Global. doi:10.4018/978-1-5225-2255-3.ch054

Trad, A., & Kalpić, D. (2018). The Business Transformation and Enterprise Architecture Framework: The Financial Engineering E-Risk Management and E-Law Integration. In B. Sergi, F. Fidanoski, M. Ziolo, & V. Naumovski (Eds.), *Regaining Global Stability After the Financial Crisis* (pp. 46–65). Hershey, PA: IGI Global. doi:10.4018/978-1-5225-4026-7.ch003

Turulja, L., & Bajgoric, N. (2018). Business Continuity and Information Systems: A Systematic Literature Review. In N. Bajgoric (Ed.), *Always-On Enterprise Information Systems for Modern Organizations* (pp. 60–87). Hershey, PA: IGI Global. doi:10.4018/978-1-5225-3704-5.ch004

van Wessel, R. M., de Vries, H. J., & Ribbers, P. M. (2016). Business Benefits through Company IT Standardization. In K. Jakobs (Ed.), *Effective Standardization Management in Corporate Settings* (pp. 34–53). Hershey, PA: IGI Global. doi:10.4018/978-1-4666-9737-9.ch003

Vargas-Hernández, J. G. (2017). Professional Integrity in Business Management Education. In N. Baporikar (Ed.), *Management Education for Global Leadership* (pp. 70–89). Hershey, PA: IGI Global. doi:10.4018/978-1-5225-1013-0.ch004

Vasista, T. G., & AlAbdullatif, A. M. (2017). Role of Electronic Customer Relationship Management in Demand Chain Management: A Predictive Analytic Approach. *International Journal of Information Systems and Supply Chain Management, 10*(1), 53–67. doi:10.4018/IJISSCM.2017010104

Vergidis, K. (2016). Rediscovering Business Processes: Definitions, Patterns, and Modelling Approaches. In P. Papajorgji, F. Pinet, A. Guimarães, & J. Papathanasiou (Eds.), *Automated Enterprise Systems for Maximizing Business Performance* (pp. 97–122). Hershey, PA: IGI Global. doi:10.4018/978-1-4666-8841-4.ch007

Vieru, D., & Bourdeau, S. (2017). Survival in the Digital Era: A Digital Competence-Based Multi-Case Study in the Canadian SME Clothing Industry. *International Journal of Social and Organizational Dynamics in IT, 6*(1), 17–34. doi:10.4018/IJSODIT.2017010102

Vijayan, G., & Kamarulzaman, N. H. (2017). An Introduction to Sustainable Supply Chain Management and Business Implications. In M. Khan, M. Hussain, & M. Ajmal (Eds.), *Green Supply Chain Management for Sustainable Business Practice* (pp. 27–50). Hershey, PA: IGI Global. doi:10.4018/978-1-5225-0635-5.ch002

Vlachvei, A., & Notta, O. (2017). Firm Competitiveness: Theories, Evidence, and Measurement. In A. Vlachvei, O. Notta, K. Karantininis, & N. Tsounis (Eds.), *Factors Affecting Firm Competitiveness and Performance in the Modern Business World* (pp. 1–42). Hershey, PA: IGI Global. doi:10.4018/978-1-5225-0843-4.ch001

von Rosing, M., Fullington, N., & Walker, J. (2016). Using the Business Ontology and Enterprise Standards to Transform Three Leading Organizations. *International Journal of Conceptual Structures and Smart Applications, 4*(1), 71–99. doi:10.4018/IJCSSA.2016010104

von Rosing, M., & von Scheel, H. (2016). Using the Business Ontology to Develop Enterprise Standards. *International Journal of Conceptual Structures and Smart Applications, 4*(1), 48–70. doi:10.4018/IJCSSA.2016010103

Walczak, S. (2016). Artificial Neural Networks and other AI Applications for Business Management Decision Support. *International Journal of Sociotechnology and Knowledge Development, 8*(4), 1–20. doi:10.4018/IJSKD.2016100101

Wamba, S. F., Akter, S., Kang, H., Bhattacharya, M., & Upal, M. (2016). The Primer of Social Media Analytics. *Journal of Organizational and End User Computing, 28*(2), 1–12. doi:10.4018/JOEUC.2016040101

Wang, C., Schofield, M., Li, X., & Ou, X. (2017). Do Chinese Students in Public and Private Higher Education Institutes Perform at Different Level in One of the Leadership Skills: Critical Thinking?: An Exploratory Comparison. In V. Wang (Ed.), *Encyclopedia of Strategic Leadership and Management* (pp. 160–181). Hershey, PA: IGI Global. doi:10.4018/978-1-5225-1049-9.ch013

Wang, F., Raisinghani, M. S., Mora, M., & Wang, X. (2016). Strategic E-Business Management through a Balanced Scored Card Approach. In I. Lee (Ed.), *Encyclopedia of E-Commerce Development, Implementation, and Management* (pp. 361–386). Hershey, PA: IGI Global. doi:10.4018/978-1-4666-9787-4.ch027

Wang, J. (2017). Multi-Agent based Production Management Decision System Modelling for the Textile Enterprise. *Journal of Global Information Management, 25*(4), 1–15. doi:10.4018/JGIM.2017100101

Wiedemann, A., & Gewald, H. (2017). Examining Cross-Domain Alignment: The Correlation of Business Strategy, IT Management, and IT Business Value. *International Journal of IT/Business Alignment and Governance, 8*(1), 17–31. doi:10.4018/IJITBAG.2017010102

Wolf, R., & Thiel, M. (2018). Advancing Global Business Ethics in China: Reducing Poverty Through Human and Social Welfare. In S. Hipsher (Ed.), *Examining the Private Sector's Role in Wealth Creation and Poverty Reduction* (pp. 67–84). Hershey, PA: IGI Global. doi:10.4018/978-1-5225-3117-3.ch004

Wu, J., Ding, F., Xu, M., Mo, Z., & Jin, A. (2016). Investigating the Determinants of Decision-Making on Adoption of Public Cloud Computing in E-government. *Journal of Global Information Management, 24*(3), 71–89. doi:10.4018/JGIM.2016070104

Xu, L., & de Vrieze, P. (2016). Building Situational Applications for Virtual Enterprises. In I. Lee (Ed.), *Encyclopedia of E-Commerce Development, Implementation, and Management* (pp. 715–724). Hershey, PA: IGI Global. doi:10.4018/978-1-4666-9787-4.ch050

Yablonsky, S. (2018). Innovation Platforms: Data and Analytics Platforms. In *Multi-Sided Platforms (MSPs) and Sharing Strategies in the Digital Economy: Emerging Research and Opportunities* (pp. 72–95). Hershey, PA: IGI Global. doi:10.4018/978-1-5225-5457-8.ch003

Yusoff, A., Ahmad, N. H., & Halim, H. A. (2017). Agropreneurship among Gen Y in Malaysia: The Role of Academic Institutions. In N. Ahmad, T. Ramayah, H. Halim, & S. Rahman (Eds.), *Handbook of Research on Small and Medium Enterprises in Developing Countries* (pp. 23–47). Hershey, PA: IGI Global. doi:10.4018/978-1-5225-2165-5.ch002

Zanin, F., Comuzzi, E., & Costantini, A. (2018). The Effect of Business Strategy and Stock Market Listing on the Use of Risk Assessment Tools. In *Management Control Systems in Complex Settings: Emerging Research and Opportunities* (pp. 145–168). Hershey, PA: IGI Global. doi:10.4018/978-1-5225-3987-2.ch007

Zgheib, P. W. (2017). Corporate Innovation and Intrapreneurship in the Middle East. In P. Zgheib (Ed.), *Entrepreneurship and Business Innovation in the Middle East* (pp. 37–56). Hershey, PA: IGI Global. doi:10.4018/978-1-5225-2066-5.ch003

About the Contributors

Maximiliano Korstanje is editor in chief of International Journal of Safety and Security in Tourism (UP Argentina) and Editor in Chief Emeritus of International Journal of Cyber Warfare and Terrorism (IGI-Global US). Korstanje is Senior Researchers in the Department of Economics at University of Palermo, Argentina. In 2015 he was awarded as Visiting Research Fellow at School of Sociology and Social Policy, University of Leeds, UK and the University of La Habana Cuba. In 2017 is elected as Foreign Faculty Member of AMIT, Mexican Academy in the study of Tourism, which is the most prominent institutions dedicated to tourism research in Mexico. He had a vast experience in editorial projects working as advisory member of Elsevier, Routledge, Springer, IGI global and Cambridge Scholar publishing. Korstanje had visited and given seminars in many important universities worldwide. He has also recently been selected to take part of the 2018 Albert Nelson Marquis Lifetime Achievement Award. a great distinction given by Marquis Who´s Who in the world.

* * *

Bayram Akay was born in Burdur province of Turkey in 1982 and finished his primary education there. He studied in the department of the front office (Reception) in Fethiye Anatolian Hotel and Tourism Vocational School between 1996-2000 including one of the educational years as a preparatory school for the German language. He majored in Zile Dinçerler School of Tourism and Hospitality Department at Gaziosmanpaşa University and graduated in 2006. He graduated with a master degree in 2009 and a PhD degree in 2015 at Sakarya University Institute of Social Sciences Tourism Management Department. He has worked as a research assistant between 2011-2015 and Asst, Prof. Dr between 2015-2018 at Kırklareli University, Faculty of Tourism. He has appointed to Burdur Mehmet Akif Ersoy University, School of Tourism & Hotel Management as an Asst, Prof. Dr. since June 2018. He has many publications as papers, articles, sections in the book. His research interests include tourism management, car rental and tourism planning. He is married and has 2 children. He speaks English and German.

Aldana Boragnio is a Doctor in Sociology from the University of Alicante, Spain (UA). Magister in Research in Social Sciences and Graduate in Sociology from the University of Buenos Aires, Argentina (UBA). Member of the Study Group on the Sociology of Emotions and Bodies (GESEC) of the Gino Germani Research Institute (UBA) and the Center for Sociological Research and Studies (CIES), led by Dr Adrián Scribano. Assistant professor in the Social Psychology subject of the Sociology career at the University of Buenos Aires. She collaborates in the Latin American Journal of Studies on Bodies, Emotions and Society (RELACES). Her research work focuses on emotions and commensalities from the perspective of Bodies / Emotions. She currently holds a postdoctoral fellowship from the National Council for Scientific and Technical Research (CONICET), Argentina.

Florencia Chahbenderian has a degree in Economics (Faculty of Economic Sciences, University of Buenos Aires - UBA) and PhD in Social Sciences on course (Faculty of Social Sciences, UBA). Deputy Researcher of the project "Consumption, emotions, social policies and education for consumption" directed by Angélica De Sena, Faculty of Education and Social Communication Sciences, University of El Salvador (USAL). Member of the Group of Studies on Sociology of Emotions and Bodies (IIGG-UBA, CIES), directed by PhD Adrián Scribano, and of the Study Group on Social Policies and Emotions (IIGG-UBA, CIES), directed by PhD Angelica De Sena. Collaborator in the Latin American Journal of Social Research Methodology (ReLMIS) and First Assistant in "Sociology of Organizations" (Faculty of Economic Sciences, UBA).

Constanza Faracce Macia is a Sociologist (UBA). Candidate for a Master's Degree in Research in Social Sciences (FSOC-UBA). Member of the Center for Research on Consumption, Sensitivities and Creativity (CICSEC) of the University of Palermo and of the Study Group of Social Policies and Emotions, of the Center for Sociological Studies and Research (CIES). Member of the Editorial Team of the Latin American Journal of Bodies, Emotions and Society (RELACES). She is currently investigating emotions and food interventions.

Babu P. George has more than fifteen years of advanced business research, university teaching, and administrative service experience, in the US and internationally. Before joining Fort Hays State University in 2015, Dr. George has worked for Swiss Management Center University, University of Liverpool, University of Nevada Las Vegas, Alaska Pacific University, and the University of Southern Mississippi, among others. He is a visiting professor at various higher education institutions around the world. He is the editor of International Journal of Qualitative Research in Services. Until recently, he was the managing editor of Journal of Tourism. He has more than a hundred peer reviewed and well-cited research publications to his credit. He has authored or edited more than seven books. He is a passionate observer of the complex dynamics of creative destruction that makes idea innovations possible. In his free time, he offers free consulting for the budding grassroots level entrepreneurs.

Ali Inanir is an Ph.D. Lecturer and head of Department of Travel Tourism and Leisure Services in School of Ağlasun Vocational at Mehmet Akif Ersoy University. His research interests are destination management and marketing, hotel management, organizational behavior in tourism, alternative tourism and sustainable tourism.

Mikail Kar is working as an academic at Bursa Uludag University, Department of Economics. He completed his undergraduate degree at Istanbul Marmara University, his master's degree at the State University of New York, and his PhD degree at Bursa Uludag University. He mainly works on economic theory, market analysis, methodological issues, economic policy, industrial economics. He has many book chapters and articles published in distinguished international publishing houses and journals in these fields of study. He is still continuing his academic studies at Bursa Uludag University and giving lectures in the field of economic theory.

Volkan Kaymaz is a graduate of Yıldız Technical University, Department of Economics and is a faculty member at Istanbul Yeni Yüzyıl University.

Pedro Lisdero holds a bachelor's degree in Sociology (U. Siglo XXI, Córdoba, Argentina) and PhD in Social Studies of Latin America (Center for Advanced Studies—National University of Córdoba). Lisdero is a researcher at the National Scientific and Technological Research Council (CONICET, Argentina), Co-director of the Program of Studies on Collective Action and Social Conflict of Center for Research and Studies on Cultures and Societies (CONICET and National University of Córdoba— UNC), and a researcher at the Centre for Sociological Research and Studies (CIES, Argentina). In addition, he is a professor at the National University of Villa Maria (UNVM) and Director of Sociological Studies Editora (ESEditora—CIES).

Maria Victoria Mairano is a Sociologist (UBA). Candidate for a Master's Degree in Research in Social Sciences (FSOC-UBA) and a specialization in Social Research Methodologies (FSOC-UBA). Member of the Study Group on the Sociology of Emotions and Bodies (IIGG-UBA), the Study Group of Social Politics and Emotions(CIES), and of the CICSEC (CIES and the University of Palermo). Member of the Editorial Team of the Latin American Journal of Bodies, Emotions and Society (RELACES).

Flavio Santos is a Ph.D. student in Tourism at Institute of Geography and Spatial Planning, Universidade de Lisboa (IGOT), Lisbon, Lisbon, Portugal. Researcher at TERRITUR of the Center for Geographical Studies (CEG), IGOT, Universidade de Lisboa. ORCID: https://orcid.org/0000-0003-3771-4579.

Adrian Scribano is a Ph.D. in Philosophy, University of Buenos Aires. MA (Master of Arts) in Developmental Science, ILADES, Santiago, Chile. BA in Political Science, Catholic University of Córdoba. Diploma in Human Rights from the Human Rights Institute at Complutense University in Madrid, Spain. Principal Researcher at CONICET Director of the Centre for Research and Sociological Studies (CIES), Argentina (estudiosociologicos.com.ar). Director of the Latinamerican Journal of Studies on Bodies, Emotions and Society (relaces.com.ar) Director of the Study Group on Sociology of Emotions and Bodies, in the Gino Germani Investigation Institute, Faculty of Social Sciences, University of Buenos Aires.http://cuerposyemociones.com.ar Director of the "Research Program on Collective Action and Social Conflict" (accioncolectiva.com.ar).

Index

A

B

C

D

E

www.ingramcontent.com/pod-product-compliance
Lightning Source LLC
LaVergne TN
LVHW061540290926
849162LV00004B/852